For Adam +
Rachie

11/4/21

Best wishes,

RHYMES WITH FIGHTER

RHYMES
with
FIGHTER

CLAYTON YEUTTER, American Statesman

JOSEPH WEBER

University of Nebraska Press

LINCOLN

The University of Nebraska Press is part of a land-grant institution with campuses and programs on the past, present, and future homelands of the Pawnee, Ponca, Otoe-Missouria, Omaha, Dakota, Lakota, Kaw, Cheyenne, and Arapaho Peoples, as well as those of the relocated Ho-Chunk, Sac and Fox, and Iowa Peoples.

∞

Library of Congress Cataloging-in-Publication Data
Names: Weber, Joseph (Professor of journalism) author.
Title: Rhymes with fighter : Clayton Yeutter, American statesman / Joseph Weber.
Other titles: Clayton Yeutter, American statesman
Description: Lincoln : University of Nebraska Press, [2021] | Includes bibliographical references and index.
Identifiers: LCCN 2021013927
ISBN 9781496230126 (hardback)
ISBN 9781496230300 (epub)
ISBN 9781496230317 (pdf)
Subjects: LCSH: Yeutter, Clayton K., 1930–2017. | Statesmen—United States—Biography. | United States. Department of Agriculture—Officials and employees—Biography. | Cabinet officers—United States—Biography. | Nebraska—Biography. | BISAC: BIOGRAPHY & AUTOBIOGRAPHY / Political | POLITICAL SCIENCE / Globalization
Classification: LCC E840.8.Y48 W43 2021 | DDC 338.1092 [B]—dc23
LC record available at https://lccn.loc.gov/2021013927

Set in Minion Pro by Laura Buis.

For Ronald A. Krieger,
an exceptional mentor in economics.

For Donna, as always.

CONTENTS

ILLUSTRATIONS

PREFACE

As a teenager tearing up and down the dusty roads of south-central Nebraska in his 1939 black Ford coupe, Clayton Yeutter might have seemed like any other hardworking midwestern farm boy destined to take over the family spread from his father. He was well liked, good-looking, and able to charm classmates in his modest rural high school with his ability to gab and to flash a broad smile. He was also a standout in 4-H, the farmland youth outfit, where he won prizes for both his cattle and his knack for public speaking. He was good at football, among other sports. Most of all, he liked working the farm.

But Yeutter would move well beyond the family farm and tiny Eustis, Nebraska. Harnessing his brainpower as powerfully as he could harness his livestock, he racked up honors as he made his way through the University of Nebraska. Then, after a stint in the U.S. Air Force, he simultaneously earned an agricultural economics doctorate and a law degree at the university, making his mark at the top of his class in both realms. Afterward, helped by contacts who were as impressed with his charm and intellect as his high school friends and university associates were, Yeutter set out on a political journey that took him from groundbreaking work in Nebraska's capital to the highest reaches in Washington DC.

He wound up with seats at the cabinet table in the White House and dealt with political and economic leaders across the world.

Yeutter served four American presidents. He never held an elective office, but he was on a first-name basis with senators and representatives, as well as with national leaders and trade ministers around the globe. Most notably, he made history as the U.S. trade representative under President Ronald W. Reagan. He counted among his banner achievements leading the way toward a trailblazing free-trade agreement with Canada, opening the markets in Japan for key American products while preserving America's all-important semiconductor industry against unfair competition, winning legislative approval for an omnibus trade bill, and overhauling Europe's protectionist farm policies as he launched the Uruguay Round of negotiations that moved the world closer toward free trade. Then, as secretary of agriculture under President George H. W. Bush, he steered the American farm belt into being more market oriented than it had been since before the Great Depression, as he helped turn once inward-looking farmers into global exporters.

Yeutter also made his mark in business as an organizational leader with few peers. Thanks to his keen grasp of markets and economics, he led the Chicago Mercantile Exchange for seven years as it grew from a Midwest power into a global bourse. And as a lawyer and businessman, he served on the boards of major corporations, helping move them even more into international arenas. When his president called, he also helped his party regain its footing in a time of tumult as head of the Republican National Committee—though he distinguished himself by his ability to work on both sides of the aisle. Reflecting an era in which many political leaders could more easily find common ground, he counted the head of the Democratic National Committee as a friend.

As he traveled the world, opening markets and making friends, the PhD economist, lawyer, businessman, and political leader remained true to his Nebraska roots. He returned to the family farm as often as he could, either to work it or just to recharge, leaving behind the stuffy halls of Washington and elsewhere. He stayed loyal to the University of Nebraska as well, often singing the praises of his beloved Cornhuskers. He endowed a garden at the school in honor of his late wife, Lillian Jeanne Vierk Yeutter, and was pleased when the university erected a statue of him, celebrating him as one of just four Nebraskans to serve as U.S. secretary of agriculture. To make an impact going forward, Yeutter and his second wife, Cristena, contributed $2.5 million to the university to establish the Clayton Yeutter Institute of International Trade and Finance, intending it to educate generations of students about global trade.

Yeutter's life story—which began during the Great Depression and ended with a vast expansion of world trade in hopes of avoiding another such debacle—is exceptional. Hope you enjoy it.

ABBREVIATIONS

AD/CVD	antidumping and countervailing duties
BST	bovine somatotrophin
C&MS	Consumer and Marketing Service
CAP	Common Agricultural Policy
CBOT	Chicago Board of Trade
CFTC	Commodity Futures Trading Commission
CME	Chicago Mercantile Exchange
CREEP	Committee for the Re-election of the President
EC	European Community
EEC	European Economic Community
EEP	Export Enhancement Program
EPA	U.S. Environmental Protection Agency
FAA	Foundation for American Agriculture
FARC	Revolutionary Armed Forces of Colombia
FDA	Food and Drug Administration
FSQS	Food Safety and Quality Service
FTA	free trade agreement
GATT	General Agreement on Tariffs and Trade
GDP	gross domestic product
LIPC	Livestock Industry Promotion Corporation
NAFTA	North American Free Trade Agreement
NATO	North Atlantic Treaty Organization

NFU	National Farmers Union
NMPF	National Milk Producers Federation
NRDC	Natural Resources Defense Council
OPEC	Organization of the Petroleum Exporting Countries
rBGH	bovine growth hormone
SIA	Semiconductor Industry Association
STR	special trade representative
TPP	Trans-Pacific Partnership
UNL	University of Nebraska–Lincoln
USDA	U.S. Department of Agriculture
USTR	U.S. trade representative
WIC	Special Supplemental Nutrition Program for Women, Infants, and Children
WTO	World Trade Organization

RHYMES WITH FIGHTER

1

Rugged Times

L ife was anything but easy at the start for Clayton Keith
Yeutter. He was born in tiny Eustis in south-central
Nebraska's aptly named Frontier County, and his early
years were framed by seismic events in the twentieth century: the
Great Depression, the Dust Bowl, and World War II.[1] His starkest
memories, as a farmer's child, were of walking to school in shoes
filled with cardboard to cover the holes, of hard farm work even as
an elementary school student, and of a father—a German American who immigrated to the United States from Stuttgart at age
two—who was perplexed by his brainy son's academic successes
and scholastic ambitions.[2] Indeed, in a defining irony of his life,
Yeutter's modestly schooled father saw little use for book learning, especially since the life he foresaw for his only child went little farther than the family homestead.

But Yeutter also could savor happier recollections, ones that had
to do with his achievements both on and off the farm, reflecting
the sort of independence and success life on a well-managed farm
can bring. As an intellectual powerhouse with few peers, Yeutter
moved through academia, law, local Nebraska politics, business at
the helm of a major commodities exchange in Chicago, and most
memorably, trade and politics at the highest levels in Washington DC. Along the way, he could recall the early experiences that

shaped him as an even-tempered, moderate-minded, and religious family man. These events—both the good and bad ones—and his political, economic, and social background were crucial in forming Yeutter's worldview, one that would serve four Republican presidents and help remake the global economic landscape far beyond Eustis.

Born sixteen months into the Great Depression, Yeutter arrived at 3 a.m. on December 10, 1930, as the lone child of Reinhold F. "Doc" and Laura P. Yeutter.[3] Throughout his childhood, national economic disaster combined with agricultural ruin across the desiccated Great Plains to drive some two and a half million people off their land.[4] Somehow, though, Yeutter's family was spared the worst and hung on to its grain and cattle-feeding operation, a spread in Dawson County between Eustis and Cozad that Yeutter helped grow over time to some twenty-five hundred acres. Led by a "hard-working German" father, as Yeutter called him, the three Yeutters lived in a comfortable bungalow down a dirt road, six miles north of Eustis. Yeutter attended the tiny Holmes school, where students in kindergarten through eighth grade shared a single classroom in a clapboard building a mile and a half from his house.[5] Unlike many young farm boys at the time, he was then able to finish high school in nearby Eustis.

Like other farm youngsters, however, Yeutter worked the land with his parents, beginning his labors when he was just six years old, driving a tractor at age ten, and doing the work of a grown man at twelve. As he told a reporter for the *Washington Star* in 1975, he learned to read by kerosene lamp. "I will always remember the hard, physical work at an early age," he said.[6] He kept baby calves alive in the icy winters by laying them on the open door of a wood-burning stove in the family kitchen.[7] He and his parents used an outhouse not far from their home and drew water from a cistern next to the house. The family bathed on Saturday nights and rarely during the week.[8] He shared a bed with a hired hand.[9] "Those were rugged times," he told a 4-H publication in 1987. His father's corn and wheat plantings, he recalled, were "terribly vulnerable to drought and grasshoppers."[10] Later, in a 2016 video for the University of Nebraska Foundation, he said the family's cattle operation sustained them, adding, "We barely survived."[11]

Early on, his Nebraska-born mother saw the brainpower that would in time take Yeutter away from the state. "He had a head on him even before he started school," Laura Yeutter told a reporter in 1985. "He knew all the state capitals before he went to school, and by the eighth grade he was almost teaching the one-room school."[12]

Too young for the military during World War II, which loomed large through his early teen years, Yeutter graduated from Eustis High School in 1948 as a member of a class of twenty in a town of about five hundred residents. He was a standout student, placing third in the class, and for decades afterward stayed in touch with classmates, corresponding with some late into his life. He also made a mark outside of school. Indeed, his mother's mementos included an account from a local newspaper of Yeutter's successes in the Dawson County 4-H Club. His long list of 4-H awards, earned while he was in high school and college, included gold medals in beef showmanship and a long string of ribbons for calves at the Nebraska State Fair and the Ak-Sar-Ben Stock Show, livestock judging awards, and trips to the National 4-H Club Congress in Chicago and the National 4-H Camp in Washington DC.

For Yeutter, who would make hundreds of speeches across the world throughout his career, 4-H was a launching pad for the public stage. He wound up winning a scholarship from Omaha radio station KFAB for his public-speaking efforts, though he noted in a 1967 letter to Marlene Timmermann, of Papillion, Nebraska, a fifteen-year-old 4-H member who had written to him, that he had taken second place in the contest. It was "the only state-wide competition which I did not win during my career as a 4-H member," he said, explaining that he had collected the scholarship because the winner declined to use it. Members of 4-H, he added, formed "a very select group of young people with a great deal of ambition and high ideals . . . the cream of the crop." He said the group was "of immense help" to him throughout his life.[13] It was also in 4-H that he suffered one of his first disappointments, when as a ten-year-old he finished last in a beef showmanship competition and wept all the way home—though he notched many wins afterward.[14] In fact, young Yeutter earned the highest award the group bestowed when, in 1948, he became one of four Nebraska delegates to the National 4-H Club Camp in Washington DC, giving him his first taste of the city that would become his longtime professional home.[15]

In an early foray into journalism, Yeutter wrote a short piece for the *Omaha World-Herald* about his experience in the nation's capital, calling it a "very neat, clean and beautiful" city. In listing adventures the 4-H'ers had on the trip, Yeutter struck a sly but diplomatic note, perhaps foreshadowing the tone of more complex arguments in which he would be immersed at high levels decades later. "We also continued our group discussions on questions and problems pertaining to the Government," young Yeutter wrote. "In several instances we nearly started another Civil War but every one is broad-minded enough so that a lot of sound ideas are brought forth in these discussions."[16] Yeutter had an earlier success with the newspaper too: midway through high school, in 1946, he won a medal from the *Omaha World-Herald* as one of the top three staffers on the 4-H Club weekly newspaper, *Cloverleaf*, for which he worked as a reporter.[17]

Yeutter's gift with words and a mischievous streak did cause problems for him at times, old friends recalled. "He was really friendly with other people," remembers Barbara Marschang-Hendry, a high school chum who was eighty-eight when we spoke in early 2020.[18] "He was a good talker, a very good speaker." Another friend, Mildred Stagemeyer, recalls the time Yeutter got in trouble for chatting with a classmate in a study session and wound up having to write a one-thousand-word essay. More respectably, he got the chance to polish his speaking skills by acting in at least one high school play, according to Stagemeyer. "He liked to have fun," says Stagemeyer, who was eighty-nine in early 2020.[19] Because his mother had bought him a small, black 1939 Ford coupe, he would give rides all around the Eustis area to such friends, who would jam into the car to travel to school sporting events, crawling up into the back-window area at times in those pre-seat-belt days.[20] He was also competitive, notes Marschang-Hendry, who says he and she would sneak over to tap one another's typewriter keys in typing class to mar each other's papers (albeit playfully). "He was an instigator," she says.[21]

The barrel-chested Yeutter was big for his age and would hover between a trim 190 and 200 pounds. He competed in several sports, lettering in basketball, baseball, track, and football; he played fullback for the Eustis Tigers, the school's eight-man football team, which at the time played in leather helmets. He was tough enough to take the hardest hits and manage to bounce up smiling, recalls classmate Ray Easterday, who was eighty-nine in early 2020. "He excelled in everything," Easterday says. "He put all the effort that he possibly could in, whether it was in studies or athletics. He was a real likeable young man and he took that right on throughout the rest of his life." Yeutter, he adds, was so popular that "he could have went with any one of the girls that was there and had no problem at all." Yeutter managed to keep an upbeat attitude, despite the hard-knock upbringing that just about all the farm children had endured only a few years before, as they got through times filled with dust storms and grasshopper swarms thick enough to block out the midday sun.[22]

By the time he was in high school, Yeutter's political ideas—and taste for the political arena—may have been jelling. President of his high school class, Yeutter became a lifetime supporter of the GOP, a viewpoint that at first blush seems surprising. Less than forty years before Yeutter was born, the Nebraska Democratic firebrand William Jennings Bryan ran three times for president, failing in those runs but managing to serve as a congressman and then as secretary of state under Woodrow Wilson. Populism swept the Great Plains and the West back then.[23] Later, during Yeutter's youth, the most influential presidents were Democrats Franklin D. Roosevelt, the New Deal leader who guided the nation, including hard-pressed farmers, out of the Depression and through almost all of World War II, and FDR's successor, Harry S. Truman, who ended that war.

But the independent farm life, his father's attitudes, and young Yeutter's relationships outside his home, along with his later education, could help explain his outlook. Like many of his Great Plains neighbors, Yeutter became a committed, if moderate, Republican, a believer in limited—though sometimes controversially active—government, and a passionate supporter of markets and free trade as the best means for growing wealth. He had a special fondness for people brought up like him, telling the *Washington Star*, "All the traditional rural values which place a premium on hard work, a premium on being open and friendly and responsive to one's fellow man, are found among the vast majority of people in the Midwest. They're basically conservative by nature. They're fiscal conservatives by and large, although not entirely."[24]

Yeutter's father was a Republican, and in his youth, Yeutter's hometown was a Republican stronghold, as it remained in 2021, with its estimated 379 residents.[25] Settled mostly by German American immigrants, Eustis in 2021 welcomed visitors with a large sign saying "Willkommen." Preschoolers in the small downtown area played in a Kinder Park, shoppers could visit Der Deutsche Markt gift shop, and diners could get the best wurst around in Nebraska's "Sausage Capital." Residents could choose between a Lutheran and a Methodist church, and Yeutter recalled services in his childhood being conducted in German until World War II approached. With the war coming on, Yeutter's parents chose not to teach him German.[26] That may have been unfortunate, since globalism would prove to be his biggest claim to fame in later days. Indeed, he would spend much of his career urging farmers to look well beyond their fence posts to seize opportunities to sell their goods to distant buyers.

The Eustis-area community was made up of farmers for whom self-reliance was a cardinal virtue. It also was—and in 2021 remained—the sort of place where a farmer driving by a motorist on the shoulder of the road was apt to stop and offer a hand. The residents saw Republicans as more likely to advocate for farmers, according to Yeutter's classmate Easterday, even as some of them condemned President Herbert C. Hoover, the Republican who led the country into the Great Depression, and praised FDR.

The parents and grandparents of those residents, like so many throughout the Great Plains, fled tyrannical leaders in Europe who taxed them heavily and were keen to draft them and their children into pointless wars. They wanted little to do with government, especially government in distant Washington DC. For many of them, the world largely began and ended on their fields, the fiefdoms they built and maintained with their own muscle, sweat, and sometimes blood—even if they or their predecessors got the land by government fiat through such measures as the Homestead Act of 1862, and even though they maintained their farms in the post-FDR days with lots of government supports and subsidies. Summing up the mindset of such farmers, former Nebraska governor and senator J. Robert Kerrey, a Democrat, cited a wisecrack made by another Nebraska Democrat, the late longtime state legislator and farmer Wayne W. Ziebarth. The attitude of such farmers, Ziebarth said, was "I own this land from the center of the earth to the top of the universe and it's only by the grace of God that I let airplanes fly over it."[27]

Yeutter's grandfather, Karl, had settled in the Dawson County area in 1900. When it was time for Yeutter's father, Reinhold, to begin farming on his own, he started out on 320 acres that the family acquired near his dad's spread. As they worked their land, the Yeutters and their neighbors prized their freedom and independence, values that likely drew them to the GOP of the time.

An early mentor of Yeutter's, moreover, was a 4-H leader who would go on to become one of the most important—and perhaps one of the most unfairly reviled—Republican governors in the state, Norbert T. Tiemann. As an assistant county agricultural agent in Lexington, Nebraska, in the late 1940s, Tiemann helped guide Yeutter to win top prizes for livestock judging, proving early on that he could be a winner in whatever area he put his mind to.[28] Yeutter was active with 4-H in high school and later headed the organization's chapter at the University of Nebraska. Tiemann, for his part, later recalled that Yeutter "was probably the most outstanding 4-H club member I ever had the privilege to work with."[29] In the 1960s Yeutter would come to work in the state capital for Tiemann—one of several older men who over time would take the brainy, hardworking Yeutter under their wing. The men, who took on something akin to father roles for Yeutter, were crucial in his life.

Along with Tiemann, Yeutter credited another early mentor with helping open his eyes to a world well beyond his farm. Harold M. Stevens, a longtime Dawson County extension agent who was involved with 4-H, was "a major influence on my life," Yeutter told a 4-H publication in 1987. As a livestock judging coach, Stevens's "great enthusiasm and support encouraged me to tackle things I might not have otherwise." The competitions he got involved in broadened Yeutter's youthful horizon: "Until I started showing beef cattle, I had no exposure outside of an area of 10 or 12 miles." County and statewide 4-H competitions "made me realize the broader world."[30]

In his 2016 University of Nebraska Foundation video, Yeutter described his father, Reinhold, as gregarious and outgoing, saying he was strong enough to lift the heavy cars of the time by their bumpers. But as Yeutter recalled decades later to his wife, Cristena, Reinhold Yeutter also was someone for whom nothing young Yeutter could do was good enough—someone who, in a fashion typical of the era, particularly among Germans, never told his only child that he loved him or was proud of him.[31]

The elder Yeutter, who quit school after eighth grade, never understood or appreciated the prodigious academic achievements that would take his boy to a global stage that Reinhold could never have imagined. Indeed, Reinhold discouraged his son from bothering with college, seeing it as unnecessary on the family farm. "He didn't really comprehend the necessity for that high fangled education in those days," Yeutter told University of Nebraska–Lincoln agricultural communications professor George S. Round in 1975. "His reaction was [that] being a successful farmer just simply requires working from dawn to dark. But he was also a very intelligent and perceptive man."[32] It was because of the influence of Stevens and others that Yeutter headed east to the university in Lincoln.[33]

By contrast, Yeutter's mother, Laura, was a warm and loving cheerleader for her boy. She created scrapbooks about his achievements from the newspaper clippings and pictures he sent home.[34] A Sunday school teacher in her Methodist church for sixty-five years, she kindled a lifelong commitment to religion in Yeutter, who moved from serving as an usher in the Eustis Methodist church to regularly preaching as a lay leader in his church in Lincoln, Nebraska.[35] He later spoke about such topics as "Religion in My Life" at another area church and was a longtime donor to and director of the Garrett-Evangelical Theological Seminary at Northwestern University.[36] Yeutter drew his first wife away from Lutheranism into Methodism, and his interest in religion endured, as he wound up attending a Presbyterian church when he worked in Washington DC.[37] His faith let him "live boldly and without fear," says his youngest son, Van A. Yeutter.[38]

Throughout his career, Yeutter was discreet about his religious convictions but didn't hide them. "He did not wear that on his sleeve at all," recalls Kelly Semrau, a press aide to Yeutter when he served as U.S. trade representative and later at the Department of Agriculture. She remembers occasional long flights on global trade missions when he pulled out his Bible as others slept, and he slept at times with a Bible at his bedside. "He was a man of great faith; it was not in your face, but I think that came through."[39] He also frequently consoled friends who had lost loved ones with warm religious sentiments in letters, especially later in his life.

Though she was always in his corner, Laura Yeutter was sometimes puzzled by the high-level jobs her son took. When he was named U.S. trade representative, he phoned her from the White House to share the news. Her response was what *Farmland News* described as less than enthusiastic. "How long do you have to stay there and do that?" she asked him. "It would be better if you'd come home to Nebraska."[40]

For much of his early career, Yeutter did return regularly to work the farm, which he would hang on to throughout his life, often coming back to oversee hired hands, and over time he would add to his landholdings with development property near Lincoln. But forty-one years after heading off to university, when he was nominated in 1989 to become the U.S. secretary of agriculture, Yeutter underscored the importance of his move to Lincoln, his departure from his father's small world into the broader academic arena. "I must add just one more philosophical note," he said in his confirmation hearing. "Education has always been the antidote to poverty, and that shall continue. So why mention it at all? Because the commitment to education and vocational training in this country is not sufficiently strong. We should not aspire to competing with the rest of the world on wage rates, in agriculture or anywhere else. We must compete on the basis of technology, innovation, entrepreneurship, creativity, institutional flexibility and personal and institutional freedoms. All those are built on education!"[41]

Certainly, Yeutter had a ready hand for schoolwork, his ticket upward in life. After graduating from Eustis High School, he distinguished himself at the University of Nebraska, through his undergraduate years, graduate school, and law school. As an undergrad, he ranked first in his College of Agriculture graduating class in 1952 and was named by the Block and Bridle Club as the outstanding animal husbandry graduate in the United States.[42] He also served as president of the university's FarmHouse fraternity chapter in Lincoln, a group whose members typically earned the highest grade point average overall among Greek houses on campus. His brainy fraternity brothers also had a sense of humor—mindful of Yeutter's voracious appetite, especially for desserts, they one day put his food into a pig trough and set it up on the dining table.[43]

He remained friends with some fraternity brothers and was a FarmHouse supporter all his life, becoming a director of its alumni group and, in time, a recipient of its highest alumnus honor, the Master Builder of Men award. He also served as chancellor of the university chapter of the Alpha Zeta scholastic honorary society and was a member of the Gamma Sigma Delta scholastic society.[44] And he served as managing editor of the *Cornhusker Countryman*, the ag college student magazine.[45]

When he graduated from college in 1952, the Korean War was raging. So Yeutter took a detour into the military, enlisting in the U.S. Air Force as a basic airman. After earning honors as the top student in medical administration in training at Gunter Air

Force Base in Alabama, he was commissioned as an officer in the Medical Administrative Corps. He lucked into a stateside assignment in Orlando, Florida, later recalling that in those pre–Disney World days, the place was much like Lincoln, Nebraska.[46] For three years he served in a hospital, where the commander, a military doctor, rotated officers though various positions to expose them to a host of jobs. Yeutter so impressed the commander that he named the wet-behind-the-ears first lieutenant as an acting successor, even though every administrator in the hospital but one outranked him. "It was almost unheard of for a responsibility of that nature to be given to a young first lieutenant, so I have always remembered that," Yeutter wrote in 1991 to a Denver man who asked about his military service. "It was a thrill to have the responsibility, notwithstanding the risk it posed for that hospital commander who selected me."[47]

Recalling his early stint in uniform, Yeutter said he "was not terribly enthusiastic" about signing up because the war was underway and he was keen to get started on his own farming operation. He chatted with a World War II veteran who told him he would either hate or like his military service, depending on his attitude. Enter with a negative attitude, the man said, and Yeutter would hate it. "If, on the other hand, I were to enter service with a positive attitude, I would have a worthwhile experience, and it would be one of the most enjoyable and rewarding periods of my life," Yeutter recalled. "Though young I had the good sense to choose the latter route, and I quickly discovered that what I had received was most sagacious advice. I have never forgotten it, and I have applied the same outlook to a lot of other subsequent experiences in my life."[48]

In all, Yeutter was on active duty for four and a half years, including three years as an officer, before switching to the Air National Guard in Nebraska. Until 1977 he remained in the active reserve—often departing his later civilian jobs for weekend and periodic duty—and rose to retire as a lieutenant colonel.[49]

While in the service, he waited for his college sweetheart, Lillian Jeanne Vierk, to graduate, and then married her in 1953. Jeanne, as she was known, was a top English and home economics student. At the time, she was also a Democrat and a daughter of Fritz Charles Vierk, an architect who was active in the Democratic Party in Lancaster County, Nebraska, and who worked hard in the 1960s to get Frank B. Morrison elected as governor of Nebraska just before Norbert Tiemann's term.[50] J. James "Big Jim" Exon, a Democratic U.S. senator from Nebraska, joked about Yeutter in 1985 that Jeanne "taught him everything he knew."[51] Yeutter and Jeanne would remain together for forty years until she died in her sleep of a presumed heart attack in August 1993, just four days after her sixty-second birthday. They raised four children: Brad, Gregg, Kim (Bottimore), and Van.

For three years after his active-duty military stint, Yeutter worked on his family farm, and he and Jeanne focused on their growing family. He expanded the farm over time to over two thousand acres by adding eight hundred acres of grassland and grew the cattle operation to include a thousand-head feedlot and three hundred Angus cows.[52] But encouraged by Jeanne and helped by the GI Bill, Yeutter headed back to school in 1960 to pursue a PhD in agricultural economics at the University of Wisconsin's flagship campus in Madison. He had to cut that short after a single semester, returning home after his father suffered a heart attack. Yeutter then wound up going back to the University of Nebraska to simultaneously pursue both his law degree and his doctorate—one of only two people in the United States that he knew of at the time who combined law and ag economics at the doctoral level.[53] He earned his LLB (later converted to a JD) in 1963, ranking first in his graduating class and serving as editor of the *Nebraska Law Review*, and he was named the outstanding law graduate in the Midwest by the Phi Delta Phi legal fraternity.

When he earned his doctorate in 1966, at age thirty-five, Yeutter was named the outstanding graduate student in ag economics, earning above an A average throughout his grad program.[54] He had focused on water law and was instrumental in helping create Nebraska's Natural Resources Districts, groups that tend to water issues in the state.[55] His doctoral dissertation, "The Administration of Water Law in the Central United States: A Legal-Economic Critique of Laws and Administrative Procedures in Colorado, Kansas, Nebraska, and Iowa," ran to 579 pages. A staunch believer in free trade, he argued that markets—with appropriate regulation—ought to guide decisions on water use. "Administrators are not omniscient decision-makers," Yeutter contended. "Where feasible, an impersonal market is a more appropriate guide for the making of decisions." He cited Frank J. Trelease, a dean of the law school at University of Wyoming, who argued, "The utilization of private initiative and the economic process has obvious advantages over complete public regulation. To the extent that the laws of economics operate as an allocative and regulatory force, there is no necessity for law that minutely regulates the activities of the people." Touchingly, Yeutter dedicated the dissertation to his late father, who died in 1965, calling him "an outstanding farmer who carried the nickname 'Doc' as well as any PhD ever will."[56]

Trained in traditional economics, Yeutter doubled down on his early faith in markets in September 1966, when he discussed his research at the annual conference of the Nebraska Association of Soil and Water Conservation Districts in Kearney, Nebraska. "First, water rights often can and should be bought and sold on a free market," Yeutter argued. "Many of my fellow economists say that this cannot be done in the field of water, because buying and selling water is simply not the same as buying and selling cattle, corn, or other commodities. Superficially, this is true, but these people ignore the possibility of developing a unique market framework for water. A free enterprise system of marketing water would achieve an efficient utilization of water resources and would maximize economic benefits to our state. Likewise, it would afford considerable opportunity for achieving flexibility in water use and water priorities."[57]

A quarter century later, in the spring of 1992, Yeutter complimented an editorialist for the *Wall Street Journal* who had pressed to end "America's water socialism" by urging that market prices, through the use of auctions, be used to allocate water in the American West. "Bob, your editorial 'Waters of the West,' was excellent," wrote Yeutter, who then was working in the White House as counselor to President George H. W. Bush for domestic policy, to editor Robert L. Bartley. "My PhD dissertation was on water administration in the central U.S., and one of the basic thrusts of that study was that we should significantly increase the use of the marketplace to allocate water. That was in 1966! We're slow learners, but maybe we'll eventually get there."[58]

While pursuing his doctorate, Yeutter taught at the University of Nebraska, drawing the notice of another in the string of mentors who would prove crucial to his career. Clifford M. Hardin, like Yeutter an agricultural economist, served as chancellor of the university from 1954 until 1969. Hardin left Nebraska when President Richard M. Nixon tapped him to become U.S. secretary of agriculture in 1969—a lofty perch from which Hardin would reach out to his protégé and jump-start Yeutter's career in Washington DC, helping set up Yeutter to take the top Ag Department post two decades later.

But first Yeutter would get his feet wet in state politics in Nebraska, also through a former mentor who rose to high office. Norbert "Nobby" Tiemann, whom Yeutter knew from 4-H activities years earlier, was elected governor in 1966, just a few months after Yeutter earned his doctorate. A dynamic former University of Nebraska football player and semipro baseball player, U.S. Army veteran of World War II and the Korean War, and a Lutheran minister's son, Tiemann was just six years older than Yeutter.[59] The governor-elect tapped the whip-smart PhD lawyer to become his administrative assistant, his "top counsel," and de facto chief of staff.[60] The move would prove challenging for both men, ultimately relegating Tiemann to a single term as governor, but it would also lead to some of the most important initiatives in Nebraska governmental history—some directly credited to Yeutter. It would also cement Yeutter's convictions as a moderate Republican, someone who eschewed the extremes in his party to see carefully delineated roles for government as crucial—a view that he would hold for the rest of his professional and political life.

2

The Clayton Grin

E ven before Governor-elect Tiemann reached out to Yeutter in the fall of 1966 to join his team, the lawyer-economist
was active in state affairs. Legislators in the state's Uni-
cameral, for instance, asked Yeutter to review a four-year-old study
about taxes and translate the major recommendations into a bill.
The result, LB797, passed by the legislature in 1965, was an unpopular
income tax, something the legislators saw as necessary because the
state lacked a sales tax and relied on controversial property taxes.[1]
But then, along with voting for Tiemann in November 1966, voters
shot down the income tax plan by just under a 70 percent margin
in a veto referendum, and voters also abolished state property taxes
by just under 51 percent in a constitutional amendment.[2] The twin
blows from tight-fisted Nebraskans left the state financially high and
dry, creating a daunting challenge for Tiemann and his new top aide.

Faced with a shortage of funds to run the state government, Tiemann, Yeutter, and others among the team of "whiz kids" that
Tiemann had assembled in his campaign moved fast. The group—
nine attorneys, including five who joined the state government—
developed a plan for a combination sales and income tax and, with
Yeutter working the legislative halls as legislative liaison, got the bill,
LB377, passed in April 1967.[3] The move flew in the face of parsimo-
nious public sentiment, tarnished Tiemann for the remainder of his

term, and ultimately cost him reelection in 1970, when James Exon, a Democrat but a fiscal and social conservative, beat Tiemann and wound up serving two four-year terms as governor and later moving on to the U.S. Senate for three terms.[4] Indeed, years later Tiemann recalled Nebraskans throwing pennies at him during parades as they derided what would come to be known as the "Tiemann tax."[5]

But the early and mid-1960s were challenging years for many Republicans in Nebraska and elsewhere. On the party's right wing, Arizona senator Barry M. Goldwater was making his mark by staking out a position against civil rights legislation, delivering hawkish anti-Communist messages, and striking a tone that critics labeled as isolationist but earned him support from a fast-growing fringe conspiratorialist group, the John Birch Society.[6] On the party's left and moderate wings, "establishment" leaders such as Governors William W. Scranton of Pennsylvania, George W. Romney of Michigan, and Nelson A. Rockefeller of New York sought to move the GOP away from what they saw as dangerous extremism, casting it more in the mold of former president Dwight D. Eisenhower. Ultimately, in the 1964 race for the presidency, the party rank and file tilted right and crowned Goldwater as their nominee—a poor choice, it turned out, since Goldwater fell in a landslide to President Lyndon B. Johnson, who had risen from vice president in the fall of 1963, when President John F. Kennedy was assassinated.

Tiemann landed on the party's left or moderate side, and Yeutter appeared to have sat squarely with him there. The *Lincoln Star*, in welcoming the new governor-elect in November 1966, complimented Tiemann for choosing Yeutter, albeit in a peculiar way. The newspaper said that Yeutter was "a man many unknowing people might well have considered a Democrat. But Clayton Yeutter is a Republican. He is, however, considered a progressive Republican, in the mold from which Tiemann himself is thought to be cast."[7] Six months into the governor's term, columnists Rowland Evans Jr. and Robert D. Novak described Tiemann as "the most progressive Nebraska Republican since George Norris bolted the party in the late 1930s," depicting him as a practical businessman who "attempted and largely succeeded in pulling Nebraska out of the political Stone Age," but someone who was "part of the nation-wide schism of the Republican party between pragmatic problem-solvers and ideological conservatives."[8]

Tiemann, aided by Yeutter working on the floor of the state's Uni-cameral legislature, proved to be an activist leader. After getting the new tax system in place, the new governor set up a state department of economic development, established and funded a new research center, and signed into law the state's first minimum wage law ($1 an hour), as *Time* magazine reported.[9] The taxes and spending made for unusual political alignments, pitting well-off Omaha residents, who would be hurt by the income tax, against farmers statewide, for whom property taxes were a bane. In a March 1967 letter to a friend in Hastings who had written him, Yeutter agreed that he had no love of a sales tax but said state officials had no choice but to enact the combination sales-and-income-tax system even though, he wrote, "some of Omaha's wealthier citizens" attempted (unsuc-cessfully, it turned out) to carve out the income tax portion of the legislation Yeutter had championed.[10] Tiemann's team did repeal a tax on intangible property, and Yeutter noted in a May 1967 let-ter to an academic friend at Iowa State University that the sales-and-income-tax bill demanded "much arm twisting on our part."[11]

With the ex-academic, education advocate, and fellow Uni-versity of Nebraska alum Yeutter at his side, Tiemann was also a big supporter of the university. The men helped bring financially stressed Omaha University into the University of Nebraska fold in a merger authorized by the Unicameral and okayed by Omaha residents in 1967 and put into place the following year under the new name University of Nebraska Omaha. Tiemann also consis-tently backed the university's funding requests, even when conser-vative legislators sought to trim funds, partly in response to campus protests in the late 1960s and in 1970 against the Vietnam War.[12]

Though moderate, Yeutter could be a scrappy GOP partisan at times, and he was troubled by efforts among both right-wing Republicans and some Democrats to scale back the tax programs he and Tiemann had labored to create.[13] In a tart April 1967 letter to Prof. Bert M. Evans, a liberal former colleague in the University of Nebraska's department of agricultural economics, Yeutter described the Democratic Party in Nebraska as one that "seems to be making an effort to become the party of the rich, particularly with its views on non-controversial issues such as taxes." Further, Yeutter wrote, "I really do not believe that the Democratic Party in Nebraska is worth saving at this point. So . . . join us, and I will attempt to use my moderating influence on your leftist views."[14]

Yeutter worked out of a windowless converted vault in the Nebraska State Capitol building, a spot that lacked air-conditioning, so colleagues would see him laboring away shirtless at times in the summer. But he managed to stay cheerful. "He was always a gentleman. He always had the Clayton grin, we called it," remembers Allen J. Beermann, who served as a deputy secretary of state when Yeutter worked for Tiemann and saw him daily. "It was always a wide grin. He was always happy. The secret to his success was he was a great listener . . . and was always exuberant about seeing people. He was a commoner, but in terms of brilliance, in terms of getting the job done, in terms of crafting ideas, he had great follow-through. He just made things happen."[15]

He took his work seriously. When opponents of the new tax system mounted petitions to put the income tax on the fall ballot, Yeutter railed against the effort, tying it to education. He called a measure to provide state aid to education one of the greatest laws ever passed in Nebraska, saying that the funding effort and moves to equalize education in the state depended on the tax system. In an impassioned speech to the Nebraska School Food Service Association, the governor's aide urged his listeners, "Think of your children and grandchildren," adding that broader efforts to curb all levels of state spending would "set our state back years." Striking a tone that might more suit Populists or many Democrats, Yeutter said the petitioners sought "to relieve the high income persons from paying their fair share of taxes."[16]

Making such speeches around the state in support of Tiemann's efforts was part of the job for Yeutter, who had grown comfortable at a podium from the days when he learned to deliver talks for 4-H as a teenager through law school and into his teaching stints at the

University of Nebraska. In April 1968 he wrote to friends that he seemed to be averaging almost one speech a day.[17] He often spoke off the cuff, sometimes making asides or wisecracks—a penchant that in time would get him in hot water with everyone from top Canadian leaders to a mayor in Chicago and to some women.

Yeutter suggested in early 1968, for instance, that faculty and students at what was then known as Kearney State College push for the embattled sales and income tax package. He pressed for a "team approach" by faculty and students, saying that was the only way state colleges would get enough support. Annoyed, a professor at the school wrote to the *Omaha World-Herald* to complain about what he called Yeutter's "political blackmail," noting that he "violently" objected to being "ordered" to lobby for the taxes just because he taught at a state school. By urging faculty and students to "become lobbyists" for the taxes, he argued, Yeutter was telling them all to join the Tiemann team or leave. For his part, Yeutter pooh-poohed the professor's argument and the contretemps, saying a "tremendous number" of faculty members had complimented him for his talk.[18] (Kearney State College joined the University of Nebraska system in 1991, becoming the University of Nebraska at Kearney.)

Around the same time as his flap with the Kearney professor, Yeutter complained about being misquoted by journalists. When the school paper at the University of Nebraska, the *Daily Nebraskan*, covered a March 1968 talk he gave about opportunities for agricultural economics majors, Yeutter complained about the "wrong" emphasis of the piece, which focused on how professionally limiting studies in agricultural economics were compared with economics more broadly. Yeutter wrote to a university faculty member that Tiemann and he had similar problems from some "mediocre" journalists at the Lincoln newspapers. Coverage of a speech he delivered at Nebraska Wesleyan University, he said, "was the worst that we have experienced in the past fifteen months. Almost every sentence was either a misquote or a misstatement."[19]

A month later, he got in trouble when the *Lincoln Star* reported that he would be moving out of Nebraska politics and that he had suggested Tiemann might not seek reelection. Citing the piece, a

Democratic friend wrote on April 13, 1968, to ask him to reconsider his plans to move, adding, "If Gov. Tiemann has any thoughts of retiring, I hope he will put them out of his mind immediately. We Nebraskans need you two like we need a good rain in the middle of a drought."[20] Yeutter answered her four days later, writing that he and the governor had a lot of support from Democrats, explaining, "Most of our philosophical problems have been with the right-wing element of the Republican Party." He further said that his comments on Tiemann's political future "were taken somewhat out of context," noting, "As you may know, I speak extemporaneously, and this gives reporters fits. It also gives me fits, in that that I am constantly misquoted." In fact, he told her, he had said the governor did not know at that time whether he would run again for political office.[21]

Two days later, on April 19, 1968, he responded to Beverly Schroeder, yet another friend in Columbus, Nebraska:

> The press did have a field day with my remark the Nobby might not run again. I distinctly remember prefacing the remark by saying that I felt certain that Nobby did not know today whether he would or would not run again. But Jack either missed the preface or decided that it would make a better story if it were omitted. I asked UPI to run a clarification just a few minutes after the original story went on the wires, and presume that they did so. However, I imagine that the newspapers figured the original story would garner the most readers, so they probably just ignored the clarification. We are getting some complimentary mail now, so maybe this will turn out alright after all.[22]

As it turned out, Tiemann ran for reelection in 1970 but lost after he was wounded in a primary where he narrowly won, garnering less than 51 percent of the party vote.

Yeutter liked and respected several Nebraska journalists, however. In another pattern he was to repeat all through his career, he sent letters to them or their editors to compliment work he appreciated. Soon after the Christmas holidays in 1967, he lauded Rita Shaw at KOLN-TV in Lincoln: "You're sweet . . . and one of the nicest people at Channel 10!! . . . We have enjoyed working with you over the past year—your efforts in co-ordinating 'Statehouse Report' and your participation in the program have made it a part of what we feel was a good year."[23] A day later, he wrote to Gary Johnson of KLIN radio in Lincoln, who had done a show on the "Tiemann Generation," calling the program "outstanding." He added, "Since it was so very complimentary to the Tiemann administration, I am sure that my opinions are biased. Nevertheless, I am also sure that the program, when evaluated on a completely objective basis, must still rate as a top-quality piece of news reporting."[24]

He wrote to two Lincoln print reporters he regarded highly, Richard "Dick" Herman of the *Lincoln Evening Journal* and Don Walton of the *Lincoln Star*, to recommend a book he had just read, *Storm over the States*, by former South Carolina governor Terry Sanford. Parts of the work were relevant to problems Nebraska faced, he advised, and he suggested they could be a source for newspaper pieces.[25]

When an editor at the *Lincoln Star* ran a complimentary editorial about Yeutter in July 1968, after he announced his plans to leave the government, Yeutter wrote to thank him. He applauded the editor, William O. Dobler, for his "progressive, forward-looking attitude toward Nebraska people and Nebraska programs," and added, "Your penetrating analysis of critical issues has been outstanding. Perhaps I am biased by almost universal agreement with you, but I would certainly encourage you to press on in the same vein. I hope that we are now on the way to achieving some of the social reforms that are long overdue." In the same note, he gave "a final pat on the back for Don Walton as one of the finest reporters that I have ever seen."[26] In August 1968 he wrote to Jack Hart, editorial page editor at the *Lincoln Journal*, who had turned down a staff job with Tiemann: "You have done a tremendous job as Editorial Page Editor of the JOURNAL. I sincerely believe it to be the best editorial page that I have ever read."[27]

Certainly, many media people recognized that Yeutter was a powerful force in his couple of years in the activist Tiemann administration. When Yeutter made public the details of his plan to leave the state government, a friend who served as the assistant to the general manager at the state's public television system sent him a tongue-in-cheek note on stationery of the Nebraska Educational Television Commission, a body that Yeutter had helped set up. "Selfishly I sincerely regret seeing you go, because I think you've been a terrific Governor," Ron Hull said in the July 1968 note.[28] Yeutter wrote back, offering his thanks "for the exaggerated, but appreciated, words of praise," and he complimented Hull and the Lincoln-based public television system manager Jack G. McBride for doing "a fabulous job in educational television."[29] Indeed, Hull's wisecrack may not have been far off the mark—Tiemann told the agricultural trade journal *Broiler Industry* in 1971 that he gave Yeutter credit for originating and drafting many of the reform proposals Tiemann pushed through in the state.[30]

As his time in state government drew to a close, Yeutter saw politics, religion, and personal convictions as all of a piece. In August 1968, when he chaired the administrative board at Christ United Methodist Church in Lincoln, he urged the church to take on social issues and to press for government roles in addressing them. Many people were personally compassionate, he argued in a provocative Sunday address to the congregation, but collectively they showed "very little compassion." He listed examples that he said he hoped would make congregants feel uncomfortable, involving government aid for the disadvantaged in areas such as helping the mentally retarded and mentally ill, providing welfare payments, and attacking racial prejudice in light of riots occurring nationally at the time. "We like to confine our church activities within four walls," he said. "Possibly the greatest thing that could happen to Christianity in the United States would be to have some of these walls fall down. Then we could start to think of the church as an institution that works in society rather than one in which we can camp for a couple of hours on Sunday morning for our weekly recharging."

Yeutter in his address castigated Democrats and Republicans alike for making a major campaign issue of law and order when the real issue, as he called it, was "what to do to deal with the ghetto problem in the United States and the ghetto problem of Omaha, Nebr.," specifically the need for combatting bigotry, which he said led to riots. "Individually and collectively, we as a church have an important role of influencing government at all levels concerning the problems of the day," he argued. "What can be more important to a Christian who really wants to live his commitment than for him to do something for the disadvantaged? There are blind, deaf, mentally retarded and ill, abandoned children, culturally and educationally deprived people, and many, many others. I merely challenge you to ask yourself what you have done in any of these areas and what are you going to do in the future?"

He called on his co-religionists to support state government initiatives to expand facilities for people with mental health issues, taking note of a study that pointed out overcrowding at the Beatrice State Home. "Unless you and I as church members individually and collectively are willing to support the conclusions of this special study committee and get them implemented into law during the 1969 session of the legislature," he urged, "we have failed in our Christian commitment."

He attacked a common right-wing argument of the day: "All of us like to be rather wise and say, 'In this country of free enterprise, people ought to pick themselves up by their own bootstraps. We ought not have programs that dole out funds to people.' How do you expect a mentally ill person with an IQ below 50 to pick himself up by his bootstraps? What do you think that person should do? As a Christian, what is your role with that individual?" He excoriated critics of government support: "Welfare is a dirty word in Nebraska and in almost every state in the nation. You have been hearing political candidates say that we must stop putting so much money in welfare and return people to where they can work for a living. What about the 10-year-old girl at Whitehall State Home in Lincoln? What are you going to do about her when you shut off her welfare payment? Do you really expect her to go out and work for a living? No, you don't."[31]

Separately, Yeutter took issue—albeit gently—with a then-emerging giant in conservative economic circles, Milton Friedman, about government support efforts. The University of Chicago economist roundly criticized poverty programs, farm programs, Social

Security, public housing, welfare, public education, state-supported higher education, and the military draft.[32] When a Nebraskan sent Yeutter a newspaper clipping that sketched out Friedman's views, Yeutter was diplomatic but cool in a letter in response: "I have read a number of Dr. Friedman's books and articles and find them to be exceptionally thought-provoking. Friedman is unquestionably a brilliant man, but very controversial. Some people believe him to be 100% right; others believe just a strongly that he is 100% wrong. As you can see from the article, he does over-simplify many of these problems." But he noted, too: "The Republican Party does need dynamic new ideas, particularly with respect to federal programs, and, even more specifically, with respect to federal farm programs."[33]

Friedman, who later won the Nobel Prize in Economic Sciences, went on to become an adviser to Presidents Richard M. Nixon and Ronald W. Reagan, the latter of whom attacked government programs in general and welfare in particular in his campaigns for the presidency. Notably, in a staple line in his rallies, Reagan derided what he called "welfare queens," women who abused the welfare system.

Yeutter made his middle-of-the-road approach clear in an interview with journalist Dennis J. "Pat" Opatrny in early 1967: "I have not been satisfied with either the philosophy or the performance of the Republican Party in recent years. The reason the Democratic Party has enjoyed success in Nebraska until recently is because it has occupied the middle of the political road. The Republican Party has moved too far to the right . . . I'm a moderate Republican in political philosophy—and have strong feelings on this. I don't like either the far left or the far right."[34]

Yeutter's moderate version of Republicanism, however, was tested in the 1968 GOP primaries. In January of that year he wrote to Opatrny, saying he favored the comparatively liberal northeastern governor Nelson A. Rockefeller for the Republican nomination. He had seen Nixon a few weeks before at a speech at Creighton University in Omaha, however, and had a chance to meet him at dinner. "I was quite impressed. Although Rockefeller would still be my choice of Republican candidates, I would not be surprised if

Nixon would wrap up the nomination in the primaries. He is projecting an entirely new image. The Nixon of 1967 hardly resembles the Nixon of 1960. It appears that he has learned from some of his past errors. He seems to have a lot of self-confidence, is able to smile and joke, and seems to have his organization well oiled."[35]

Yeutter also provided a reference for graduate school for Opatrny, whom he had befriended. Throughout his working life, Yeutter provided many such letters of reference for schools or jobs for people he respected. "It was a pleasure for me to lend a hand in your recent application to become a graduate student at UCLA," Yeutter wrote. "Although the field of journalism will be losing a very capable young newsman (at least temporarily), I am sure that the additional education will be a fine long-run investment for you. We miss you around the State House."[36] Opatrny, a Marine Corps veteran who had attended the graduate school of journalism at the University of California–Berkeley, skipped over UCLA, though he went on to a distinguished career at the *San Francisco Examiner*.[37]

Nationally, Nixon defeated Rockefeller and Reagan, the conservative-wing candidate, and others in nearly all the 1968 primaries around the country to become the party's nominee. Nixon took Nebraska with 70 percent of the vote to 21 percent for Reagan and 5 percent for Rockefeller, though neither Reagan nor Rockefeller visited Nebraska that year.[38] Nixon then went on in the fall of 1968 to defeat Democrat Hubert H. Humphrey Jr., then the sitting vice president, and independent George C. Wallace Jr., the segregationist and former governor of Alabama, in a three-way race for the presidency. Yeutter would later take a leading regional role in helping get Nixon reelected as president in 1972 and would support Reagan's successful election drives in 1980 and 1984. He wound up working in Washington under both men. But neither man was Yeutter's top choice for the presidency at the outset. (He favored the more moderate George H. W. Bush, rather than Reagan, in the 1980 primaries, which Reagan won.)

Back in Nebraska, after he helped Tiemann put his controversial taxing and spending programs in place, Yeutter's major work in the state's politics was largely done by early 1968. So when he was offered an opportunity that would bring his educational, political, and economic expertise to bear far from the halls of state government, he leaped at it. Officials at the University of Nebraska asked him to take charge of a program in Bogotá, Colombia, to upgrade agricultural education, research, and extension in the country by creating a graduate agricultural program much like that in Nebraska and across other parts of the United States.

The University of Nebraska Mission in Colombia, as it was called, was funded by the Kellogg and Ford Foundations, operated in conjunction with the U.S. Agency for International Development, and involved five other midwestern universities. The project was the brainchild of Yeutter mentor and then-chancellor of the University of Nebraska, Clifford M. Hardin, with whom Yeutter had worked closely on university budget matters while in the governor's office. As Yeutter recalled about Hardin's role in the Colombia effort in 1971, "He was primarily responsible for its creation and fortunately it has turned out to be one of the most successful foreign aid efforts that this country has ever had."[39]

For the little-traveled Yeutter and his family—which by then had grown to include four children, about three to thirteen years old— the international adventure would be an eye-opener. The experience would confirm Yeutter's view that free-market capitalism and open trade provided the best route for people to prosper and for countries to grow. Even more important, his experiences in South America would set the stage for the central roles he would in time assume as he worked to revolutionize the global trading system. The program immersed him in a foreign culture for two years and gave him the chance to develop fluency in Spanish, something he would later use with Spanish-speaking diplomats and trade officials—and a skill that, unlike so many others he had, did not come naturally to him. As he later told his wife, Cristena, learning a second language in his late thirties challenged Yeutter, but, characteristically, he mastered Spanish by bending his shoulder to the plow, logging long hours of working at it, and getting lots of practice.[40] In Colombia, he spoke Spanish at work and watched Spanish-language television at home.

3

More Self-Help

For both Colombia and Yeutter, the time he and his young family spent in Latin America with the University of Nebraska Mission was transformative. Those years would presage dramatic economic growth in Colombia, particularly in agriculture. They would also set Yeutter on a path that would establish his bona fides in bureaucracy and politics in Washington DC, as well as give him the international chops that would serve him well still later in his career.

Yeutter directed the Colombia program from September 1968 until October 1970, and he and his forty or so academic colleagues from several universities built an agricultural education and extension program on models that had been successful in the United States. Some two hundred of the Colombian students came to the United States for master's and doctoral degrees during that period, and many came for short-term extension training programs. Yeutter and his team developed a master's program for the Colombians at National University as well, enabling them to train their own graduate students. They worked, too, with the Colombian Agricultural Institute, a body akin to the U.S. Department of Agriculture. By Yeutter's account, five years later, the program proved to be "probably one of the best foreign aid efforts the United States Government has ever had in an agriculturally related endeavor. . . .

Colombia now probably has more well trained agriculturalists than any other nation in South America with the exception of Brazil."[1]

In addition to training people in the latest farmland techniques, the program was aimed at helping Colombia diversify its agricultural economy, moving beyond just coffee. Over time, the country moved into cut flowers, bananas, sugarcane, rice, maize, cotton, beans, oil palm, tobacco, and tropical fruits. Cattle also became prominent, along with guinea pigs.[2] Colombia's gross domestic product (GDP) more than doubled in current U.S. dollars from $5.8 billion in 1967 to $13.1 billion in 1975, soaring to peak at $381.8 billion in 2013 before slipping to $282.8 billion in 2016 amid problems with terrorists and drug cartels. With some of those problems subsiding, the GDP bounced back to $331.1 billion in 2018, according to the World Bank.[3]

For the Yeutters, the Colombian adventure was life-changing. While Yeutter developed his Spanish, his two older sons, Brad and Gregg, did so as well, and they worked to maintain their language skills after returning to the United States. Yeutter in his 1975 interview with the University of Nebraska's George S. Round called the time "probably the finest experience that we had as a family in all our lives," saying, "I wouldn't sell those two years for a million dollars. They vividly and persuasively illustrated to me the value of international programs. Not just to the recipient country, but perhaps even to a greater extent to the participants therein."

The program was good for Nebraska, too, Yeutter maintained. It and international efforts like it enriched participants, who returned to their universities and other stateside positions as "broader and broader people." He likely was speaking from personal experience in adding, "It gives them a perspective on life and living that is altogether different from anything they can ever achieve in Nebraska. The total exposure of living in another culture is simply invaluable."[4] It also gave him a chance to shine as an administrator of what he said was the largest such U.S. project of its kind at the time.[5]

Yeutter was taken with what he called "fascinating" Bogotá, then a city of about two million people. The sprawling city was a far cry from tiny Eustis, where the population of five hundred when he was born had dropped to four hundred by 1970. It was much larger, too, than Lincoln, which that year had fewer than 150,000 residents, or even Omaha, with fewer than 350,000. "The architecture is advanced considerably beyond that of this country, so the suburban homes are beautiful," he wrote to a friend in Gordon, Nebraska, after he and Jeanne flew down for a visit. "All of them have interior gardens, lots of stone work, fireplace, etc." He said his wife, tending to their home, would have two maids and a gardener, "so we'll be spoiled rotten by 1970." The cost for the help would be $20 per month each. He joked to his friend, attorney Michael V. Smith, "I suppose that would be about a half hour of legal work in Gordon."[6] Before heading out to stay in Bogotá, he also wrote to a colleague in the program, asking that he keep an eye out for attractive homes in his neighborhood, adding with his characteristic, sometimes mildly randy wit, "Likewise for maids. (I told Jeanne that I was going to spend December and January interviewing sexy maids, but she doesn't seem to believe me.)"[7]

After a year in Bogotá, Yeutter had developed deeper and more nuanced impressions of the place. Gaps between the very wealthy and the poor were wide, leading to social instability, he told the *Lincoln Evening Journal and Nebraska State Journal.* Unemployment, at 20 percent, plus widespread underemployment could make for a highly explosive situation, he suggested to the newspaper. But he also said that the University of Nebraska program he was leading was making a big dent and that the potential for agriculture in the country was "tremendous," as were its natural resources and "people resources."[8]

Over the years after the Yeutters left, Colombia suffered from the emergence of drug cartels and armed conflict with the Revolutionary Armed Forces of Colombia (FARC). Even though the government struck a deal to end FARC terrorism in 2016, terrorism from the National Liberation Army continued to plague the country as of 2020.[9] The country developed into a leading supplier of cocaine for the United States and the rest of the world, an illicit trade that has persisted well into the first decades of the twenty-first century, posing a danger to farmers like those Yeutter's group trained.[10] As author and documentarian Toby Muse reported, coca co-opted and supplanted parts of the agricultural economy that Yeutter sought to build. "You had these dignified towns of cattle ranchers or coffee growers," Muse told the *Atlantic* in mid-2020 after releasing his book *Kilo: Inside the Deadliest Cocaine Cartels—from the Jungles to the Streets*. "Coca takes over. Then social decay comes." He added that officials in Bogotá couldn't control the remote territories, where some farmers plant as little as one or two hectares of coca, thus avoiding government forces that tried to eradicate bigger plantings and entrenching cocaine in the farmland economy.[11]

Nonetheless, years earlier Yeutter and his group made inroads into Colombia that have endured, and the marks that the time there made on his family also persisted. After she returned to Lincoln, Nebraska, in August 1970, Jeanne Yeutter told a reporter for the *Omaha World-Herald* that her life and that of her children would never be the same. They were touched by the warmth of the people they dealt with, such as when the family chauffeur gave Jeanne and the children a basket of orchids as they prepared to leave. She was impressed at how the role of a maid in Colombia was a high calling and that doing without one—as midwestern homemakers such as herself might prefer—would deprive people of honorable jobs. Foreshadowing volunteer efforts she would make all through the rest of her life, Jeanne and other foreign women ventured into a Bogotá slum to set up a day care center. She drew on her home economics training to help boost protein in the diets of people they worked with, using beans instead of unaffordable eggs. She also worked with a program for foster parents and at a family planning clinic. Overall, the experience was an education for her. As she told journalist Ruth Thone, "Everybody should be a foreigner once in his life . . . to feel what it's like to be a foreigner."[12]

Yeutter's second son, Gregg, had similarly powerful memories from the eighteen months he was there. He attended part of sixth grade and all of seventh in a school in Colombia. "It was an incredible experience for me," he says. "I did not want to come back to the United States, I loved it that much." He was smitten by the international school he attended, the city, and the Colombians he dealt with, but he also found it an education to see the deep disparities in wealth. People lived in makeshift tents on a vacant lot next to the house they lived in, he recalls, musing that if it weren't for the accident of his birth to a couple of successful Americans, "that could be me." It fostered a sense of compassion in him for people in need. "I would forever recommend a foreign living experience to anyone," Gregg Yeutter says.[13]

As Yeutter's time in Colombia drew to a close, he had a few top-notch options to choose from for his next career move: working as dean of international programs at the University of Nebraska, taking a spot at the U.S. Department of Agriculture (USDA) as administrator of the Consumer and Marketing Service (C&MS), or serving as agricultural adviser for President Nixon, a job that Nebraska senator Carl T. Curtis had pressed for specifically for Yeutter. At first Yeutter was intrigued with the idea of working in the White House, but he ultimately rejected the early chance. "When I visited the White House, thrilling as that experience is for anyone, I was not impressed by Mr. [John D.] Ehrlichman," assistant to the president for domestic affairs, Yeutter recalled in a 2015 note in his personal files. "I simply thought he was over his head in the job he was occupying, and that made me unconvinced that I should work under his jurisdiction. The prestige of the job was appealing, and I was most grateful for all the support from Senator Curtis, but I concluded that accepting that post (were it offered) would not be a good move."[14]

Ehrlichman certainly had impressive credentials, though. Like Yeutter, he was a U.S. Air Force veteran, even winning the Distinguished Flying Cross as a navigator in World War II. After the war, he earned his undergraduate degree in political science at UCLA and his law degree at Stanford Law School. But Yeutter's instinct in not wanting to work for Ehrlichman may have been prescient—or he was just very lucky. The president's assistant was convicted of conspiracy, obstruction of justice, and perjury in 1975 for events involving the June 1972 break-in at the Democratic National Committee headquarters that ultimately felled Nixon. Ehrlichman had put together and oversaw the Plumbers, the secret group that carried out the botched break-in.[15]

In the fall of 1970, though, all that was yet to come, and Washington appealed more to Yeutter than returning to Lincoln. So when mentor Clifford M. Hardin, then the secretary of agriculture under Nixon, offered him the C&MS administrator spot, he took it. The position would establish Yeutter's chops in the regulatory world of Washington DC and school him in dealing with agricultural and political issues well beyond his state and university experience and his days on the family farm. The job, which he took in October 1970, made him responsible for such crucial functions as meat and poultry inspection, the grading of agricultural products, development of product standards, market news, the administration of market orders, and the procurement of food for commodity distribution and school lunch programs.[16] "I have never regretted that decision," Yeutter later recalled. "I loved the Consumer & Marketing Service appointment, and it led to all the other positions I held in the Federal government."[17] Still later, he said, "C&MS was one of my favorite jobs in D.C. because it was an executive position, and I liked to run things!"[18]

The new move was a big jump in responsibility for Yeutter, who was thirty-nine when he took the post. C&MS, then one of the government's largest consumer protection agencies, included some eight hundred offices nationwide with fourteen thousand employees and an annual budget topping $250 million. His challenge was, in part, to split up and reorganize the agency, as Nixon planned to shrink his cabinet and fold parts of C&MS and the Food and Drug Administration into a new Department of Human Resources while carving off some parts of C&MS into a new Department of Economic Affairs.

While Nixon did not get the congressional authority he needed to set up his new departments, Yeutter still was charged with streamlining C&MS. "We've rewritten the job descriptions for a lot of people," Yeutter told the trade journal *Meat Management* half a year into his tenure. He looked at cutting midlevel supervisory roles, for instance, but he wanted to avoid wholesale sacking, saying, "No one should deliberately hurt anyone. . . . There's no point in being tough just to show that you can be, particularly when a man's future is at issue. We don't try to harm anyone, financially or position-wise, if it is at all possible to avoid."[19] He planned to consolidate his staffers by preserving eight regional offices and deploying staffers among thirty-five area offices around the country, each in a state capital.[20]

Philosophically, the job would also help set the tone for further steps in Yeutter's career. As he moved up through governmental posts, he wouldn't try to yank government out of the agricultural and global trade marketplace altogether—something some Libertarian critics sought. But he would aim to rein in government, preferring markets over government-led decisions. One case in point: starting with an FDR initiative to shore up agriculture as prices collapsed in the Depression, the USDA had helped some commodity groups develop marketing order programs, and those continued when Yeutter took the helm at C&MS. The orders allowed producers of various commodities—including dairy products, fruits, vegetables, and tree nuts—to set base prices for their goods, as well as regulate the quality and quantity of the products, and thus to collectively influence supply, demand, and price. Yeutter accepted such programs, saying USDA involvement was minimal and arguing that the orders were "in the best tradition of our free enterprise system" because industry players developed the terms.

To an economist, such producer groups are little more than government-coordinated cartels, but this did not appear to trouble Yeutter. He held that producers, not the USDA, decided when to phase in and out marketing order programs, and they would be both initiated and terminated by producer votes. Striking a moderate—and diplomatic—tone, Yeutter told *Broiler Industry* magazine, "Marketing orders are not a panacea for all of agriculture's ills. But they can provide a very useful and effective mechanism for dealing with *some* marketing problems for producers of at least *some* agricultural commodities. We should be careful not to claim too much for marketing orders, but not too little, either."

Further, Yeutter contended that such government programs helped develop "some semblance of supply discipline in some commodities." He expected that over time, government involvement would decline, however, throwing that "discipline" in production into jeopardy. He warned, "If that discipline is to be gradually abandoned, someone must devise an alternative, or the price consequences could be disastrous."

The USDA at the time was coming under pressure from consumer advocates to abandon some longtime practices and strengthen others. Yeutter's unit, for instance, periodically published marketing guides for commodities including broiler chickens, eggs, and turkeys. These provided price and supply guidelines that some critics opposed, holding that they propped up prices to the detriment of consumers. Yeutter defended them, arguing that they were tools for helping producers plan their operations and vehicles for helping improve efficiency in production and marketing, thus benefiting consumers. "Personally, I hope that we will be able to do even more with marketing guides in the future than we have in the past," he said. Some poultry producers, though, were troubled by regulations that C&MS proposed, as it implemented legislation that mandated tougher meat and poultry inspections, and Yeutter maintained that the changes kept pace with the industry's progress.

In his revealing *Broiler Industry* interview, Yeutter took an oblique shot at consumer advocates such as Ralph Nader, then one of the government's major critics. Such advocates were calling on the government to force industry to provide more information on product labels. "I have no quarrel with asking processors to include label information that consumers truly want," Yeutter said. "But I sometimes wonder if it is the average consumer, or only his advocate, who wants some of the information that has been under discussion in recent months." Reflecting his economics background, Yeutter argued for cost-benefit analyses to make sure that consumers knew the costs involved in gathering and maintaining all the information required for labeling. "As label requirements become more complex, product costs will inevitably increase," he argued. "The question then becomes whether the benefit is worth the cost, and that analysis is frequently omitted."[21]

Nader and his student task force, known as "Nader's Raiders," had focused most of their ire on the Food and Drug Administration (FDA), criticizing its food protection programs as servile to industry and in a state of "total collapse." In *The Chemical Feast: The Ralph Nader Study Group Report on Food Protection and the Food and Drug Administration*, a 273-page report written by Nader associate James S. Turner and published in the spring of 1970, the group charged that the FDA had succumbed to political pressure and was unwilling to protect consumers. The group excoriated the use of additives and the adulteration of much of the food supply.[22] Presaging his later battles with activist groups—especially environmental organizations—Yeutter had little good to say about Nader in a talk at the end of April 1971 in Lincoln, Nebraska, marking Law Day. He called the consumer advocate "a man who made his reputation on gross exaggeration and oversimplification."[23]

Labeling requirements and practices would only grow over time, of course, and would become widely accepted. But Yeutter's view of a reduced government role in agriculture would also take hold in many areas—and he would play key roles in that shift. Even as early as 1971 he was predicting changes, some of which he would drive over the coming years. "Since we live in a society that is becoming more complex each day, it would be naïve to assert that government will not play an important role in agriculture (or any other industry for that matter) a decade from now. But that role may well be substantially different in 1980. I would doubt, for example that government will be as involved in the production process as it has been in recent years," he said. "Some of government's past involvement in agriculture can undoubtedly be eliminated and never missed. But some essential functions may well be abandoned, and these must then be carried out by the private sector. . . . In my judgment, agriculture is ready for less governmental involvement and more self-help."[24]

For all his advocacy that government play a smaller role, however, Yeutter certainly was a dedicated government worker. He averaged more than a hundred hours on the job each week, according to *Meat Management* magazine. Long days were a hallmark of his career, especially in government, when travel to far-flung places around the world would stretch his working time around the clock. "Work is my hobby," Yeutter told the magazine.[25] Years before, Yeutter had credited his farm upbringing—particularly his "ultra hard-working" father—for his work ethic. "You just didn't work any harder than we did. Daylight saving time would have been irrelevant to our family," he told a journalist in 1967, though his words applied throughout his life. "I've always tried to just plainly outwork competition."[26]

At C&MS, he was able to indulge his "hobby" to a fare-thee-well—in part because he lived in an apartment while working in Washington DC, as Jeanne and the children stayed at the family home in Lincoln. The family lived in a house that Jeanne's father, an architect, had designed. Jeanne's father and mother lived just across a small lake that backed up to the house. Yeutter's family saw him during the summers and when he returned to Lincoln on weekends, sometimes as rarely as every other weekend.[27] His children didn't want for family company, though, and had fond memories of cutting across the water to visit their grandparents. "We kept that house for years and years and years," recalls Van A. Yeutter, Yeutter's youngest son.[28]

After Yeutter spent just over a year at the helm of C&MS, politics intervened to bring him a new challenge. This one would set him up for future GOP roles and would also bring him closer to the White House. Yeutter's move was triggered by the resignation in November 1971 of his mentor, Clifford M. Hardin, as secretary of agriculture. Nixon's White House had decided Hardin was not "political" enough, so he took a job with Ralston-Purina, leading to speculation that Yeutter might follow him to join the company.[29] However, when Yeutter got the call to take a major role in Nixon's reelection effort in late 1971, he answered it. At the time, some of the president's darkest deeds—the ones that would drive him from office under threat of impeachment—were yet to come.

4

Character Flaws

For Republicans and the nation overall, the years from 1972 to 1974 were tumultuous and largely bleak ones. Richard M. Nixon was facing reelection to a second term in 1972, at a time when national turmoil over the Vietnam War was intensifying. The war had led Nixon's predecessor, Lyndon B. Johnson, to decline to seek reelection in 1968. And Nixon that year won his first term, defeating Vice President Hubert H. Humphrey Jr., in part by claiming to have a plan to end the war. But Nixon failed to deliver on his promise during his opening term, even as he was beset by widespread fury over the war.

Things had grown ugly while Johnson was in office and worsened all across America during Nixon's first years on the job. In May 1970 Ohio National Guardsmen shot thirteen students during a demonstration in the heartland at Kent State University, killing four of them. Radical leftists in the Weather Underground bombed the Capitol in Washington DC in March 1971 and the Pentagon in May 1972.[1] As the president first sought victory on the Vietnam battlefield and later pursued what he called "peace with honor," hundreds of thousands of demonstrators repeatedly marched in Washington. In his reelection fight in 1972, Nixon faced South Dakota senator George S. McGovern, a Democrat who pressed for withdrawal from the war.

After working to carry out Nixon's policies in agriculture at the Consumer and Marketing Service, however, Yeutter felt loyal to the president and the GOP. So when Attorney General John N. Mitchell tapped him to help Nixon keep his presidency for a second term, he took up the task.[2] He quit the Department of Agriculture and from January to December 1972 served as Midwest regional director of the president's national reelection committee. He oversaw all facets of the president's campaign in seven midwestern states and did double duty as the campaign's director for agriculture, responsible for the president's reelection efforts in farm country across all fifty states.[3] "I just couldn't say no to running the Nixon agricultural campaign nationwide," he recalled in 2015. "I was the only person in the now notorious Committee for the Re-election of the President (CREEP) to fill two of the major campaign positions. Fortunately, I avoided the Watergate scandal, and was unaware of what happened until long after the campaign ended."[4] Immersed in national electoral politics, as he was for Nixon in the new position, Yeutter made his bones for later partisan roles.

The CREEP job was a challenge, with inflation driving up farm costs as farmers struggled with low corn prices and uncertainty about whether Hardin's successor as secretary of agriculture, Earl L. Butz, would cut farm supports and force farmers to rely more on markets.[5] Many farmers were unhappy with some Nixon administration policies, as reflected by a North Dakota poll in the spring of 1972 in which 72 percent of some six thousand farmers surveyed disapproved of the policies, and 90 percent said price supports on grain should be raised, against administration wishes. Nonetheless, between 60 and 65 percent of forty-nine hundred responding farmers preferred Nixon over his potential rivals, Senators Edmund S. Muskie, Hubert H. Humphrey, and George McGovern. Yeutter told an agriculture reporter that the polls were "relatively accurate," arguing that nonfarm issues such as foreign policy and "labor union arrogance" would figure more heavily than agricultural issues among farmland voters.[6]

But Yeutter also saw that post-election, the administration would have to deal with the widespread dissatisfaction among farmers. "I don't see how any administration can ignore the fact that we have not developed farm programs which are satisfactory to farmers," he told the agriculture reporter. Still, he struck a cautious tone, perhaps not wanting to alienate farmers during the election year. "Perhaps we should reappraise farm policy from the very beginning, but we should not make major changes in what we have now unless we can design a better program."[7] Indeed, that reappraisal would come for Yeutter and would mark some of his signature achievements in farm policy in the future, but all that lay well down the path, long after Nixon's reelection and eventual fall from office.

Winning over farm country for Nixon would require persuasive policies, but even more, it would demand deft organizational skills. Republicans and Democrats both made broad and far-reaching promises in their party platforms for 1972, but with only a few sharp differences. They both pledged to support family farms, for instance. But while the GOP aimed to do that with tax law changes, the Democrats encouraged farmers and ranchers to organize and bargain collectively, in part by extending marketing orders to all farm commodities. Both sought to protect family farmers from rapacious corporations, with the Republicans vowing to shield families from "the unfair competition of farming by tax-loss corporations and non-farm enterprises," while Democrats would "prohibit farming, or gaining of monopolistic control of production, on part of corporations financed by non-farm sources," "investigate agribusiness interlocks and prohibit tax shelters in agriculture," and end farm benefit programs for units larger than family farms.

On another point, the Republicans pledged "realistic environmental standards" that would not unduly burden farmers. They also promised to "keep farm prices in the private sector, not subject to price controls." For their part, the Democrats promised higher prices and income for farmers, in part by barring price ceilings on farm products until prices hit 110 percent of 1910–14 parity (an oddity of agricultural economics in which the USDA sought to maintain parity between farmland and industrial product prices, using a ratio of the index of prices farmers got for their goods to the index of prices they paid for inputs and expenses). While the

GOP pledged to open foreign markets, the Democrats similarly promised to build stronger export programs and, in a protectionist fillip, backed "rigid standards of inspection for imports of meats and dairy products." In one area that likely pleased some farmers less, Democrats pledged to support the United Farm Workers as it sought collective bargaining in dealing with growers. And in an unintentionally ironic note—since it foreshadowed Yeutter's own later role as U.S. secretary of agriculture—the Democrats called for appointing a farmer or rancher to that post.[8]

Party platforms aside, the organization that Yeutter built delivered the farm country vote for Nixon. By Yeutter's own immodest account in a CREEP press release from October 24, 1972, shortly before the election, the effort was "the most intensively organized farm and ranch Presidential campaign in the nation's history." He set up nearly two thousand county committees headed by husband-and-wife teams across farming and ranching areas to deliver the message to friends and neighbors that the Nixon administration was bringing progress. The committees, accordingly, were called Farm or Ranch Families for the President. Yeutter made a special effort to reach younger farmers, noting that fifteen of the husbands who chaired fifty state committees were under forty years old. In a comment that might seem patronizing to modern ears but may have seemed natural, witty, or even chivalrous to a man who came of age in the 1950s, Yeutter said, "Understandably, I hesitated to attempt to log the age of the farm wives jointly chairing state committees with their husbands." The release noted that Yeutter believed that farm wives had never before played such a leading role in a political campaign.[9]

Yeutter and other economists who supported Nixon had to put aside one of their cardinal free-market principles the year before the election, though, when the president ordered a ninety-day freeze on all prices and wages throughout the country—a draconian measure that he dramatically announced on a televised Sunday evening broadcast on August 15, 1971. Nixon feared inflation, which notched upward at a 4.3 percent rate that year. The president created the Pay Board and Price Commission, designed to control increases on an ongoing basis after the election. He also stuck an extra 10 percent tariff on dutiable imports, hoping to drive other countries to revalue their currencies upward against the dollar. He wound up all but repudiating the commission's actions shortly before his second inauguration in January 1973, when he ended mandatory wage and price controls on everything but food, health care, and construction.[10]

Nixon also wanted to restrain the overvalued dollar and the global currency tumult that had plagued him and Presidents John F. Kennedy and Lyndon B. Johnson. So he ended the gold standard, which had long set the value of gold at $35 an ounce. Following Nixon's summertime move, the world's ten major democracies in late 1971 agreed to a set of fixed exchange rates, based on a further devalued dollar, only to spawn another devaluation in February 1973 and, in time, floating exchange rates.[11] The devaluations tended to drive up inflation, as imports commanded higher prices and demand for exports rose.

The price controls were a bust with most economists. Breaking with Nixon, whom he had advised, economist Milton Friedman said the president's move ended "in utter failure and the emergence into the open of the suppressed inflation."[12] When prices climbed again, Nixon reimposed a temporary freeze in June 1973, even though it had become obvious that price controls didn't work, as critics later noted. As authors Daniel Yergin and Joseph Stanislaw describe it, "Ranchers stopped shipping their cattle to the market, farmers drowned their chickens, and consumers emptied the shelves of supermarkets."[13] Heavy spending on Vietnam, coupled with rocketing oil prices thanks to the Organization of the Petroleum Exporting Countries (OPEC), the devaluation of the dollar, and lingering "stagflation," led to a sixteen-month recession that began in the fall of 1973 and stretched into March 1975.[14]

When Yeutter was stumping for Nixon throughout the Midwest in 1972, the results of the president's economic package, known as the "Nixon shock," lay in the future.[15] Indeed, Yeutter, who likely knew better as a classically trained economist, told a reporter for the *Sunday Oklahoman* that the wage and price control program would succeed. He predicted that food prices would rise just 2 to 3 percent, instead of 5 to 6 percent, although he said the long-term trend would be upward.[16] He praised Nixon to a reporter in Lincoln, Nebraska, as "the only President who has made a real effort to control inflation."[17] Yeutter also appeared to accept the Nixon administration's market-meddling moves in agriculture, particularly efforts to boost wheat and feed grain prices through a 1970 farm act program in which farmers were paid to keep land out of production, a "set-aside" program in the bill that Yeutter told a reporter was "unquestionably the most popular piece of farm legislation that we've had in my lifetime."[18] Soon after taking the reelection committee position, Yeutter explained to a reporter for the *Denver Post*, "The President's election chances of prevailing in the agriculture sections of the country will be enhanced if food grain prices are at satisfactory levels."[19]

At the outset of the year, however, Yeutter was cautious about how well Nixon would do in the farm belt. He told the *Post* reporter that the race would be tighter than Nixon's 1968 campaign, when the candidate won overwhelming support from farmers. Yeutter warned that low grain prices would have a depressing effect.[20] As it happened, major commodity farm prices strengthened through the year, and grain prices, in particular, were boosted by a big mid-year grain sale the government made to the Soviet Union, according to an internal campaign postmortem analysis.

But the analysis suggested that agricultural issues were not decisive for farmers in the election. Yeutter's team dealt less with such matters and instead drove home Nixon's views on issues including inflation, drugs, busing for racial diversity in schools, welfare, crime, and the courts—issues that seemed to be front and center for many farmers.[21] Yeutter told a farm editors' conference in Washington DC in April 1972 that the Vietnam War was more important to rural people than farm policy. The agricultural campaign was buttressed, moreover, by speeches across the Midwest by Agriculture Secretary Butz, a blunt-to-a-fault speaker who had grown up on an Indiana dairy farm and proved to be popular on the stump at the time. Unlike many others across the country, farmers and ranchers appeared to appreciate Butz's pleas for support for Nixon as U.S. forces stepped up action against enemy forces in Vietnam.[22]

Yeutter's early caution may have been smart and appropriate, but he did deliver the farm belt for Nixon. The president took more than

70 percent of the farm and ranch vote—a ratio that was "probably the strongest support ever received by a Presidential candidate
in history," as Yeutter put it in a congratulatory thank-you note to
CREEP supporters in the farmland. "It was a magnificent victory;
the President is very pleased, and very proud of you and all the
others who worked so hard on his behalf," Yeutter wrote. "Never
before has a campaign of this intensity been conducted in American politics. We countered the opposition at their point of greatest
strength—organization—and beat them at their own game. We out-
organized, out-worked, and out-performed the McGovern forces."[23]

After helping engineer Nixon's big win over McGovern, Yeutter
got his reward. He headed back to the Department of Agriculture,
this time to take a bigger job as assistant secretary of agriculture for
marketing and consumer services, working closely with Butz. Starting in January 1973 and lasting until March 1974, Yeutter was responsible for all regulatory and domestic market service functions of
the USDA. The agencies reporting to him included the Animal and
Plant Health Inspection Service, Agricultural Marketing Service,
Commodity Exchange Authority, Food and Nutrition Service, and
Packers and Stockyards Administration.[24] In that time, Yeutter—
who had long backed government efforts to feed the most needy,
even when critics derided welfare—helped birth the Special Sup-
plemental Nutrition Program for Women, Infants, and Children
(WIC), a major support program for the poor that still exists as of
this writing. WIC had been created by legislation sponsored by then-
senator Hubert H. Humphrey Jr. in 1972, and in the fall of 1973 Yeutter joined California officials to launch a pilot of the program in San
Diego before rolling it out nationally.[25] Yeutter wrote in 2015, "The
WIC program, whose first budget was only a few million dollars,
now is budgeted in the billions annually, but it probably does more
good nutritionally than any food program the nation has ever had."[26]

Despite his earlier support of Nixon's broad-based price control efforts, Yeutter in 2015 recalled that he and Butz had fought
against such controls on food, battling a strong-willed top adviser,
Donald H. Rumsfeld, and his deputy, Richard B. "Dick" Cheney,
who ran the inflation-fighting Cost of Living Council. "Secretary

Butz and I challenged them, and the policy decision went all the way to the President," Yeutter wrote. "We won! That was one of Rumsfeld's rare losses!"[27]

Under Nixon and Butz, who pressed to end many New Deal approaches put in place by FDR, farm policies shifted away from the most heavy-handed government involvement. The Farm Bill of 1973, formally known as the Agricultural and Consumer Protection Act, moved agriculture away from the coupling of high support prices and production that had dictated U.S. farm production for most of the prior forty years. Instead, it set up target prices, with price guarantees and deficiency payments, and created disaster payment and disaster reserve inventories, all of which incentivized farmers to produce to their maximums.[28]

As Yeutter later described the change, mistrust of market forces dating back to the Depression had shaped the government's approach to that point. "The theory was that government planners could better allocate supply and demand than the marketplace could," he said in "The New American Agriculture," a 1974 speech. "Frankly, the plans didn't work very well. We either had a glut of government-owned grain carried at high expense to the taxpayers, or the inability to adjust planning quickly enough to meet changing marketing situations. Thankfully, with the more flexible farm legislation now in effect, farmers are once again free to make their own management decisions and to respond quickly to any changes in the marketplace."[29] The bill also expanded food stamp coverage and benefits, which Yeutter administered.

The 1972–74 period in the Nixon administration, however, was darkened by two scandals, the first and more infamous of which was Watergate. Watergate began in mid-1972, even as Yeutter—who said he was unaware of the sordid events—was marshaling his troops to help Nixon march to victory in the election. Five men, operating at the behest of top CREEP and Nixon administration officials, broke into the Democratic National Committee office at the Watergate complex on June 17, 1972, to photograph campaign documents and install wiretaps. They were caught, and when the action came to light—in large part because of the investigative reporting of *Washing-*

ton Post journalists Robert U. "Bob" Woodward and Carl Bernstein—Nixon and others tried to cover it up, paying the burglars to keep the president's involvement secret. Scores of administration and CREEP officials were indicted and convicted of various offenses in the scandal, including the president's chief of staff, Harry Robbins "H. R." Haldeman; White House counsel John W. Dean III; Special Counsel Charles W. Colson; Domestic Affairs Assistant John D. Ehrlichman; Communications Adviser Jeb S. Magruder; Deputy Chief of Staff Alexander P. Butterfield; and Attorney General Mitchell.[30]

The Watergate break-in trial of the burglars and some of their CREEP backers began before Nixon's inauguration, in January 1973, and convictions and guilty pleas soon followed. Through the spring of the year, prosecutors methodically climbed up the chain of officials, some of whom cooperated in the investigation and some of whom resigned or were fired by the White House. After damning tapes of White House conversations about the break-in and the cover-up came to light, in mid-1974 the House Judiciary Committee drafted articles of impeachment against Nixon, but they never moved to a full House vote. Instead, Nixon resigned on August 8, 1974, after revelations in televised hearings eroded support from his Republican colleagues in the Senate and House.[31]

Nixon's tenure was marred still further in 1973 by scandal involving his vice president, Spiro T. Agnew. Agnew, former governor of Maryland, quit the nation's second-highest office that year after he pleaded no contest to a single count of federal income tax evasion. The plea sprang from an investigation of alleged bribery and extortion during his governorship and a term as Baltimore county executive. He denied the bribery and extortion charges, in which he was alleged to have accepted at least $87,500 in bribes and kickbacks from architects and engineers working on state and county highway and bridge projects, and in the plea deal the government agreed not to prosecute him. He resigned on October 10, 1973, was fined $10,000, and was sentenced to three years of probation for evading income tax payments. He later had to pay the state of Maryland $268,482 after officials there brought a civil suit, along with $150,000 in back taxes, interest, and penalties demanded by the IRS.[32] Gerald R. Ford Jr., a congressman from Michigan who had been born in Omaha, rose to the vice presidency on Nixon's nomination in December 1973.

Despite the scandals, Nixon may have seemed like a Tiemann-like figure to Yeutter in some respects. Regarded as a moderate in the Republican ranks, the president—like Tiemann and Yeutter—believed that government could serve useful functions. Nixon created the U.S. Environmental Protection Agency (EPA) and Occupational Safety and Health Administration. His EPA spawned the Clean Air Act, Clean Water Act, and Marine Mammal Protection Act. Nixon also signed Title IX, a civil rights law that prevented gender bias at colleges and universities receiving federal aid. He backed lowering the voting age from twenty-one to eighteen, ended the military draft, and gave Native Americans the right to tribal self-determination by ending forced assimilation and returning their sacred lands.[33] Indeed, with some overstatement, economist Friedman called Nixon "the most socialist of the presidents of the United States in the 20th century," criticizing him for creating those agencies and for doubling the roster of government regulations on business in the Federal Register. Charged the late Friedman, "You had the biggest increase in government regulation and control of industry during the Nixon administration that you had in the whole postwar period."[34]

Nixon, moreover, was an internationalist in ways that appealed to Yeutter, who would later make his biggest professional marks on the global trade stage. Early in his reelection year, Nixon opened the door to China with a weeklong visit in February 1972, when he met Chairman Mao Zedong and other top leaders. In May of that year, the president also visited Moscow for a summit, which led to the Strategic Arms Limitation Treaty, restricting the number of antiballistic missiles in the United States and Soviet Union.[35] The Soviets in July 1972 also bought huge quantities of wheat and corn from the United States at government-subsidized prices, which drove up global grain and food prices, perhaps helping farmers but also notching up the troublesome inflation rate. The deal—controversial at the time—involved about 25 percent of the total American wheat crop.[36] Years later, in 1977, Yeutter hailed the grain sale to the USSR for bringing the country into the global market "essentially for the first time."[37] Nixon also ended U.S. involvement in the Vietnam War, albeit belatedly in 1973, by signing the Paris Peace Accords, and during that year's Yom Kippur War, he backed Israel with substantial aid, which Prime Minister Golda Meir credited with saving her country.[38]

After Nixon's resignation in August 1974, Yeutter avoided condemning his former president, instead expressing sorrow at his fall. "Many of us here spent literally thousands of hours of our lifetime working with and for the (former) president," Yeutter told the *Lincoln Journal.* "So it's inevitable that we feel a great sadness at his departure." Further, he said, Nixon's first term was productive, especially in foreign policy, and he expected Nixon to go down in history as one of the greatest presidents of all time. Added Yeutter, "It's a tragic end to a magnificent career." Tiemann, who at the time had moved to Washington to serve as administrator of the Federal Highway Administration, declined comment on Nixon, saying, "I've done what I've exhorted my people to do: keep your head down, keep an eye on your job and work." Tiemann praised Nixon's successor, Ford, however, as someone people could trust.[39]

Nearly seventeen years afterward, when Nixon was undergoing a public rehabilitation of sorts, Yeutter waxed warmly about his former president in a note to him. At the time, in early 1991, Yeutter was working as chairman of the Republican National Committee, and Nixon sent him a copy of a speech he had made in December 1990 to a Republican group in New York, along with an op-ed he had written for the *New York Times* about U.S. policy in the Persian Gulf in the lead-up to the January 1991 U.S.-led offensive against Saddam Hussein's Iraq, called Operation Desert Storm.[40]

"I've been telling people for years that you have the finest foreign policy mind this country has ever produced," Yeutter said in a letter to Nixon in March 1991. "It was also a delight to chat with you at Washington National Airport for a few minutes a month or so ago. It had been a long time since we've crossed paths, and it was good to see you doing so well." Still gracious toward his former leader, Yeutter wrote effusively of their early association, though he seemed to feel obliged to mention the Watergate scandal, albeit without criticizing Nixon directly. "I still take great pride in first having come to Washington D.C. (in late 1970) during your Administration, and I still believe the 1972 Presidential campaign was the best organized of any that this country has ever seen. I would not expect you to remember this, but I directed the agricultural campaign nationwide that year and the entire campaign in the midwestern states. It was tragic, particularly for you, to have all of that good effort tarnished by Watergate."

Yeutter urged Nixon to stay in touch during the impending presidential campaign, which would pit incumbent Republican president George H. W. Bush against Democrat William J. "Bill" Clinton and Independent H. Ross Perot. "You also have one of the best political minds around, so I hope you'll give me your counsel from time to time as the 1992 campaign season unfolds," Yeutter told Nixon. "When you next have an opportunity to come to Washington, D.C., we'd be delighted to have you stop for a few minutes here at the RNC. I know our top people here would love to see you, and I'd like a chance to absorb some of your insights."[41] It's not clear whether Nixon ever took him up on the offer, but with or without Nixon's advice, Bush fell to Clinton in that election.

With the benefit of hindsight and time, Yeutter in late 2005 offered both damning criticism and fulsome praise for Nixon. "He would have had a far more successful presidency and may not even have had Watergate, had he been more open and transparent with everybody, including the press," Yeutter told high school student Jenna Riemenschneider for a report she did for a U.S. history class.

> It was not unfortunate for President Nixon that the Watergate scandal surfaced; it was unfortunate that he became personally connected with its cover-up. Watergate should have surfaced; all crimes of that nature are ultimately discovered. But the cover-up should never have occurred. It reflected character flaws in the President and some members of his top team, and the media properly publicized those character flaws. . . . Had President Nixon handled the press in a more forthright way, with a lot more congeniality and respect than he ever demonstrated

for them, he would have gone down in history in a much different light than he will now. In foreign policy he may well have been the best President this country has ever had, but the history books may never show that. Those foreign policy achievements, regrettably, will probably be overwhelmed by Watergate.[42]

Before all that, however, Yeutter would labor again for the Department of Agriculture during mid-1970s, when Nixon was gone from the scene. His efforts would school him well for major trade and agricultural positions, and for business leadership opportunities, which all were still to come his way. And the times would test his free-market views, underscoring anew how he saw that pragmatism and compromise sometimes had to trump ideological purity.

5

Free Farmers

For Yeutter, for others toiling in agriculture, and for the nation in general, the mid-1970s brought still more challenges. Contending with "stagflation"—a peculiar blend of stagnant economic conditions and inflation—the country slipped into a scorching recession from November 1973 until March 1975. The jobless rate nearly doubled from 4.6 percent in October 1973 to 9 percent in May 1975, as the inflation rate leaped into double digits, topping out at 12.3 percent in December 1974.[1] Politically, the tumult of Nixon's final days in office gave way to a hiatus with Gerald R. Ford Jr., the vice president who stepped into the Oval Office when Nixon left. Seeking to calm the roiled waters, Ford in September 1974 pardoned the former president for any crimes he may have committed. Trying to build unity, Ford also tapped a liberal northeastern Republican, former New York governor Nelson A. Rockefeller (whom Yeutter, coincidentally, had backed initially for the presidency years before), to become his vice president.

As economic problems deepened, however, solutions from Washington seemed in short supply. One much-ridiculed idea that Ford promoted in the fall of 1974 was his Whip Inflation Now campaign, replete with campaign-style buttons. He asked the public and companies to restrain price increases and take conservation measures to contain the price spiral that was reignited when Nixon's wage and price controls dissipated. But such voluntary restraint proved to be tougher than capping an oil gusher, as manufacturers of all sorts struggled to preserve their profit margins as the costs of their supplies rose. The effort failed, and economists such as Alan Greenspan, Ford's chairman of the Council of Economic Advisers, later explained that "it didn't reflect any practical, conceivable policy that could be implemented."[2]

But Yeutter found grappling with the challenges of the time to be compelling and professionally expanding. Guided by his instincts and education, as well as by political leaders and colleagues, he set a path for himself ideologically—away from New Deal approaches to agriculture and toward market-oriented ones—that would shape his future efforts in farm legislation in years to come. Moreover, he showed his independence from those elected leaders by invoking his intellectual polestar, classical economic theory, in talks that departed sharply from the approaches his two presidents during this period took. At times he contradicted his earlier, election-time rhetoric on behalf of candidate Nixon.

Yeutter served under Nixon as the assistant secretary of agriculture for marketing and consumer services, filling that post for fifteen months until March 1974. He then took up a global portfolio when he became the assistant secretary of agriculture for international affairs and commodity programs, serving under Ford until June 1975. As the economy improved, Yeutter then fatefully shifted gears even more deeply into the international realm to serve as deputy special trade representative in Ford's Executive Office of the President until February 1977.[3] Along with many other political appointees, Yeutter left this trade post after former Georgia governor James Earl "Jimmy" Carter Jr. defeated Ford in 1976 and the Democrats swept into the White House again, ending eight years of GOP control, in January 1977. Yeutter's move out of government while the Republicans were in political exile would prove temporary, but it also opened him more broadly to the corporate world.

In his Department of Agriculture roles, Yeutter hammered away at the familiar economic idea that free markets—when left unmolested—served people far better than government meddling would. Perhaps chastened by Nixon's caps on wages and prices from 1971 to 1973, Yeutter in July 1974 delivered an address to the American Association of Agricultural College Editors titled "Prices: Power to the People," a talk that he described as a "ringing endorsement of the free enterprise system." In it, he derided efforts that he said would have disregarded the role of prices in a market-based economy, such as moves to put government-imposed ceilings on beef prices and government-guaranteed loans for cattle producers. "Prices are the signal system that makes it possible for 200 million Americans to live and work and interact in the world's most complex economy without tripping over each other. Prices make it possible for this fantastically complex organization to produce the things we need," Yeutter thundered. "Prices permit consumers to bid for what they want—be it food or heating oil or electric toothbrushes. Prices make it possible for a man to judge whether he can make a better living producing cattle or rutabagas."

At the time, soaring oil prices had hobbled the U.S. economy, pushing it into recession, as they drove up production costs of everything from cattle to electric toothbrushes to food to gasoline. Inflation was raging. But Yeutter counseled patience, saying that energy prices would self-correct despite the OPEC cartel's power over pricing and supply. "Higher energy prices and profits are now stimulating more energy production and less energy consumption, and this will, in time, bring prices back down," he said. "That is how the pricing system works. It is self-regulating—but only if it is allowed to operate."

Yeutter drew a bold contrast between U.S.-style free-market pricing and systems in other countries. The centrally planned economies of the Soviet Union and other Iron Curtain countries spawned inefficiency, he said, with even the Russians admitting that they lost up to one-third of their potential economic output each year through poor decisions. Whereas they could once make simple choices, such as producing 20 million pairs of shoes, after forty years planners needed to produce 150 million pairs in ranges of styles, colors, and sizes, he explained—all without the price signals that consumer demand delivered to govern supplies. "The shoe store manager simply sells the shoes he gets. The manager of the manufacturing plant is responsible for turning out a certain number of shoes. The central planner allots raw materials for the shoes he thinks consumers should have. But no one has to listen to what the consumer wants."

Because of the absence of price signals, he argued, the Soviets had particular trouble at that time with proper distribution of small consumer items such as shoelaces and meat grinders. "They wind up with too many in Minsk, too few in Pinsk," Yeutter cracked. By contrast, in the United States, consumer demand dictated production and distribution decisions. When a consumer asked for particular goods, store managers could call a supplier for more. The plant would order more raw materials and boost its production schedule. "The market system responds," Yeutter said. As a result, the U.S. economy responded to consumers more quickly and effectively than any other in the world.

He highlighted differences even with some capitalist countries, such as the more managed economy of Japan—a country with which he would later wrangle over import restrictions. Japanese consumer prices on most items, he said, were very high by U.S. standards because the government sought to export as much production as possible. This would plow profits back into businesses to keep growth high, but on the backs of Japanese consumers. "Japanese housewives pay $12 a pound for sirloin steak," he observed. "The average family of four lives in an apartment the size of an average American living room. Again, the consumer has little direct say in how the economy performs."

In decrying the notion that government could make better decisions than markets, the cerebral, farm-bred Yeutter cast his argument in lofty historic terms. Citing the writings of neoconservative New York University professor Irving Kristol, Yeutter traced social history from the pursuit of heavenly perfection in the medieval yearning for the Second Coming to the age of reason, then the age of science, and up to the contemporary age of government. Yeutter argued, "Unfortunately, there is little hope that government can produce perfection either." Perhaps surprisingly, in light of Nixon's creation of various agencies, he complained about "an endless proliferation of government agencies, and government involvement in more and more of our activities."

Bringing his message down to the agricultural level, Yeutter criticized efforts by cattle producers and consumers alike who looked to the government for solutions when markets turned against them. "Unfortunately, too many farm interests have spent the past forty years justifying federal farm subsidies on the premise that market forces do not work in agriculture," he said, striking a theme that he would hit repeatedly in future years, as he sought to reduce the government role in the farmland economy. "When our consumers feel that prices are too high, they demand that the government bring them down. When an industry is losing money, it demands that the government bail it out."

Yeutter told the agricultural college editors that they needed to educate their readers to appreciate the market price system. Americans needed to have faith in it or it wouldn't work, he said. "The heart of our economic system is prices," Yeutter counseled. "We may not always like the level of our prices, but they give us all the power to choose—and that is the ultimate economic power."[4]

He preferred to get Washington out of agriculture as much as possible and to allow decisions to be made at local levels. In early 1974 he wrote a memo to his boss, Secretary of Agriculture Butz, recommending that they consider ending the federal commodity procurement program, in which Washington bought food and provided it to schools under the National School Lunch Program. Yeutter suggested replacing it with a program to provide cash to state and local governments, thus decentralizing purchasing and distribution and, in Yeutter's view, making the system more efficient—a view in line with Republican ideology about state versus federal programming. When the *St. Petersburg Times* editorialized against the idea, going so far as to suggest that Yeutter "be bounced out of government," he struck back in a letter to the editor: "My view is that Federal support should continue until there are no more poor schools, poor orphanages and disaster victims, but such support should be provided in the most efficient way possible. To reject a new and better method out of hand, as you do in your editorial, may be acceptable in the newspaper business, but it is indefensible in government."[5] In the end, Yeutter's suggestion didn't fly, however.[6]

Perhaps because of his past role as an educator, Yeutter seemed to feel that he needed to teach farmers—who were long used to turning to government for both paychecks and guidance on what and how much to produce—that they should trust in the wisdom of markets. He pulled no punches. "Freer Trade: Key to the Future for Grain" was the title of an April 1974 talk he gave to the National Federation of Grain Cooperatives. "We have made impressive gains for farmers with market orientation—but we are meeting new problems and there is still the danger of sliding back into the old solutions," he said. "The new patterns are still not familiar, and our experience with free markets is still limited. There is danger that we may retreat from the market in the face of new pressures, and so lose the benefits we have gained."

While American farmers responded to the 1973 legislation and were planting and producing at higher and higher levels, the world grain crop from the prior year had come up short. That, together with the devaluation of the dollar that occurred when Nixon eliminated convertibility of the dollar to gold and let the currency float on global exchanges, drove up food prices. As a result, demands abounded for export controls, calls rose for consumer boycotts and price rollbacks, and pressures mounted to cap farm prices. But Yeutter, always an optimist and a student of markets, predicted that the growing American supply of grain would meet demand in time. "Consumers will be encouraged, because we will be able to add to current stocks, and food price pressures will moderate somewhat," he predicted. "Consumers' fears about a new era of perpetual food shortage will be eased."[7]

A few weeks later, in a May 1974 talk at the Merchants Exchange of St. Louis, he argued that once-soaring commodity prices likely had leveled off and could hold through 1975. His reasoning: based on recent plantings, supplies of grains would rise through the year. Cotton plantings likewise were up, helping still other farmers. And while soybean acreage had declined, a large carryover of old-crop soybeans ensured high stocks even while big catches of anchovies over the coast of Peru would make fish meal more important as feed for livestock, reducing world demand for U.S. soybeans. "It appears that the world grain situation is returning to a more normal supply and demand balance," Yeutter maintained. As American farm incomes rose, he said, the world was "recovering from the short-crop year of 1972."[8]

He hit hard on the main theme that would guide his future efforts in agriculture and other realms—globalism. American farmers could no longer focus solely on the domestic market but needed to reach out to foreign buyers, forging links to sell their products overseas. "Anyone doubting the growing interdependency of the world's nations will have his eyes opened quickly if he looks at what's happening in agriculture," Yeutter told participants in the 1974 annual meeting of the Animal Health Institute. "A hard rain hits the Soviet Union in the middle of spring planting season and the commodity prices in Chicago soar upward the daily limits. The first fishing boat of the new season pulls into a Peruvian harbor and unloads a record catch of anchovies—and the price of soybean meal drops on the Rotterdam market. A peasant farmer in India looks anxiously to the sky, waiting for the overdue monsoon rains—and accordingly, a Montana wheat farmer plants more wheat in 1974."

But the challenge—and opportunity—for American farmers was to market their goods well to buyers in countries and regions as far-flung as Japan and China, Latin America, and eastern Europe, he said. "The demand for American farm goods grows with every new day, with every new human being added to the world's population, with every dollar of increased buying power that people now earn." Americans, operating in a competitive international arena and facing off against rivals across the globe, would have to adjust their selling habits to tap into that demand.[9]

Already, some agriculturalists, particularly large organizations, were shifting gears. "American farming has become increasingly oriented toward export markets in recent years, and the speed of the trend in the past ten years has been phenomenal," Yeutter said in keynoting the 1974 annual banquet of the Kern County Farm Bureau in Bakersfield, California in late May. "California farmers were among the first to recognize the trend and among the first to actively promote their export products in overseas markets." They were helped, he added, by proximity to fast-growing import-minded Asian markets.

Foreshadowing some of his later actions in the trade arena, Yeutter drove home the message that government policy must support global trade, which would benefit American producers. Further, nations that erected barriers to such trade must be punished. "We must liberalize world agricultural trade, so that food supplies can flow where they are needed," Yeutter argued. "Trade barriers—whether import levies, export embargoes or export taxes—must be made more expensive for countries that resort to them."

And he again invoked his classical economic training to educate his listeners. "We must make full use of comparative advantage—the fundamental economic principle that each product should be produced in the country where it can be produced more efficiently," he said. "In the United States, we have to free farmers to produce for their markets. In developing countries we will need to offer technical assistance. In every country, we will need to offer price incentives and guaranteed access to markets. If we do, then the production that is needed will be forthcoming."[10]

Despite Yeutter's optimism about American crops in spring 1974, bad weather intervened later that year to cut soybean and grain production below expectations. This drove up prices, further ratcheting up inflation, which Yeutter acknowledged in an August 1974 speech in Texas as "our most serious problem."[11] The problems renewed calls for controls on exports, something Yeutter railed against. Other countries had produced big crops, and he argued that these would make up for the U.S. shortfall. He took a global view, saying in an August 1974 talk in Illinois, "This sharing of available supplies through the world market is far superior to export controls, which force each country to be self-sufficient and to deal with weather and crop production problems by themselves."[12]

Yeutter and his boss, Agriculture Secretary Butz, were of like minds on most things—though not all—about markets and trade liberalization. Butz's views made political enemies for the often-confrontational secretary, as they would, over time and to a far smaller degree, for the generally popular Yeutter. Like Yeutter, Butz was an agricultural economist and an academic, and Butz had served as dean of agriculture at Purdue University, as well as in several political posts dating back to the Eisenhower administration. Back then, Butz had worked for the controversial agricultural secretary Ezra Taft Benson, who the *New York Times* reported "had presided over huge grain surpluses, low farm prices and the start of the great exodus from American farms."[13] Critics also thought Butz was too close to big agricultural corporations, such as Ralston Purina, on whose board he served until he took the secretary of agriculture post after Yeutter's mentor, Clifford M. Hardin, stepped down to become vice chairman of that company. As a result of skepticism on Capitol Hill about him, Butz had been confirmed in the secretary's job in 1971 with a narrow Senate vote of fifty-one to forty-four.

Controversy dogged Butz, as he and Yeutter pressed farmers to produce more and to sell abroad. As the *Times* reported, the men's approaches succeeded in helping drive up farm income— which rose from $14 billion in 1970 to $26 billion by 1975—and in sharply boosting exports while subsidies fell. The remaining subsidies were concentrated in protected crops, such as cotton, peanuts, rice, and tobacco, as grain farmers planted from fencerow to fencerow and didn't need the supports. Indeed, Butz scrapped the set-aside program under which the government paid farmers not to plant all their land in corn—a program that Yeutter ironically had praised during the 1972 election as enormously popular with farmers. Set-aside programs would return, however, and Yeutter—taking the part of the pragmatist, not the ideologue— backed them: in early 1978 Yeutter criticized the Carter administration for making its set-aside program on feed grains, set at 10 percent of a farmer's land, too small by half and further said farmers should be pressed to comply, faulting the voluntary program for having "no teeth."[14]

In the mid-1970s, when agricultural conditions were comparatively good, Butz's enemies remained unappeased by rising farm incomes. Groups such as the Farmers Union and the National Farmers Organization, which tended to back Democrats, were still troubled by Butz's market-oriented approaches. His support of presidential vetoes of higher price supports for dairy farmers may have hurt him, leading to a *Des Moines Register* poll in 1975 that showed that less than half of Iowa's farmers thought Butz was doing a good job. He was criticized for preferring Big Ag over family farmers, something he denied, even as the numbers of small farmers were shrinking amid globalism and modernization.[15] Furthermore, his reputation remained tarnished by the secretive 1972 grain deal with the Soviet Union— nicknamed the Great Grain Robbery—because six multinational companies profited while food prices climbed and many farmers were shut out.[16]

Rumors abounded in 1974 and 1975 that Butz might resign or be ousted, and Yeutter was vaunted in some circles as his successor. Some in the Washington rumor mill suggested Yeutter could be vulnerable as well, however, and in both cases his biggest liability was said to be his association with the Committee for the Re-election of the President in the Nixon campaign in 1972, even though he and others on the farm campaign had nothing to do with Watergate. As he put it in a 2015 email to a friend, the fall 1972 successes, with more than 70 percent of the farm vote going for Nixon, made people involved in the campaign "all mighty happy. And then came Watergate! Fortunately, none of us who were involved with the farm campaign were in any way tarnished by the abominable series of events."[17]

Nonetheless, Yeutter was thinking in the spring of 1975 of leaving Washington the coming summer. He was weary of flying back and forth to Lincoln to see his family, which had continued to stay in Nebraska. The four and a half years of commuting, he confided to a reporter, had just about done him in.[18] Indeed, he had felt like an absentee father at times, with a local newspaper article from 1981 reporting that he credited "his wife Jeanne, a home economics major from UNL, with the raising of their family of four, three boys and a girl."[19] Yeutter recalled years later, in 2015, "[Jeanne] returned to Nebraska to be both mother and father for our four children for a good number of years. She did a sensational job, but living apart so much was certainly not ideal."[20]

But then ambition—and duty—called again, as it would so many times. President Ford tapped him for a newly created job, the post of deputy special representative for trade negotiations in the Executive Office of the President. So Yeutter left the Department of Agriculture in June 1975 for that ambassadorial post, which immersed him deeply in global trade issues. He did manage to bring at least some of his family members to the Washington DC area with him for a while. Because the city was celebrating the nation's Bicentennial in 1976 and was alive with cultural and historical events, Yeutter and his wife rented a home and took their younger two children out of school in Nebraska (the older boys had commitments that kept them in Nebraska), and the four lived together in the Lake Braddock area of Virginia for the year. "There was so much going on, so much patriotism," recalls Yeutter's daughter, Kim Y. Bottimore, who spent seventh grade in a local public school and later returned to Washington to earn two master's degrees. "That year was what created the passion in me to want to do graduate school in DC."[21]

Soon Yeutter was busy with contracts and negotiations with foreign governments and coordination of U.S. policy with other federal departments, with Congress, and with private-sector organizations, and he was focusing on strategy planning for global trade talks in Geneva. Those talks, known as the Tokyo Round because they had been launched in Japan in late 1973, would bring together about a hundred nations to try to scale back trade barriers. Until February 1977 Yeutter served in the Office of the U.S. Trade Representative, learning the ropes under Frederick B. Dent. The move would set the stage for bigger things for Yeutter later on, including becoming the U.S. trade representative in 1985.[22]

Yeutter drew on his agricultural experience in the new trade post, maintaining his ties to farmers and ranchers. In early 1976, for instance, he forecast growing demand for U.S. beef domestically and overseas in both 1976 and 1977, and he urged American cattle producers to crack the global market. "You have a quality product at competitive prices, and a unique opportunity to develop foreign consumer demand, not only in hotels and restaurants but in supermarkets, too," he said in a speech at the National Livestock Feeders Association in Omaha, Nebraska. "Now is the time for us to raise our sights and expand our export potential."

He urged the cattlemen to back U.S. efforts in the multilateral trade talks then underway and in bilateral talks with trading partners to remove government restrictions hampering agricultural trade—an issue that he would hammer at vigorously in future years with the European Union and protectionist-oriented countries. He said, "We must find a better way to manage national agricultural production and trade policies in order to bring both producers and consumers worldwide the benefit of a freer flow of products at reasonable prices with monetary rewards going to those who are the most efficient."

Even then, Yeutter was beginning to battle such market-distorting techniques in trade as export subsidies and such barriers as levies, import quotas, and health standards in which health concerns merely masked protectionism. He banged a drum he would often strike loudly and successfully in the future, contending, "What would help U.S. agriculture on these issues is the emergence of a good, strong voice of consumer advocacy abroad to press foreign governments to join in negotiating a liberalized international market for food."[23]

A few months later, in May 1976, he took his message global. In a luncheon talk for the World Trade Writers Association in New York City, he called on all countries taking part in the Geneva multilateral trade talks to get specific. They should develop a formula for cutting tariffs, for instance; should name sectors suitable for discussions; should develop codes for subsidies and countervailing duties, as well as product standards, safeguards, and government procurement practices; should develop dispute settlement rules and procedures; and should figure out how to deal with developing countries. Both agriculture—a much-protected realm for all countries, including the United States—and industrial trade should be part of the approach, he said.

The United States, Yeutter argued, was not out to destroy the European Community's Common Agricultural Policy (CAP), something he would chip away at later in his career. But it did want to negotiate rules and limits on export subsidies, import levies, and what he called other devices of the CAP system. He contended that it was necessary to resolve distortions of agricultural production and marketing worldwide if world food problems were to be met.[24] He took on the European Community (EC) in 1975 over its subsidies on cheese, which prompted the "cheese war," which he won by forcing the EC to pull back on some of it subsidies. "That was the first time in Common Market history that they agreed to withdraw some of their agricultural subsidies," he recalled a decade later. "It made some of the Common Market's agricultural ministers very unhappy."[25]

Over time, he grew more fervent in his opposition to such subsidies. In February 1983 he wrote a letter to the *Farm Journal* deriding the more than $7.5 billion in export subsidies the community used in 1980 "to market (dump might be a better word) its farm product throughout the world." He added, "EC export subsidies have devastated the U.S. in a whole host of markets on a myriad of agricultural commodities. The situation has simply become intolerable." Things were so bad, Yeutter argued, that the United States should develop a subsidy program of its own to "neutralize the unfair advantages of the EC subsidies."[26] He had no trouble going to the mat over issues in trade he cared about, showing a feistiness that would become as much of a hallmark as his ability to make concessions when opponents needed them.

In a talk in the summer of 1977, he conceded that nations had legitimate reason for some protective measures in agriculture, but he thought them overdone. "Some protection is understandable, for no nation wishes to be completely dependent on another for the major portion of its food. That would make it inordinately vulnerable in the delicate arena of international politics," the ever-pragmatic Yeutter said at a meeting of the National Institute on Cooperative Education at Texas A&M University. But he added, "In my judgment, most importing countries, particularly in the developed world (Japan, western Europe, etc.), are overly sensitive on this point."

Indeed, Yeutter argued, nations that were overly protective of domestic farm interests could likely boost their economic growth rates by shifting human and capital resources from agriculture into industry—a message that likely would have been coolly received among foreign farmers, as similar messages would have dropped with a thud on American farmers. However, he said, "This would be mutually beneficial in that their standard of living would rise, and our farmers would benefit from expanded exports." At the time, American farmers were struggling again with low U.S. farm prices for such products as wheat, of which there was a global surplus.

Critical of embargoes and the use of food products to achieve political ends, Yeutter also lambasted restrictions on U.S. sales to the Soviet Union and eastern European countries. He had left the government at that point, in August 1977, and denounced the Jackson-Vanik Amendment of 1974, which denied most-favored nation status to those countries as a way to encourage them to let Jews emigrate:

> Though the intent of this amendment (to help Jewish residents of these countries to leave if they wish) is laudatory, there ought

to be other and better ways to achieve that objective. Denying these countries most favored nation treatment in international trade, and also denying them access to certain credit programs, simply makes it more difficult for them to export to us, and in turn impedes their imports. Since one of their prime needs is for agricultural products and agricultural technology, U.S. farmers are indirectly hurt by this amendment as much or more than any other segment of the American economy. If this amendment were repealed or substantially altered, we should be able to significantly expand our farm exports, particularly to eastern Europe.[27]

The amendment, which Ford had signed into law in early 1975, was designed to counter the Soviet Union's "diploma tax," which imposed hefty fees on people educated in the USSR who sought to leave. Long after the 1991 fall of the Soviet Union, the law was repealed with respect to Russia and Moldova in late 2012.[28] But such embargoes, to Yeutter's mind, did little more than give the United States a bad reputation as an unreliable supplier, forcing such nations simply to turn to other countries.[29]

Even before leaving the government, Yeutter bluntly spoke his mind on sensitive matters. He raised the alarm domestically in 1976 about whether the United States was prepared to conduct the Geneva talks, for instance. In a July appearance before a group of economists in Fort Collins, Colorado, he warned that the United States had too few trained experts to conduct far-reaching trade talks such as those in Geneva. "We are much too thin—in the government, in the academic community, and in the private sector—in people who truly understand international trade policy issues," he said. The United States, he complained, had a "paucity of international trade talent."

As the *Journal of Commerce* reported, some forty U.S. negotiators were participating in the Geneva talks at the time, but only a handful had been involved in the last major trade round of talks, the Kennedy Round, which lasted from 1963 to 1967. Critics told the newspaper that the American group was inexperienced, though learning fast, and some warned that savvy European and Japanese negotiators would outfox the Americans. Yeutter said he longed for the day when such rounds of negotiation would end and, instead, a permanent group of well-trained professionals would serve U.S. trade policy in continuous consultation with trading partners.[30]

As Yeutter's career soared in this period, Butz's professional life was plummeting like a stone. In the end, Butz's plain—perhaps tactless—way of speaking and his fondness for coarse, sometimes vulgar, jokes did him in in Washington. Butz irked Catholics when he mocked Pope Paul VI in 1974 for the pope's stance against birth control, using a fake Italian accent. Then he offended African Americans with a racist joke that he told on a flight after the GOP convention of August 1976, and when the uproar went national, Butz quit as agriculture secretary in October 1976, a month before the presidential election. Though it came to naught, an executive at Beatrice Foods put in Yeutter's name to take over for Butz at that point.[31]

Despite Butz's problems, Yeutter remained on friendly terms with his old boss for years afterward, and the men often corresponded, particularly after Yeutter took the secretary of agriculture job in 1989. Butz, ever the Indiana farm boy, sometimes wrote Yeutter notes on stationery depicting an outhouse with the caption "The job is never finished until the paper work is done." Butz wrote his former assistant secretary just such a note in 1990, when then-secretary Yeutter was coming under heat for cuts to farm programs proposed in a new farm bill. A small group of wheat growers in Washington State had demanded Yeutter's resignation.[32] Butz mocked the group in his outhouse-graced note to Yeutter, saying it had not done its paperwork in seeking Yeutter's departure.[33] Then in mid-1992 Yeutter wrote to an official of the campaign to reelect George H. W. Bush as president that Butz, who was eager to get involved in the campaign, could "still be a very fine attraction" with certain specific audiences.[34]

When Butz and Yeutter were working well together in the early and mid-1970s, Yeutter's optimism about economic conditions in agriculture was well founded. But his upbeat attitude couldn't forestall broader political developments moving fast against the Nixon administration. With his presidency demolished by Watergate and his anti-inflationary economic intervention efforts a failure, Nixon resigned in disgrace in August 1974, just a few months after Yeutter's several agriculture industry talks. And soon after that, in October 1974, Ford launched his ill-fated Whip Inflation Now program to cajole people into voluntarily restraining price increases (apparently, Ford was oblivious to Yeutter's arguments about prices). Just as Nixon's mandatory controls only temporarily capped prices, however, so did Ford's bid for voluntary efforts fail.

Ultimately, national economic conditions turned upward, but they did so too slowly and too late to keep Ford in the White House. Inflation rates slipped from a 12.3 percent annual rate at year-end 1974 to 6.9 percent at the end of the following year, and then to 4.9 percent at the end of 1976.[35] But it was the slowed growth and sharp rise in unemployment in the recessionary economy, rather than jawboning by a president, that contained the price spiral. While the recession ended in March 1975, the jobless rate continued climbing—as is typical in recoveries—to peak at 9 percent in May of that year before inching down to 7.8 percent by the election month of November 1976.[36] The economic troubles and the shadows cast by Watergate, together with the appeal of the religiously committed Carter in the post-Nixon period, drove the Republicans out of the White House in that fall 1976 election.

The electoral upheaval pushed Yeutter, a political appointee, out of the government in early 1977, and he embarked on the first major segment of his career in the private sector. He joined a law firm that was headquartered in Lincoln, Nebraska, and had offices in Washington DC and elsewhere. Based in Washington, Yeutter served as a senior partner of the firm, known variously as Nelson, Harding, Yeutter, Leonard & Tate and, in Washington, as Nelson, Harding & Yeutter, and he was responsible for its agriculture-related practice. He also coordinated elements of the practice involving

Washington and international interests. After practicing law for sixteen months, in July 1978 he moved to yet another new private-sector job, accepting a post as president and chief executive officer of the Chicago Mercantile Exchange.[37] Throughout, Yeutter kept his hand in on government-related matters and in politics.

During this period and long after, Yeutter had no shortage of professional opportunities, especially academic ones. Despite the travails of the Nixon and Ford administrations, he had built a solid reputation by crisscrossing the country to deliver his free-market messages. So appealing job offers and feelers came in regularly for the lawyer-academic turned public official. A search committee for the presidency of Kansas State University pursued him in early 1975.[38] In the fall of 1976 a friend suggested him for the presidency of the University of Nebraska, noting in his letter that Oklahoma State University was considering Yeutter for its top spot.[39] Still later, after he had risen to lead the Chicago Mercantile Exchange and moved on to serve as U.S. trade representative, a headhunter for the business school at the University of Southern California approached him in 1987 about the deanship there, and a headhunter for Texas Tech in 1988 broached the idea of his taking the university's presidency.[40] Late that same year, heading the University of Minnesota became a possibility.[41]

After he had moved on to the secretary of agriculture post, several schools would come knocking for Yeutter again, though none would win him over. In 1990 he was nominated for the presidency at Iowa State University even as the University of Nebraska pursued him for its top post, and he was approached by the University of Arizona.[42] In 1992 a distinguished alumnus of Miami University of Ohio who had known Yeutter when he ran the Chicago exchange suggested him for the presidency of that school.[43] Still later, in 1993, Yeutter was nominated to lead Michigan State University, and he wrote to a headhunting firm that the University of Nebraska again was "pressuring [him] hard"—even before a search was opened—to lead it.[44] Nebraska's law school dean, Harvey S. Perlman, had personally made the case for Yeutter.[45] Then in 1996 an official at the University of Missouri broached the idea of its presidency to him, only to have him turn thumbs down on the idea, saying he was enjoying his professional activities and "the income level resulting therefrom."[46]

Yeutter was characteristically candid in rebuffing his alma mater in 1993, writing to the headhunter, "I have told the University of Nebraska folks that I do not wish to be considered for the presidency, but they've pleaded for an opportunity to talk with me again at a later stage of their proceedings. I've told them I'd certainly grant them that courtesy, but want them to understand that the door is open only a small crack. I might well come to the same conclusion with respect to Michigan State, but just don't know that situation well enough at this point." At that point, in the spring of 1993, Yeutter said he had agreed to serve on seven corporate boards, join a Washington law firm on an "of counsel" basis, and travel making speeches. He complained, "To do a university presidency I'd obviously have to turn a lot of that topsy turvy."[47] Still, he told a friend that he had seriously considered leading schools in Nebraska and Minnesota, as well as Purdue University.[48]

As was typical of him, Yeutter was gracious in leaving the deputy trade representative post in 1977. He offered his resignation to Ford in January, noting that he left with sadness and pride. "The sadness comes from knowing that our tasks are not yet completed; but that is a part of our democratic process that all of us must willingly accept," he wrote. "The pride comes from being associated with an Administration that leaves with the deep respect of the American people. For that, Mr. President, you are primarily responsible. I know of no man who could have restored faith in the Presidency so quickly."[49] Yeutter maintained a cordial relationship with Ford for years afterward, taking part at times in global leadership discussions that the former president put together in his beloved post-presidential retirement town of Vail, Colorado.[50]

6

Juicy Corn-Fed Nebraska Sirloin

Life outside of government in the late 1970s and early 1980s would prove lucrative and intellectually enriching for Yeutter and would pave the way for when Washington's revolving door returned him to the highest reaches of the federal system. He made corporate and global political connections that would pay off well in the future, including with trade officials in the new administration whom he continued to advise. Indeed, though he was not on the government payroll, the lines between the government and the private sector—at least as practiced by Washington law firms—could be quite blurry. For Yeutter and those in the federal bureaucracy he worked with, that often proved helpful.

Yeutter's adventure in practicing law, Washington-style, began in April 1977, when he joined the twenty-year-old Republican-connected law firm of Nelson, Harding, Marchetti, Leonard & Tate, based in Lincoln, Nebraska. Yeutter's name replaced Marchetti's in the firm's masthead, as he became a senior partner charged with building and running the firm's Washington DC office as its resident managing partner. He split his time between his home in Lincoln, where his family remained, and Washington but often was jetting around the country or world. Through the DC office, Yeutter—who held the title of ambassador because of his trade representative work—dealt with foreign ambassadors from countries such as Brazil and Mexico and top trade officials from Hungary, Japan, and elsewhere. He worked with corporate clients on legal problems or difficulties with regulatory agencies, particularly those associated with the U.S. Department of Agriculture (USDA).

In assembling the Washington office, Yeutter built an impressive team stocked with former administrative and regulatory figures. For instance, he brought in thirty-six-year-old Dick Cheney, who had been President Ford's chief of staff, on a part-time basis in August 1977. Cheney, who happened to have been born in Lincoln, Nebraska, was not a lawyer but could consult on matters related to the government. Other figures in the office included former deputy assistant secretary of state William W. Geimer, former deputy assistant secretary of agriculture James H. Lake, and former Environmental Protection Agency (EPA) assistant administrator for air and water Donald M. Mosiman. The firm also had a working relationship with another firm headed by former Texas Democratic congressman Graham B. Purcell Jr. and former Idaho Republican congressman Orval H. Hansen.[1]

Yeutter sought a bipartisan approach, something crucial for dealing with regulators and clients of varying political stripes. When he discussed the firm, moreover, he liberally dropped names, bragging about the connections that are the stock-in-trade in DC. "Aside from our heavy involvement in the labor, transportation, and corporate elements of the practice, the firm takes quite a strong interest in the political world," he wrote to a lawyer who was interested in having his California law firm, Baker, Manock & Jensen, join forces with Yeutter's.

> At the moment, we are heavy on the Republican side, with Dick Cheney and I both being involved with the Party at the national level. In addition, Bill Geimer is a close associate of Don Rumsfeld [Ford's secretary of defense], and Don Mosiman a similarly close associate of Bill Ruckelshaus [first administrator of the EPA, former acting director of the FBI, and former U.S. deputy attorney general]. Jim Lake, as you know, worked closely with Governor Reagan during his presidential campaign. We also

have some people in the Lincoln office who have been key figures behind the scenes in both domestic and national politics.
Our association with Graham Purcell provides the only major
entrée on the Democratic side, but we expect to beef that up in
the Washington, D.C. office in the near future.[2]

Yeutter was proud of the firm. In mid-1977 he boasted to the
chief of the minister's cabinet in Brazil, Luiz Augusto Pereira Souto
Maior, about how unusual it was, "with a geographic distribution
that probably goes beyond that of any law firm in the United States."[3]
At the time, the firm had offices in Denver, Houston, Omaha, and
Salt Lake City, as well as its headquarters in Lincoln. Along with
Yeutter's new Washington office, it planned to add offices in Rapid
City, South Dakota, and Los Angeles. Working as a classic rain-
maker, Yeutter tried to add Brazil to his client roster.

With Yeutter's contacts, the firm packed its client roster with
major agricultural names. He served on the board of Tri-Valley
Growers, a giant California-based tomato- and fruit-processing
cooperative owned by many growers, and his firm did legal work
for the outfit. He brought in Land O'Lakes, a Minnesota-based dairy
cooperative. The firm also represented Sun-Maid Raisins, the biggest raisin-processing cooperative in the world, as well as the entire
California olive industry, including the big Lindsay Olive Growers cooperative.[4] Closer to home in Nebraska, Yeutter won over
Lindsay Manufacturing Company, a global irrigation and infrastructure company now known as Lindsay Corporation (no rela-
tion to the olive grower group), on whose board he later served.

He also kept beating the drum for American businesses of all
sorts to boost exports, following the model of the raisin industry,
which sold as much as a third of its crop abroad. "U.S. businesses
need to be much more aggressive—and much better prepared—in
all facets of their export endeavors, as well as their battles over
unfair trade practices," he wrote to an executive of a packing company in Fresno, California. "I do not fully understand why we have
not yet honed our international marketing skills in the same way
that we have honed those in the domestic market. My hypothesis,

however, would be that export markets just have not been all that important to most companies and most industries, either agricultural or industrial. We have too often used our export markets as a dumping ground for our surpluses, rather than seeking to develop them on a permanent and long-term basis."[5]

Yeutter advocated for his clients with the U.S. trade officials who had come into office under President Carter, often sharing helpful information that he had learned when he was in those officials' shoes. For instance, when his successor, Deputy Special Representative for Trade Negotiations Alan Wm. Wolff, asked for a briefing from Yeutter in May 1978, in advance of a trip to Latin America, Yeutter plumped for Sun-Maid Raisins. "I gave Ambassador Wolff a full briefing on some of the key personalities on the Mexican scene, and put in a few good words for raisins in the process," Yeutter informed California raisin executive Clyde E. Nef. He had urged Wolff to set up a bilateral trade deal with Mexico and explained to Nef, "I told Ambassador Wolff that the U.S. raisin industry, as one example, was very interested in penetrating the Mexican market, but could not do so because of Mexico's prohibitive licensing program. I said that opening up the Mexican market to high quality U.S. raisins would not be severe competition for present Mexican production, and that there might even be opportunities for joint ventures between Mexican and U.S. firms if the Mexican government were to display some flexibility on such trade issues."

Yeutter was well connected and that showed. When Wolff asked whether he thought Mexico would be willing to join the General Agreement on Tariffs and Trade, predecessor to the World Trade Organization, Yeutter said he had often encouraged Mexican officials to do so. "I then said that I thought the Mexican attitude was one of being open-minded on this issue," he told Nef. "In fact, I said that my friend, Secretary of Commerce [Jorge] de la Vega, was an internationally-oriented individual who would probably be sympathetic to Ambassador Wolff's comments in this regard."[6]

He realized, too, how much negotiating trade issues was like a poker game—complete with bluffs, tells, and personalities—though in the end everyone had to walk away with some winnings. He told Wolff, for instance, "The Mexicans have a tendency to give with one hand and take away with the other. You'll need to watch that, particularly on the non-tariff measure side. Keep the pressure on for them to convert from a restrictive licensing system to duties. They keep talking a good show on that issue, but progress has come slowly."[7]

He cautioned clients, moreover, about how shrewd European bargainers could be. He explained in a mid-1978 memo to a California olive executive, Jud Carter, how European Community (EC) officials had manipulated an American trade representative, first telling him by phone before a meeting that the outlook for any concessions was "very bleak," but then telling him in person that they were prepared to move. "They had prepared [Richard R.] Rivers for a non-productive session, and then sent him home elated with what probably were relatively minor concessions. In other words, he thinks he achieved a much greater victory than probably was actually obtained. The EC people are very skilled negotiators!"

Yeutter also saw how U.S. negotiators could be undone by a domestic industry's political clout, complicating the trade-offs that often were crucial in trade deals. EC officials were showing surprising flexibility in discussing agricultural trade issues, particularly subsidies that Yeutter had long railed against, he suggested in that same memo to Carter. Subsidies by Greece, Turkey, Spain, and other nations were troublesome to California specialty crop exporters, so getting them scaled back would be a big step forward. "I have a hunch, however, that the Europeans will want to extract a pound of flesh from the U.S. dairy industry by asking for a significant increase in our dairy import quotas," he speculated. "That will cause STR [the special trade representative] a lot of difficulty, since the U.S. dairy industry is very strong politically."[8]

But he was aware that trade was a two-way street and that to get something, one needed to give something. Polish officials, for instance, were keenly interested in marketing sixteen types of canned fish in the United States in 1978. So Yeutter tried to broker a deal, working with a Washington attorney representing the Poles, in which Land O'Lakes could distribute such fish in exchange for the right to export soybean products to Poland.[9] Deals had to be win-win arrangements, especially when political officials with veto power waited back home. He saw that dynamic at play in dealings between Mexico and the United States, writing to a raisin industry executive that Mexicans who wanted to boost their exports to the United States "could be accommodated to at least some extent by the United States if we receive comparable concessions in return."[10]

Yeutter knew, as well, how much personalities could complicate matters. He complained in a March 1978 memo to Carter that he had made no progress in attacking European subsidies when he worked in the trade representative's office: "At that time, the Commissioner for Agriculture at the EC was Pierre Lardinois, a hot tempered individual with whom negotiations were all but impossible. Fortunately, in late 1976 he was replaced by Finn Gundelach, a much more sensible individual who is not only knowledgeable in agriculture but also in international trade."

As Yeutter made clear, he appreciated the strengths of American trade officials, irrespective of their political affiliations. He thought highly, for instance, of Robert S. Strauss, the former chairman of the Democratic National Committee who had taken over as special trade representative from 1977 to 1979. "As you know, Strauss is very astute politically, and he displayed that characteristic in a fascinating way during the Gundelach visit," Yeutter wrote in the memo to Carter.

> Strauss told Gundelach that he [Strauss] was at the height of his popularity in the U.S. government. [Strauss has been featured in a whole host of complimentary newspaper and magazine articles in recent days.] But he also told him that this would not last. No political figure in this country can maintain his star in the stratosphere for very long. Ultimately, it begins to fall, and Strauss candidly conceded that at this point he really has nowhere to go but down. Realizing this, Strauss said that he needed to consummate a multilateral trade agreement within

the next several months. . . . Gundelach apparently responded positively to the Strauss plea.[11]

Even as he worked outside of government, Yeutter maintained his ties to foreign leaders. For instance, when Janos Nyerges, a top Hungarian trade official, wrote to him in 1978 about a trade pact that provided for most-favored-nation status for Hungary, Yeutter responded warmly. He praised the agreement and told Nyerges that Hungary had been discriminated against in the Jackson-Vanik Amendment, which limited dealings with Eastern bloc countries in a bid to pressure them to permit Jews to leave Russia and elsewhere. Yeutter advised Nyerges, however, that a full legislative agenda in Congress 1978 would make it unlikely that other needed changes to facilitate trade could be made that year. "There might, however, be a possibility to do so in 1979," he added. "I hope so, for this could certainly expand trade between the United States and all the countries of eastern Europe." Yeutter added that he planned to visit Geneva in early May 1978 to meet with delegations to the ongoing multilateral trade talks on behalf of some clients and hoped then to grab lunch with Nyerges.[12]

Clients benefited from his high-level personal relationships. He was friendly with a top-level Mexican commerce official, Hector Hernandez Cervantes, for example, and sympathized with domestic political challenges he and President José López Portillo grappled with as they sought to expand international trade for Mexico. "Your philosophy is sound, and your actions will clearly prove to be in the long-term best interest of the people of Mexico," Yeutter wrote to Cervantes in the fall of 1977. "But such issues are always politically sensitive, and you will inevitably receive some criticism for not protecting your local industries as much as they would like to be protected. We receive[d] that same criticism when President Ford was in office, and the Carter Administration is under even more pressure now. But I hope the United States will likewise maintain its open trading philosophy." He went on to sketch out prospective joint ventures between Mexican firms and Sun-Maid Raisins, which was eager to boost raisin sales in the country.[13]

His trade contacts could grease the wheels for the firm's clients. For instance, Nebraska's Lindsay Manufacturing Company in mid-1978 wanted to provide parts to pilot an irrigation project in Brazil and sought a break on the country's import and industrial products taxes. Yeutter was friendly with Alvaro da Costa Franco, a top minister, and after a visit and an exchange of letters, Franco let Yeutter know that an 80 percent cut in the taxes was possible. The minister urged Lindsay to pursue that.[14]

Certainly, Yeutter had developed warm personal relationships abroad. He was close enough to a Swiss commerce official, Arthur Dunkel, to strike a folksy tone with him even in a business letter. At the time, Switzerland was considering opening its border to a mere 450 tons of U.S. beef imports, less than half of the 1,000-ton quota the U.S. sought as a minimum. "I would certainly like to be able to buy a tasty, juicy, cornfed Nebraska sirloin on my next trip to Geneva, Berne, or Zurich," Yeutter wrote. "If you will put prime beef in all your ski resorts, they will attract everybody in the world! I really do believe that a quota of 1,000 tons would have little or no impact on your own domestic cattle industry." He closed by saying that he and his wife would love to host Dunkel and his wife on a visit to the United States.[15]

Colleagues say he developed such warm personal relationships with negotiating partners—even those with whom he differed sharply on policy—simply because he liked dealing with people. He could generally see things from others' viewpoints while hewing to his own, and he showed an upbeat and can-do attitude that drew others in. "He was the classic, quintessential, irrepressible optimist," says William A. Reinsch, a senior adviser at Washington's Center for Strategic and International Studies who crossed paths with him in trade circles. "Always looking for the bright side, always trying to find a basis for agreement, for moving forward. Always open. . . . He always struck me as classically midwestern. That injected a note of . . . niceness, if nothing else, into the debate. . . . He was always just a ray of light and optimism when other people were being gloomy."[16]

But Yeutter was also clear-eyed about the risks involved in the global bargaining at the multilateral trade talks underway in the late 1970s in Geneva, and he could be brutal in his assessments of the work of some of his successors. "Finally, all this discussion with the EC and Japan to date has not yet achieved anything of significance in terms of agricultural concessions by either trading partner," Yeutter said in a June 1978 memo to his law firm file, after lunching in Geneva with a U.S. trade ambassador, Alonzo L. McDonald Jr. "Unless that changes for the better in the next few weeks, the outcome of the MTN [multilateral trade negotiation] will not really be very beneficial to U.S. agriculture. In other words, our delegation really hasn't done the job to date, but I am not at all sure that Ambassador McDonald realizes this."[17]

On that same trip, Yeutter heard a problematic assessment of McDonald's performance, which he shared with his law firm colleagues. Yeutter got the dishy assessment from James Starkey, an agricultural adviser who worked as an assistant U.S. trade representative. "Jim is not at all high on McDonald's performance, particularly in agriculture. He says that McDonald just has not spent enough time on the scene in Geneva, and that this has reduced his effectiveness," Yeutter wrote of McDonald, who had served as global managing partner for the McKinsey & Company consulting firm before joining the trade office. "Apparently, McDonald has been doing lots of speeches throughout Europe, and also a lot of personal appearances and speeches here in the U.S. . . . Jim says that a lot of people feel he is campaigning for the STR [special trade representative] position in anticipation of Ambassador Strauss' departure."

The problem complicated life for the STR office in Washington and for firms such as Yeutter's, as it represented clients with big stakes in the success of the Geneva trade talks. "Starkey also feels that McDonald is cozying up too much with the EC. Apparently, he spends a lot of time with Roy Denman, a former British governmental official who now occupies the #2 trade policy position at the EC," Yeutter noted. "Starkey says that dissatisfaction with McDonald's performance has led to an unwillingness by STR-Washington to provide much negotiating discretion in the Geneva delegation. What this means is that anything we want to sell at STR will have to be done in Washington, at least in the immediate future, if it is to be implemented in Geneva."[18]

In the end, McDonald was denied the top STR position. His efforts as a leading negotiator led to modest cuts in import duties and reductions in other trade barriers in the Tokyo Round. But critics such as Clyde V. Prestowitz Jr., Alan Tonelson, and Robert W. Jerome later assailed the round, saying it "manifestly failed to live up to its promise." Tariffs were expected to be slashed by as much as 60 percent, for instance, but came down at half that level, they wrote.[19] McDonald, however, rose to become an assistant to President Carter and the president's White House staff director. He later worked as president of Bendix Corporation and taught at Harvard Business School.[20]

Yeutter had read the tea leaves correctly about the negotiations, drawing on his conversations with various players to get a sense of where they all stood. "The Japanese do not expect to gain anything from these negotiations; their basic objective is to cut their losses. The EC has essentially the same objective, and they too are doing a lot of stalling. In their case, however, it is not so obvious because of their experience and shrewdness as negotiators," he wrote in a June 1978 memo to raisin executive Nef. "As to agriculture, it does not look like as if we will obtain any major concessions on the big ticket items—feed grain, wheat, soybeans and soybean products, etc. There will be some give, of course, but if we go the commodity agreement route in most of these areas, that give will be more apparent than real."

While he complimented the U.S. bargaining team in general in Geneva, he faulted those at the top levels in both Geneva and Washington for their lack of experience. "In addition, they are a bit naive with respect to the true intentions of the European Community," he told Nef. "The EC, as usual, has done a good job of lulling the U.S. negotiators into a sense of security. In other words, we are probably being out-negotiated by the EC once again, and perhaps even out-negotiated by Japan." Yeutter correctly predicted the 30 to 35 percent level in average tariff cuts—which he said overall

would be a "good result," contrary to the assessment by Prestowitz and colleagues—but said the tariff trims would likely prove
lower for agriculture, even as tariffs were less of a problem than
nontariff barriers.[21]

Yeutter's relationships with European and Asian trade officials,
which deepened in this stretch of his career, would pay off well over
time. Ultimately, the groundwork he laid here led to the breakthroughs that opened European markets to goods from the United
States and the rest of the world. In turn, that would make possible
the Uruguay Round of global trade talks, which spawned "the most
ambitious trade agreement in history," as journalist and Council
on Foreign Relations senior fellow Edward Alden describes it.[22]

At home, Yeutter also immersed himself in sometimes ticklish
client issues, as happened with the Dubuque Packing Company
of Denison, Iowa, a client he had picked up in the middle of 1977.
Yeutter proved crucial in helping the company deal with the USDA,
especially when it was denied the department's all-important meat-
grading services after it turned out that boxes of ungraded meat
in one of its plants were being labeled and marketed as graded.
The executives of the firm came clean and promised to avoid a
repeat, and Yeutter both publicly and privately acknowledged the
problem, telling USDA officials that company managers would
"take whatever action is appropriate to completely clean the slate
at Denison," including firing implicated workers.[23] In a February
1978 letter about the case to Dr. Robert Angelotti, administrator of
the USDA's Food Safety and Quality Service (FSQS), Yeutter wrote,
"I am sorry that FSQS will have to spend so many man-hours on
that one, but apparently even the top companies are not immune
to dishonesty in the ranks! . . . The Dubuque people want to handle the matter thoroughly and decisively, and they will certainly
cooperate fully with you."[24]

Yeutter had met with several USDA officials about the case and
was concerned that it would become an example that top officials,
Angelotti and Assistant Secretary of Agriculture Carol Lee Tucker-
Foreman, would use to tighten up labeling practices. He was told
as much in a meeting with agency officials he had worked with

when he served as administrator of the USDA's Consumer and Marketing Service. "What they were saying, in a subtle and diplomatic manner, is that their supervisors would be elated over the opportunity to use Dubuque as an example of the industry sins that must be corrected through aggressive regulatory action," Yeutter explained in a January 1978 memo to his law firm file. "Regrettably, this incident provides them with a ready-made case that fits at least some of the proposals that were to be propounded the following day."[25] Indeed, a lawyer for the agency later told him, "Both Foreman and Angelotti are likely to use this case as an example of ills that must be treated within the meatpacking industry."[26]

With a lawyer's skill, Yeutter could size up his opponents well. After an early February 1978 meeting with Angelotti, Yeutter wrote that the official seemed to empathize with Dubuque management but was resigned to take strong action in the case. Yeutter thought a follow-up with Foreman would be "imperative" to try to get her to "moderate her reaction," saying, "If we can get her to display as much empathy as Dr. Angelotti, perhaps we can affect the sanctions in a positive way. It looks as if we now have a situation where Dr. Angelotti wishes to show Assistant Secretary Foreman how tough he can be, and vice versa. We need to try to simmer both of them down!"[27]

As it turned out, the Dubuque case was one of several that led the USDA to propose changes in grading and labeling. Under plans sought by Tucker-Foreman, meat would be marked either with the traditional quality grade, such as USDA Prime or Choice, or with a new stamp, U.S. Ungraded.[28] Such grading was not mandatory but provided meat marketers with key edges in selling their products. In the end, the U.S. Ungraded stamp proposal did not fly, but to this day Standard and Commercial grades of beef are sold as ungraded or as store-brand meat.

Yeutter had been keeping an eye on Tucker-Foreman's work because of her interest in pressing the poultry industry to remove additives. She had left the Consumer Federation of America, an activist organization, to join the USDA in March 1977. The following month she asked the Food and Drug Administration to rule on the safety of nitrates and nitrites from poultry. But by July 1977 she was persuaded that the additives may have helped prevent botulism and thus did not warrant the "precipitous action" of barring them.[29] Yeutter warned officials at Dubuque Packing that despite this softening of her stance, eliminating such additives was "probably still her long-term objective. Unless and until the industry comes up with a good substitute in the way of a color additive, and also as a curative, doing what she has in mind would be devastating."[30] Indeed, Tucker-Foreman had long been a critic of industry regulation, saying in a 2020 email to me, "Then and now, the laws are less powerful than Congress initially intended and the public deserves. . . . The regulated industry has disproportionate power to see that industry was not too bothered by the federal laws."[31]

Taking a lawyerly approach to building bridges among adversaries, nonetheless, Yeutter sat down with Tucker-Foreman several weeks after the Dubuque Packing contretemps to discuss grading and other issues in a conversation he described as "most amicable and useful." Recounting the meeting in a memo to Erving H. Priceman, an executive at the MBPXL Corporation meatpacking company and head of the National Independent Meat Packers Association, Yeutter said Tucker-Foreman was troubled by hostility among meatpackers toward the proposed grading changes. "Secretary Foreman stated that she had been receiving a considerable amount of flak from her consumer constituency in recent weeks, and that it might be nice to get a bit of recognition and praise from the meatpacking industry occasionally," Yeutter told Priceman. She needed access to industry executives who displayed what he called "positive, rational, and reasonable thinking," and Yeutter said he assured her that MBPXL took a "much more enlightened view" than industry peers. Priceman, he suggested, could be among industry figures who could helpfully advise her, and Yeutter would help put together a list of such people.[32]

Moving quickly to make good on his promise, Yeutter brought Priceman and others to Washington to meet Tucker-Foreman, and he wrote her an effusive letter of thanks: "Everyone from MBPXL was genuinely impressed with your knowledge of both the meat grading and net weight issues, your willingness to listen to their views, and the sincere and objective way in which you are approaching these delicate issues. I know they return to Wichita with a positive and favorable impression of the Honorable Carol Tucker Foreman."[33] In a note to Priceman, Yeutter said, "[I am] especially pleased with Carol Foreman's positive attitude and her obvious display of interest in what you had to say."[34] For Tucker-Foreman's part, she recalls Yeutter as "an extremely talented lawyer and a masterful politician."[35]

Given his contacts and his experience in agriculture and trade, Yeutter was much sought after on the lecture circuit. But he could be high-handed—even with federal agency officials—if not accorded the prominence and respect he felt he deserved. When an official of the USDA's Agricultural Marketing Service proposed that he appear for thirty minutes as part of a two-hour presentation at the service's Market News Conference in June 1978, for instance, he balked. The Chicago Mercantile Exchange, which he planned to join the following month as president and chief executive officer, had agreed to pay his honorarium because the organization valued its working relationship with the marketing service. But the money was secondary for Yeutter. "I really do not believe, Dennis, that I can justify either my time or the CME budgetary expenditure for only a 30 minute general session appearance," he told the official, Dennis E. Stringer. "As I told you when we first visited, I have a heavy speech-making schedule, and usually ask for an honorarium in the $1,000 to $1,500 range. Ordinarily, such events involve either luncheon or dinner speeches, or else a keynote address at the beginning of a conference or convention."

Yeutter turned Stringer down. He said he had a "tremendously busy schedule" and just could not "afford to make the time and expenditure commitment that would be necessary for such a brief presentation," adding, "I am sorry to give you a negative response on this, Dennis, but had thought you probably had a more substantial presentation in mind."[36]

Yeutter may have felt burned by some of his speaking engagements. He sometimes noted in memos when the crowds were disappointingly small. One session close to home especially irked him. In the fall of 1977 he appeared at a conference arranged by Nebraskans for Peace and a few allied groups at a hotel in Lincoln, Nebraska, that addressed the theme of "Citizen Participation in International Policy: Making a Just World Order." Yeutter had no use for the ideas espoused by the keynote speaker, Richard J. Barnet of the Washington-based Institute for Policy Studies, a critic of globalization and of multinational corporations. "I do hope that some of your audience went away with a better understanding of how the world functions," Yeutter wrote to organizer Betty Olson.

> If they did not do so, it was a wasted day for all of us. There is certainly no harm in being exposed to the ideas of Barnet or anyone else of his ilk. But many of those ideas, and many of his criticisms of society, are so ill-conceived and so far from reality as to be irrelevant if not counter-productive. . . . Groups such as yours will be much more effective if you seek incremental changes in society, rather than the wholesale restructuring of its very fabric, as was discussed this past week.[37]

Even as he traversed the world while working for his law practice, dining with ambassadors and trade ministers, still more impressive dealings were in store after he took leave of his firm to become a corporate executive. He took the helm of the Chicago Mercantile Exchange, then the second-largest futures exchange in the world (and now, under the name CME Group, still one of the largest).[38] There he deepened his understanding of trade and financial flows while mastering agricultural and financial futures trading and building important links to other corporate executives. While there, he would suffer the biggest professional disappointment of his career, but it would turn out to be a boon and only a temporary setback.

7

Our Fellow Man

The Chicago Mercantile Exchange of the late 1970s and 1980s was a freewheeling, raucous place where traders in colorful jackets mingled for hours each day in great "pits," octagonal multistepped arenas where the traders bought and sold contracts on such things as hogs, cattle, currencies, and various financial instruments. The pits were so loud that the traders had developed arcane hand signals to communicate and could be so rough that few women dared at the time to join the broad-shouldered men jockeying for deals. For ranchers and farmers nationwide, the "Merc" (more formally, the CME) was a place where they could lock in prices on their animals or other products by pledging their production by selling futures contracts, in essence locking in the price for their herds months before slaughter. Typically, the traders would deal the pigs and beeves off to giant processing companies. The CME, which dated back to 1898, was a place of capitalism red in tooth and claw, seemingly a perfect spot for a free marketer like Yeutter.

But the CME also had baggage. Scandals had tarnished the image of the futures exchanges over the years, most notoriously in 1955, when two traders cornered the market on onions, which at the time accounted for 20 percent of the commodities traded on the CME. The pair pushed up the price of onions by garnering nearly all the onions available in Chicago, some thirty million pounds, and they then forced down the price by selling their hoard, driving the price from $2.75 for a fifty-pound bag in August 1955 to 10 cents in March 1956. The traders had sold short, betting on prices to drop, and their gambit made them millionaires while pushing onion producers out of business. This led to a bill banning trading in onion futures, sponsored by Congressman Gerald R. Ford Jr. and signed into law by President Dwight D. Eisenhower in 1958.[1] The CME "had a sordid history," recalls Leo Melamed, an attorney who had nonetheless become intrigued with the CME when he worked there part-time while in law school in the mid-1950s.

By 1969 Melamed had left a law practice to trade at the CME and had risen to become chairman of the exchange. In 1971 he pushed through revisions to the exchange's rules to end what he called "shenanigans" by some members. Nonetheless, allegations of manipulation dogged the futures exchanges into the 1970s, leading Congress and President Ford—with Yeutter's help—to create the independent Commodity Futures Trading Commission (CFTC) in 1974. Previously, the industry had been loosely regulated by a short-staffed group within the U.S. Department of Agriculture (USDA) called the Commodity Exchange Authority, a group that had been under Yeutter's purview when he worked at the USDA.

As the CME sought out a president and CEO in 1977 to succeed a long-standing leader who was retiring, officials came across Yeutter. His background in agriculture, law, and regulatory affairs, and especially his familiarity with Washington and his connections there, including with the USDA, made him the perfect candidate. But particularly in light of his burgeoning law practice, Yeutter was reluctant. "It was very difficult for me to convince him to take over the CEO's role in an institution that had such a sordid past and very little future, but he did come around," recalls Melamed.[2]

By mid-November 1977 Melamed's persuasive arguments that things had changed and the prospect of a $200,000-a-year salary with growth potential and executive responsibility proved appealing. So Yeutter took leave from his law firm the following July to take the helm at CME. The exchange, he told a reporter from Lincoln, Nebraska, was "the free enterprise system operating at its best, a major bastion of American capitalism." Soon the garish plaid sport jackets, mismatched ties, and white shoes that the sartorially challenged Yeutter had favored for much of his time in DC—particularly at the USDA—gave way to a CEO's proper dark suits and white shirts. In time the move also meant the Yeutter family would live together again, as Yeutter bought a spacious home on a lake in Golfview Hills, near the affluent western Chicago suburb of Hinsdale, proudly sending his mother a 1984 newspaper clipping with a photo of his backyard.[3]

By 1984 his annual income had risen to $344,395 (the equivalent of nearly $889,000 in 2021), according to a loan application he filed.[4] With such resources, he was able to indulge a family passion for skiing with a $150,000 condo in Keystone, Colorado. (Some of the Yeutters had skied in St. Moritz in the Alps in the winter of 1974.)[5] He also had condos in Clearwater, Florida, and Scottsdale, Arizona. It was all a remarkable climb for someone who as a child had stuffed his shoes with cardboard to cover the holes. Nonetheless, as a child of the Depression, he didn't splurge on $900 suits, says his longtime Nebraska friend Allen J. Beermann, who fondly remembers asking in their early years working together, "Clayton, who dressed you?" Beermann adds, "He had the weirdest things in combinations."[6]

But just as corporate members of the CME hedged their positions with futures contracts, so did Yeutter hedge his bets on the job at first, even though it paid far better than the $40,000 from his prior government job.[7] Yeutter signed on for just a three-year stint, leaving an opening for him to move into a top government job should a Republican be elected to succeed President Carter—something he expected.[8] In an April 1977 letter to a Republican National Committee official, Yeutter wrote, "I will want to maintain my activity within the party from now until the 1980 election, so offer you my services if and when I can be useful. The Carter Administration has been making lots of blunders. I hope he continues, so long as they do not jeopardize the basic well-being of our country. And I hope we can effectively use those blunders about three years from now."[9]

Yeutter seemed to be angling down the road for the secretary of agriculture spot, one for which his training and experience, both in the USDA and outside, qualified him. Supremely self-assured, as always, he knew he was well suited for the office that one of his mentors, Clifford M. Hardin, had held under President Nixon from 1969 to 1971. Hardin, a former chancellor at the University of Nebraska, had been trained, like Yeutter, as an agricultural economist. And Hardin had brought Yeutter to Washington in October 1970 to take his first USDA job as administrator of the Consumer and Marketing Service, which in turn led to two successive assistant secretary positions at the department before Yeutter's stint outside the USDA as a deputy special trade representative.

Keeping his hand in GOP matters even as he arranged to take the CEO spot at the CME, Yeutter in early 1978 wrote to another official of the Republican National Committee, volunteering to serve on party advisory committees dealing with economic affairs, particularly tax policy, and agriculture.[10] Party leaders put him on their agriculture subcommittee, where he worked again with Earl L. Butz, the former secretary of agriculture with whom he had been close. Butz had been forced to quit that post after he was caught making a racist joke and was seen as a liability for President Ford's ultimately unsuccessful election campaign in 1976. Now Butz was happy to have Yeutter on his party advisory committee team, writing in his characteristic acerbic manner, "Welcome aboard. Things are really going for us in Agricultural Districts. Our best allies are the Democrats."[11]

Later, from his perch atop the Chicago exchange, Yeutter felt free to give GOP leaders advice on how to run the next campaign. At the end of May 1979, for instance, Yeutter brutally assessed the shortcomings of President Carter and his cabinet. Yeutter offered his counsel on how GOP candidates could best attack the Democrats in a letter to Republican National Committee chairman William E. Brock III. He sent a blind copy of his note to George H. W. Bush, his favored candidate to take on Carter in the 1980 race. In the end, Bush quit the presidential race after falling behind Ronald W. Reagan in the primaries that year and soon became Reagan's running mate. Bush ultimately served as Reagan's vice president for eight years.

Yeutter cast his criticisms in personal and political terms, advising Brock on how presidential and congressional candidates should attack the Carter administration's flaws. He told Brock that the Carter administration had been "weak and inept" in the "general question of skill, toughness, and all the other attributes that are required for one to become an effective negotiator." He backhanded Treasury Secretary W. Michael Blumenthal as "effective but abrasive." Secretary Cyrus R. Vance was "highly respected, but tough and strong he is not." Yeutter saw Secretary of Agriculture Robert S. Bergland as "extremely erratic and inconsistent." National Security Adviser Zbigniew K. Brzezinski was "enigmatic" and lacked the "international reputation of a Kissinger." But Yeutter was especially tart about Carter: "And the President himself has been nebulous, ambivalent, inconsistent and a lot of other things as he has undergone on-the-job training as this nation's chief executive."

Yeutter was also sharp in criticizing areas he knew well, such as the Geneva trade talks in the Tokyo Round, as they neared their conclusion. "Ambassador [Robert S.] Strauss has generally done a fine job there, but President Carter has had him so busy doing other things that a lot of loose ends still remain," he told Brock. "The negotiations have not yet produced a safeguards code; the attempt to reach agreement on wheat and feed grains programs, including an international grain reserve, has collapsed (perhaps fortuitously from our standpoint); we still have not reached agreement with the European Community on citrus; we have not yet reached agreement with Japan on the government procurement code (though this may finally come a few days from now); and we have no agreement with Mexico either in the MTN [multilateral trade negotiations] or bilaterally on energy issues." He said Carter's secretary of energy, James R. Schlesinger, had so mishandled talks with Mexico "that all Americans will ultimately pay an enormous price for the Secretary's arrogance. That tab will undoubtedly be in the billions."[12]

But politics and personalities would get in the way of Yeutter's Washington ambitions the first time around. Another unsuccessful candidate in the Republican primaries, Kansas senator Robert J. "Bob" Dole, who chaired the Republican National Committee in 1971 and 1972 and became the vice presidential candidate on the ticket with President Ford in 1976, was irked that Yeutter had not backed him for the presidency in the 1980 race but instead favored George H. W. Bush. After Reagan was nominated, Yeutter chaired the agricultural task force for the nominee, sketching out farm belt policy recommendations for the new administration in a position that should have given him an inside shot at the job.

Indeed, Reagan supported Yeutter for the top ag post. But Dole was in line after the election to chair the powerful Senate Finance Committee while continuing to serve on the Senate Agriculture Committee.[13] And Dole pressed for Illinois director of agriculture John R. Block to get the secretary of agriculture slot, faulting Yeutter for not being a working farmer and for his ties, through the CME, with Big Ag businesses.[14] Dole told reporters that he would object to Yeutter's appointment, saying Yeutter was "not a hands-on farmer" and adding he would prefer someone "not tied to interest groups in the corporate sector."[15] An *Omaha World-Herald* reporter quoted Dole as saying, "I don't think we need someone out of big business making $200,000 a year."[16]

When Reagan beat Carter to take the presidency, Dole won the day on the ag secretary appointment. While Yeutter was ambivalent about returning to government service for family and financial reasons, he had suffered few, if any, professional setbacks before, and this one must have stung. He wrote to Congressman Douglas K. Bereuter of Nebraska, thanking him for his support for the ag secretary spot and adding, "The financial sacrifice would have been enormous, and we would have had to return to a commuting arrangement since our youngest son is still a high school sophomore. None of us were very excited about that possibility. At the same time, I would have appreciated having the opportunity to make the decision!" He commented that "Senator Dole decided to extract his pound of flesh" because of his unwillingness to back Dole for the presidential race. Yeutter noted that he had been told he headed "almost every kitchen cabinet list, including Governor Reagan's personal list, so that is gratifying." He added, "But these things usually work out for the best, so I am not terribly concerned about it."[17]

Yeutter struck a similar tone in a letter to a Korean friend in January 1981: "I would have been invited to become Secretary of Agriculture but for the opposition of Senator Dole, who was angry because we would not raise money for his Presidential campaign a year ago. The Reagan people did not wish to challenge Senator Dole, because of the importance of tax legislation to their governmental program in 1981. Senator Dole will strongly influence that legislation by virtue of his chairmanship of the Senate finance committee."[18]

Yeutter had worked with Block, the man Dole preferred, and gracious as always, he sent Block a personal note to congratulate him on the appointment. But he also wrote condescendingly about the Illinois state agricultural official to a high-ranking Japanese minister, Mamoru Sawabe, calling Block "a fine man" but adding, "You will also find, however, that he is very inexperienced in both national and international affairs. Consequently, it may be a few months before he is prepared to respond to some of the issues we discussed during my Tokyo visit." Yeutter reassured the minister that he would offer as much counsel as possible to the incoming Reagan team.[19] He hit a similar note in a letter to an agricultural industry colleague in California, saying he thought highly of Block but noting, "He has no knowledge of western agriculture, nor of the Washington, D.C. scene. Consequently, he has a lot to learn in the next year or so, unless he surrounds himself with sub-cabinet officials that fill these gaps. Time will tell. All that any of us can do at this point is hope, for the sake of the country and for American agriculture, that he learns quickly and performs well."[20]

However disappointing the snub may have been, it would turn out to be a lucky setback for Yeutter, whom Reagan would tap in 1985 to serve as U.S. trade representative. The role would prove far more consequential for Yeutter and for global trade. Indeed, after Yeutter was nominated for the trade position, he wrote to a friend who had congratulated him, "Now I am glad that Bob Dole was being vindictive in 1981! He was very supportive this time around, as were an enormous number of other people."[21]

Yeutter mended fences so well with Dole that the senator backed him for the trade job.[22] Later, in 1989, the senator supported Yeutter for the secretary of agriculture post under President Bush, calling him "a strong and intelligent voice" for American farmers.[23] For his part, Yeutter returned the favor in the 1996 presidential race by backing Republican nominee Dole in his unsuccessful attempt to beat incumbent President Clinton, with Yeutter serving on the GOP candidate's task force on international trade and investment and serving as honorary chairman in a Nebraska Dole fundraiser.[24] Furthermore, when Dole—who had a hand injury from his wartime military service—stumbled at one point in the campaign and the *Washington Post* published a photo of his fall, Yeutter angrily canceled his subscription. He wrote to *Post* chairman Katherine Graham, a friend whose seventieth birthday party he had attended in mid-1987, "Were I the editor, compassion alone would have dissuaded me from ever running such a photograph. . . . Incidents such as this make one wonder whether we've begun to lose our moral compass in this country."[25]

Despite deferring to Dole in 1980 in passing over Yeutter for the ag secretary job, Reagan kept an eye on Yeutter as he led the CME. Through Secretary of State Alexander M. Haig Jr., the president asked Yeutter in the spring of 1982 to lead an agricultural task force to Peru, an effort that built on Yeutter's expertise from his days in Colombia. The two-week mission, which included meetings with the top officials of the country, assessed market-oriented changes the Peruvian government put in place. "You have moved a long way in a very short period of time to correct many of the policy shortcomings of your predecessor government," Yeutter told Prime Minister Manuel Ulloa Elias, a fellow lawyer and economist, afterward. "That is inevitably somewhat traumatic, and I certainly hope you can ride the waves of discontent until the benefits of your own programs begin to be realized." He also complimented officials in the country's Ministry of Finance: "Their analysis of agricultural policy issues is first rate, and they are professional in their approach as well as being very vigorous and dynamic. It was refreshing to see a team of that caliber working in a developing country."[26]

The work of the Peruvian mission may have had broader influence. In 1983 Yeutter asked an official of the U.S. Agency for International Development to share a copy of the group's report with a

Chilean agricultural leader, Rodolfo Arbat, a businessman the Chilean government repeatedly pursued to serve as minister of agriculture (though he declined). Arbat was troubled by "the present disarray of Chile's agricultural policies" under President Augusto Pinochet Ugarte, Yeutter said, and had suggested that a U.S. presidential mission like Yeutter's to Peru might be helpful for Chile.[27] At the time, Chile was struggling with a recession that had idled more than a third of its workforce. Pinochet had taken advice on how to liberalize the country's economy from economist Milton Friedman, and the country's agriculture officials also got advice on agricultural credit issues in 1982 from former U.S. secretary of agriculture Clifford M. Hardin and former under secretary of agriculture Clarence Palmby. By the second half of the 1980s the free-market policies the dictator put in place led to impressive growth, though it was overshadowed by Pinochet's brutality and corruption.[28]

The White House in 1982 also seated Yeutter on the President's Export Council, a group charged with boosting U.S. exports. The move drew praise from, among others, Illinois Republican representative Charles H. Percy. "You could not have selected a better candidate for the vacancy on the P.E.C.," Percy wrote. "Clayton has served previous Republican administrations with distinction in formulating agricultural and foreign trade policies. Few Americans have the grasp of issues and ability to deal creatively with them as Clayton."[29] The praise echoed that of a group that had presented the balding Yeutter with a wig when he left a government job because, they said, the only thing he could not do was grow hair.[30]

Yeutter often cast his eyes abroad from Chicago, sometimes visiting overseas to build personal connections. On a fall 1980 trip, he visited several people in China whose lives had been disrupted by the Cultural Revolution, but who by then were helping reopen and redevelop the country. "It is tragic to have lost the use of your talents for so many years, but I know you will do everything in your power to now make up for that lost time!" he reassured one official he met in Shanghai, the Harvard-educated Dr. Chen Ding, vice chairman of the Shanghai Federation of Industry and Commerce and a national committee member of the Chinese People's

Political Consultative Conference. "The potential of China is just enormous, for you not only have natural resources in abundance, but an intelligent human population as well. If that combination can be harnessed in an effective way, China will become a major part of the world economy."[31]

He struck a similarly compassionate theme in writing to Mr. and Mrs. Charles Wang, a couple who had hosted him and who similarly had been targeted during the Cultural Revolution: "What a tremendous waste of valuable human resources that must have been, and what a travail to you and all the other families who suffered so much." Sharing his personal plans with them, he noted that he would consider taking "one of the top positions" in the U.S. government if one opened up after his youngest child graduated from high school in June 1983 but otherwise would stay at the CME at least until after the 1984 elections.[32] (As it happened, the Wangs wound up moving to California because of politically difficult situations for them in China. They stayed in touch with Yeutter, writing him about their move, a decade after their first contact.)[33]

Yeutter also generously advised American trade officials who bargained with foreign governments, as he had done. In June 1981, for instance, he wrote a six-page memo to David R. Macdonald, the new deputy U.S. trade representative, sketching out his advice on how the United States should approach talks with the Soviet Union about a long-term grain-purchasing agreement. Yeutter touched on such diverse subjects as economic theory about markets, American public reactions to Soviet deals, and the likely positions the Russians would take, depending on the health of their own crops.[34]

Presumably with the blessings of U.S. trade officials whom he later briefed, Yeutter even undertook personal diplomatic missions. When he visited Minister of International Trade Shintaro Abe in Japan in 1982, they discussed how Japan should open its markets to the United States. Yeutter followed up with a detailed eight-page memo titled "Steps to Relieve Bilateral Trade Tensions between the United States and Japan," which included suggestions that the Japanese should phase out import quotas of certain agricultural products; open their market to American beef and citrus, a long-standing bugaboo; make loans and grants to U.S. universities; improve information for would-be exporters seeking to crack the insular Japanese market; reflect on the Japanese attitude toward imports; open financial markets; make long-term grain arrangements; and endeavor to understand American thinking and the U.S. political process.[35] In just a few years, Yeutter would take up many of these issues in an official capacity.

As he tracked world affairs, Yeutter took an evenhanded, lawyerly approach to some conflicts. After England and Argentina went to war for ten weeks in the spring of 1982 over the Falkland Islands, also known as the Malvinas, he wrote to a friend in Peru:

> The controversy over the Malvinas was just ridiculous. It is unfortunate that both Peru and the United States had to become involved, and you are correct in asserting that the only winner of that kind of conflagration is the Soviet Union. I am very displeased with both England and Argentina for permitting the controversy to erupt into war. The Argentinians should have been intelligent enough to realize that the British were not going to sacrifice that property without a fight, and the British should have been sensitive enough to realize that Argentinian patience was beginning to run out. Not a very good performance on the part of either country.[36]

He joined such groups as the New York–based American Council on Germany, making note of his German heritage in accepting the group's invitation. In 1983 he and others on the Chicago Council on Foreign Relations visited Europe as guests of the North Atlantic Treaty Organization (NATO), and he told the head of the German friendship group, "We had an excellent session with Chancellor Kohl during our NATO trip, and I was very favorably impressed by him (much more than would be indicated by the American media). We are fortunate indeed to have him in the Chancellorship at a time when defense issues will be exceedingly sensitive. On the negative side, we were hosted at dinner by several Social Democrat members of Parliament, and I was terribly distressed by how far they have moved to the left."[37]

Such global matters riveted Yeutter, whose job at the CME often took him back into the international arena by way of Washington. In September 1981, for instance, he and officials of the South Africa Foundation feted Jeane D. J. Kirkpatrick, the U.S. ambassador to the United Nations, for dinner and a boat ride on the Potomac River. "Having had a lot of involvement on the international side during both the Nixon and Ford Administrations, it was a special pleasure for me to meet you," Yeutter wrote. "You are obviously doing a very fine job in your present post, and I wish you every success in the future. If I can ever help on agricultural, international trade, or international financial issues, just let me know."[38] Kirkpatrick, for her part, thanked him for the "rare moment of relaxation" at the dinner.[39] In later years, Yeutter and his wife, Jeanne, grew to know Kirkpatrick well, as they attended the same church in the Washington DC area.[40]

As Yeutter's job tilted toward political chores, it involved people of all partisan stripes. For instance, he wielded his powerful personal Rolodex to invite politicians and other leaders to a January 1982 meeting in Florida of the Foundation for American Agriculture (FAA), an arm of the conservative farm industry advocacy group, the American Farm Bureau. One of those he invited was Carol Lee Tucker-Foreman, the longtime consumer advocate and frequent government critic who became an assistant secretary of agriculture under President Carter. "You have no hesitancy coming into what might be a lion's den for you, and that earns you a great deal of respect," Yeutter told her in a January 1982 letter of thanks. "I thought you did a superb job in Florida, and I know the group would have asked you questions for another hour had you been able to stay longer. They may still not agree with all your policy positions, but there is no question about their admiration for your basic competence and your courage in taking on tough issues." He offered her a "red carpet tour of the Merc," should she visit Chicago.[41]

Working both ends of the political spectrum, Yeutter also helped bring to the FAA meeting California representative Anthony L. "Tony" Coelho, an influential Democrat on the House Agriculture Committee who served as the chamber's majority whip at-large, as well as the controversial Republican former secretary of agriculture, Earl L. Butz. Coelho thanked Yeutter for inviting him, saying, "I enjoyed the trip, especially the chance to visit with you and Earl Butz. Earl is a great individual and he charges up my battery. I only wish that people like you and him were in this administration. Not only does the administration need it, but agriculture needs it."[42]

Coelho had visited the CME in December 1981, bringing in tow Thomas R. Harkin, a fellow Democrat from Iowa who then was serving as a member of Congress. Harkin, who was elected to the Senate in 1984, was someone Yeutter would later tangle with over agricultural issues. In a January 1982 letter to Coelho, Yeutter thanked him for their visit: "Thanks especially for bringing Tom Harkin with you to Chicago, since Tom's level of knowledge on futures trading is very low." He added that Coelho's appearance afterward, at the FAA meeting in Florida, was "clearly a highlight." He also joked with the California Democrat, who was a member of his party's steering and policy committee: "We will be coordinating with you on both political campaign and legislative issues during the coming months. I fear you may win so many seats in November that Republicans like me may not even be welcome in Washington, D.C.! Aside from that, have a great year and let me know when I can ever be helpful. You were just superb on futures industry questions during 1981."[43]

Busily maintaining good relations with industry groups, with foreign officials, and with Washington, Yeutter chiefly served the CME as its "Mr. Outside," leaving many internal exchange matters to the chairman and the board—a characterization former CME chairman Melamed ("Mr. Inside") agreed with. Yeutter told one interviewer, "I was there [in Washington] for six-and-a-half years and a lot of the people in power in Washington either in the Executive branch or in Congress are longtime friends, many close personal friends. . . . I simply cannot devote the time to day-to-day management that other exchange presidents can. . . . So what we have here at this exchange is more of a Mr. Outside, Mr. Inside relationship." As always, Yeutter was confident in his skills and that of his lobbying team in DC, saying, "I don't want to be immodest about it . . . but I've been around Washington for a long time and I really believe I can evaluate Washington performances as well as anybody in the country. And I would say that as of right now, we probably do our job as well as anybody in Washington."[44]

Officials at the CME also knew that financial support for friendly politicians was invaluable in keeping them acting in line with industry desires—and that transcended party lines. The CME's Commodity Futures Political Fund distributed $324,000 in 1985 among allies including Democrats Daniel D. Rostenkowski, who chaired the House Ways and Means Committee and was a longtime supporter of the exchanges, and James C. "Jim" Wright Jr., the Texan who rose to become Speaker of the House in 1987, as well as Kansas senator Dole, a Republican. At the time, the CME's fund was the biggest contributor among corporate political action committees without stock. Distributing its ample largesse to members of both parties was useful realpolitik, but good-government advocates faulted the generous support that the CME, the Chicago Board of Trade (CBOT), and the Futures Industry Association gave such politicians. *Common Cause* opined, "The story of the commodity industry's Washington lobbying operation, fueled by the industry's well-timed, well-placed and increasingly generous campaign contributions provides a textbook example of what's wrong with the legislative system." For his part, Yeutter took umbrage at the suggestion that the CME was buying influence, telling a reporter, "We don't make quid pro quos on campaign financing for any member of Congress on any issue ever. . . . We don't buy votes and don't intend to buy votes."[45]

Yeutter always sought the high road, but some of the politicians he and the CME dealt with proved to be ethically challenged. Rostenkowski wound up serving fifteen months in federal prison and paying a $100,000 fine after cutting a plea deal, pleading guilty to two counts of mail fraud, to resolve seventeen counts of abusing his congressional payroll by paying people who did little or no work, converting stamp vouchers to cash, and misusing office expense accounts, along with other violations alleged by federal investigators in 1994. Rostenkowski denied guilt in the crimes, and Clinton pardoned him belatedly in 2000, as the president prepared to leave office.[46] After rising to the speakership, Wright resigned from the House in the spring of 1989 when a House ethics committee found "reason to believe" that he had broken congressional conduct rules sixty-nine times. He was accused of taking $145,000 in gifts from a Fort Worth developer and accumulating about $54,000 in royalties from bulk sales of a book he had written, *Reflections of a Public Man*, to groups with business before the House.[47]

Coelho, the California Democrat, also wound up quitting Congress in 1989 under a cloud related to a 1986 purchase of junk bonds in which he was aided by a savings and loan executive, an investment he failed to disclose. He denied wrongdoing and was never charged with a crime, saying he quit to spare the Democratic Party embarrassment.[48] Yeutter at the time wrote to Coelho about the "mixed and ambivalent emotions" he had over the congressman's resignation. "The Congress will lose an individual with outstanding leadership capabilities, and that makes me sad. In the democratic society which we hold so dear, it has become almost impossible to defend oneself against attack, whether or not the attack has any merit." He added that he was pleased, however, that Coelho would have the chance to make a mark in the private sector.[49] Coelho went on to run the firm Wertheim Schroder Investment Services and remained active in Democratic Party affairs.

Working with elected officials at times nevertheless tempted Yeutter to seek office himself, especially since Washington proved to be such a magnet for him. But family matters got in the way. During the spring of 1983, for instance, he looked into running for the U.S. Senate from Nebraska in response to a plea from Ralph J. Knobel, a fraternity brother from the University of Nebraska who chaired the state Republican Party. But Yeutter reasoned that he would need at least two six-year terms to make a difference, plus a year to run—thus carving out thirteen years at a point when Jeanne, his wife, was wearying of the demands his career was putting on his time and he was hoping for more family time. "My political interest still remains very strong, Ralph, so it is conceivable that I would run for an executive office at some time in the future, and perhaps even more likely that I would accept a top level Presidential appointment at the appropriate time," he told Knobel in April 1983. He also said that business and academic options appealed to him, but a U.S. Senate spot would foreclose those. So he declined to seek the senate role.[50]

Later, in 1987, Nebraska Republicans mentioned him as a challenger to Senator Edward Zorinsky the following year, but he demurred.[51] Just two years earlier, Zorinsky, who had switched from the Republican to the Democratic Party, had praised Yeutter's nomination to serve as U.S. trade representative.[52] Moreover, Yeutter's daughter Kim had interned in Zorinsky's office. Then, in 1990, when an executive at Citibank wrote Yeutter to offer support, should he ever run for office, Yeutter responded, "I will, however, probably stay on the appointive side of politics, which has at least a few less headaches than running for public office."[53]

Still, Yeutter's knowledge of Washington and his contacts—as well as his agriculture, economics, and law background—were pivotal for the CME, which had a long history of hiring leaders suited to particular challenges of the moment. Political relations and, specifically, efforts to counter the threat of an often-broached tax on transactions were top of mind for CME officials, recalls John J. Lothian, head of an online media and financial services firm in Chicago that covers the exchanges. "Every time it [the transaction tax] has been proposed in Washington, it's been defeated," Lothian says. With a touch of hard-boiled Chicago realism, he notes, "But it's a little like Whac-A-Mole—politicians like to propose it, then the exchanges and others throw a lot of money at them to not do that. It's a good way to get campaign contributions."[54] Such transaction taxes repeatedly were shot down as damaging to trading volumes and tending to drive trading to competing nontaxed bourses, particularly those overseas, but the idea resurfaced as recently as 2016.[55]

Yeutter also proved helpful in preserving the autonomy of the futures industry regulator, the CFTC, which he had helped birth. When he served at the USDA, he had tutored legislators about the commodities industry, helping them create the commission. *Futures* magazine called him the chief troubleshooter in the commission's creation.[56] But when he was hired at the CME, the commission was under assault by Congress, the General Accounting Office, the

Office of Management and Budget, and the industry itself, as the *New York Times* reported.[57] Critics outside the business regarded it as lax on enforcement and captive to the industry, even as insiders balked at heavier oversight and the perennial proposals to tax transactions to fund the commission. Some critics thought the Securities and Exchange Commission, which regulated the New York Stock Exchange and other equity markets, a more appropriate regulator, especially as the CME moved more aggressively into the financial products that in time would become its major source of trading volume, far outstripping agricultural contracts.

To better advocate for its interests in Washington, the exchange set up an office there and appointed Yeutter's law firm as its Washington counsel. Plugged-in attorneys and former regulators at the firm, from which Yeutter was on leave, could help the exchange deal better with congressional oversight committees and the CFTC.[58] Nearly four years into his tenure at the CME, in February 1982, Yeutter pressed for reauthorization of the agency and argued for a blend of taxpayer and industry support to fund it. He also tipped his hat to the CFTC's leadership, saying, "The agency has performed over the past twelve months in a manner far superior to what it had done in the prior seven years of its history. . . . We have our differences, and we certainly disagree vehemently and vigorously with some of the CFTC proposals before you today, but in terms of overall performance, the agency is vastly improved over what transpired earlier."[59] President Reagan renewed the CFTC's authority to regulate futures trading in January 1983, when he signed the Futures Trading Act of 1982, and the transaction taxes were not part of the final bill.[60]

Industry insiders preferred having the CFTC regulate them because, in part, they felt that its small size and sophistication could help it move faster on new-product approvals in the competitive futures arena. The CME contended with rivals across town at the bigger CBOT, as well as with competitors such as the Amex Commodities Exchange in New York. The CME wanted to expand into trading in a broad swath of assets, for instance, supplementing its offerings in agricultural products, gold, and currencies.[61] With the CFTC as a backstop, moreover, much of the regulation was self-regulation by the exchanges. And CFTC commissioners typically tended to be supportive rather than adversarial—though not always, as disciplinary actions over the years demonstrated.

Like other officials of the CME, Yeutter was determined to keep regulation to a minimum. "The exchange is capitalism at its best, pure capitalism. A true interaction of supply and demand with no government-imposed frills," he told a reporter for the *Kansas City Star* shortly after his appointment to the CME, but before he stepped into the job. "If the exchanges do an excellent job of regulating their own operations, then there is a small role for the government to play."[62]

For Yeutter, the internal and external lines were often blurred, though. When John F. "Jack" Sandner, the CME chairman, tussled in 1980 with Nelson Bunker Hunt and W. Herbert Hunt, a pair of Texas billionaire brothers who infamously had tried to corner the market on silver, Yeutter helped him and other officials understand the techniques the twosome used. The pair used futures contracts to buy huge quantities of silver and drive up its price. While their silver dealings were on the CBOT and the New York Commodity Exchange, they also were heavily involved in cattle contracts on the CME until the silver bubble they created burst and they were left needing credit and time to meet a margin call—extensions that the CME had never offered.[63] Sandner refused their request, even though he wound up losing a fortune himself on his cattle contracts when prices moved against him. Yeutter counseled CME officials on how the Hunts were pulling off their schemes, advising Sandner so he could testify in Washington about their maneuvers. "Clayton was a great resource at that time to understand the dynamics of the squeeze," Sandner said. "He was there right in the eye of the storm."

Indeed, work at the helm of CME could be stormy. Along with the political challenges from the outside, it was place of strong personalities, both among chairmen and traders. After a hardscrabble upbringing, for instance, Sandner had dropped out of high school and become a Golden Gloves boxing champion before going on to Southern Illinois University and the law school at Notre Dame University.[64] For their part, traders were often swashbuckling risk-takers used to making and losing millions based on their gut instincts. Typically, the president and CEO in the mix was a hired gun who operated at the behest of the chairman and the exchange's board—a difficult balancing act for anyone accustomed to being in charge, Sandner told me. "It's very hard to handle," said Sandner, who died in March 2021. "Clayton was the perfect person for that. He could walk through all those raindrops without getting wet. He knew how to deal with people; he had a tremendous talent. He was so damn smart, but he never came off that way. He could really connect with traders and the board."[65]

Even as he kept up his political liaisons and outside work, in the CME Yeutter was leading an entity that was fast becoming a major global financial force. Trading volumes soared at the exchange, nearly quadrupling from 15.1 million trades in the year he joined, 1978, to 56.6 million by 1985. New products—based on assets as diverse as T-bills and Treasury notes, fuel oil, leaded gasoline, plywood, along with options on the Standard & Poor's 500 index—surged onto the floor in that period. And membership expanded, with seat prices climbing from a low of $150,000 in 1978 to as high as $380,000 in 1980, before dipping again to a low of $155,500 in 1985 as the membership rosters swelled.[66]

The exchange's International Monetary Market unit, which Melamed debuted in 1972, was growing quickly as well. Increasingly, the CME looked for growth abroad—a sweet spot for Yeutter—as it diversified into products based on foreign assets, such as British pounds and Eurodollars. It opened an office in London in early 1980, the first U.S. exchange to do so. Yeutter and other CME leaders also crafted an alliance with officials in Singapore to create the Singapore International Monetary Exchange in the fall of 1984, a move that helped protect the CME's Eurodollar contract from a European rival.[67]

To accommodate all the growth at home, the CME built a twin-towered forty-story building in downtown Chicago that would give it one million square feet of office space and seventy thousand square feet of trading space. On Yeutter's watch, the $350 million project, which opened on November 28, 1983, went up smoothly.

"People squabble more about putting up a three-story building than we have," Yeutter said. On the opening day, officials and politicians saluted the exchange at a champagne breakfast. "The Merc is to Chicago what oil is to Texas and Oklahoma, what milk is to Wisconsin, and what corn is to Iowa," declared the Illinois congressman, Rostenkowski, with whom Yeutter got on well, despite their partisan differences.[68]

While he cemented good relations with regulators and politicians, Yeutter also reached out to farmers and ranchers and industry groups to preach the value of futures. He was barnstorming as aggressively as he ever had in any appointive office or political role. In one year he gave sixty-seven presentations of various sorts around the world, as recounted by Bob Tamarkin in *The Merc: The Emergence of a Global Financial Powerhouse.* "On one day he was the lead-in for President Reagan at the National Corn Growers Association convention in Des Moines; then he left for a presentation to the New York Society of Security Analysts and, shortly thereafter went to the annual meeting of the National Livestock Producers Association. From there, he moved on to Washington, where the Merc hosted a dinner in honor of retiring CFTC commissioner David Gartner."[69]

Yeutter's public appearances could be fraught with risk at times for him, however. He had long tended to shoot from the lip and got in trouble in Chicago because of attempts at humor or flashes of impatience—flaws Melamed attributed to "a little bit of naivete." Melamed recalls that when he introduced Yeutter early on to a large group in the city, Yeutter joked that until he got to Chicago he had never met a Jew and he was now "inundated with Jews." Melamed, who was Jewish, remembers, "Clayton meant it in the nicest way possible, but a lot of Jews took it as an insult. Clayton would be the last guy to insult anybody."[70]

Indeed, later, when he served as U.S. trade representative, Yeutter presided over the implementation in 1985 of the first U.S. bilateral free trade agreement, which was with Israel. He counted major leaders in Jerusalem among his friends, after visiting the Jewish capital in 1986, and wrote to Israeli minister of tourism Abraham Sharif, "Because of the religious heritage that is involved, the travel through Israel was one of the most moving experiences we have had in a long time. It is truly a trip that we shall never forget, and I may now be the best spokesman for Israel tourism that you have in the United States!"[71]

For his part, Melamed became Yeutter's biggest advocate in lobbying his high-level contacts to land Yeutter the job as trade representative, calling him "a valuable asset for the nation."[72] Melamed also stayed in touch with Yeutter long after the CEO had left the exchange. When Yeutter honeymooned with his second wife, Cristena, Melamed let him use his house in Scottsdale, Arizona, where he and Cristena would later get their own place. "I truly loved Clayton," says Melamed, noting that he later led an effort for the CME to donate $500,000 to the Clayton Yeutter Institute of International Trade and Finance at the University of Nebraska–Lincoln.

More problematically, Yeutter once grew impatient when Harold L. Washington, Chicago's first African American mayor, was late to a function Yeutter was chairing. With Washington's staff in attendance, Yeutter remarked that the mayor may not have cared about the niceties of etiquette because he was Black, recalls Melamed. "I almost died at the table," the former CME chairman says. "If you insult a guy who is the first Black mayor of the city, you're going to have trouble." It was left to Melamed to patch things up, which he did by visiting the mayor to assert that Yeutter had unintentionally slipped up and "didn't mean anything by it." To ease the mayor's hurt feelings, Melamed prompted the exchange to create a program in which the CME would fete the city's best graduating high school students with lunch and give the top student an award named for the mayor, plus $500 and a temporary job at the CME.[73]

Relations between Yeutter and the mayor, however, remained strained, with Yeutter faulting Washington for his management style. "The business community basically told the mayor that he's running a big, big business and that he has to exercise some management skills," Yeutter told a reporter for the *Christian Science Monitor* in 1984. "There aren't many accolades that could be handed out over the first year. . . . Harold Washington has not been a Tom Bradley [the first African American mayor of Los Angeles] in the way this city has been run."[74] Washington, a lawyer who had been an assistant city prosecutor, a state representative, state senator, and a U.S. congressman, served as mayor from April 1983 until November 1987, when he died in office seven months into his second term.[75]

Despite what Melamed calls his tendency to commit such verbal faux pas, Yeutter impressed most people he dealt with at the exchange and outside with his warmth and genuine friendliness. "When you mentioned his name, what it conjures up is that big booming laugh and smile," recalls Terry Savage, a TV reporter, commentator, and longtime trader who became an outside director at the CME. "You think about this expansive, booming, laughing, grinning [person], always with a broad smile on his face. His voice was so distinctive, it had a laugh in it. . . . That was his natural life skill. It came from the inside out." But he also was nobody's fool, she says, with an ability to bring his powerful intellect to bear on difficult exchange matters as he served as the CME's public face in Washington and around the world. His brainpower and geniality could draw people's attention. "He was like the North Pole and all magnets spun in his direction when he walked into the room. He did it without effort." That helped him get on with everyone from elected officials to traders and farmers, she says.[76]

Toward the end of Yeutter's time at the exchange, however, some farmers were cool toward the city slickers at the CME and CBOT, angrily blaming traders for driving down farm product prices. Conditions were tough in agriculture in the mid-1980s, with the low prices combining with rising production costs, falling land values, and high interest rates to drive up farm foreclosures, leading to such events as a twelve-thousand-farmer march in January 1985 on the state capitol building in Minnesota. Forty-seven farmers led by the American Agriculture Movement were arrested protesting at both Chicago exchanges on January 21 and 22, 1985, as some of them tried to shut down trading. Farmers had picketed the CBOT the prior September and met repeatedly with officials, but they were unhappy when the executives refused to ban speculative trading on crop contracts and put a floor on prices. The protesters were unpersuaded that the futures markets just reflected supply and demand and thus were vehicles for discovering, not hammering down, prices.[77] As Savage puts it, "You don't blame the thermometer for your temperature."[78]

As a farmer, Yeutter could talk comfortably with the protesters, but he also pulled no punches. He called Wayne Cryts, president of the American Agriculture Movement of Missouri and an organizer of the Chicago protests, someone who "likes to be on TV and is prepared to go to jail to be on TV," saying, "It's a bit of the Jesse Jackson syndrome."[79] Reverend Jackson, an African American Chicago-based civil rights leader, sometimes courted arrest to make his points. Nonetheless, Yeutter met with Cryts and others, later saying they had a "very amicable discussion." Yeutter sympathized with their economic plight, calling it "very serious," but he said their solution was not in Chicago but in Washington, if anywhere.[80] Yeutter blamed farmland woes on the high dollar, which limited exports, and a lack of credit, and he argued that the farmers actually saw how the futures markets worked to their benefit. "Deep down they understand that these [futures] markets are helpful to them," he said at a press conference. "We provide a convenient forum for protest."[81]

Certainly, Yeutter had his finger on the pulse of discontent in farm country. Only days before the January 1985 Chicago protests, at a meeting of turkey producers in Arizona, Yeutter had predicted demonstrations by farmers in the coming spring, as Congress considered a new farm bill. Yeutter and others, such as Senate Agriculture Committee chairman Jesse A. Helms Jr., a Republican from North Carolina, were pressing for legislation to be more market oriented. "We're at the edge of a catastrophe," Yeutter argued at the meeting. Failed farm programs to that point had led to the economic problems in the farm belt, making farmers "terribly frustrated," he said. For his part, Helms contended that price supports, government purchases, and land set-aside programs had failed, driving worldwide surpluses and slashing profits. Further, Yeutter called for trade policy to attack subsidies and trade barriers in Europe and elsewhere that shut out American products. Despite doing a good job at home, U.S. farmers were "getting killed" in the global marketplace, he said.[82]

As he moved beyond the CME and upward through several important jobs, Yeutter stayed loyal to people he dealt with, and he kept up his warm relationships with colleagues at the CME long after he left. In the fall of 1989, when he was serving as the U.S. secretary of agriculture, he even went to bat in a highly publicized legal proceeding involving a former CME chairman, Brian P. Monieson, over the objections of both Nebraska U.S. senators and a former Missouri senator. Monieson chaired the exchange board during the second half of Yeutter's tenure there, from 1983 to 1985. The CFTC accused Monieson of failing to supervise two employees of his brokerage firm when the pair bilked customers out of thousands of dollars by routing losing trades to customers while directing winning trades to their personal accounts—a gambit known as "bucketing the trades."[83]

Monieson, who was not accused of personal wrongdoing, fought the charges and asked Yeutter to serve as a character witness. Yeutter did so, despite a letter from Democratic senators James Exon and Robert Kerrey, who called his testimony "inappropriate at best," and suggested that his high government position would "unduly influence" the administrative law judge. "Further, the message that will reach the American people by your action will be one of special privilege," the senators wrote. "The word will go forth, as described in the attached letter from former Senator Thomas Eagleton, that the bigger you are the less likely it is that you will fall."[84] Eagleton, a Democrat who in 1972 briefly ran as a vice presidential candidate with nominee George S. McGovern, had served as an outside director at the CME, and he quit the board in protest over the testimony by Yeutter and other exchange leaders.

Yeutter took a beating in the press for his testimony. "Some suggest that instead of testifying as a character witness, a member of the Cabinet ought to be demanding that any abuses be rooted out and punished as harshly as possible. Unless the president disavows Yeutter's actions and demands that he retract his testimony or resign, they say, the markets will get the message that political interference is part of the Bush administration's policy on market regulation," wrote Jerry Knight of the *Washington Post*.[85] The

Wichita Eagle picked up Knight's piece from the *Los Angeles Times–Washington Post* news service, headlining it "Friends in High Places: Yeutter's Testimony in Investigation Raises Questions."[86]

When a Wichita couple wrote to President Bush, criticizing Yeutter for what they called "obvious tampering with the justice system," Yeutter wrote back, giving them a tutorial on the purpose of character testimony. He said such testimony was designed to give

> an appraisal of whether the person charged with wrongdoing has a reputation of being fundamentally honest, or a reputation of being a crook. In this case, I felt it important that the Commodity Futures Trading Commission, the regulatory body, know that Brian Monieson is an honest man. My character testimony, and that of others, does not, of course, demonstrate that Mr. Monieson violated no CFTC rules. He may well have done so, and it is up to the CFTC to determine that. I consider my own integrity to be unimpeachable, but I have violated rules from time to time and have some traffic tickets to illustrate that. Mr. Monieson may have done the same. I cannot judge that, and I do not in any way seek to do so, and my five minutes of character testimony will be of no relevance to the CFTC's deliberations on that point. If Mr. Monieson is found to have violated rules, and if the offense is a serious one the CFTC should mete out whatever punishment they deem appropriate. Mr. Monieson must accept the result, whatever it may be.[87]

In a stinging rebuke to the Nebraska senators after he testified, Yeutter reminded them that Americans were presumed innocent until proven otherwise. Furthermore, he pointed out that his testimony did not deal with the case, but rather with Monieson's character.

> Brian Monieson may or may not have satisfactorily supervised his employees, but I believe deeply that he is an honest human being. Testifying to that, when asked, is in my judgment the mark of a good citizen. Had I chosen not to do so and were it later to appear that a paucity of character witnesses may have

had an influence on the final outcome, I would never have forgiven myself. Life is too short for us to avoid or ignore our responsibilities to our fellow man. If that conflicts with my position as Secretary of Agriculture, then I would give up my position before I would shirk my responsibility as a human being.[88]

Only a year before, after the election of 1988 brought former Nebraska governor Kerrey to Washington, Yeutter had wished Kerrey well on winning the senate seat. "Heartiest congratulations on the election victory! I'd like to change your party affiliation, Bob, but I suspect it is now a bit late for that!" he wrote. "Everyone tells me that you ran an excellent campaign, and that certainly was demonstrated in the final result. I hope the transition to Washington, D.C. life will be a smooth one, and I look forward to seeing you on Capitol Hill, at meetings of the Nebraska Society, and in other incarnations. If Jeanne and I can help you in any way as you make the big move, just let us know."[89] Soon, however, the men would battle over issues ranging from trade to farm policy, with Yeutter at times accusing Kerrey of demagoguery. For Yeutter at least, the Monieson flap seemed to mark a low point from which their professional relationship—contacts over several years—never recovered.

Publicly, Yeutter often shrugged off such controversies and slights—though the length and depth of his responses suggested he was troubled by them. When a friend wrote supportively of his actions in the Monieson affair, Yeutter responded, "That generated some criticism here in Washington, D.C. but it shouldn't have so I just ignored it! As you know, human relationships are everything in this world, much more important than power bases and a lot of other things that serve as motivating forces for far too many people."[90]

In the end, the authorities ruled that Monieson had failed to supervise the brokers, barred him from the futures industry for life, and fined him $500,000. On appeal, the trading ban was cut to two years and the fine was trimmed to $200,000.[91] William J. Brodsky, who succeeded Yeutter as CEO of the CME, wrote him to say how much he was moved by Yeutter's letter to the offended senators. "It certainly has been a difficult time for everybody involved but you really stood up to the plate and hit a home run. We are constantly in awe of your talents, fortitude and independence. There is not much of any of those characteristics in Washington and you seem to be doing well on all of those."[92]

Shortly after the Monieson brouhaha, Yeutter in April 1990 wrote a character reference for another former CME associate who sought a presidential pardon for various offenses. Yeutter wrote that the disciplined brokerage chief, Joseph E. Siegel, "paid the price through rather harsh sanctions that were meted out to him, and has since conducted himself in an exemplary manner."[93] Siegel and an associate had been convicted of conspiracy, fraud, and violating the Commodity Exchange Act in connection with a tax-avoidance scheme, and Siegel was fined $500,000 and given probation.[94] Despite Yeutter's effort, President George H. W. Bush denied the pardon request by Siegel, who died at seventy-nine in 2005.

Yeutter was proud of his time at the CME and particularly enjoyed working with Melamed, who had recruited him there. When Melamed was honored in Chicago in 1990 for his work at the exchange, Yeutter said that he had been "tremendously impressed" by Melamed's insights into the futures industry and in the national and global economies when he first him years before, and he credited Melamed with convincing him to join the Merc "for what turned out to be a glorious and productive seven years." Yeutter wrote, "We accomplished a lot together during those years, and the world of futures trading will never again be the same! Futures markets became a major factor in the operation of the global economy, and the Chicago Merc was clearly identified as the most innovative and dynamic private sector financial institution in the world. It was a privilege for me to be a part of that, but it never would have occurred without your personal leadership, creativity and intense personal involvement."[95]

During Yeutter's tenure at the CME, the exchange took big steps toward becoming one of the largest bourses in the world, going so far as to discuss a merger with its crosstown rival, the larger

CBOT. Egos and money got in the way then, however, and for a couple of decades afterward. Ultimately, the exchanges did merge in 2007, when the CME acquired the CBOT. Like others, including editorialists at the *Chicago Tribune*, Yeutter had seen the virtues of such a deal long before. In 1996 he complimented N. Don Wycliff of the newspaper for pro-merger editorial:

> The Merc and Board of Trade have phenomenal competitive instincts and uncommon institutional energy. They are great institutions, but they are not infallible or indestructible. Their extraordinary energies need to be focused on their external competitors, not on each other. If that is not done soon, Chicago could take the same blow in these markets that Detroit took a few years ago in automobiles, and it will take years to recover. Chicago's odds of winning in the global competition of the 21st century will be significantly enhanced if it puts one powerful futures/options exchange on that playing field.[96]

Even as he helped guide the CME toward a more influential and important future, Yeutter also took big steps that would help him in his later top jobs in Washington. The corporate, political, and global relationships he cemented while running the exchange helped him prepare for the stiff challenges to come—challenges that would test his ample diplomatic and intellectual skills far more than anything he'd done before.

1. Reinhold F. "Doc" Yeutter, Clayton's father, was gregarious, hardworking, and unusually strong, but the German immigrant whose schooling ended after eighth grade was perplexed by his brainy son. He never told the boy he loved him.

2. Laura P. Yeutter, Clayton's mother, was committed to her church and devoted to her only child. As he advanced in Washington, she preferred that he return to Nebraska.

3. The Yeutter family home was part of a small farm between Eustis and Cozad, Nebraska. Growing up in the Depression, Yeutter shared a bed there with a hired hand.

4. (*opposite top*) Yeutter came along in 1930, relatively late in his parents' lives.

5. (*opposite bottom*) Times were tough for farmers and most other Americans during the Depression, but pets such as a dog named Sport and a cat, along with the occasional toy, were still available.

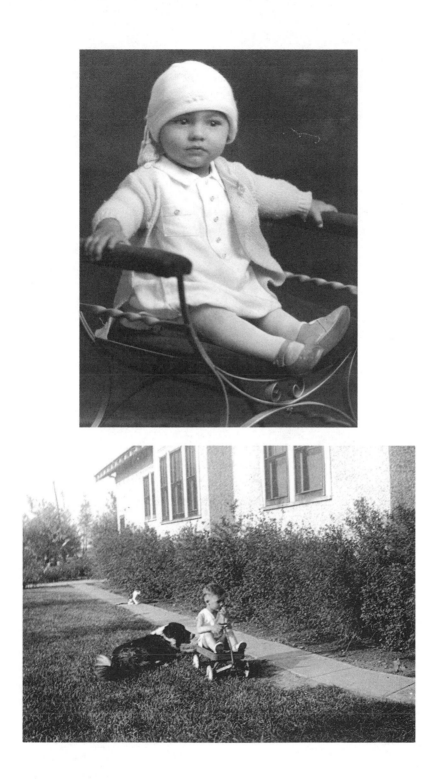

6. As the war loomed, Yeutter's parents opted not to teach him German, which might have helped him greatly later in his career. He struggled with languages, learning Spanish in his thirties.

7. Even as a child, Yeutter was showing off the smile that would later be his trademark.

8. By the time he graduated from high school,
Yeutter was known for his charm and talkativeness.

9. As a teenager, Yeutter was big for his age and a standout in football and other sports in his small high school. He proudly stayed fit his whole life.

10. Showing a hint of a smile among his stern-faced fraternity brothers in the FarmHouse chapter at the University of Nebraska, Yeutter (*fourth row up, third from the left*) was popular in the group, serving as its president. He supported the fraternity throughout his life.

11. Yeutter led the Chicago Mercantile Exchange as president and CEO from 1978 to 1985. The job kept him in touch with Washington and with global trade issues.

12. The moderate Yeutter did not initially support Ronald W. Reagan in his first run for the presidency in 1968, preferring Nelson A. Rockefeller, or in Reagan's 1980 bid, favoring George H. W. Bush. But he came around to back the successful Reagan-Bush ticket, and Reagan named him U.S. trade representative, a key role in the president's cabinet.

13. Yeutter joined Treasury Secretary James A. Baker III in keeping President Reagan informed about talks on the U.S.-Canada Free Trade Agreement.

14. Yeutter developed and shepherded an omnibus trade bill President Reagan signed in August 1988 in Long Beach, California. The legislation became the heart of U.S. trade law.

15. President Reagan signed the U.S.-Canada Free Trade Agreement into law in September 1988 in the White House Rose Garden, joined by Canadian ambassador Allan E. Gotlieb, Yeutter, and Baker.

16. As trade issues with Japan loomed large, Japanese prime minister Noboru Takeshita and President Reagan conducted full-team discussions in the White House Cabinet Room. Yeutter had warm relations with Japanese leaders, paving the way for breakthroughs in trade with the country.

17. President George H. W. Bush thought so highly of Yeutter that he tapped him to become his secretary of agriculture.

18. Heading the U.S. Department of Agriculture, Yeutter dealt with thorny issues, sometimes finding the job a great strain.

19. One of Yeutter's most important tasks at the USDA was guiding the 1990 Farm Bill through the legislature, garnering the support of key Democrats and Republicans.

20. As chairman of the Republican National Committee in 1991, Yeutter kept the president and his chief of staff, John H. Sununu, up to date on issues of the day.

21. Yeutter and President Bush remained close during and after Bush's presidency.

22. Yeutter and his first wife, Lillian Jeanne Vierk, raised a daughter, Kim, and three sons, Gregg, Van, and Brad (*from left to right*). Jeanne, as she was known, died in August 1993.

23. Yeutter and Cristena Bach, whom Yeutter knew casually when she worked in the White House under President Reagan, married in October 1995 and here marked their birthdays in December of that year.

24. The Yeutters adopted and raised three daughters, Victoria, Olivia, and Elena (*from left to right*). Here the young women celebrated Olivia's quinceañera celebration in January 2020.

25. Throughout his life, Yeutter projected self-assurance and optimism.

8

Macho Man of Trade

W hen word got out about Yeutter's appointment in the spring of 1985 as U.S. trade representative (USTR), congratulatory letters poured in from all over the world, sent by friends, industry leaders with trade issues, politicians, and foreign officials with whom Yeutter would bargain—and contend—over the following three and a half years. As a veteran of the trade office where he had served as a deputy representative nearly a decade earlier, and someone who followed news of the deteriorating global trade situation regularly, he was under no illusions about the difficulties he faced. But he also attacked the task with his typical enthusiasm and shoulder-to-the-wheel approach.

"It is an atrocious time to become U.S. Trade Representative! But, that is also what makes it fun," he wrote to a trade association friend.[1] When he requested an indefinite leave from a partner at his law firm, he said, "The trade arena will be brutal, but that is what makes the job exciting. The interest at the moment is just incredible, probably at the highest level it has been in 50 years."[2] And he told a friend in the insurance industry, "You are correct that this is a far more attractive and exciting position than the post of Secretary of Agriculture. As Jeanne says, I should thank Bob Dole for doing me a favor! These things do seem to work out for the best in the long run, which is why all of us need to learn patience and tolerance. The USTR position will be a murderous one, but that is also what makes it enticing."[3]

Perhaps his most sober assessment of the job, however, came in a letter to Milton Friedman, the economist who advised presidents and consulted with foreign governments and U.S. companies. "Trade issues will be incredibly difficult to manage over the next few months," Yeutter wrote in response to Friedman's congratulatory note. "I really wish I could have gotten here a little sooner. There are a lot of things that needed doing within the Administration in order to blunt or neutralize some of the protectionist pressures on Capitol Hill. You are certainly correct in your assertion that not many people in Washington, D.C. can take the long view. And with the 1986 election approaching, the view of Members of Congress is becoming shorter by the day!"[4]

He was similarly frank with Japanese business leaders who congratulated him. "Trade frictions are very significant at the moment, not only between Japan and the United States, but in many other parts of the world as well. As you can tell, the entire world is becoming much more protectionist, a trend that we must try to arrest," he told Yoshifusa Watanabe, who chaired the Tokyo Commodity Exchange for Industry. "In our relationships with Japan, it is just imperative that the trade deficit begin to correct itself. That will take a concerted effort on the part of both the public and private sectors of each country, and a definitive commitment on the part of Japan to expand its imports. That will not be easy, but I have confidence that progress will occur."[5]

Yeutter's political, trade, and economics experience—and particularly his negotiating skills and knowledge of agriculture—equipped him well for the job, which opened up when the Reagan administration decided to move U.S. trade representative William Brock to the helm at the Department of Labor. Yeutter rose to the top in a field of some thirty candidates the White House considered, as the *New York Times* reported. Among them were the former chairman of Citicorp, Walter B. Wriston, and a former Republican congressman from New York, Barber B. Conable Jr., both of whom pulled out of consideration. Several other congressmen were on the list, the newspaper reported. Part of what appealed to the White House was the way Yeutter helped boost exports to the Soviet Union in 1974, when he co-chaired the America-Soviet Committee on Agriculture as the deputy trade representative. Even more persuasive, the following year he resolved the cheese war with Europe, pushing some countries there to end some of their subsidies on cheese.[6]

The Reagan administration set a high bar for him in the post. When Yeutter agreed to take the job, President Reagan's chief of staff, Donald T. Regan, escorted him out of the White House with a tall order. "And Don Regan says to me: 'your job is to change the world,'" Yeutter recalled in 2016. "Isn't that something? And we did, we did it. Not just me. It took a lot of other people helping, but we did things in trade that had never, ever been done before. . . . I kinda took that to heart. When somebody says your job is to change the world, you better pay attention."[7]

By the fall of 1987, two and a half years into the trade representative's job, Yeutter's 130-person operation in Washington's historic Winder Building was heralded in the *New York Times* as the government's "elite force" on global commercial issues. As he led the comparatively tiny outfit through a bevy of trade fights across the world, Yeutter was called the squad's commander.[8] Earlier, in February 1987, he was applauded in *Business Week* for his twelve-hour workdays in the second-floor corner office—long days on which he typically also brought work home—as well as his "determined yet good-natured persuasiveness." One staff member said he "[has] a marvelous way of saying no or hanging tough with a pleasant smile. He doesn't elicit anger on the other side."[9]

He was relentlessly upbeat, according to Susan K. Nelson, his executive assistant on and off from the late 1970s until near the end of his career. About the only thing that could send a cloud across his brow at Monday morning USTR office meetings was when the University of Nebraska's football team, the Cornhuskers, lost on the Saturday before, she says, and even then his sunny demeanor quickly broke through. Nelson, who handled his correspondence, was deluged regularly with Dictaphone tapes, both after his busy weekends and during the week, on which he had recorded scores of letters for her to type. Each week she would handle between twenty-five and several hundred letters, many on sensitive matters and addressed to world leaders; reflecting his good manners, he also would dictate legions of thank-you and congratulatory notes to people ranging from legislators who had done work that impressed him to drivers who had made special efforts for him. On special documents, he often did the typing himself, hammering away on his IBM Selectric, the pre-PC electric typewriter of choice for many professionals.

Nelson started working for Yeutter in 1977, when she was an assistant at the Lincoln, Nebraska, law firm he joined at the time. The Nebraska-born Nelson and her husband moved to Illinois, where she worked for Yeutter at the Chicago Mercantile Exchange, then to Washington at the USTR office and the Department of Agriculture. And then, after a time doing other things, she rejoined him—working from her home—when he went to the Washington law firm Hogan & Hartson. Citing his midwestern work ethic and the fairness and decency with which he treated everyone—from parking lot attendants to presidents—she says he was an inspiring boss worth following around the country. Like Yeutter, Nelson grew up on a farm and found common ground with Yeutter in the values they shared. "You learned to persevere and you learned to work hard, but the biggest part of it was caring for people; you treat people as you would want to be treated," she says. "Those all were the characteristics I saw in this man. We absolutely just jelled."[10]

Indeed, Yeutter earned the loyalty of his teams with both his personal work habits and his personality. "Clayton is a bigger than life guy," recalls Roger Bolton, who worked with him as an assistant U.S. trade representative for public affairs and fondly remembers him in the present tense: "He bounds into the room, bigger than life, booming voice, big smile: 'Hi, Rog!' Backslapper, a little handsy . . . big personality, always, always, always positive . . . generous to a fault, very, very driven. Problems to him were just challenges to be solved, not things to wring your hands over. And his leadership of trade policy of the United States at that critical point in history changed the world in profound ways."[11]

Yeutter inspired those he worked with, says Ambassador Alan F. Holmer, who came with him to USTR as general counsel and then rose to deputy USTR. "At his first senior staff meeting, Yeutter told the story of a major midwestern company whose chairman was going to retire in two years," Holmer remembers. "He had three top contenders to be his successor. The chairman told them: 'I'm going to judge you based on two things: first, how well you do your job; second, and equally importantly, I'll judge you on how much you do to help the other two succeed.' That was the kind of collaboration Clayton expected from his team. And he got it."[12]

Such plaudits were yet to come, of course, when Yeutter took the USTR job and headaches loomed. In the mid-1980s U.S. political and business leaders were apoplectic about the mushrooming trade deficit the United States was running. American consumers and businesses were snapping up more goods from Japan than American businesses were exporting there, in value terms. Though small by 2021 standards, the figures were unprecedented then. While the trade balance in goods and services had been modestly negative going back to 1971, the red ink began soaring in 1984, nearly doubling on a balance of payments basis from $57.8 billion in 1983 to $109.1 billion in 1984. The deficit climbed to $121.9 billion in 1985, when Yeutter took his new job, and peaked at $151.7 billion by 1987 before turning downward in 1988 ($114.6 billion), just before he left the trade position in January 1989. The deficit then steadily cascaded downward, dropping to a low of $31.1 billion by 1991 before beginning a nearly relentless climb to $616.4 billion in 2019.[13]

Fairly or otherwise, many in Congress felt that the Reagan administration in its first term had neglected trade issues. Sentiment for protectionist legislation was growing, and as the deficits climbed, the clamor was bipartisan, as the *New York Times* reported. Democratic senator Maxwell S. "Max" Baucus of Montana argued that Congress was reacting to the absence of a trade policy and the claim that "virtually every American industry is going down the drain." On the other side of the aisle, Republican senator Henry John Heinz III of Pennsylvania charged that the administration "has no game plan, not even a team."[14] Reagan's critics accused the president of "almost willful blindness and indifference" to the trade problems, columnist David S. Broder wrote.[15] Trying to seize the initiative, members of the Democratic-controlled Congress introduced more than three hundred protectionist bills, and only Republican control of the Senate ensured that most didn't get far.[16]

Given the looming 1986 election and the tendency of politicians of all stripes to push for protectionism, as well as the sheer volume of issues he faced, Yeutter felt he was racing against the calendar when he settled into the job. The issues on his plate included Japan's swelling trade surplus with the United States because of its anti-imports, pro-exports policies, particularly its refusal to accept U.S. farm products and U.S.-made semiconductors; intellectual property and insurance issues with Korea; bilateral trade negotiations with Hong Kong, Taiwan, and Korea; renegotiation of a textile agreement (protecting the U.S. textile industry through quotas on imports into the United States) that would lead to bruising congressional battles; disputes with the European Community over citrus and pasta; bilateral free trade agreements with Israel and Canada; and laying the groundwork for all-important efforts for the world to scale back tariffs and nontariff barriers in the Uruguay Round of trade talks. When a friend wrote to say he looked tired in TV appearances a year into his job, Yeutter in August 1986 replied, "I must reluctantly concede that the tube does not lie! We had about half a dozen major negotiations underway simultaneously, and there was a lot of stress and strain attached to all of those. Fortunately, they all came out well—though some of our political opponents would only confess to that privately, while being critical publicly."[17]

On the very day that President Reagan nominated Yeutter, the Senate Finance Committee voted for a bill directing the president to retaliate against Japanese imports in ninety days unless Japan opened its markets.[18] Yeutter, for his part, acknowledged the worries: "There is a substantial level of feeling that the executive branch has not been as responsive as it should have been in handling some of these problems."[19] At an April 3, 1985, press conference, he stated, "The U.S. has not been as strong as it should have been on trade issues."[20] Then, at his June 25 Senate Finance Committee confirmation hearing, Yeutter said that "on trade issues we have turned the other cheek for many years, perhaps too many, and it has cost . . . dearly."[21]

To build trust and confidence, Yeutter made dozens of trips to Capitol Hill to meet with leaders in the House and Senate, listening to their concerns, recalls Holmer.[22] Still, Yeutter and the Reagan administration overall suffered through a hot summer in 1985, as trade took center stage in Washington. At home, anger about trade issues and calls for protections for American industries percolated through the Democratic-controlled House and in many quarters of the Republican-dominated Senate, as well as in business circles outside of Washington. Overseas, trading partners were similarly restive. "Nineteen eighty-five was the year that really put trade on the map," says Judith H. Bello, who served as a deputy general counsel and later general counsel for Yeutter's office.[23]

Right off the bat, Yeutter inherited a long-simmering "pasta war" with Europe. On June 20, a few days before Yeutter's confirmation hearing as USTR, President Reagan announced that he would boost duties on European pasta because the European Community (EC) discriminated against American lemons and oranges by giving preferential tariffs to certain Mediterranean countries; infuriating the United States, the EC had ignored a ruling against those tariffs handed down by a panel under the General Agreement on Tariffs and Trade (GATT). The Europeans slapped back by imposing more tariffs on U.S. lemons and walnuts (both grown in California, Reagan's home state).

Trying to head off a tit-for-tat battle, Yeutter negotiated a short-lived truce in that squabble in July 1985 that was reminiscent of his success a decade before in resolving the cheese war with Europe.[24] He brokered the truce over a weekend filled with conversations between him and the EC commissioner for external relations and trade, Willy De Clercq, someone he would deal with extensively in coming years. But their truce—a complex deal tied to settling a separate dispute over American citrus exports—didn't end the war.[25] The following November the United States imposed higher tariffs on imported EC pasta. At the time, the United States had a complaint pending under the GATT procedures against export subsidies that the EC provided to boost pasta exports, so the American actions were shrewdly aimed at both the subsidies and the discriminatory tariffs, as Leonard W. Condon, who was then deputy assistant U.S. trade representative for agricultural affairs, recalls.[26]

As the tempest escalated, both sides threatened more measures and countermeasures, and it took until August 1986 for all the contenders to cut an initial, albeit flawed, deal. That deal proved to be an awkward compromise in which the United States tolerated—for the time being—the EC's preferential tariffs with eleven countries, including Israel, Morocco, Algeria, and Tunisia.[27] In the knotty arena of global trade, that pact only aggravated the problems American pasta makers had, because it called for removing the retaliatory tariffs on competing EC pasta imports.

A year later, the United States and the EC reached a deal that resolved the pasta problems. Finalized in August 1987, this compromise mandated that half of the Common Market's pasta exports would no longer be subsidized, and the subsidy on the other half would be cut by 27.5 percent at first, with further cuts later. The pact ended six years of squabbling. While still short of what American pasta industry leaders wanted, the deal was better than the mere 20 percent cut in their pasta subsidies the Europeans had sought.[28]

During his opening summer on the job, in 1985, pasta was far from the only hot item Yeutter dealt with—but some of the heat he took was surprising. Unexpectedly, an American denounced and undercut him on August 19. Donald E. Petersen, the chairman of Ford Motor Company, told the Midwest Governors' Conference that day that it was a "tragedy" that Brock had been removed as trade representative, called the Reagan administration's record on trade "appalling," and said he and other business executives had no confidence that Yeutter would fight for American interests against the Japanese. Apparently irked that Yeutter seemed to be taking a moderate line on Japan in public speeches, Petersen also endorsed Democratic legislation that would slap a retaliatory tariff on imports from Japan and other countries if they didn't open their markets to American goods, a move that would limit the administration's flexibility in negotiations.[29]

Yeutter's response to Petersen was swift and sharp: "Bill Brock was an outstanding USTR, and he will likewise be an outstanding Secretary of Labor. But do you really believe it is fair to crucify his successor, no matter whom he may be, after he has served for five or six weeks? And after having met him on only one occasion? I have just spent seven years heading one of the most successful corporate entities in this country, and I would not even consider such a modus operandi. Beyond that, we've had a very productive six weeks!" Yeutter, no shrinking violet in corporate politics, continued, "Your comments would seem to indicate that Ford Motor Company is declaring war on the Reagan Administration generally and USTR specifically. I would appreciate knowing if your view is representative of the entire automobile industry. If so I should reconsider committing time and effort to issues such as trade in automobile parts which was a priority item for me in Tokyo."[30]

Yeutter reached out to CEOs of major companies to join USTR advisory groups, meeting with them regularly. But anger from some American business leaders only grew at the end of August 1985, when Reagan threw down the gauntlet for free trade. Suffering under the onslaught of cheaper imports, American shoemakers asked the president to limit imports of foreign shoes, as permitted by section 201 of the Trade Act of 1974. Reagan refused. He told Congress in a message and Yeutter in a memo that he wouldn't inflict a cost of about $3 billion on American consumers by limiting such imports and thus reducing price competition. The stance could have been politically costly, since it infuriated a fellow Republican, Missouri senator John C. Danforth, a key member of the important Senate Finance Committee. Furthermore, Reagan's clarion call for free markets also marked a split with some of his own cabinet members: leaders of the Departments of Agriculture, Commerce, and Labor, along with Yeutter, had all favored hiking the tariff on nonrubber footwear, according to an anonymously sourced report in the *Washington Post*.[31] (Perhaps not coincidentally, the Senate Finance Committee oversaw the USTR office.)

But Reagan fretted that if he granted such protection to shoe-makers, which were widely seen as uncompetitive, other industries would line up for similar shields. The president reasoned that such moves then would just hurt consumers and worsen already strained global trade relations. "Protectionism often does more harm than good to those it is designed to help," the president said. "It is a crippling 'cure,' far more dangerous than any economic illness." The president did, however, couple his move with orders to Yeutter to investigate any unfair trade practices harmful to the United States. Such probes could have led to punitive responses under section 301 of the Trade Act—as they did in time—and Reagan may have swung that club both to placate protectionist-minded legislators and to send a tough message to countries that flouted the rules.[32]

Despite the anonymously sourced report in the *Washington Post*, it's likely that Yeutter did not, in fact, side with the cabinet pro-tectionists in backing a tariff, according to a longtime colleague, former USTR lawyer Charles E. "Chip" Roh Jr.[33] Indeed, Yeutter quickly hewed publicly to Reagan's view, which would have been more consistent for him. He told reporters that many U.S. shoe-makers were profitable and could compete with imports without any help, according to a news report that reflected Yeutter's view about how tough free markets could be on the inefficient: "There will clearly be some attrition in this industry irrespective of whether or not relief is provided. In a capitalist society we do not have all survivors."[34]

Yeutter took to heart both the president's respect for markets and his toughness on countries that acted improperly. And if Yeutter harbored any resentment at being passed over for the ag secretary post, he kept it to himself. Indeed, because so much of the negotiating Yeutter dealt with involved agricultural products, he lent a hand to Reagan when the president mulled over a change in his cabinet that month. Yeutter suggested the former governor of Iowa, Robert D. Ray; American Farm Bureau Federation chief Robert B. Delano; or even a Democrat, former U.S. senator Walter Darlington "Dee" Huddleston of Kentucky, who had been involved in agricultural issues in the Senate.[35] In the end, when

John R. Block left the secretary's spot in February 1986, the administration installed a former deputy secretary of agriculture, Richard E. "Dick" Lyng, a longtime personal friend of Yeutter's and someone with whom he would work closely.

But Reagan's market-friendly approach put him and Yeutter on what could have been a crippling collision course with Congress. "While that was a principled stance for a freer-trader, that drove many Democrats in Congress bonkers," Bello says.[36] Thanks largely to the diplomatic savvy of Yeutter, his deputy trade representatives, and such colleagues as Bello and Holmer, however, things turned out far better, and even most in Congress wound up happy with most of the results.

Backed by the president's principled commitment to free trade, Yeutter threw himself passionately into the U.S. trade representative's role. And the deals he immersed himself in—small and large—would prove to be global game changers. Consider, for instance, the free trade agreements (FTAs) with Israel and Canada, the sort of deals the United States had long resisted. American policymakers had preferred to try to lower trade barriers across the board through multilateral negotiations in the GATT, rather than set up binational FTAs. But Yeutter's predecessor, Brock, had gotten the ball rolling by arranging an FTA with Israel and having preliminary conversations with Canada about such a deal. Israel had tight military and political links with the United States and was regarded as strategically crucial, while neighboring Canada had long been America's biggest single trade partner.

Brock viewed the Israel pact as a template for other such bilateral arrangements. It was fairly short in the birthing process, with Brock launching the talks with Israel in January 1984 and wrapping them up by February 1985. U.S. and Israeli officials then signed the agreement on April 22, 1985, a week before Brock left the trade office to become secretary of labor on April 29. The U.S. House of Representatives approved the agreement shortly afterward, on May 7, and the Senate concurred on May 23. Brock knew that an Israel-friendly Congress would swiftly okay the deal, and he felt it would serve as an example to the world of the benefits of free trade. "I said, 'We have got to show people that it's good to do business with the United States and it's good to do so with open borders,'" Brock recalls.[37] The pact took effect on August 19, 1985, several weeks after Yeutter had been sworn in to the trade representative job on July 1, and it fell to him to make sure the arrangements worked out.

Certainly, the deal with Israel proved to be a winner. Israel's exports in goods alone to the United States rose from $2.1 billion in 1985 to $3.3 billion in 1990, while exports from the United States to Israel climbed from $2.6 billion in 1985 to $3.2 billion in 1990.[38] Goods ranging from bathing suits to metal pipes for Texas oil drillers flowed tariff-free into the United States from Israel, and American exports such as automobiles became more competitive in Israel. The U.S.-Israel FTA created "a first-class incentive to make American markets more attractive to Israeli businessmen, who are used to looking to Europe for trade, and to make our industry more competitive," Ariel Sharon, Israel's minister of industry and trade, said at the time.[39] Since then, trade between the countries has soared, with American exports of goods to Israel jumping to $14.4 billion in 2019 and imports from Israel soaring to $19.5 billion.[40]

Each deal was unique. The pact with Israel, for instance, scaled back export subsidies, import permits, and nontariff barriers to trade, adding requirements to gradually eliminate customs duties, while dealing with security issues.[41] But Brock saw the deal as a precursor to an arrangement that could be made with Canada, though several knotty political and commercial concerns clouded the prospective deal with the United States' northern neighbor. He had begun talking with Canadian officials, including Prime Minister Martin Brian Mulroney, about such pacts with them, as well as with Mexico and with countries in the Association of Southeast Asian Nations. Much of the heavy lifting on the Canadian talks soon fell to Yeutter, though, and Brock asserts that it would be appropriate to regard Yeutter as the father of the U.S.-Canada agreement. "He made it happen," Brock says.[42]

Even before he took up the trade representative's post, Yeutter was pressed to pay attention to Canada's interest in a deal. Just after he was nominated, the Canadian trade minister stopped in on him in Chicago to talk about it. Yeutter made plans to visit him in Ottawa in July 1985, shortly after he was sworn in.[43] A few weeks before, he had written to the chief economist at Bank of Montreal, Lloyd C. Atkinson, to say he would read a paper Atkinson had published about a possible trade agreement, adding, "I would very much like to see our two countries move to a free trade area, or something closely approximating a free trade area, just as quickly as we can."[44] In the end, it took nearly two and a half years to reach an agreement, in early October 1987, and then a couple of months to sign the deal, on January 2, 1988. It went into effect on January 1, 1989. From the outset, the intention was to eliminate all tariffs on trade between Canada and the United States by January 1, 1998, although the three-country North American Free Trade Agreement (NAFTA), which included Mexico, superseded the U.S.-Canada FTA on January 1, 1994.[45]

The drive for the U.S.-Canada arrangement came from the top in both countries. Mulroney, a conservative like Reagan, chafed at Canada's tradition of government intervention in the economy and wanted to chip away at the country's economic insularity, which was based on exporting natural resources and protecting the Canadian industrial base, as journalist Steve Dryden details in his 1995 book, *Trade Warriors*. For his part, President Reagan had championed a North America–wide free-trade area in his 1980 run for the White House. Mulroney and Reagan discussed a deal at a pair of "shamrock summits"—so called because both men were Irish and the first meeting took place the day after St. Patrick's Day—in the spring of both 1985 and 1986.[46]

But the talks on the U.S.-Canada FTA nearly came undone when the U.S. Commerce Department reversed its 1983 ruling that Canadian lumber products were *not* unfairly subsidized by Canada, determining in 1986 that they were. Countervailing duties to offset the subsidy were preliminarily applied on imports of Canadian cedar shakes and shingles, prompting Ottawa to retaliate with tariffs on computer parts, books, and even Christmas trees. Then, in October 1986, the United States imposed a 15 percent tariff on Canadian softwood lumber imports after the Commerce Department concluded the Canadian government was subsidizing such products—a bugaboo in U.S.-Canada trade relations that required special agreements and persisted for decades after the FTA and NAFTA were signed.[47] In addition, Canadian corn producers alleged that imports of corn from the United States were bolstered by U.S. government subsidies, so the Canadians began collecting a duty of $1.05 on each bushel of American corn imported into their country.[48]

Driven in part by personalities and the differing ranks of the negotiators involved, moreover, the Canada-U.S. talks took troublesome detours. The chief Canadian negotiator, Sol Simon Reisman, and Yeutter's negotiator, Peter O. Murphy, were "polar opposites" in approach and in personality, according to trade lawyer Warren H. Maruyama, a colleague of Yeutter's at USTR and later elsewhere. Reisman, widely seen as a domineering bargainer, wanted a far-reaching agreement that would have abolished U.S. antidumping and countervailing duties (AD/CVD) and created an arbitration mechanism.

But as Maruyama describes it, Murphy was wary on two counts. First, the AD/CVD approach had broad political support in the United States, and second, the man who chaired the Senate Finance Committee and who would be in charge of any U.S.-Canada FTA, Senator Robert W. "Bob" Packwood, hailed from Oregon, where the lumber industry competed with Canada's lumber industry. So Murphy adopted what some in the USTR office called a "rope a dope" strategy, sitting back and letting Reisman talk.[49] Murphy also wanted Canada to address specific grievances the United States had, among them limiting government spending on such areas as support for softwood. The different approaches held up agreement for months, Dryden reports. The at times acerbic Reisman criticized Murphy publicly, moreover, prompting Yeutter to compliment Murphy's "great class" and to add, "If Canada hadn't chose Reisman, we would have had this agreement six months ago."[50]

Other protocol-oriented frictions ensnared the talks as well. The Canadians, who chronically felt like they lived in the shadow of the United States, saw themselves as engaged in the discussions at the highest levels of their government, with their representatives reporting directly to the Canadian prime minister and a special committee of his cabinet. They felt the Americans had relegated affairs to lower-level officials, even though Murphy had been a former USTR ambassador to the GATT, according to Derek H. Burney, who became Mulroney's chief of staff and later served as Canada's ambassador to the United States. Against that backdrop, relations between Murphy and Reisman—who was almost twice as old as the American—were strained. Burney, who worked in Canada's foreign office at the time of the talks, repeatedly called for his contacts in the White House to try to get more involved to even the playing field and put more balance into the bargaining. He calls the Murphy-Reisman sessions "a negotiation between a guy who wouldn't talk and a guy who wouldn't listen."[51] Roh, the USTR lawyer who was involved in the talks, says, "It wasn't great chemistry."[52]

But Yeutter's tendency to make quips also triggered a flap that went all the way up to Mulroney. Canadians had long been sensitive about preserving their cultural identity, which they thought they could do in part by limiting the ability of U.S. companies to sell magazines, newspapers, books, and movies in the country and restricting their ownership of Canadian outlets producing such material. Seemingly dismissing that, in early 1987 Yeutter joked at a Brookings Institution conference on trade, "Both of us have our cultures at stake. . . . I'm prepared to have America's culture on the table and take the risk of having it be damaged by Canadian influence after a free-trade arrangement. I hope that Canada's prepared to run that risk too." The crack, along with a comment that he knew about Canada because he and his wife had honeymooned there, prompted such an uproar that Mulroney condemned Yeutter's words in the Canadian House of Commons: "His comments betray a stunning ignorance. . . . His remarks are completely insensitive and totally unacceptable to the government and the people of Canada."

Yeutter's wisecrack, moreover, prompted Canadian commentators to indulge in brutal, if cliched, caricatures of Americans in print. "The U.S. Trade Representative is the classic stereotype of the unthinking American, ignorant of anyone or anything outside his own backyard. He's the loud talker in the Parisian restaurant, the guy in the Hawaiian shirt and camera who expects the whole world to speak English, the tourist who arrives at the Canadian border in July with skis on the roof of his car," fumed columnist John Ferguson in the *Ottawa Citizen* in February 1987. "Stories of Yeutter's pushy, bullying tactics with his counterparts abroad are a regular feature of the diplomatic cocktail circuit."[53]

That cartoonish image was probably more the product of an angry journalist's imagination than of any personal dealings with Yeutter—and indeed, the bargainers likely shrugged off the misstep. John M. Weekes, a former Canadian trade official, instead remembers Yeutter as someone who was warm, open, and lively, and who would remember the names of even junior officials he dealt with. Still, Yeutter had a couple of things going against him, according to Weekes, who later went on to serve as Canada's chief negotiator for NAFTA and the country's ambassador to the World Trade Organization. First, Canadians were quite aware of the imbalance of economic power between the two countries and therefore were sensitive about pejorative comments by American leaders concerning their country. "When an American leader says something, it becomes top news," recalls Weekes. "It's not the same the other way around."[54]

Second, and more important, with an economy and a population each roughly one-tenth of those in the United States, Canadians feared being culturally and economically swamped. Free trade played into Canada's long-standing fear of being overwhelmed by its much larger southern neighbor, so Mulroney was taking a major political risk by pursuing the FTA. The issue was so sensitive in many quarters in Canada, especially in the left-leaning media, that Canadian officials were directed never to use to the term "free trade" in their official communications, Burney notes.[55]

The Canadian public paid far closer attention to the negotiations than Americans did. Holmer once accompanied negotiator Murphy on a trip to Canada. Murphy was not especially well known in Washington, Holmer says, "but he was a rock star in Canada. Everyone seemed to know him and recognize him."[56]

Unlike the comparatively simple talks with Israel, the Canada FTA negotiations were complex, involving vastly higher volumes of trade and a comprehensive agreement, as described by Maruyama. For instance, they dealt with rules of origin that would bar Japanese automakers from assembling Japanese parts in Canada and then exporting the finished vehicles to the United States. And political sensitivities were complex: bowing to Quebec farmers at a time when separatism was running high, the Canadians objected to U.S. demands to open their protected dairy and poultry markets, and they balked at letting their state-run liquor stores sell U.S. wines and spirits. They worried, too, about U.S. cultural exports, ranging from movies to magazines. More broadly, the negotiators wanted to create a far-reaching FTA that addressed everything from trade in services, agriculture, and investment to technical standards and dispute remedies.[57]

American officials were deeply skeptical about whether the deal would come to anything, according to USTR lawyer Roh. Attempts at a pact had failed several times before, he says.[58] And opposition in Canada was strong, including from such national luminaries as author Margaret E. Atwood, who wrote, "Canada as a separate but dominated country has done about as well under the U.S. as women, worldwide, have done under men; about the only position they've ever adopted towards us, country to country, has been the missionary position, and we were not on top."[59]

The talks nearly foundered in late September 1987, only days before an early October deadline for U.S. fast-track authority to expire. (Under that authority, granted by Congress, the president could propose an international agreement that legislators could approve or deny but not amend or filibuster.) As the deadline approached, Canada's Reisman walked out, saying U.S. officials had not been responsive to Canadian demands on antidumping and countervailing duties (AD/CVD) laws. He specifically pointed to Canada's demand that both sides set up a special tribunal to resolve trade matters, thus shielding the country from U.S. trade laws at a time when American politicians were toughening them.[60] Reisman warmed to the idea floated by Sam M. Gibbons, a Florida congressman who chaired the House Ways and Means subcommittee on trade, that such a binational panel be created to hear AD/ CVD dispute appeals while respecting the laws of each country.[61]

To break the impasse, Treasury Secretary James A. Baker III stepped in. Recollections differ about just how big a role Baker played, with people close to Yeutter suggesting the treasury secretary interceded largely to placate the Canadians while leaving the heavy lifting to Yeutter. For his part, Baker in a 2004 oral history interview with the University of Virginia's Miller Center recalled that Yeutter and the Canadian trade minister

> were at loggerheads, and they weren't going to make it. Brian Mulroney picked up the phone and called President Reagan and suggested that he put me in charge of that. I'd known Brian as Chief of Staff, and he knew I was close to the President. And the President did. He called me and said, "Would you take the lead on this? Try to see if we can get this done." Brian gave the lead to his Chief of Staff, a guy named [Derek] Burney and Michael Wilson, on the Canadian side, and Yeutter and I on our side, through some long-night negotiating sessions finally got agreement on the U.S.-Canada Free Trade Agreement.[62]

USTR and Treasury negotiators worked late into the night as the deadline neared and ultimately found a solution. The American bargainers picked up on Gibbons's idea, making sure that U.S. trade remedy law and, more generally, the laws of each country would continue to apply. Despite grumbling, both sides could live with the resolution, Maruyama says.[63] And it would likely fly with American legislators, according to USTR lawyer Roh, who notes that William W. "Bill" Bradley, a senator from New Jersey who sat on the Senate Finance Committee and was a "quiet behind-the-scenes hero" in the discussions, thought the idea was "salable."[64]

Baker and Yeutter co-chaired the closing negotiations in the historic Secretary's Conference Room in the Treasury Building. Burney remembers that Yeutter was not as "front and center" as

Baker in closing the deal, and indeed Baker recalled being "actually involved in the specifics of that Canada-U.S. Free Trade Agreement."[65] But as Maruyama sees it, Baker's presence mainly showed how committed Reagan was; Baker was the most powerful member of the Reagan cabinet and a close proxy for the president.[66] Yeutter was the master of the details and nuances involved, and afterward, the work fell mostly to him and his USTR team to make the case for the deal in Congress, which held the whip hand on the implementing legislation.

Selling Congress was challenging. Democrats controlled both the House and the Senate. And many members felt consultations with Congress about the free trade agreement had been inadequate and were unhappy about the administration's trade policy. Many had been focused since 1985, moreover, on omnibus trade legislation. By early 1988, in fact, most members of the Senate Finance Committee expressed opposition to the agreement.

Yeutter and his team went to work with Congress to hammer out the implementing bill. Busy with preparations for the upcoming global trade talks, Yeutter relied heavily on Holmer and Bello. Holmer, a graduate of Princeton University and the Georgetown University Law Center, had served in the Reagan White House and run the AD/CVD program at the Department of Commerce before coming to USTR with Yeutter. He was close to Senator Packwood, as the senator's former administrative assistant, and Packwood had chaired and later served as ranking Republican on the Senate Finance Committee. Bello was a Yale-educated lawyer and University of North Carolina valedictorian who had extensive trade experience at the Departments of Commerce and State and as deputy general counsel. She also chaired the Section 301 Committee, which brought together representatives of a bevy of federal agencies to deal with unfair trade issues.[67]

Yeutter gave his trusted lieutenants a long leash, but he would help as needed. Holmer remembers getting ready to testify before the Senate Agriculture Committee when, unprompted, Yeutter brought Holmer a list of key points he had typed up himself to make sure the testimony went smoothly.[68] Yeutter explained the intricacies of the pact to the House Agriculture Committee, discussing how the Canadians would not use export subsidies—his long-standing target—to penetrate the U.S. market with grains, along with opening their market to such U.S. exports as wine and distilled spirits. He also explained how some issues, such as Canada's protectionist dairy regime, would have to be dealt with later on in multilateral trade talks in the Uruguay Round, the sessions that Yeutter and others intended would lower tariffs and liberalize trade across the world.[69]

The collaboration between the Republican administration and Democratic Congress was extraordinary, Holmer observes, especially in contrast to the polarization that arose over NAFTA during the William J. Clinton and George W. Bush years—a split that endured and erupted into a full-scale partisan schism in the second decade of the 2000s.[70] After months of intense negotiations, on July 14, 1988, the Speaker of the House and the majority leader of the Senate sent draft implementing legislation to Yeutter and Baker. Then, just eleven days later, President Reagan transmitted formal implementing legislation to the Congress—item for item, clause for clause, word for word, as he had received it from Congress.

President Reagan credited Yeutter for getting the deal done with Canada. "Your leadership and expertise in negotiating the Free Trade Agreement with Canada and the implemented Act with the Congress have served the nation well," the president wrote to Yeutter in October 1988, a couple of weeks after he signed the deal on September 28. "With appreciation for your success in achieving these free trade milestones for America, I am pleased to present you with a pen to commemorate its enactment."[71] Baker, moreover, called Yeutter's role "indispensable," adding that the deal "sparked the liberalization of trade, not only between those two countries but also around the world."[72]

Along the way in the negotiations with Canada, Yeutter managed to repair his strained relations with Petersen, the Ford CEO who had criticized him soon after he first took the USTR job. He even turned to Petersen for help in getting the deal through both the U.S. Congress and the Canadian Parliament because Ford had substantial operations on both sides of the border. "Those negotiations were brutal, but they finally turned out quite well," Yeutter told the CEO, thanking him and others at Ford for their help.[73]

The rest of the world paid attention to the deal. Indeed, Canada's Burney felt that the Reagan administration looked on the agreement with Canada as a strategic tool for prodding the reluctant Europeans to move forward in the Uruguay Round. Yeutter's predecessor, Brock, had tried in 1982 to get such a global round of talks going but couldn't persuade other countries to join in.[74] The Canada pact, in particular, moved the ball forward. "That woke them up," Burney recalls.[75]

Certainly, Yeutter saw the importance of both the deal itself and the precedent-setting power it would have. As early as February 1987, at a Brookings Institution conference, he called the talks about the FTA "the most important bilateral negotiation this country has ever had" and said it would provide "an excellent example for the rest of the world." He added, "To me, that is constructive bilateralism, and that is the kind of bilateralism that fosters and facilitates multilateralism. . . . It will set an example for the Uruguay Round of the MTN [multilateral trade negotiations]."[76]

The U.S.-Canada pact did not eliminate all trade challenges and had "carve outs" that allowed both sides to protect politically sensitive constituencies (such as sugar for the United States and dairy and poultry for Canada). By tolerating such exceptions, Yeutter proved again that he was a pragmatic and skilled negotiator and was willing to accept an agreement that met many, but not all, U.S. goals. "His commitment is to the freest possible trade, but he's not one to go down with the ship for the sake of a lofty goal," John C. L. Donaldson, a former colleague in Yeutter's first stint in the trade office, said after Yeutter's appointment as trade representative. "He's not above cutting a deal. . . . He has a questioning mind, and basically he's a negotiator."[77] In the U.S.-Canada pact, the final agreement allowed Canada to shield its publishing and film industries and permitted the United States to protect its maritime industry.[78]

Nonetheless, the trailblazing deal let Yeutter move on quickly to develop a trade agreement in November 1987 with Mexico—a nonbinding "understanding" that set up special mechanisms for resolving disputes.[79] That effort represented Mexico's initial market-opening overture to the United States after a half century of policies championed by Mexico's ruling Institutional Revolutionary Party that discouraged imports. Together, the two pacts set the stage for the creation of NAFTA several years afterward, in which Yeutter played a supporting role.

The U.S.-Canada FTA, moreover, paid off enormously in increased sales between the countries. American exports of goods alone to Canada more than doubled from $45.3 billion in 1986 to $100.4 billion in 1993, before NAFTA, while imports of goods from Canada grew from $68.3 billion in 1986 to $111.2 billion in 1993. After that, U.S. exports in goods to Canada soared to $292.7 billion in 2019, while imports from Canada jumped to $319.7 billion.[80] "The proof is the pudding in terms of volume of trade," Burney says, adding that once-resistant Canadians in the 2000s became overwhelmingly pro–free trade.[81]

Several years after the deal was put in place, when Mulroney stepped down as prime minister in 1993, Yeutter wrote to say he would be missed. (Readers here may recall Mulroney's tongue-lashing of Yeutter in the Canadian parliament.) Yeutter sympathized with the Canadian leader about brickbats political rivals tossed at Mulroney soon after the trade pact went into force, which unfortunately occurred just on the brink of the 1990–91 recession. "You've had to face the assertion that every job lost since we negotiated the U.S.-Canada Free Trade Agreement was attributable to that accord—and every job gain since then was attributable to other causes!" Yeutter said. "Yet we both know that the Agreement is working essentially as we had hoped and that it is stimulating additional commerce between the two countries, which inevitably leads to more jobs in both. NAFTA will simply build on that foundation, and it'll be a winner too if we can turn back the short-sighted opposition that presently prevails in too many quarters."[82]

While he labored diplomatically to seek a win-win deal on the Canadian FTA, Yeutter also worked—at times two-fistedly—to fulfill Reagan's mandate that cloistered foreign markets had to open their doors to American companies, even if they had to be pried open by legal action or threats of retaliation. The president maintained that free trade had to be a two-way street and chafed at countries that failed to uphold their end of the bargain. "I believe that if trade is not fair for all, then trade is free in name only," Reagan told business and congressional leaders, as well as cabinet members, in a White House address on September 23, 1985. "I will not stand by and watch American businesses fail because of unfair trading practices abroad. I will not stand by and watch American workers lose their jobs because other nations do not play by the rules. . . . Let no one mistake our resolve to oppose any and all unfair trading practices. It is wrong for the American worker and American businessman to continue to bear the burden imposed by those who abuse the world trading system."[83]

Just a few weeks before that talk, Reagan directed Yeutter to launch unfair-trade practice investigations against Korea, Brazil, and Japan, the first time a president had done so. Using the section 301 process under the Trade Act of 1974—a previously less effective and less often used provision—Yeutter attacked a law in Korea that limited U.S. insurers from picking up business there. He went after Brazil for restricting imports of high-tech computer products from the United States. And he pursued Japan for, among other offenses, curbing imports of U.S. cigarettes and other tobacco products, along with leather and leather footwear. The United States also brought actions against European Common Market rules that limited canned fruit imports.[84] The aggressive initiatives, together with later battles Yeutter waged, earned him such headlines as "Yeutter: The Nation's Macho Man of Trade," as the *Santa Rosa (CA) Press Democrat* described him in February 1987.[85] The California paper had picked up the story from the *New York Times*, which in its archives used the headline "Washington Talk: Working Profile: Clayton K. Yeutter; A Trade War Veteran with Tales to Tell."[86] For his part, Yeutter used to tell reporters that his name rhymed with fighter—a phrase that then vice president and later president George H. W. Bush used to introduce Yeutter.[87]

Such actions would help establish Yeutter's reputation as a hard-charging but gentlemanly advocate for open markets and for American trade. But nothing cemented this role more than an all-important fall 1986 gathering in the Uruguayan casino-resort town of Punta del Este. Representatives of seventy-four of the ninety-two countries that were parties to the prevailing international trade agreement, the GATT, gathered amid wintry rainstorms in the resort to set the table for years of negotiations to come in Geneva. They were charged with setting the agenda for the upcoming eighth global round of trade liberalization talks. As the world threatened to slide ever deeper into protectionism, the GATT countries would either halt that slide through what would be called the Uruguay Round or yield to rising tariffs and trade barriers.

The five-day session in Punta del Este, a cramped place where transportation among the venues was difficult, proved critical. An effort to launch a new GATT round had failed in 1982. So the Uruguay meeting was akin to an opening game in the NFL play-offs, with a twist. If the negotiators succeeded, they would move on; if they failed, there would be no Super Bowl.[88] What's more, the early scrapping would set the agenda for the battles to come. If Yeutter couldn't get U.S. priorities onto the agenda, they wouldn't be addressed. With some two thousand trade ministers and officials on hand, watched by about five hundred journalists, the talks would also thrust Yeutter ever more into the global spotlight. The United States was regarded as what the *Economist* called the *demandeur* of the talks, the main party pressing for markets to be more open and for rules under GATT to be strictly enforced after years of being flouted by nearly all parties.[89] Yeutter's tall order included dealing with services, intellectual property, and agriculture.

The Europeans, through their Common Agricultural Policy, were seen by many in the talks as the villains in trade matters. Their farmers were building up huge surpluses of grains and other products as officials jacked up prices and then sought to dump the excesses on the world markets with subsidies for exports. For their part, Americans shied away from export subsidies but did subsidize production at home, bolstering prices. The approaches, while different, gave both sides much to haggle about. "American agriculture was incensed about these European Union export subsidies," recalls former deputy assistant USTR Condon. He says that a key breakthrough in the bargaining was Yeutter's willingness put domestic U.S. subsidies on the negotiating table along with the foreign export subsidies.[90]

The stakes were enormous for everyone at Punta del Este, but particularly for Yeutter. He had ratcheted up the drama by saying beforehand, in a speech at the U.S. Chamber of Commerce, that he and the rest of the sixty or so members of the U.S. delegation would walk out if they didn't see progress in their demands—a threat to other nations and reassurance to the protectionist-minded U.S. Congress. Yeutter led the American delegation, which included Secretary of Commerce Howard Malcolm "Mac" Baldrige Jr., who happened to be a fellow Nebraskan by birth (hailing from Omaha), and Secretary of Agriculture Lyng. At the gathering, Yeutter sketched out his priorities in an opening presentation that he said "sent the message to the world that if we didn't get them, we were going to go home," as he later told USTR special assistant Diane Yu, who edited an oral history of the talks. "We projected U.S. strength and leadership, and the fact that I did it extemporaneously also helped set the tone for what came afterwards. And then just the fact that we had a good game plan and executed it well in Punta was very, very important. I had the game plan pretty well thought out before we got to Punta del Este and it was just a matter then of putting it into effect."[91]

The United States wanted services to be on the agenda, for instance, including such big-ticket areas as insurance, banking, credit cards, and telecommunications—all American strengths. The existing global trade agreement, the GATT, had no rules for such exports, and American companies faced steep hurdles in penetrating some markets. Some countries—notably Brazil and India—opposed the U.S. proposal, fearing that American competition would throttle their infant businesses. Agricultural subsidies, another ticklish arena—and a longtime vexation for Yeutter—had to be on the table, too, though this would pit the heavily subsidizing European Community against at least fourteen other major agricultural exporting countries that were known as the Cairns Group (named for the Australian city where a group of smaller free trade–minded exporting nations met first in August 1986).[92] Other U.S. demands included stronger intellectual property rules, such as protections against counterfeiting of films and sound recordings and trade-linked aspects of U.S. direct investments—all of which developing countries wanted to keep out of the round. After its frustrating experience with the GATT's dispute settlement mechanism, which let the loser block decisions by GATT panels, the United States also wanted improved procedures for settling and enforcing disputes under the GATT umbrella.[93]

Yeutter and his team attacked the issues methodically, with Yeutter operating in his customary fashion of letting colleagues steer their own ships according to a course he laid down. Lyng, for instance, took up agricultural matters, working "off to the side" to broker between the EC and rival farm-goods exporters in the Cairns Group. "The outcome was a major victory for the U.S.: full-scale negotiations on agriculture that include not only subsidies but also import barriers—quantitative restrictions as well as those arising from sanitary and phytosanitary regulations," Yu reported.

Baldrige thrust intellectual property issues on the agenda. Indeed, the three cabinet officers brought clout to the talks that Yeutter said awed or at least impressed the other trade ministers. As Yeutter told Yu, "It wasn't just myself—we had three American ministers there—that's a lot of force. . . . And they did their jobs very well, cooperating beautifully. It was easy, of course, with Dick Lyng because he was such as long-time personal friend, and that was a smooth relationship. It could have been otherwise with Secretary Baldrige because of the past rivalries between Commerce and USTR, but it didn't turn out to be the case."[94]

Lyng's friendship with Yeutter, in particular, was crucial as the pair pressed for liberalization in agricultural trade, both during the Punta del Este talks and afterward, particularly in later dealings with Japan and the EC. Both men were far more knowledgeable about global and domestic agricultural issues than trade generalists or politicians were, and each could rely on the other to sing from the same hymnal. "They were friends, they trusted each other, they worked together extremely well, and that was very, very helpful to accomplish things in agriculture," says Condon.[95] Such personal bonds, which the almost always convivial Yeutter forged with many figures domestically and globally, went far to smooth the way for trade deals.

At Punta del Este, the services area proved to be especially fractious, and Yeutter opted to compromise on the format for handling such fast-growing exports. India and Brazil demanded that rules on trade in services be negotiated outside of GATT, meaning no trade-offs in goods would be possible. Such tense moments were also occasions for political theater, such as one point toward the end of the conference when a frustrated Yeutter had notices posted in the elevator areas where the American delegation stayed, telling his fellow Americans to pack their bags and be ready to leave early—a not-so-subtle message to officials of the other countries to find a way to break impasses. Yeutter was serious. "He certainly hoped that it would result in improvement and, if it didn't, he wasn't going to sit around and do nothing," recalls USTR lawyer Roh.[96]

In the end, on the last night of talks—after the famously high-energy Yeutter had been up well past midnight haggling with his opposite numbers—they all compromised, allowing talks about services to proceed on an ad hoc basis that Yeutter said would force them back in time under the GATT umbrella. Yeutter, in fact, didn't sleep at all on the Thursday night before the closing Friday sessions, as he pondered how to avoid having the meeting crater on the services issue, which he said was the "real fist-fighting" matter. Representatives of Brazil and India met with Yeutter privately in sessions in which he "kept saying over and over again" that he "could not accommodate on substance but was prepared to be accommodating on the cosmetics or the presentation." As it all unfolded, last-minute deals were worked out to resolve their issues, along with loose ends in agriculture, investment, and intellectual property, to put all the matters the United States cared about into the mix for talks in the Uruguay Round.[97]

Yeutter and his cabinet partners Lyng and Baldrige earned their victory at the close of the gathering. But even for the tireless Yeutter, the sessions were exhausting. He staggered back to his hotel room at 5:30 a.m. on Saturday, grabbing two hours of sleep before boarding his flight home, as *Time* magazine reported. He emerged ecstatic, saying, "The launching of the Uruguay Round is a major victory for the principles of free and fair trade."[98] As the *Far Eastern Economic Review* explained it, the five days of bargaining led to a sweep for the United States: "The US went to Punta del Este with five objectives and achieved them all, though not without difficulty." The new round would for the first time include negotiations on trade in services such as insurance, tourism, stronger intellectual property rules to safeguard U.S. pharmaceutical and entertainment products, and trade-related aspects of direct investment abroad. It would commit countries to tackling the havoc wreaked by protectionist agricultural policies. And it would cover stronger procedures for settling disputes under the GATT.[99]

"Punta had been historic," Australian diplomat Alan Oxley, an ambassador to the Geneva-based GATT organization, writes in his 1990 book, *The Challenge of Free Trade*. "Developing countries had participated actively in negotiating the mandate for the Round. It was as much their round as anybody else's. There was agreement to negotiate on agriculture and services. They were tied. There was a compact that one could not move without the other. It was one of those remarkable meetings where everybody considered that they had achieved something."[100]

The meeting—especially the last forty-eight hours of intense talks—amounted to Yeutter's tour-de-force, says Roh. "It was because he did have such a command of so many issues." Among the challenges, Yeutter had to coordinate moves among a clutch of his senior officials and cabinet partners, all negotiating separately with their counterparts, as he sought to hammer out an acceptable package. Yeutter had to make the trade-offs in which some officials would have to yield on some points while others gained. The meeting overall "was his singular accomplishment," Roh asserts. "In the end, it was really Clayton."[101]

In some respects, the negotiations Yeutter was involved in during this period amounted to high-stakes poker—appropriately enough, given Punte del Este's gambling ethos. The administration of President Reagan, who favored free trade, formally proposed in Geneva trade talks in July 1987 that all nations drop all forms of government farm subsidies by the year 2000. It was a bold and unrealistic plan that would have killed off even such long-standing U.S. programs as the agricultural extension service and crop insurance, leaving only the options of direct cash payments to farmers not tied to crop production or marketing and food aid programs. It was perhaps an aspiration, rather than a true goal; a way for the administration to lay down a marker.

Reagan, in fact, was willing to compromise when needed, as he did on such matters as steel quotas. The president also deferred to advisers, hearing various views ranging from those of staunch free traders such as Deputy Treasury Secretary Richard G. "Dick" Darman to U.S. industry advocates such as Commerce Secretary Baldrige. Yeutter, who hewed to a middle course in cabinet debates, brought expectations down a peg, cautioning that the United States would not drop its farm programs until other nations, especially Japan and those in Europe, did so too. Yeutter said, "We have no intention whatsoever of unilaterally disarming in the agricultural area."[102]

Later, as the U.S. prepared for the Uruguay Round, Yeutter would show even more how well he could play the game—and how much of that turned on his personal relationships. Yeutter asked Condon and other USTR ag specialists to draw up a detailed plan for all GATT member economies to reduce their blends of subsidies, tariffs, and market-access barriers over time. Playing it conservatively, the USTR staffers brought in a plan for a 50 percent cut over ten years, only to have Yeutter scratch out the 50 and scrawl in 100 percent, saying, "If you want to get to fifty, you need to start at one hundred."

Then, accompanied by Condon, Yeutter took the plan to his friend Lyng, the USDA secretary, the day before Thanksgiving in

1986. Condon, who felt like he was a "fortunate witness" at the meeting, calls it a "historic conversation" between the two cabinet members. No USDA staffers were on hand, as Yeutter wanted to get out ahead of the staff, fearing any proposal from them would be too timid.[103]

Lyng okayed Yeutter's plan. Then USTR and USDA staffers fleshed it out over several months, getting clearances from other executive branch agencies. In July 1987 the audacious plan was submitted to the GATT and circulated among all the negotiating partners, and Yeutter and Lyng detailed the effort in a White House press conference. When the deal was finally done in 1994, developed countries agreed to an impressive 36 percent cut over six years. Yeutter "had the trust of the Secretary of Agriculture, which is immensely important if you want to change agriculture from outside the Department of Agriculture," Condon recalls.[104]

While Yeutter succeeded in setting the table in Punta del Este and in subsequent meetings for the multiyear Uruguay Round, the main course was yet to come. And there would be setbacks. One of the first came in December 1988, when the trade ministers met in Montreal for a midterm assessment of the round's progress. The purpose seemed simple enough: clarify the agenda for the following two years. But the talks ended in a deadlock that wasn't resolved until the following April at a meeting in Geneva.[105] That session set the stage for the final deal.

Indeed, in the complex trade talks, each couple of steps forward seemed to bring at least one backward. The process would bring challenges that would keep Yeutter busy through the end of his time as U.S. trade representative, during his subsequent job as secretary of agriculture, and even into his time outside of government, as it took until the end of 1993 for all the terms to be agreed on and into April 1994 for the final global trade deal to be inked.[106] Because they involved politics, national pride, big-moneyed corporations and labor unions, foreign and domestic policy, national security, and armies of lobbyists and news media from around the world, trade issues were especially knotty. Some took years to resolve, as the Uruguay Round of talks demonstrated.

But with successes such as Punta del Este in 1986 and his victories in dealing individually with troublesome trading partners, Yeutter was able to blunt—for that time, anyway—the protectionist drive that animated Congress, particularly many Democrats with close ties to organized labor and Republicans from steelmaking states. Many members of Congress proposed legislation to greatly expand the power of USTR and to impose automatic penalties on other countries that broke the rules. This led to a snarky lead editorial in the *Wall Street Journal*, headlined "President Yeutter," that slammed Congress for the bill's "sabotage of presidential authority."[107] In the end, Yeutter won balanced bipartisan legislation that empowered and obligated the USTR to work out trade problems, according to Holmer.[108]

One of Yeutter's major coups in his legislative work was to win approval for the Omnibus Foreign Trade and Competitiveness Act of 1988, which had begun as a Democratic measure to mechanistically curb surpluses that foreigners racked up in trade with the United States but wound up as something more productive and moderate. House Ways and Means chairman Daniel D. Rostenkowski of Illinois, a friend of Yeutter's from his Chicago Mercantile Exchange days, had teamed up with another Democrat, Senate Finance Committee chairman Lloyd M. Bentsen Jr. of Texas, to draft a major trade bill in 1987. House Majority Leader Richard A. Gephardt of Missouri—another Democrat and a presidential hopeful who saw trade as his signature issue—added an eponymous amendment that would have required countries that were accused of unfair trade practices and ran "excessive" trade surpluses with the United States (i.e., Japan) to cut those surpluses by 10 percent a year through at least 1992.[109]

In the end, the trade act was the culmination of a brutal multiyear legislative battle. With Yeutter busy with the Uruguay Round and Canada talks, he turned to Holmer and Bello for the day-to-day lobbying. After much back and forth, and a veto of the first version of the act by President Reagan, the final bill recast the Gephardt Amendment into a tool for using section 301 of U.S. trade law to challenge specific foreign barriers rather than automatically impose quotas or tariffs. As Maruyama describes it, this effectively codified Yeutter's approach to using that section of trade law to challenge specific unfair trade practices and was a major accomplishment.[110]

With political differences over trade erupting at the time, the 1988 act represented an important compromise between Congress, which constitutionally has the power to set tariffs and regulate foreign commerce, and the executive branch, which Yeutter represented with cabinet partners.[111] Among other things, the bill secured fast-track authority for the president, which later administrations used in pursuing such monumental deals as NAFTA and the Uruguay Round Agreements. "While I know you didn't enjoy dealing with Congress as much as a good trade negotiation, the 1988 Act was a huge political breakthrough," Maruyama wrote for a book of letters that friends put together near the end of Yeutter's life. "It represented one of the last times that an Administration was able to bridge the deepening partisan divide over trade policy that continues today."[112]

Experts applauded the act's restraint and the flexibility it gave the USTR. "The act does not direct the U.S. trade representative to declare any nation's actions unfair or, having done so, to respond with any particular penalties, but it clearly puts on the trade representative the burden of proof that it is doing enough to combat unfair trade practices," explains Ronald A. Cass, dean of Boston University's School of Law. "The act does not command trade sanctions against Japan, but expresses the sense of Congress that Japan has not played fairly and that it deserves to be made to pay a price if it will not play by our rules."[113]

Japan, of course, figured heavily into legislators' concerns as they authored such legislation. Indeed, the protracted and complex dealings Yeutter had with the country encapsulated many of the challenges that U.S. trade officials wrangled with for years.

9

Saving a Major Industry

Yeutter's long and winding dealings with Japan were especially charged because the country at the time was a bête noire for many American critics. As the bilateral trade imbalance rose, Japanese companies were exporting cars whose high quality was leaving Detroit angrily in the dust. Alarmist accounts appeared in the press about how Japan's investors were buying up such American icons as New York City's Rockefeller Center. When companies such as Sony snapped up American music producers and movie studios, critics fretted they would take over the previously all-American realm of entertainment.[1]

Imports of American goods into Japan, meanwhile, faced huge hurdles. One Japanese diplomat went so far as to tell Yeutter that he had just visited New York and found nothing in the stores Japanese would want to buy (though in fact, formal and informal barriers kept many American goods out of Japan).[2] At times in the mid-1980s the trade deficit the United States suffered with Japan amounted to about one-third of the deficit America ran with the world overall. The U.S. deficit in goods traded with Japan climbed from $46.2 billion in 1985 to $57.3 billion in 1987 before turning downward steadily until 1991 ($43.4 billion). The red ink in trade then swelled again to peak at $89.7 billion in 2006 before settling down to just under $69 billion by 2019.[3]

From the outset of Yeutter's time as U.S. trade representative, Japan was very much on legislators' minds—and on Yeutter's. At his Senate confirmation hearing for the job on June 25, 1985, he said it would be a "tragic mistake" if Japan tried to restrict exports rather than open its markets—as the Japanese were considering, according to news reports from Tokyo. But, perhaps trying to turn down the heat, at least publicly, Yeutter also struck an evenhanded tone, saying he was concerned "that the level of rhetoric has become increasingly harsh" between Japan and the United States. He even criticized some U.S. industries for their lack of competitiveness and expectations of a U.S. government bailout.[4]

When he gave speeches, first in Minneapolis and then in August 1985 in Tokyo, he took a light touch publicly—earning him some criticism at home. Secretary of Commerce Baldrige critiqued Yeutter's comments, leading Yeutter to thank him. "Though I was deliberately attempting to take a moderate line, it was too soft in a few places, and your input helped," Yeutter wrote. "I took a harder line in the private discussions, both in terms of their becoming serious in opening up markets, and in avoiding the easy solution on their part—export constraints. Some of our friends in industry and in the Congress would find the latter action acceptable, but we will never get those markets opened if we let them off the hook that way."[5] Yeutter wrote a similar thank-you note to Treasury Secretary James A. Baker III.[6]

As it turned out, Yeutter's wrangles with Japan persisted throughout his tenure as trade representative and beyond. He fought the Japanese on everything from semiconductors to beef, along with cigarettes and leather goods. No battle was more challenging, however, than that over semiconductors, the crucial chips that lay at the heart of computers. The fight there touched on national security issues and the maintenance of a vital industry, as companies tussled with one another and officials in both countries pushed to preserve their domestic manufacturers.

Yeutter inherited the semiconductor fracas but fast made it his, as journalist Dryden details in *Trade Warriors*. Before Yeutter joined the trade office, the writer reports, the U.S. Semiconductor Industry Association (SIA) had complained that the Japanese were unfairly shutting out American sales of the computer microchips. They also dumped their chips in the United States, selling them below Japanese market prices or even below cost, the Americans maintained. Such efforts kept the U.S. share of the market in Japan at around 10 percent or below, even as the U.S. companies made deeper inroads in other countries. Jobs in the U.S. industry disappeared by the tens of thousands as American companies exited such sectors of the market as the basic dynamic random-access memory chips. Yeutter's predecessor, William Brock, told SIA officials to file a section 301 case against Japan, and they did so just around the time Yeutter took the reins from Brock.

As it took many twists and turns, the battle reflected Yeutter's pragmatism. Even if the free trader in him initially bristled at negotiating market share arrangements, for instance, he wound up embracing them as the price of preserving an industry deemed essential to U.S. national security. Matters had grown so dire that the National Security Agency, the U.S. government's high-tech surveillance outfit, had taken to making its own chips rather than depend on foreign companies. Negotiations proceeded fitfully throughout Yeutter's first year as trade representative, leading to a marathon thirteen-hour session in Tokyo in May 1986 in which he told balking Japanese officials, "Listen, getting you from eight to twenty percent isn't interfering with your marketplace. It really ought to be at fifty. So don't argue you are making any gifts to us." It took another two months, until a July 30 deadline, to land a signed agreement. The pact provided for the Japanese government to boost penetration in their home market by American companies. In a side letter that at first was kept secret, the Japanese government said it "recognizes" the expectation that the foreign share of Japan's market would rise from about 8 percent to above 20 percent in five years.[7]

But the deal ran into trouble almost as soon as it was signed, as *Time* magazine reported in an April 1987 issue with the cover line "Trade Wars: The U.S. Gets Tough with Japan." Even after the July 1986 accord was reached, Japanese manufacturers continued to dump semiconductors in Hong Kong, Taiwan, and Singapore, the U.S. government charged. By January 1987, the Reagan administration privately warned Japan that retaliation was likely, and a U.S. investigation found that not only had dumping been under way, but the Japanese had failed to ramp up purchases of foreign microchips.[8] Indeed, the Japanese were also said to be dumping their chips in Europe, where manufacturers planned to take their complaints to the European Economic Community. Third-party buyers of Japanese chips were offering them below the fair market values, as determined by the U.S. Commerce Department, pursuant to the July 1986 agreement.[9]

And some Japanese officials made no bones about the refusal of Japanese organizations to buy even the most sophisticated American high-tech products that used American-made chips. Makoto Kuroda, vice minister of Japan's Ministry of International Trade and Industry, told a visiting American trade delegation in February 1987 that it would be a waste of time for Americans to try to sell supercomputers to Japanese government agencies or universities, no matter how superior they were in price or quality. As the *Washington Post* reported, a U.S. State Department account about the comment circulated widely in the administration and on Capitol Hill, spurring demands for retaliation.[10] Members of Congress faulted Japan for not playing fair in trade or negotiating honestly. Caricaturing the Japanese in racist fashion, Representative James Jarrell "Jake" Pickle, a Texas Democrat, suggested he might introduce what he called an "ah-so amendment," targeting Japanese negotiators "who say 'ah so' to everything and then don't do anything" about the complaints.[11]

By April 1987 the brouhaha worsened to the point that President Reagan announced plans to slap hefty tariffs on $300 million worth of Japanese electronics exports to the United States, moves that would double the prices of televisions, computers, disk drives, hand-held tools, refrigerators, electric motors, even X-ray film.[12] As *Newsweek* reported, the effort was America's first trade sanction against Japan since World War II. Ever the diplomat, Yeutter tried to be both tough and encouraging at the time, apparently in hopes he could persuade the Japanese to change their ways. Said Yeutter, "Japan is a great friend, and we take this action out of sorrow, not because we want to demonstrate American machismo."[13] Even as Yeutter pressed the efforts against Japan, however, his moves were not unanimously applauded by government officials. For instance, Gerald M. Marks, who directed the U.S. Commerce Department's Chicago office and was a Republican backer of President Reagan, resigned in protest over what he publicly called the "myopic" approach the administration was taking.[14] At a press conference Marks staged—against department policy—he predicted that the sanctions "would have disastrous results."[15]

Certainly, the United States was turning up the heat. At the same time that the United States was pressuring Japan in the high-tech realm of semiconductors, the Rice Millers' Association filed a section 301 petition, challenging the country in one of its most culturally sensitive and traditional areas. The move in effect urged the U.S. trade representative (USTR) to force the Japanese to open their market to American rice. The push on rice came along with U.S. pressure for Japan to eliminate quotas on imports of beef, cheese peanuts, tomatoes, and citrus products and to boost wheat imports. Yeutter, who worked in tandem with Secretary of Agriculture Dick Lyng on the agricultural matters, argued at Japan's April 1987 Shimoda Conference that the chip dispute was "a small bullet in the screen" of the overall U.S.-Japan relationship, soothingly stressing the close bonds between the countries. He told the group of more than eighty Japanese and American politicians and business leaders there that boosting imports of American agricultural products would go far to trim the U.S. deficit in trade with Japan.[16]

For their part, leaders in the Japanese parliament pummeled Yeutter and Lyng with reasons about why they could not liberalize trade in the politically sensitive area of agriculture. "We spent three hours today listening to members of the Diet tell us again and again why it was impossible to open Japan's markets for agricultural products," Yeutter said at a Tokyo press conference at the time with Lyng. "When one hears that argument consistently from people who are in positions of political leadership one wonders how we in the [Reagan] administration can be expected to continue to defend a free and open trade policy in the United States."[17] Indeed, some Democratic politicians in the United States pressed for protectionist legislation that Yeutter and other administration officials resisted, such as the Gephardt Amendment.

At times the food fight turned comical. A major farm official in Japan, Tsutomo Hata, told American political leaders in December 1987 that Japanese people had "much, much larger" digestive systems than Americans and thus found it harder to eat U.S.-produced beef. Speaking at a steak luncheon given by the Congressional Beef Caucus in Washington, Hata also said Buddhist restrictions against meat and a preference for fish in part explained declining Japanese consumer interest in American beef. At the time, Japan was the largest overseas market for U.S. beef, with nearly $500 million worth of it shipped there in 1986. Hata chaired the Japanese ruling party's agricultural committee and was a former agriculture minister. Outside of food, another Japanese official defended import barriers on foreign skis in 1986 by saying Japanese snow differed from snow in other countries.[18] Japanese baseball officials even stymied the sale of American baseball bats in the country.[19]

Shortly after Yeutter and Lyng huddled with Japanese officials in Tokyo in the spring of 1987, President Reagan and Japanese prime minister Yasuhiro Nakasone met in Washington for two days of inconclusive talks about the trade conflict. Nakasone wanted Reagan to lift the tariffs he had imposed, but Reagan said any relaxation would depend on Japan complying with the semiconductor pact. Still, Nakasone admitted in a speech at the National Press Club that the U.S.-Japanese trade imbalance had "escalated into a serious problem" that he was "deeply concerned" about. The problem, in fact, was global: the Japanese Finance Ministry disclosed at the time that Japan's worldwide trade surplus had soared to $101 billion in the year ended March 31, 1987.[20]

Both sides were working toward another deadline to resolve their differences, a multinational summit meeting slated for Venice in early June 1987.[21] American officials planned before then to review the trade statistics to see if they could lift the sanctions, as indeed they did—at least partly—when the sales numbers looked better. "The sanctions have clearly gotten the attention of the [Japanese] government and hopefully also of the firms," Yeutter told the *Christian Science Monitor* in mid-June. He added that the tougher U.S. approach would likely spawn more confrontations and said he hoped the Japanese paid "due attention to some of the messages we send, as in the semiconductor case. And hopefully that will affect the decision-making."

The stakes in the semiconductor battle were huge, amounting to no less than the survival of a crucial American industry. "I really believe that this may be a case where we saved a major high-technology industry in this country from its demise," Yeutter said. "That industry had one foot in the grave and the other almost there at the time we negotiated that in the semiconductor agreement, and there have been very dramatic improvements in the financial well-being of the industry since then." He noted that Japanese companies were practicing predatory pricing, selling chips for as much as 40 percent below cost, and had "the basic objective of putting the competition down the tubes—and were doing very well at it." At the time of his interview with the paper, the Japanese had halted such dumping, and while sales of chips in Japan were flat at first, they soon accelerated.[22]

The Semiconductor Industry Association lobbyist in Washington at the time of the battle with Japan was Alan Wolff, who had succeeded Yeutter in the late 1970s as a U.S. deputy trade representative and later, in 2017, became a deputy director general of the World Trade Organization. He and Yeutter had worked together on the chip fight, and three and a half years later Wolff was effusive in praising Yeutter's efforts. "The semiconductor folks owe you a debt of gratitude on what has been achieved," Wolff wrote to Yeutter in late 1990, after Yeutter had moved on to become secretary of agriculture. "This is an Agreement which has actually produced results. The increase in sales per year under the Agreement is now running at over $1 billion. It would not have occurred without your negotiating success."[23] By the fourth quarter of 1995 the foreign share of Japan's semiconductor market rose to 29.6 percent, with American firms leading the globe in the industry.[24] After that experience, Japanese officials reportedly vowed never to do another market share agreement, according to Yeutter's longtime colleague Warren Maruyuma, who worked with him as associate general counsel at the USTR's office and several years later served as USTR general counsel. (The men also worked together at the Hogan Lovells firm and the White House, where Maruyama served on the policy staff under President George H. W. Bush.)

Yeutter was able to point, too, to similar negotiating success to resolve the food fracas with Japan—though it took more time, perhaps because Japan's agriculture industry was especially politically powerful, much as the American industry was. And again, the resolution was not the full monty that a doctrinaire free trader might have wanted, but rather reflected Yeutter's pragmatism. In February 1988 a General Agreement on Tariffs and Trade (GATT) dispute settlement panel ruled that Japan should remove import quotas on ten of twelve agricultural categories; the ruling undercut the country's long-standing restrictions on farm imports, which it had long tried to justify on sanitary, phytosanitary, and balance-of-payments grounds. That led to negotiations between Yeutter and Japan's agricultural minister, Takashi Sato, that failed twice—in March and April 1988. So in May, the United States took another beef case to the GATT, asking that quotas be outlawed and seeking approval to retaliate against an equivalent amount of Japanese goods.

By June 1988 the Japanese cried uncle. After a rare daylong Sunday bargaining session, Yeutter cut a deal with Sato in which Japan agreed to end its quotas on beef and orange imports in three years and on orange juice in four years. The agreement promised to boost American beef and citrus exports to Japan by $1 billion once the quotas were lifted, as the *Los Angeles Times* reported.[25] The United States then dropped its beef case with GATT.

The 1988 Beef-Citrus Agreement provided a model for future U.S. efforts to open Japan's agricultural markets in the Uruguay Round and Trans-Pacific Partnership, according to Maruyama.[26] Under the Japanese system, a government-run buying agency, the Livestock Industry Promotion Corporation (LIPC), acted as the principal importing agent for beef, using quotas. In some years, the LIPC didn't import any beef at all. So Yeutter targeted the LIPC's iron control over imports. His U.S.-Japan Beef-Citrus Agreement phased out the quota system, replacing it with Japanese tariffs that started at 25 percent in 1990, rose to 70 percent in 1991, and then fell to 60 percent in 1992 and 50 percent in 1993. Given the extremely high cost of Japanese beef production, much higher tariffs would have been needed to block U.S. imports. So Yeutter's calculation that trading off the LIPC for modest increases in Japanese tariffs was vindicated by sharp increases in U.S. beef exports, which leaped by nearly 90 percent in value and 50 percent in volume from 1988 to 1990. Japan remained the leading export market for American beef in 2020.

The haggling over oranges showed how complex such bargaining could get and how competing domestic interests could snarl matters. California producers of oranges, through the Sunkist Growers cooperative, initially opposed anything more radical than raising the quotas Japan had on orange imports. Why? Because the Japanese shielded sales to the country from competition from other orange growers. They feared rocking the boat and complained publicly, through ads, and personally in letters to Yeutter and Lyng when the pair rebuffed Sunkist's narrow demands in favor of a bigger goal.[27] Yeutter and Lyng aimed to pry open the Japanese market for hundreds of agricultural products, and they succeeded. With his blend of multilateralism and negotiation, Yeutter "really set the template for opening up the Japan market," says Maruyama.[28]

As always, however, Yeutter was gracious in victory. "There was tremendous political resistance in Japan," he told a reporter for the *Billings (MT) Gazette* in July 1988. "But the government did it anyway. It shows they are prepared to make the tough decisions." The newspaper reported that the food deal was backed in the United States by both Republicans and Democrats. Senator Baucus, the Montana Democrat, had pressed to boost meat sales to Japan since the early 1980s, and he called the pact "potentially the biggest market-opening agreement in the past decade," something that would lead to as much as 5 percent of American beef production going to Japan. "We took a page from Japan's book," Baucus added. "We were persistent—Republicans, Democrats, the administration and Congress. We stuck together. Japan was not allowed to divide and conquer. They got the same message over and over. That is the major reason it passed."[29]

Sharing the credit generously for the deal on meat, Yeutter applauded Baucus and Wyoming Republican senator Malcolm Wallop, who co-chaired the Congressional Beef Caucus, for their efforts. Later, when Baucus won reelection in 1990, Yeutter offered his "heartiest congratulations." He added, "We didn't give you as much competition as we had hoped!" and said he looked forward to working with Baucus on other issues. (Yeutter sent similar post-election congratulatory notes at the time to Democratic senators David L. Boren of Oklahoma, J. James Exon of Nebraska, Thomas R. Harkin of Iowa, Paul M. Simon of Illinois, and John D. "Jay" Rockefeller IV of West Virginia, and to Democratic congressmen Ben Nighthorse Campbell of Colorado, Glenn L. English Jr. of Oklahoma, Alphonso Michael Espy of Mississippi, and James R. Olin of Virginia, as well as congratulating victorious Republicans.)[30]

A savvy diplomat, Yeutter was always measured in the amount of pressure he would apply to those he bargained or dealt with, at home or overseas, recalls A. Ellen Terpstra, a former deputy under secretary for international activities at the USDA and international economist at USTR with Yeutter. Particularly with Japanese officials, and those in Asia more broadly, he was careful to avoid humiliating them by appearing to bludgeon them with American demands. "He was stabbing a knife in the heart of their ag policy, the linchpin of their ag policy and the way they protected farmers, which was sacred in Japan, and yet he tried his best to have them not lose face," Terpstra says. "He found a way to be a friend and to look for the best outcome for everybody. He's well remembered . . . in Japan for his graciousness."[31] He was also known there, though, as the "dreaded Yeutter-san."[32]

Indeed, according to colleagues, he could make difficult demands without being difficult. "When it comes time for countries to make really hard calls, the chemistry at the table matters. Clayton was known for being very tough, not being afraid to flex his muscles. But also he was a good and decent person who had a lot of respect for the other side of the table," says Darci L. Vetter, who worked in several key positions at USTR, at the USDA, and on Capitol Hill and dealt with Yeutter mostly after he left government. "It was no picnic for the Japanese when he was pounding on them to open their beef and citrus markets. He was pretty relentless, but it didn't have to be personal. He had lifelong friendships with some of the people in Japan that he worked with."[33]

Yeutter was so well regarded in Japan that in November 2017 the country posthumously awarded him the Grand Cordon of the Order of the Rising Sun, one of the greatest honors the nation could bestow.[34] A few months earlier, at a memorial service for Yeutter in April 2017, Cristena Bach Yeutter was handed a condolence letter from Japanese prime minister Shinzo Abe praising Yeutter's contributions to enhancing relations between the United States and Japan and memorializing him personally. "Mr. Yeutter remains alive in the heart of many Japanese people, as a tough counterpart at the negotiating table, but at the same time, as a partner who is versed in the importance of the Japan-U.S. alliance and who seeks the common ground together," wrote Abe, a son of foreign minister Shintaro Abe, whom Yeutter worked with in the early 1980s. "The current strong relationship between Japan and the U.S. has been built upon his endeavors. As a profound bridge between Japan and the U.S., he will be remembered forever by people of both of our countries."[35]

His people skills were among the things that set him apart, friends and colleagues recall. Yeutter told his children—and said in speeches to students—that the world was filled with smart people, but it was the ability to get on well with people that made the difference in succeeding, as his daughter Kim says. Yeutter had an exceptional memory for names, showed his personal warmth by touching people on the shoulder or back, and more abstractly, could put himself into another's shoes in negotiations to see how they could reach common ground.[36]

Yeutter knew how crucial personal chemistry among global leaders was. He made a point in June 1988 of bringing trade leaders from Canada, the European Union, and Japan—which together with the United States formed what was known as the Quad group—to a resort area in Brainerd, Minnesota. There, far from a busy and distracting city Yeutter could have chosen as the venue, the leaders could relax as they contemplated major changes that would come about through the Uruguay Round of talks. Such diversions as golf, biking, fishing, boating, and hiking would have helped leaders develop the personal connections Yeutter saw as essential. Even when they tackled tough issues, talks in shirtsleeves in a placid setting would be easier than buttoned-down bargaining in some urban conference room.[37]

Yeutter and his USTR colleagues also had a sense for the theater involved in negotiations. When they met with Japanese representatives on one occasion in the USTR facilities in Washington, the team borrowed a portrait of General Douglas MacArthur to hang on the wall facing the visitors. It served to remind the Japanese of how much the United States had done for their country during the 1945–51 postwar occupation, when MacArthur oversaw sweeping changes there while supervising the occupation.[38]

Atmospheric elements also figured into the calculations by Yeutter's European counterparts at times. On one occasion, Willy De Clercq, the European commissioner for external relations and a Belgian nobleman, hosted Yeutter and other American trade officials for negotiations at his lavish estate outside Brussels. As USTR lawyer Chip Roh recalls, a resolution of differences eluded everyone in the morning, and the Americans were scheduled to leave in the afternoon. So De Clercq feted his visitors with a sumptuous feast well supplied with wine. Yeutter and De Clercq chatted amiably for a while at their end of the table, while Roh and his European counterpart could hear little of the conversation at their end.

"Both delegations were getting pretty relaxed," says Roh. "Just as dessert was being served, suddenly boomed out Clayton very clearly from the other end of the table: 'Well, I think Willy and I have got what we think might be a way to solve all this, and we'd like you lawyers to get together right away and work this up.' I remember my EC counterpart and I just looked at each other and it was a feeling of, 'uh oh, time to get serious again real fast.'" Eventually, the parties did cut a deal. The lesson Roh took was "never [to] assume that a negotiation led by Clayton was ever on a break."[39]

Still, Yeutter, who had been in the trade representative's job since April 1985, also reflected in his 1988 interview with the Montana paper on how challenging the USTR post was. "It has been more brutally difficult than I imagined," he said. "It has been three rugged years, but rewarding. I think we have turned the train around and are going the right direction." Both the devalued dollar and stepped-up exporting by U.S. companies were helping trim the American trade deficit at that point. Indeed, the United States was selling steel again to Japan, Yeutter noted.[40]

Nagging issues with Japan persisted for several years, as companies and the government there sought ways to circumvent agreements. In the mid-1990s the "abrasiveness" in trade between the countries, as Yeutter called it, endured in disputes over automobiles, airline routes, and various service and manufacturing issues, he wrote to a Japanese businessman in 1995. By then agriculture was less of a battleground, with Yeutter saying he heard fewer complaints about Japanese trade barriers in agriculture than at any time in his career to that point. Still, rice lingered as one of the stickiest areas, and Yeutter maintained that opening Japan to American exports of rice would have to wait for global trade negotiations.[41]

Because rice was so central to Japanese culture, resistance to imports was deeply entrenched. Some Japanese feared that the domestic industry would wither under the onslaught of cheaper American rice, and they cast the issue in almost spiritual terms. "Rice cultivation, which is the base of many traditional events and ceremonies, forms an integral part of the Japanese consciousness," a Tokai University professor of political economics, Susumu Yamaji, wrote in the *Japan Times* newspaper in 1986.[42]

But framing the dispute as anything but raw economics and politics did not sit well with all Japanese. A professor at Aoyama Gakuin University, Kenichi Ito, in November 1986 sided with free traders at a dinner cosponsored by Georgetown University's Center for Strategic and International Studies. Ito, the center's Tokyo representative, told Yeutter publicly at the affair, "There are many Japanese who support liberalization of rice imports; yet, the existing interest groups [e.g., the rice-growers' organization] have such enormous political power that it is necessary for Japan to be pressed by foreign countries in order to liberalize its rice imports. I want you to know that not all Japanese people agree with the Japanese government."[43] Indeed, Japanese consumers paid up to six times world prices for domestic rice as the government propped up domestic producers with subsidies.[44]

Shortly before, the Rice Millers' Association in the United States had filed a complaint under section 301 of U.S. trade laws, seeking to toss out Japan's ban on imports or allow for trade retaliation.[45] But Yeutter rejected the complaint—as he had rejected calls for a similar complaint two years earlier—killing the filing and irking some in the American rice industry. One industry official, Ralph S. Newman Jr. of the Farmers' Rice Cooperative of California, even obliquely accused Yeutter of timidity, saying, "This is less than a politically courageous way to deal with our complaint."[46] Indeed, Yeutter complained of the "verbal lynching" he got from rice organizations and their congressional representatives. But his move also yielded supportive editorials in the *New York Times*, *Washington Post*, and *Washington Times*, along with backing by some columnists.[47] It earned him a letter of approval, too, from former secretary of agriculture Earl Butz, who took a shot at the rice organizations. "These rice boys are already among the most heavily subsidized groups in all Agriculture," his old friend wrote. "Thank goodness you had the courage to stand pat on sound principle against their political onslaught."[48]

With all the troubles getting American products into Japan, at least one corporate CEO stepped forward to say he could do a better job as USTR than Yeutter. Chrysler Corporation chief Lido A. "Lee" Iacocca told reporters in Tokyo, "I don't think many countries would like me in that position because I am an unabashed patriot. I would come home with the bacon for the United State more often than not."[49] Yeutter wrote to a friend who sent him a newspaper story about Iacocca's comments, scoffing about his chances of getting the job, "Though Mr. Iacocca has some chameleon-like quality when it comes to political affiliation, I doubt that he's going to be getting any calls from George Bush!"[50] Bush had just won the 1988 election and took over from Reagan in January 1989. For his part, Iacocca retired from Chrysler at the end of 1992, with whatever interest he had in the trade slot unfulfilled.

Confirming Yeutter's views about forgoing the 301 process for rice, on October 28, 1988, President Reagan wrote a letter to Japanese prime minister Noboru Takeshita explaining his trade representative's decision. It was no endorsement of Japan's resistance to American rice exports, the president said, but rather an invitation to open the markets in upcoming multilateral trade talks. "I understand that Japan cannot make sweeping unilateral concessions in sensitive negotiations," Reagan said. "But until now Japan's position has been so carefully hedged as to raise questions about its negotiating commitment. Intentionally or not, Japan's cautious stance has decreased the chances for agricultural reform."[51]

While Reagan wrote such leader-to-leader letters to top foreign heads, he generally deferred to experts such as Yeutter on the ins and outs of trade talks. "Reagan was a delegator," recalls Roh. "Reagan was very much a 'set the direction and I want my people to do it' [president]. And he would stand behind his people when they did it . . . he and Clayton were intuitively sympatico."[52]

Yeutter's view, in fact, was practical. He saw a negotiated deal, under the umbrella of the global trade talks launched at Punte del Este, Uruguay, as more likely to boost Japanese imports of rice. "In my judgment, we would win the GATT [dispute settlement] case, but we might lose the ultimate objective of the case—market access," Yeutter said at an October 28, 1988, press conference. "As a sovereign nation, Japan can refuse to implement the GATT decision, in which case the US could and, undoubtedly would, retaliate. That will level the playing field, but it will not sell any more US rice. Would it not be better to find a solution that has a greater probability of expanding our rice exports?"[53]

Looking beyond just commercial concerns, moreover, Yeutter was sensitive to wider political implications. After he took on the job of secretary of agriculture in February 1989, he regularly updated President George H. W. Bush by memo on his work and on current issues. In a November 1989 memo he called the Japanese policy "indefensible," "embarrassingly protectionist," and "desperately in need of change." Plugged in as he was to Japanese leaders, however, he also said most of them conceded the problems and recognized that they needed outside pressure to "correct the situation," even as he added that the Japanese leaders were "under a lot of political strain at the moment." He warned, "We are beginning to observe more America bashing in Japan as a concomitant to the Japan bashing that occurs here." He said the degree of outside pressure needed was something Carla A. Hills, who succeeded Yeutter as U.S. trade representative, "must answer with great care." The Japanese would prefer to avoid the issue in the ongoing Uruguay Round of trade talks, he added, but he cautioned that taking it off the table would kill agricultural bargaining if not the entire round of talks. "Japan will have to open up to rice imports over time," Yeutter advised Bush. "If Japan is to be a responsible trading nation, it must be able to handle adjustments such as this even though they entail some political pain."[54]

Yeutter wrote the memo in response to a letter that a former adviser to President Reagan, journalist Jude T. Wanniski, sent Bush to warn that he was "growing alarmed at our trade frictions with Japan." Wanniski complained that "continued threats from Carla Hills and [Commerce] Secretary [Robert A.] Mosbacher [Sr.] are infuriating the people of Japan. For the most part, pushing and shoving them to open their markets helps do just that, but there is a point of diminishing returns."[55] Responding by backing his people, Bush said he supported Hills's and Mosbacher's efforts, adding, "As I am sure you know, the only way to avoid protectionist legislation at home is to have open markets abroad." He added that the rice issue was difficult, saying he would discuss Wanniski's suggestions "with our top people."[56]

Diplomatically, as always, Yeutter continued to put his oar in on rice and Japan, where he had built a deep reservoir of credibility with political officials. He advised Bush by memo in April 1990 that he had met with Japanese officials and added, "I believe they are gradually beginning to soften a bit." And he said signs of that would likely emerge at the end of the Uruguay Round.[57] A bit later, in August 1990, he traveled to Asia for two weeks, where, he said, the "entire Japanese leadership structure graciously turned out for my visit." Prime Minister Toshiki Kaifu and his family welcomed Yeutter and his wife, Jeanne, to their home on a Sunday morning. and other officials cut their vacations short to meet with him. Yeutter noted that "two major power brokers" in Japan's governing party, Shin Kanemaru and former Prime Minister Takeshita, "seem to be tilting in our direction."[58]

The Japanese treatment of Yeutter seemed to go well beyond the country's vaunted politeness. Yeutter's standing in the country was likely bolstered by his several years of dealing with business and political leaders there, first at the USTR office as a deputy, later when he ran the Chicago Mercantile Exchange and served as USTR, and still later as secretary of agriculture. It may have helped him, too, that his daughter Kim and her husband, John S. Bottimore, lived and worked in Tokyo for three years in the early 1990s; she had studied in Japan, was conversant in Japanese, had interned at the major trading company Nissho Iwai Corporation, and was then working for Eastman Kodak in Japan, while her husband worked there for Honeywell.[59] The Japanese press paid attention to Kim, chronicling her work experiences and feelings about Japan.[60]

Yeutter took umbrage when critics, such as Charles Lewis of the Center for Public Integrity, drew attention to his children. Yeutter said, for instance, that some news reporting about Kim's Japanese experiences was "unfortunate and very unfair to her." He added, "I do not perceive why they are of any relevance because the children of public servants should be able to lead their own lives."[61] But Yeutter at times used the example of his daughter to make a point to Americans. At a Farm Women's Leadership Forum in Washington in June 1989, he detailed Kim's knowledge of Japan and plans to work there to encourage farm women to have their children educated globally. "And we just need encouragement—it takes a lot of discipline to get kids out in farm country, or anywhere else for that matter, to work on languages and to think internationally and to think about living in other countries," he said. "But it's something that we ought to stimulate and I hope you will stimulate in some ways when you have a chance to do so."[62]

Despite Yeutter's personal ties in Japan, tensions between the United States and Japan over rice brought embarrassing confrontations. Japanese officials threatened staffers of the United States Rice Council with arrest in the spring of 1991, for instance, for displaying ten pounds of American rice under glass at a food exhibition in Tokyo. The exhibitors were also handing out bumper stickers that said "Have a Rice Day." For a few days, Japanese Food Agency officials told the exhibitors to shut down their efforts, but the Americans ignored them until the Minister of Agriculture notified the American Embassy that everyone associated with the exhibit would be arrested, according to an account in the *New York Times*. The Americans then removed their rice.[63] The contretemps annoyed the normally unflappable President Bush, who wrote a memo to several top officials, sharing a copy of the news story and saying, "The attached story really burned me up. Inasmuch as it says that the Japanese Ag Minister took the action against a 'display' of our rice, I think our Ag Dept. should weigh in with Japanese Ag Ministry, but other departments should also advise their counterparts that this is a tawdry performance."[64]

In the end, Japan did open its borders to some American rice, though not enough to satisfy American producers. The president of the Rice Millers' Association in February 1991 wrote Yeutter complaining about a Japanese proposal to accept certain amounts of American rice but to limit imports to rice used only in processed products, something the official said was "not an acceptable outcome."[65] Nonetheless, by the mid-1990s Japan became a major market for U.S. rice, and by the early 2000s it was the biggest market for U.S. medium/short grain rice, with more than half of California's annual rice exports typically going to Japan.[66] Ironically, Japanese American farmers in the state's Central Valley grew much of that American rice.[67] Japan agreed to import American rice under commitments it made through the World Trade Organization, the outfit created after the Uruguay Round, although American producers complained afterward that they wanted to sell even more than the Japanese permitted. Rather than going directly onto Japanese tables, much of the American rice went into noodles, beer, or sake.[68]

Yeutter was realistic about how far he could push on certain issues, such as rice in Japan. He was fond of saying that "every country has sacred cows and most of them don't have four legs," recalled Carole L. Brookins, a trade consultant whose expertise Yeutter often tapped. "He did understand the reality of reaching agreement and the priorities that were the most important."[69]

Yeutter got quicker results in prying open the market in Japan and in other countries for American-made cigarettes—but that put him at odds with a growing view that tobacco was essentially poison. The tobacco affair, which also troubled some on the USTR staff, pointed up a surprising personal inconsistency in Yeutter's words and actions. It started when tobacco put Yeutter on the wrong side of Surgeon General C. Everett Koop, who was quoted in a Reuters news story in late 1988 as saying he was disturbed by the USTR office's efforts to open up overseas markets to U.S. cigarette companies. Dr. Koop said, "It does bother me as a health officer that this country is involved in exporting disease, disability and death to countries that can ill afford that price down the road."[70]

Yeutter responded to Dr. Koop that larger principles were involved in his office's advocacy for tobacco producers in challenging Japan, Korea, and Taiwan for restricting U.S. companies that wanted to sell cigarettes there. He said he supported the physician's efforts to "sensitize the American people to the health dangers of this troublesome habit." He added, "I totally agree with what you have done, commend you for it, and I personally hope that you and others who might occupy your position in the future will become even more aggressive as time passes. I have never smoked, have no desire to do so, and believe this addiction to be a terrible human tragedy."

But he argued that "what we are about in our trade relationships is something entirely different," and that U.S. tobacco makers should be treated just the same in other countries as domestic tobacco companies were in those countries. He said he was bound to challenge discriminatory practices against cigarette makers or risk that other U.S. products would be subject to discrimination. "We have learned by harsh experience that any time the United States failed to challenge an unfair trade practice that practice proliferates widely," Yeutter wrote. "It is essential that we attack discriminatory practice, as a matter of principle, and I hope you will be supportive of that."[71] With the U.S. government subsidizing tobacco production, moreover, he reasoned that it would be inconsistent for him to treat requests by cigarette makers for relief under a U.S. law available to fight unfair trade practices less favorably than requests by other industries.[72]

Despite his lawyerly response to Dr. Koop, Yeutter grew close to the tobacco industry—incongruously so, given the contradiction between Yeutter's free-market views and the industry's long-standing subsidies. Within weeks of Yeutter's letter to the surgeon general, the Philip Morris company hosted a reception for Yeutter in conjunction with the inaugural celebrations for President Bush, which also marked Yeutter's move from the Office of the U.S. Trade Representative to the Department of Agriculture. "Once again,

Philip Morris has outdone itself!" Yeutter wrote to CEO Hamish Maxwell. "Jeanne and I were gratified by such a send-off and the wishes of so many old and new friends. . . . Thanks, Hamish, for your friendship, your advice, and all the thoughtfulness you have shown us." Yeutter handwrote on the note, "A fantastic event! One of the best I've ever attended."[73] The party was less enthusiastically received by some critics quoted in the media, with the *Washington Post* publishing on February 2, 1989, a news story headlined "Yeutter Fete Sponsored by Philip Morris, Acceptance Raises Ethical Questions."[74]

While he served as U.S. trade representative, Yeutter also owned stock in RJR Nabisco and, for his children, in Philip Morris—though he promised to divest himself of those holdings when he became secretary of agriculture. He denied there was any conflict of interest for him in owning such stocks, noting that the investment decisions about most of his holdings were made outside his direction and were part of his Chicago Mercantile Exchange deferred compensation program. Critics, such as Charles Lewis of the Center for Public Integrity, disagreed: "The actions and policies of USTR under Clayton Yeutter had helped Philip Morris and RJR Nabisco reap an enormous bonanza which brought those companies several hundred million dollars of added revenue in just a few years. If Yeutter and the Office of Government Ethics thought there was enough of a conflict issue in owning the stocks to require Yeutter to sell them as a condition to becoming Secretary of Agriculture, why was there not similar sentiment and sensitivity while he was the U.S. Trade Representative?"[75] After leaving government service, Yeutter still further deepened his relationship with the industry, despite its central role in what he labeled the "terrible human tragedy" spawned by smoking. He joined the board of BAT Industries, formerly known as British American Tobacco and one of the world's largest tobacco sellers, serving on it until the fall of 1998.[76]

After three and a half years of knocking on the world's doors to open markets, battle protectionist policies, and wrestle with political and business leaders at home and overseas as the U.S. trade representative, Yeutter got the call to serve under newly elected President George H. W. Bush as his secretary of agriculture. Yeutter felt drawn again to the private sector, so Bush reached out to others to help him persuade Yeutter to take the job.[77] Bush pressed Hills into service to succeed Yeutter as U.S. trade representative, and at a post-election reception at the vice president's residence in the fall of 1988, he enlisted her help in winning over Yeutter for the new job. According to Hills, "He drew me aside and he said, 'I've invited Clayton Yeutter to be my Secretary of Agriculture, but he hasn't said yes. Do you think you could persuade him?' I had never even met Clayton, so I went over and introduced myself and I said, 'you know the president wants you very much to take this position.' And he said, 'I've sort of decided I will.' So then I told that to the president and he said, 'I knew you were a good negotiator.'"[78]

Yeutter had come close to leaving government. He was offered one job that guaranteed him an annual income of $1.5 million, compared with the roughly $100,000 a cabinet post would provide. "We don't do everything in life for money, however, and in this case, other considerations were paramount," Yeutter said in an April 1993 forum at the University of Virginia's Miller Center of Public Affairs. And one of those considerations was his relationship with Bush, as he explained: "Had he not been George Bush, I would not have done so; I accepted the appointment out of affection for him and a desire to help his administration."[79]

He had also come close to taking an academic post, as he told a friend in a 2012 email. Other friends had tossed his name into the search for president of the University of Minnesota, and Yeutter had what he called a "really good session" with the search committee. The committee members were worried that faculty would be troubled by his comparatively thin academic experience, however; they had eliminated former vice president Walter F. Mondale, who hailed from Minnesota, from consideration at least partly because Mondale lacked academic credentials, he wrote. To ease such worries, Yeutter flew to Chicago to meet with a group of the school's faculty members, who unanimously recommended him for the job. But when word leaked out, it triggered a furor in the Democratic-controlled state legislature. "The reaction was: 'You dumbos have rejected Vice President Mondale as a candidate, and now you want to offer the university presidency to a Reagan Republican! Are you out of your minds?'" The search committee head called to say apologetically that Yeutter couldn't get the job. A few days later, Yeutter wrote, President Bush asked him to stay on to lead the Department of Agriculture.[80]

Certainly, the top ag post was a job the farm boy turned lawyer, economist, businessman, and trade expert had long sought. It would prove by turns to be exhilarating and frustrating, as he sought to put his philosophical and intellectual imprint on the nation's agricultural industry. Along the way, he would have to deal with ambitious politicians, restive farm groups, competing economic interests, and a host of sometimes surprising controversies.

His ag appointment started out in much the same way as his USTR post. For both jobs, he was sworn in by Supreme Court justice Sandra Day O'Connor, whom he admired and who, in turn, thought highly of him. Just as Yeutter hailed from a farm, so had O'Connor grown up on a cattle ranch in Arizona. They had known one another since the Nixon campaign days, when she co-chaired the president's reelection effort in Arizona, and shared moderate Republican views.[81] In both ceremonies, moreover, Yeutter had used a Bible belonging to his daughter Kim.[82]

But the ag ceremony, on February 16, 1989, did get off on the wrong foot—albeit trivially so—when President Bush said that his cabinet ambitions had implausibly deep roots. "Many kids want to grow up to be President; not Clayton," the president said. "When he was a boy, he wanted to be Secretary of Agriculture. And here he is, and that's a lucky break for America."[83]

News reports had earlier picked up the erroneous idea that the post was something Yeutter had dreamed of since childhood. And a Baltimore writer, Christopher Graybill, responded with a column in the *Wall Street Journal* poking fun at the idea: "All I can say is, Mr. Yeutter's childhood aspirations certainly put the rest of us to shame. The kids in my neighborhood wanted to be astronauts, cowboys and sports heroes. Most, as I recall, had only two goals in life: to bat clean-up for the Yankees and marry Tuesday Weld."[84] Amused, Yeutter wrote to Graybill to say he hadn't really had such a dream as a youngster. "We were trying to survive in those days when the dust was swirling and the grasshoppers ate all the crops. But somehow we made it, thanks to living in a country where hard work still pays off. . . . Your article was terrific! My children will be quoting it to me forever!"[85]

10

We Barely Survived

While Yeutter had not yearned for the secretary of agriculture post from his schoolboy days, he did seek it as far back as the late 1970s, in his early days at the Chicago Mercantile Exchange. But when he finally won the prize, he soon found the $99,500-a-year job to be something of a poisoned chalice. Just like his trade representative's post, the appointment brought knotty challenges—a new farm bill, the ongoing Uruguay Round of trade talks, and a string of prickly environmental and animal rights issues. And in 1990, after just a year on the job, Yeutter faced what he called "probably the most demanding year in the history of the United States for a secretary of agriculture."[1]

Beyond the issues, he contended with scorching heat from farm groups, environmentalists, and politicians as he pressed to deepen agriculture's reliance on markets instead of on government at a time when grain surpluses made farming financially ruinous. "I knew full well when I accepted this post that some criticism would be inevitable," he told a reporter for Reuters in a story that one newspaper headlined "Ag Secretary Yeutter Finds Praise Is Scarce." Yeutter added, "It is impossible for a secretary of agriculture to make everyone happy. . . . I'd rather take the political risks, try to achieve as much as possible. That high level of activity is bound to generate some criticism."[2]

Indeed, the job entailed reconciling the interests of so many varied constituencies that it may well have been impossible to avoid making enemies. In a sense, the job is riddled with contradictions. Such secretaries, after all, must balance the needs of family farmers and giant corporate agribusinesses, producers and consumers of all sorts, and the hungry in nutrition programs. They tend to areas as far-flung as forestry, conservation, water policies, export policies, utility, and infrastructure in rural America and global economic development. The portfolio Yeutter took on was not only sprawling but filled with competing interests, some of which grew vehement in their disputes with him.

Yeutter also had to deal with cynics on Capitol Hill and elsewhere in Washington who didn't know quite what to make of his straight-shooting approach. "He had a sincere Midwest cheerfulness and kindness. That's so unusual in Washington," notes Gary Blumenthal, who joined Yeutter as his executive assistant at the USDA and rose to become his chief of staff. "He always had a big grin and a strong handshake."[3]

Yeutter touched those he dealt with because he genuinely cared about others, friends said. After the late Carole L. Brookins, a trade consultant whose expertise he regularly tapped, underwent surgery for breast cancer in the mid-1980s, Yeutter was the first person to call her in the hospital. "I never, ever forgot that. I would have gone to the end of the earth for this man," she said. "This is not Washington. Washington is you eat what you kill and as long as you're edible and of value to people, they keep in touch with you. . . . But it's not the humanity that Clayton expressed. It's truly virtues that I was taught coming from the Midwest."[4]

USTR lawyer Chip Roh recalls that he and Yeutter once flew back from a tiring European trade negotiation session in Brussels and were both exhausted. As was routine, Yeutter's driver picked up the men at the airport, and Yeutter noticed that Roh was "down at the mouth" because the flight had arrived back late. Roh's son, Michael, then nine years old, was scheduled to solo in a choir performance, and the proud dad feared missing it. So, reversing protocol, Yeutter had the driver drop Roh at the church first and then was driven home himself. "It was a very kind thing," Roh says.[5]

Yeutter paired his personal warmth with an ability to absorb great quantities of information—a propensity he had first shown years before in earning his doctorate and law degree simultaneously and a feat that sometimes awed staffers. "Clayton was really a speed reader," remembers Blumenthal, who reviewed mountains of material sent to Yeutter each day before passing it on to him. "He could consume amazing volumes of paper, and I would joke that if you look at the pictures of me back then, I didn't wear glasses, but after working for him I had to wear glasses."[6]

Throughout his two-year tenure, Yeutter was clear about his mission, which transcended Washington and national borders. He felt, for instance, that the Uruguay Round of global trade talks would be crucial for the health of American agriculture, giving farmers new outlets for their crops, beef, and other products. Prying open foreign markets was their salvation, he maintained. "What happens in the Uruguay Round between now and December is infinitely much more relevant to the success or failure of American agriculture over the next 20 years than anything that happens in this or any other farm bill," Yeutter told the Reuters journalist. "We have to keep our priorities straight and know where it is that the future income potential of American agriculture lies."[7]

As a former colleague at the Department of Agriculture puts it, Yeutter came into the department with two broad aims. "He had goals both on the domestic side and the international side," recalls Richard T. Crowder, who served as under secretary of agriculture for international affairs and commodity programs for Yeutter and later as chief agricultural negotiator for the USTR in the mid-2000s. "On the international side, he wanted the Uruguay Round to be successful and reduce all trade barriers. On the domestic side, he wanted to reduce the operational impact of government on domestic programs." At home, Yeutter wanted to put an end to such heavy-handed Washington practices as allotting the numbers of acres of wheat, corn, and other crops that farmers could plant.

Globally, he wanted to scale back government supports and tariffs, which also entailed the politically hazardous moves of reducing domestic supports.

Indeed, philosophically, Yeutter had long held to the idea of setting ambitious goals. Crowder sums up Yeutter's aims in trade generally and in agriculture in particular as "zero-zero-zero: zero tariffs, zero domestic supports and zero export subsidies." As a realist, however, Yeutter knew that the best he could hope for would be to approach such stretch goals, attaining as much as possible. "He knew what he wanted, he knew the principles he was working for and toward," Crowder says. "He understood markets. He was outstanding in terms of preparing himself. And he was a really good negotiator."[8]

Up until that time, U.S. domestic agricultural policy was largely a matter of Washington battling over subsidies, recalls Bush's chief of staff, John H. Sununu. "The president realized—and Clayton was very much a part of helping shape these thoughts—that it was important for American farmers to be more aggressive with exports." He explains that the legislation the men drove in that period moved away from commitments to subsidies and more toward facilitating exports, a pattern that he says endured through many years and administrations afterward. It was, Sununu notes, "a major policy redirection in terms of agricultural policy."[9]

But that major redirection was bound to run up against deep skepticism among many in the farm belt and disagreement over the idea of less government support—and it did so fast. Gene Johnston, the managing editor of *Successful Farming* magazine, welcomed Yeutter to his new job in April 1989 with a snarky open letter that began by saying, "Few of us out here on the prairie asked you to be Secretary of Agriculture." Johnston, then contended that Yeutter had only one constituency: "It's farmers. Not consumers. Not the military. Not big business nor agribusiness. Not even the taxpayers. They have their own representation in the system, and they don't seem particularly concerned about the plight of farmers." Johnston went on to defend farm subsidies and loans and told Yeutter he "blew it" at GATT meetings in pursuing President Reagan's declared goal of eliminating trade subsidies globally.[10]

Yeutter was sharp in his response to the Iowa-based editor:

I will speak up for farmers, Gene, vigorously but not blindly. All
public servants have a responsibility to the American taxpayer,
and I do not believe it is healthy for farmers to get a large per-
centage of their income from the Federal government. I want
to do everything I can to help them get more from the international marketplace. If we can accomplish that, farmers will feel
a lot better about themselves, and so will their families. That is
why I pressed so hard to get agriculture in the forefront of the
Uruguay Round of trade negotiations, and why I'll do a lot to
help Amb. [Carla A.] Hills as she carries forth in the final 18
months of that exercise.

He added that GATT meetings were not failures, but were part of a
long-term effort, "and journalists need to understand that moves
which are made or not made at a particular time represent tactics
defined within an overall strategy." Yeutter said he was willing to
take political risks and would admit mistakes when he made them,
concluding that he and Johnston should stay in touch and he would
be sure to "provide some fodder" for Johnston's "journalistic mill."[11]

In his job running the Ag Department, though, challenges that
could have derailed Yeutter's big aims came hard and fast. Soon
after he was unanimously approved for the post by the U.S. Senate, critical Congress members—and some senators—tossed barbs
at him. "Our worst nightmare would be to have the archenemy of
the American farmer as Secretary of Agriculture, and that's exactly
what we have with Secretary Yeutter," Iowa Democratic congressman David R. Nagle told syndicated columnist Jack Anderson
when Yeutter had been on the job for only six months. Reflecting
scattered bipartisan hostility, an unnamed Republican congressman told a reporter for Anderson that Yeutter was more often an
adversary than an advocate for farmers. For his part, the columnist argued that Yeutter was boosting the interests of corporate
agriculture, "thumbing his nose at family farmers," and spending
too much time and money promoting Republican Party interests.[12] Yeutter could take comfort in notes he got afterward from

friends in agriculture, such as one from the CEO of Blue Diamond Growers, a California almond group. The executive, Roger J. Baccigaluppi, wrote, "In response to his article, I have just one word—HOGWASH!! You have proven time and again your concern for farmers and the agricultural industry."[13]

Still, it was true that Yeutter and others at the Department of Agriculture did stump for GOP candidates, especially in 1990, as an appreciative note from Sununu made clear. "You sacrificed a great deal of time and energy for our candidates and I wanted to stress to you how critical it was to our efforts," Sununu wrote to Yeutter in late November 1990. "During the past year, Administration officials participated in nearly 900 events on behalf of Republican candidates. . . . You personally made a difference for more than fifty candidates. Overall, during this election year, more Republican candidates received more help from more top Administration officials than ever before. This would not have been possible without the dedication and commitment of you and your staff."[14] Responding, Yeutter thanked him, adding, "I wish I could have done more, but the farm bill and the Uruguay Round tied me down a lot this year."[15]

Yeutter managed the many pressures of the job in part by working out—a lot. "With muscles bulging in his thighs, calves and shoulders, Yeutter has a physique most marines would envy—regardless of their age," *Successful Farming* magazine wrote in an adoring profile of him in the fall of 1989. "At 58, Yeutter is clearly the oldest one pumping iron at the gym this day and most other days," the magazine reported. "Besides working off stress, Yeutter says he lifts weights to 'develop an energy level.'" As he pushed three hundred pounds on leg lifts in the White House Athletic Club, clocked a dozen sit-ups, and then set the rowing machine humming, he meticulously recorded his performance in written notes.[16] Indeed, as Yeutter stayed fit, he challenged others at the USDA to do so too. In mid-1990 he launched a fitness challenge, inviting any USDA employee to compete against him on a rowing machine.[17]

Yeutter also took heart from his warm relationship with President George H. W. Bush, whom he had long admired as a fellow traveler in moderate Republican circles. The president phoned to offer condolences soon after Yeutter's mother, Laura, died at age ninety-two on April 27, 1989. In a memo, Yeutter thanked Bush for the call, saying, "That meant a lot. It was tough losing her, as a mother and as a marvelous human being. She taught Sunday School for 65 years, painted her own house at 90, and mowed her own lawn—which is large—during the day she passed away."[18] Laura Yeutter's work ethic had deeply impressed her son all his life, much as his father's had. Yeutter remembered her milking the family's cows far faster than he or his father could, as her hands were "amazingly strong."[19]

Laura passed her religiosity on to her son, as reflected in a letter he wrote to a friend of hers with whom she had volunteered at her church's clothing thrift shop in Cozad, Nebraska. "I know my Mother will be cheering you on from her position in Heaven," Yeutter said. "She'll be watching, and she'll certainly be hoping someone does the ironing properly! One of you mentioned to me that you would now have to retire her ironing board, and that was the nicest compliment you could possibly have given my Mother."[20]

Shortly after Yeutter was sworn in as secretary of agriculture, on February 16, 1989, Bush hosted him for lunch. The session prompted Yeutter to write to the president, "I thoroughly enjoyed the discussion and the good fellowship, and I hope you'll find time for comparable occasions in the future. . . . Please feel free to call me, or to invite me over on short notice, if and when you have questions or concerns about anything related to agriculture. I'll try not to bother you with demands on your time, since I should have the background to do this job properly. But I want to be responsive to you, so be sure to ask whenever you feel the need." He also complimented the president on appointing Dick Cheney as secretary of defense, calling Cheney a "longtime friend, former business associate, and a fabulous talent."[21]

Just as Yeutter was stepping out of the blocks in his new job, only a few days after his start, he ran headlong into the first of many thorny issues. Incongruously, this battle pitted him against actress Meryl Streep, as well as colleagues in the U.S. Environmental Protection Agency (EPA). In late February CBS's *60 Minutes* set off a national alarm when it broadcast the claims of an environmental group, the Natural Resources Defense Council (NRDC), that the chemical additive Alar on apples posed a serious health risk to children.

Schools nationwide pulled apples and apple juice from their menus, and the issue became a cause célèbre when Streep appeared in an NRDC-created public service announcement advising people to wash their fruits and vegetables.[22] Then Streep told a Senate subcommittee that the use of the chemical should be suspended immediately. Yeutter fired back, referring to "a self-proclaimed nutritionist who ought to stick to acting" and saying the NRDC report was based on a study undercut by other research. "I have no hesitancy in eating apples," Yeutter countered, asking schools to reconsider their moves. The NRDC report, Yeutter said, "did great damage to the apple growers of this country, damage that can never be withdrawn."[23]

The EPA maintained that the risk from Alar, used to keep apples fresh and crisp, was too small to justify immediately suspending use of the chemical, which may have been used on as little as 5 percent of the apple crop in 1988. But the agency began the process to phase Alar out if the final data justified doing so.[24] According to government agency talking points in Yeutter's papers, nearly all suppliers to the USDA no longer accepted apples that used the chemical, formally known as daminozide.[25]

Nonetheless, Yeutter worried about the impact the flap would have on the apple industry, and he stuck to his guns about the low risk Alar-treated apples posed. "We do not live in a risk-free world," he said at a March 17, 1989, meeting of the National Newspaper Association in Washington.

> I don't think you should be concerned about Alar, even though the EPA has proposed that it be banned. Because in my judgment, the health risk of consuming apples that have been treated with Alar is nominal. It is minuscule. As I said, if you want to try to avoid every food that has some potential health risk, you

are going to have an awfully narrow diet; and you may be down to 75 pound[s] pretty fast. . . . [T]he fact that EPA is going to take Alar off the market does not say to me that there is a risk there. It says to me that they are being exceptionally prudent, and they are taking it off the market simply because there have been some tumors in rodents as result of consumption of Alar.[26]

As it turned out, the environmentalists were probably right, at least regarding long-term and cumulative exposure to the chemical. After an extensive review, the EPA decided in late 1989 to ban Alar, determining that long-term exposure posed unacceptable risks. Studies and reviews, including one by Alar manufacturer Uniroyal Chemical Company, confirmed the research the NRDC had relied on. Furthermore, CBS was vindicated in the courts, with the U.S. Supreme Court ultimately upholding an appeals court decision that dismissed a $250 million class-action suit that Washington state apple growers brought against the network for its report, alleging that *60 Minutes* falsely disparaged their product. In the end, moreover, the apple industry rebounded, and an industry official said that losing Alar proved not to be a catastrophe.[27]

But the Alar garboil pointed up a larger one: Yeutter and officials at the EPA at times rubbed one another the wrong way, leading to palace intrigue. In July 1989 the *New York Times* ran a story about how the agency was pushing for the ability to remove potentially dangerous agricultural compounds from the market more quickly. Yeutter fired off a memo to EPA administrator William K. Reilly complaining about it. "Bill, this story had to have been generated by comprehensive discussions between the reporter and one or more people at EPA," Yeutter wrote in a note he blind copied to seven other officials. "I question the wisdom of engaging in such discussions before an Administration position has been reached on these very sensitive issues. We ought not to be having our internal debates in the newspapers. Beyond that the article makes the EPA the hero of this exercise and USDA the villain. That just isn't fair. Our people have been working in good faith with yours to try to develop a sensible consensus in this highly emotional arena, and this kind of media attention makes things a lot harder for us."[28]

Environmental groups, indeed, proved to be a thorn in Yeutter's side for much of his time at the Department of Agriculture and afterward. They had grown far more powerful and better financed in the decade leading up to his appointment, he explained to a South Carolina man who had written to him, so they wielded a lot of influence in Congress, both through campaign contributions and lobbying, along with notching victories in the courts and regulatory agencies. Yeutter contended that such groups used or manipulated the press, citing Alar as an example. "I suspect that the media has been a willing compatriot in some of those efforts, perhaps an inadvertent helper in others. After several days of a well-orchestrated attack, the manufacturing of alar and the EPA were both faced with impossible situations. The only feasible response was for alar to be withdrawn from the market by one or the other. Had that not occurred the apple industry would almost assuredly have suffered far greater damage than what occurred." He said the Bush administration was better prepared to handle such assaults in late 1990 than it had been earlier and by then could coordinate well among the EPA, FDA, and USDA. "But it is still much easier for the environmental advocacy groups to get their story out than it is for us to communicate ours. As you well know, the media focusses [sic] on bad news; it is not enthusiastic about articulating good news."[29]

Several environmental issues dogged Yeutter. A year after he started in the job, he was even concerned that such matters would dominate congressional debate over the 1990 Farm Bill, eclipsing traditional price and income support issues. "There will be wide differences of opinion as to what is practical to achieve," Yeutter told a journalist at the Farm Credit Council's newsletter, the *Insider*. "Some of the advocacy groups will want to put restrictions and regulations on production agriculture that will go much too far. These would be restrictions that would hamper agricultural production in a very substantial way and probably make it very difficult for many of our farmers to make a living." Striking an evenhanded note, however, he added, "At the same time, agriculture as an industry has to recognize that environmental protection must be a high priority for us. In many respects we are going to have to do a better job in the future than we have in the past."[30]

One issue that plunged Yeutter hip deep into complex ideological, scientific, and economic arguments was the dispute over genetically engineered bovine growth hormone (rBGH), also known as bovine somatotrophin or BST. Health and financial issues vied for prominence in the fight over the synthetic hormone, which could boost milk production in dairy cows by as much as 25 percent. The Food and Drug Administration (FDA) in 1985 had okayed the hormone for testing in dairy cows, ruling that it was safe to drink in milk. But anti-rBGH activists launched a boycott, spurring major companies to blacklist the test milk. Small dairy producers supported the activists, fearing that the hormone would put them at a competitive disadvantage with large producers and would lead to surpluses of milk, driving down prices. Yeutter favored innovations that drove agriculture to be more productive, even if that put less-efficient producers at risk, and he argued that the hormone ought to be approved if new scientific reviews again found it safe. "Our job is to try to—is to protect the health of the population of America," he said at a September 15, 1989, press conference. "It's not our job to make marketplace judgments."[31]

Only a few days before that press conference, Yeutter took his case on the hormone to Vermont, where he got a mixed reception at a special hearing of the U.S. Senate Agriculture Committee in Montpelier. A Republican congressman, Peter P. Smith, accused him of "insensitivity to the concerns of Vermont farmers and about what BST will do to the marketability of milk." But the head of the Vermont Farm Bureau, who was a dairy farmer, said Yeutter was "facing the reality of the issue" in wanting science, not economics, to dictate any decisions. Yeutter told some one hundred farmers and others at the hearing that he would not support halting production of the hormone based on fears that it might spawn a milk glut and drive down prices.[32] Later, Yeutter derided BST critics in a note to someone who had written to him about the meeting: "A lot of the folks at that hearing were very far to the left side of the political spectrum. Apparently that reflects some of the influence of wealthy New Yorkers moving into the Vermont area, thereafter becoming very liberal in political philosophy. Some have obviously reached the point where they are just not sensible any longer."[33]

In late 1990 a private watchdog group led by author Jeremy Rifkin sued Yeutter and officials of the department's National Dairy Promotion and Research Board, accusing them and four major drugmakers of illegally promoting rBGH to boost milk production in cows. The group, the Foundation on Economic Trends, alleged that the board improperly financed and took part in a public relations effort to persuade the public that the hormone was safe. The stakes were huge, since the four companies had spent some $100 million developing the hormone and foresaw a $500 million annual market for it.[34] Consumers Union, publisher of the respected *Consumer Reports* magazine, weighed in soon after, urging the FDA to stop the sale of milk from such test cows, saying it saw little or no benefit to consumers from the hormone.[35]

A federal judge dismissed Rifkin's suit on April 30, 1992, saying his foundation had not shown sufficient harm.[36] Despite the objectors, moreover, experts including a panel convened by the National Institutes of Health found in the end that rBGH milk was safe for people.[37] So the FDA okayed the hormone for cows in 1993. Nonetheless, it remained taboo in the European Union, Canada, and some other countries. While the hormone caused some health problems in cows, evidence for harm in people was inconclusive, according to the American Cancer Society, which took no formal position on the hormone.[38]

Another contentious and headline-grabbing issue Yeutter faced involved spotted owls in the Northwest, a species that had been listed as potentially endangered in 1973. In the spring of 1990 Secretary of the Interior Manuel A. Lujan Jr. faced the question of whether to declare the owl endangered, which would protect it in the national forests that Yeutter oversaw and in the national parks that Lujan oversaw. A panel of government scientists in April 1990 declared that timber-harvesting practices did not protect the species and said old-growth forests in Washington, Oregon, and Northern California would have to remain undisturbed if the owl were to survive, as Yeutter advised President Bush in a memo. "That will provoke an enormous controversy in that part of the country over the next few months, for it looks as if 20,000 jobs or so are in jeopardy in order to preserve about 8,000 owls. We'll do our best to keep folks calmed down and look at the policy options in a methodical way," he wrote. Yeutter noted that the scientific report came in response to a lawsuit environmental groups had brought against the government, one of many on a host of issues. He said nearly three thousand lawsuits were pending against the Forest Service alone, "nearly all of them by environmental advocacy groups who seem to have lots of money at their disposal."[39]

Pressure to save the owls grew, even as Yeutter labored to balance the economic and environmental concerns involved. In June 1990 the U.S. Fish and Wildlife Service declared the species threatened. In September Yeutter sought a compromise, though he expected it would be a tough sell. "We've taken a middle of the road position that will probably generate some criticism from both the timber industry and environmental groups. But I'm prepared to defend our package to anyone because it is sound. We've contemplated about every trade-off I can imagine, and we've dealt with both the short run (FY 91) situation and the long term process," he wrote in a memo to President Bush, noting that the Department of Agriculture spent a lot of time trying to make Republican senators Thomas S. Gorton III of Washington and Robert W. Packwood and Mark O. Hatfield of Oregon comfortable with the plan. "The issue is very emotional in the Pacific Northwest, and the press will be inclined to sensationalize and polarize the outcome. We'll be trying to low key it as much as possible, calm people down, and persuade folks that we'll continue to work on these issues in a rational, objective way."[40]

But the compromise didn't fly, and the issue lived on to plague both the Bush and Clinton administrations. In May 1991, several months after Yeutter had left the ag secretary's post to chair the Republican National Committee, a federal judge in Seattle ruled that the federal government had not done enough to protect the owls, and he temporarily halted most logging rights sales in old-growth habitats.[41] In May 1992, when Yeutter oversaw domestic policies for Bush as his domestic counselor, Interior Secretary Lujan unveiled another plan, proposing that the owls be captured from certain areas and moved to wilderness areas in national parks, even though that would mean it might take centuries for the population to recover.[42]

Then in 1993 federal scientists said the populations appeared to be declining. President Clinton and Vice President Albert A. "Al" Gore Jr. hosted a forest conference in Portland, Oregon, that later gave rise to the Northwest Forest Plan. In 1994 logging was cut dramatically and two-thirds of remaining forests were protected. Federal agencies were required to survey for more than one hundred rare species before proposing timber sales, so loggers were denied the right to cut one billion board feet of timber they said they were promised.[43]

Much as Yeutter advocated for industries and for free markets, Gore passionately advocated for the environment, and his conviction grew over the years into his defining issue. But Yeutter had little use for Gore's strident approach. When a scholar at the American Enterprise Institute in 1993 wrote a critical review of Gore's book *Earth in the Balance* for the *Yale Law Journal*, Yeutter thought it was right on target. "I loved the article! I'd have been even tougher on the Vice President, but that's because I had to tolerate his harassment while he served in the Senate!" Yeutter wrote in a letter to the reviewer. Yeutter, who was then out of government and practicing law in Washington again, added, "He really is 'off the wall' on most of the critical environmental questions of the day, and he was singularly unhelpful to President Bush before and during the Rio Conference. I thought his behavior during that time period was downright repulsive!"[44]

The Rio Conference, formally known as the United Nations Conference on Environment and Development, or the Rio de Janeiro Earth Summit, was a seminal meeting in June 1992—a time when Yeutter was serving as counselor for domestic policy for President Bush. The meeting gave rise to the United Nations Framework Convention on Climate Change, which led in later years to other major global environmental pacts, including the Kyoto Protocol and the Paris Agreement on emissions and global warming.[45] Gore chaired the U.S. Senate delegation to the summit, at which Bush spoke, much to the consternation of conservative Republicans. Bush balked at setting specific emissions reduction targets at the gathering, however, and Gore later sharply criticized the president's environmental record.[46]

During his time at the Department of Agriculture, Yeutter's job went well beyond tending to domestic farm issues. It often bled into foreign policy, something for which his prior diplomatic experiences had prepared him. At the end of 1989, for instance, Bush tapped Yeutter to lend a hand on dealings with Poland, which was then opening itself to the West. Lech Walesa, the union leader who led the way to Poland's repudiation of Communism and in December 1990 would be elected as the country's president, addressed the U.S. Congress in November 1989, pleading for foreign investment. So Bush asked Yeutter to lead a high-level fact-finding mission to the country two weeks later. Labor Secretary Mary Elizabeth "Liddy" Dole, Commerce Secretary Robert Mosbacher, and Michael J. Boskin, who chaired the President's Council of Economic Advisers, tagged along on the trip, along with twenty corporate and labor leaders, economists, and other experts. Their mission was to study where the United States could lend a hand in rebuilding the country's agriculture, business management, industry, and financial services sectors.

The mission, the first of many contacts for Americans interested in helping recast the country's economy, was right up Yeutter's alley philosophically. "All of us on this mission are committed to furthering the transition of the Polish economy from one that has been crippled by central planning to one that gives free rein to the enterprising spirit and creativity of the Polish people. Central planning, even by the largest and most sophisticated computers, can never equal the market for matching supplies to the varied needs of a nation's consumers," he wrote in a statement released on the eve of the group's departure. "Never before has a country attempted a successful transformation of a state-controlled economic and political system into one of political pluralism, democracy and a market economy."[47]

In short order after the trip, the U.S. helped Poland set up a bevy of post-Communist institutions, encouraged thousands of Poles to study in the United States and elsewhere, created the Polish-American Enterprise Fund (a private equity fund), and supported nongovernmental organizations that helped the country. The Poles also got direct aid from the United States, as well as multilateral aid through the World Bank and the European Bank for Reconstruction and Development.[48] With all that help and the economic surge that came along with embracing capitalism, Poland's gross domestic product, in current dollars, more than doubled from under $64 billion in 1987 to $142.1 billion by 1995, and later soared to top $592 billion in 2019.[49]

Yeutter turned his diplomatic touch mostly to efforts at home, though, developing a new farm bill for 1990 that would govern farm policies and practices for five years. Selling U.S. farmers, along with legislators in Washington, on the bill was a Herculean task that preoccupied Yeutter throughout much of his tenure at the Department of Agriculture. He launched the debate over the measure in February 1990, planning about seventy changes to the 1985 Farm Bill, which stunned some legislators who had expected incremental tweaks. "The Hill was startled by the comprehensiveness of our proposals and the analysis that accompanied them," Yeutter wrote to President Bush. "One longtime Washingtonian called it the highest quality farm bill submission by any Administration in 20 years, and perhaps ever." Republicans were largely united behind the plans, he said, but Democrats were "utterly frustrated" because the bill didn't specify target price levels for commodities but left such details to negotiations.[50]

The bill would sting many farm country recipients of federal largesse. President Bush wanted to cut federal costs for agricultural programs by $13.6 billion over five years, ensuring that the debate over the measure would prove loud and lively—with critics painting a bull's-eye on Yeutter's back. The arguments grew shrill at times because the economic ground in that period shifted against farmers. Bumper crops of such commodities as wheat drove prices way down in 1990, leaving lots of farmers in distress. That, along with poor rains, cut yields on wheat and sugar beets in areas in North Dakota and Minnesota, for instance. One agriculture reporter for the North Dakota farm magazine *Agweek* wrote a snide column urging farmers to mail Yeutter a Christmas card that year telling him how poorly they were doing. "It seems as though sometimes you're out of touch with farmers," the columnist, Ann Bailey, said. "I don't agree with your 'survival of the fittest' mentality, Clayton." She said she understood that Yeutter wanted to wean farmers off government payments, making them more independent. "But it's darn hard to subsist on nothing and that's why farmers participate in the program."[51]

Yeutter was not one to take such affronts lying down. He grew passionate in his two-page riposte to her:

Ann, I've been involved with agriculture from the day I was born until now, more than 60 years later. I've lived through some mighty tough times too, having grown up in your neighboring state of Nebraska during the depression and dust bowl days of the '30s when our farm policy safety net was only a fraction as generous as it is today. There were years when we barely survived. My parents and I prayed for rain too, on a lot of occasions over a lot of years, just as many of your North Dakota farm families are doing today. I hope the rains come, to everyone's satisfaction, in 1991.

Yeutter added that he wanted farmers to be less dependent on Uncle Sam, and prying open foreign markets would help.

While saying he had never suggested eliminating the safety net for U.S. agriculture, Yeutter would not back down in his defense of a more market-oriented approach to farming. "You said that you don't agree with my 'survival of the fittest' mentality, but that's what we call capitalism in this country," he wrote, adding that he had visited many socialist states and never met a farmer in any of them who "wouldn't give his right arm to move to North Dakota." But he acknowledged the risks in a market-oriented approach: "Not every farmer in America will make it through 1991, nor every automobile dealer, hardware store owner, or barber. The losses are sad, in any business, but change often works out for the best. God seems to have a way of guiding us through life, and He may even take you in a different direction a decade or two from now." He said he and others at the USDA were putting in long hours trying to open markets for farmers such as Bailey's father and brother, whom she had mentioned. "If your dad and brother are unhappy with me because they want bigger farmer subsidies, that just isn't in the cards—under any Secretary of Agriculture."[52]

Indeed, the calls for Yeutter's scalp came fast and hard late that year, largely because some commodity prices were falling so sharply. After reading Bailey's column, one wheat farmer wrote to Yeutter anonymously:

> I am an avowed life long Republican, but you make me ashamed of my political party with your snobbish attitude towards farmers. It's easy to discern that you are more of a lawyer than you ever were more of a farmer. . . . If farming is so damned profitable, why in the hell don't you resign from your plush dream world job in D.C. and try making a good living on the farm, with no off-farm income? YOU ARE A DISGRACE AND AN AFFRONT TO EVERY HONEST, DEDICATED, HARD WORKING FARMER IN THE U.S.! . . . I hope you lose a little sleep knowing there are farmers who not only disagree with you, they thoroughly despise you and your attitude.[53]

Wheat farmers, in particular, were hopped up. A two-hundred-member group of farmers in Washington State called for Yeutter's resignation in October 1990 because, they said, his Export Enhancement Program (EEP) failed to boost wheat sales. The program—which Yeutter had held his nose to create, largely to pressure the European Community—provided an export subsidy designed to let the American growers compete with subsidies from Europe. Wheat at the time was fetching $2.47 a bushel, only 40 cents more than growers got in 1920, according to a leader of the Douglas County Association of Wheat Growers. The group was also troubled by a planned 2.5 percent reduction in wheat support programs in the 1990 Farm Bill.[54] A columnist for the *Hutchinson News* in Kansas joined the chorus against Yeutter, arguing, "Now it seems as though Yeutter is a man on a mission. His mission is not on behalf of farmers but on behalf of free marketers. Yeutter makes no bones about his desire to sign a new General Agreement on Trade and Tariff [*sic*] pact and has become all but blind to his first responsibility of improving conditions for American farmers. Yeutter should be replaced with someone who truly cares about farmers."[55]

Piqued by the *Hutchinson News* piece, Yeutter sent a strong two-page response, asserting:

> My mission is on behalf of farmers. I've been one most of my life, and I have a hunch I've gone through much tougher times on the farm in my lifetime than you have in yours. I want Kansas farmers and all other American farmers to have a chance to increase their earnings as the years unfold. But they'll not do that by being on the federal dole. Federal financial support for agriculture will decline in the future, irrespective of the Administration in power and of who is Secretary of Agriculture. . . . What that means is we must generate more income from the marketplace, and I've been devoting a lot of hours over the past several years to doing that. We've succeeded in several major areas—beef, citrus, tobacco products, and a number of processed foods. We need to keep working on that, particularly in the Uruguay Round. In my view we have no viable alternative.[56]

In time, Yeutter and his trade-minded allies put American domestic subsidies of farm products under the knife as part of the global negotiations, applying restraint for the first time to such U.S. internal supports. "This was first time we had ever, ever touched domestic subsidies," says Yeutter's USTR ag expert Condon. "This was revolutionary. The thought that we might put disciplines on domestic support was unheard of."[57]

Others who worked with Yeutter seconded the idea that by attacking subsidies globally, he was putting the domestic supports into the crosshairs as well. "Remember that the international front was a way to change the domestic front," consultant Brookins told me. "The constraints of the Uruguay Round of negotiations were to reduce subsidies and everybody had to cut back their subsidies and cut back their trade barriers and cut back their non-tariff barriers. . . . We were not going to disarm unilaterally."[58]

Certainly, Yeutter had the Uruguay Round near the top of his mind when—counterintuitively—he ramped up the Export Enhancement Program (EEP), setting aside his longtime loathing for export subsidies. He did so in early 1991 by increasing the amount of money available to support wheat exports under the program. He opted to delete the program's limit of $425 million, opening the door to more support to make American wheat more competitively priced globally. The move likely was tactical, aimed at prodding the export-subsidizing countries of the European Economic Community (EEC) to support agricultural reform efforts in the Uruguay Round of trade talks, but some allies saw it as a risky gambit prone to backfiring, and it brought Yeutter criticism from overseas that was more genteel than the domestic sort, but perhaps more troubling.

Referring to an ongoing "subsidy war" in wheat that had helped drive down the global price, officials of Australia pushed back on Yeutter's move. "We find the timing of your request particularly unfortunate in the context of our mutual efforts in the Uruguay Round," Australian ministers wrote to Yeutter.

Your own expert analysis and ours demonstrates that EEP primarily affects non subsidising exporters, such as Australia, not the EEC. Therefore we dispute your contention that the removal of the funding limit will assist in breaking the deadlock on the agriculture negotiations in the Uruguay Round. Rather it is both counterproductive in our bilateral trade relations and in our view may well harden EC [European Community] attitudes in the Uruguay Round negotiations if only by example. . . . In

Australia's view, the US could show real leadership on international agricultural reform by reducing subsidies at this time rather than increasing spending as you are proposing to do.[59]

Yeutter suggested in a letter to the leader of an Australian farm group that the EEP was a way to pressure the Europeans. "We believe the Export Enhancement Program (EEP) is consistent with our goal of imitating worldwide reforms of agricultural policies under the General Agreement on Tariffs and Trade round," he wrote. "Without this persuasive tool, there would be little incentive for such parties as the EC to curtail its heavily subsidized agricultural practices. In the long run, trade unencumbered by trade barriers or distorting subsidies would benefit all nations."[60]

At home, the EEP move—and related changes in President Bush's proposed budget—drew applause from some hard-pressed American wheat growers. The Nebraska Wheat Board, for instance, backed plans to raise the spending cap and boost financing on export credit guarantees. "The U.S. farmer's share of the world wheat market has fallen from 43.4 percent to 29 percent while the EC's share has climbed from 14 percent to a record 21.8 percent since 1987," the Lincoln-based group wrote to Yeutter in February 1991. "The reasons for these changes are simply that the EC has spent nearly $12 billion per year on export subsidies compared to only $312 million last year by the U.S. The U.S. must not stand by and let the EC and others take advantage of U.S. farmers."[61]

As it turned out, Yeutter's tactic did succeed in moving the U.S. and the European Community to eliminate export subsidies, though it took a few years after Yeutter's tenure at the USDA for that to happen. "He laid the foundation," says Yeutter's former USDA chief of staff Blumenthal.[62]

While he was on the job, however, some U.S. farmers just couldn't be persuaded that Yeutter's efforts globally and domestically would help them. A Kansas man ratcheted up the hostile rhetoric against Yeutter in 1990, suggesting he be replaced by an Arkansas jackass. "All Secretaries of Agriculture seem to receive such recommendations from time to time, so perhaps I should not be surprised—

particularly during a downtrend in prices," Yeutter responded. Further, he gave the man a tutorial in economics: "Wheat prices have been falling for a very simple reason, namely that we have huge crops all over the world. Markets work, and when supply increases dramatically prices decline. . . . The good Lord gave us excellent weather in 1990, and there is not much the U.S. Secretary of Agriculture can do about that. In fact, many folks would consider that to be a blessing since a lot of that wheat will go toward feeding the people of this world." Yeutter added that American farmers still had "solid protection" through a target price program and that net farm incomes for Kansas wheat farmers would actually rise in 1990, compared with 1989.[63]

Some of the critics, however, wrote to Yeutter more in fear than in fury. "Farm conditions have deteriorated drastically in the last two years, and we are being eaten up by inflation, rapidly rising production costs and ever increasing taxes at every level. Meanwhile the prices for our products, with the exception of livestock, have fallen far below the cost of production," Keith E. Portenier, a third-generation wheat farmer from Guide Rock, Nebraska, told Yeutter in September 1990. "We need to know if you and the Bush Administration are comfortable with this situation, or if agriculture can be returned to a profitable endeavor. I am at retirement age but our son needs some assurance that agriculture will be more than second rate as a lifetime career."[64]

Taking the time to compose a two-page response, Yeutter said he knew the farm outlook in Nebraska from regular conversations with the tenant on his family farm in Dawson County. "Not only do we have one of the largest crops in history this year, but a lot of other countries have had the same experience," he explained. He noted that the Soviet Union had been out of the market until recently, and the ability to sell to Iraq had vanished because of troubles there. But Yeutter also said that farmers who used the futures markets to hedge or forward-contract their production were better off than others and pointed out that if Portenier participated in the federal farm program, he had income protection.

Indeed, he said, "a good many farmers" would enjoy a higher

income in 1990 than they had in 1989 because of the federal program. But Yeutter added that federal budget deficits meant that higher farm subsidies were "just not in the cards" for the future. The answer, he said, lay in the global trade talks, provided they would open more markets. Yeutter declined to advise the Nebraska farmer about his son's future but told him that "efficient, well-managed operations" would always find room. "They'll have their ups and downs though, for that is the nature of farming. So your son will need to be able to adjust to the volatile times as they occur."[65]

If Yeutter was taken aback by both the sorrow and anger heaped on him by some wheat farmers, he probably was not surprised by it, at least with respect to Japan. The Japan Food Agency had bought American wheat for years on an unsubsidized basis, even taking lower-quality wheat than they did from other countries, Yeutter wrote to a colleague in August 1990. He said the American wheat industry was reluctant to raise problems with Japan's wheat policy, such as its "stratospheric support price." If the Japanese lowered their support prices, Japan's farmers would grow less wheat, Yeutter said, noting that resale prices for imported wheat were triple the cost of the imports, which cut consumption. "We might lose some wheat sales to Japan in the short run if they were to reform these programs, but we'll be better off in the long run. Our wheat organizations may not favor a more aggressive course of action, but that would not dissuade me."[66]

American wheat growers and exporting companies were loath to upset trade relations with Japan in general because the country was such an important importer of American wheat. "The prevailing attitude at USDA and probably in the farm community was 'Don't mess with Japan. We don't want to see anything that's going to threaten our access for wheat,'" recalls Ellen Terpstra, the former deputy under secretary for international activities at the USDA and international economist at USTR with Yeutter. Indeed, because of the interlocking push-and-pull nature of global trade, she says that American wheat interests eyed efforts to pry open Japan's markets for other goods and services suspiciously, for fear that the Japanese would retaliate by cutting back wheat purchases. The Japanese government called the shots on such wheat purchases.[67]

Yeutter held fast to his conviction that American farmers relied too greatly on Washington. In a January 1991 letter to a Montana farmer who had written to him, Yeutter responded, "It would be a lot healthier for everyone in American agriculture if we could reduce our dependence on financial support from the government. I don't know many farm families who like receiving government checks, and I doubt that you do. That's why I've been working so hard, both as U.S. Trade Representative and as Secretary of Agriculture, to open up markets around the world for products such as your wheat and barley, and simultaneously discipline some of the unfair practices that today impede your export sales." He acknowledged that low wheat prices were "disconcerting" but blamed the world glut of wheat for them.[68]

While Yeutter's philosophy and methods stoked some farmers to demand his ouster, not everyone in farm country agreed. When people at a Rural Strategy Summit in Kansas City, Missouri, issued a news release in the fall of 1990 saying participants called for him to step down, he got a curious response from the head of the National Farmers Union (NFU), a group that he had been at odds with at times. NFU president Leland Swanson assured Yeutter that even though several union members attended, "the National Farmers Union was not a participant in, or a signatory to, any call for your resignation." Swanson apologized for any misunderstanding.[69] Yeutter responded with thanks, adding, "We'll always have plenty of challenges in American agriculture, but it takes people working together to effectively confront them. Regrettably, agriculture (in all countries) has often been marked by far more divisiveness than cooperation."[70]

Yeutter had developed cordial relations with Swanson and others in his organization in the spring of 1990, when he spoke at the group's annual meeting. "We do have some major policy disagreements but, as I noted in my presentation in Oklahoma City, we also have many areas of agreement," Yeutter wrote to Swanson afterward. "I particularly wanted to thank you for the gracious way in which you handled my appearance. I know you worked very hard to make sure that your membership demonstrated respect for me and the position I hold, and you succeeded. All the questions were constructive and substantive, and that assuredly is not always the case!"[71] When one farmer sent him a respectful note about his presentation, Yeutter thanked him and admitted it "was a bit like walking into the lion's den!"[72] He echoed that language in a letter to Oklahoma governor Henry L. Bellmon, adding, "However, I doubt we'll ever convince them to move away from some of their radical positions. The Oklahoma Farmers Union people seem to be quite sensible, but those folks up in the Dakotas are really off on a tangent!"[73]

Nonetheless, Yeutter found fault with NFU. In 1993, after he had left the Agriculture Department and the Democrats controlled the White House, Yeutter told a friend in Lincoln that the union was "still living in a dream world of production controls, artificially high prices, and massive government subsidies that has long since passed. If they can't see the signals coming from the Clinton administration, they are truly blind. Clinton, as you've undoubtedly perceived, wants to cut farm programs far more than did any of his Republican predecessors. That should be an eye opener for the Farmers Union, the AAM [the American Agriculture Movement], the NFO [National Farmers Organization] and a few others."[74]

While running the Department of Agriculture, Yeutter got crosswise with some dairy producers as well. He delivered a scathing speech at a meeting of the Chicago Farmers group in the fall of 1990 in which he lambasted farm legislation passed by the House and Senate as containing a "belly full of malodorous policy cadavers left over from the pre-1985 farm bill."[75] He predicted that setting a rigid price floor on dairy products, for instance, would lead to production quotas or other supply control measures and would hurt opportunities for opening export markets. And he called on producers of corn, soybeans, cotton, rice, and other farm products to pay mind to Congress on the matter. James P. "Tom" Camerlo, a Colorado dairyman who served as president of the National Milk Producers Federation (NMPF), charged that Yeutter was "pitting farmer against farmer" and argued that the dairy industry was the only major commodity without a needed supply management program.[76]

But not all dairy producers sided with the trade group leader. A producer from Clifton Springs, New York, personally delivered a handwritten note to Yeutter at a meeting in Buffalo in late September 1990, conveying his disgust with the NMPF leader's criticism. "Free trade is the secret to world prosperity and national prosperity," dairyman George B. Mueller wrote. He quoted an English historian: "Nothing can I [sic] a nation more than free trade and nothing is opposed more vigorously by a nation's people." Mueller affirmed, "As a daryman [sic], I fully support free trade even if means more dairy products will come in from abroad!"[77] When Yeutter met with Camerlo, he discussed Mueller's note with him, telling Mueller in a response, "Thanks for the ammunition!" Yeutter added that he had found that a "substantial number" of producers agreed, saying many were young and had not risen to positions of authority in their dairy organizations. "Hopefully more positive and sensible voices, such as yours, will be heard with more frequency in the future. The U.S. dairy industry simply has to get its head out of the sand and realize that it is competing in a global market."[78]

The Chicago Farmers speech also brought attacks from Nebraska senator Bob Kerrey, who was then being bruited as a potential presidential contender. Kerrey's criticisms appeared to have gotten under Yeutter's skin. John Block, who had served as secretary of agriculture when Yeutter worked in Chicago, told Yeutter, "[Kerrey] did a good job of distorting and taking your remarks out of context."[79] Yeutter responded, "Bob Kerrey seems determined to attack me two or three times a week, so we've become accustomed to that!" He told Block, who then was serving as president of the National-American Wholesale Grocers' Association, that Kerrey "is just an incredible demagogue, and it would be tragic if he were to move to any higher position in this government. It is time for the RNC [Republican National Committee] to begin to take some blasts at him."[80]

The two Nebraskans did not see eye to eye on farm policy. Kerrey, in a handwritten note to Yeutter, took issue with comments Yeutter had made about how the federal deficit could double or triple if all requests for agricultural funding were honored. "Clayton, you genuinely are not coming across as an advocate for agriculture with many in rural Nebraska, who like me, know that you have been. Briefly, let me also suggest that our philosophies toward ag policy are different in some key ways. These differences perhaps appear to be demagoguery.... I assure you this is not my intent."[81]

But Yeutter's critical view of Kerrey only grew sharper over time. In August 1991, when he was serving as chairman of the Republican National Committee and preparing for the fall 1992 presidential election, Yeutter advised President Bush that Kerrey could jump into the race, though he thought it more likely that the decorated Vietnam veteran would wind up as a vice presidential candidate. "Kerrey will get attention as a Congressional Medal of Honor winner, and through his liaison with Debra Winger and his prairie populism," Yeutter wrote to the president. "He'll push the health care agenda, with his proposal being essentially the Canadian system. And he'll demagogue on everything, at least as much as Tom Harkin." Harkin was then a presidential hopeful. Yeutter added, "Neither he nor Kerrey is likely to be civil in their attacks on you and the Administration. They'll be the two hatchet men of the primary campaign season."[82]

The following month, Yeutter wrote that Kerrey and Clinton would both join the race. "Both will get some immediate attention—Kerrey on glamour, Clinton on Republican-like substance!"[83] Soon after that, Yeutter called Kerrey "the more glamorous figure" and predicted a "Kennedyesque campaign" from him.[84] And Yeutter maintained an extensive opposition research dossier on Kerrey at the Republican National Committee. But as the race turned out, Harkin and Kerrey lost in the primaries to Clinton, who chose Gore, then a U.S. senator from Tennessee and another longtime thorn in Yeutter's side, to be his vice presidential running mate.

Kerrey and Yeutter continued to joust long after Yeutter left the government. In late 1998 Yeutter was working with a law firm again and was quoted by the *Omaha World-Herald* as telling hard-pressed farmers and ranchers to roll with the punches in the bad farm economy of the day. Kerrey wrote him a letter, which the senator made public, arguing that the problems in farm country were "knock-out blows," not mere "punches," and he took issue with Yeutter on farm policy, advocating a loosening of marketing loan rates and new incentives for taking land out of production.[85] Yeutter responded that he found it "discouraging to work so hard for so long to open up market opportunities around the world, and then have those opportunities jeopardized by our own political processes." He also said it was "terribly poor form" for Kerrey to make his letter public long before it even reached Yeutter. "In thirty years of being in and around Washington D.C., I don't believe I've ever done that. Life is too short for cheap shots."[86]

For his part, Kerrey was surprised at the vehemence with which Yeutter responded to him, at least in his letters to Republican National Committee leaders and others. He found Yeutter's letters criticizing him to be "startling." He recalls thinking that they got on well and likely would have agreed on such issues as soil and water conservation. "I never thought of Clayton as a partisan," Kerrey says, adding that their one-on-one dealings were always cordial and he never saw mean-spiritedness in Yeutter. "Clayton was very much a free-market advocate," Kerrey remembers. "We had some disagreements about the role of government in agriculture. [But] every time I had a conversation with Clayton, I realized I [was] in the presence of someone extremely smart, and he was. . . . I admired him a lot."[87]

To be sure, Yeutter complimented Kerrey when he felt it was appropriate—or when Kerrey's views comported with his. In early 1997 he dropped Kerrey a note after Albert R. Hunt, a columnist for the *Wall Street Journal*, wrote a laudatory piece applauding Kerrey's desire to partly privatize Social Security as part of an overhaul of entitlement programs, as well as recounting criticisms Kerrey had of President Clinton.[88] Yeutter's note called the piece "splendid" and said to Kerrey, "You had some mighty substantive, worthwhile things to say. Congratulations on a terrific piece."[89]

There was also some bad blood between Yeutter and Harkin. In April 1989 the Iowa Democrat accused Yeutter of "telling Iowa just to kiss off" after Yeutter told Harkin in a Senate Agriculture Committee meeting that federal budget restraints would make it difficult to meet a request for aid for drought-ravaged farmers in southern Iowa. Harkin told reporters afterward that he was shocked by Yeutter's attitude that state government should pick up the tab.[90] Yeutter fired a note off to Harkin:

> Tom, the attached [newspaper clip] is a cheap shot. You know very well that finding money for water programs in Iowa or anywhere else is enormously difficult under present budgetary constraints. And it is tough not just for the Secretary of Agriculture but for the Appropriations Committees as well. Nor do I believe it is unreasonable for Iowa and other states to provide support in this area. Most state government budgets these days are in far better shape than is our budget here in D.C. Your statements may make good politics back home, but they are grossly unfair to me. What goes around comes around![91]

Congressional debate over the farm bill was lively, sharp, and time-consuming for Yeutter and the Bush administration. As Yeutter told a friend, U.S. ambassador to Greece Michael G. Sotirhos, in August 1990, "We've been inundated by the farm bill debate, which has been a rugged exercise. In an election year, farm state congressmen have no self-discipline at all!"[92] When the dust settled on the argument in the fall of 1990, Yeutter wrote to President Bush, making note of the "psychological and political warfare" that surrounded the bill, which clocked in at 719 pages, more than twice as long as the 306-page 1985 farm legislation.

In the end, however, Yeutter told Bush it had turned out well for those committed to market approaches. Price supports were higher on some commodities than Yeutter would have liked, and federal support programs on sugar and peanuts were not changed. "But we did sustain the market oriented direction of the 1985 Bill, and we were able to build in more planting flexibility than farmers have [had] in many years." The bill didn't sit well with everyone, he noted. "Not surprisingly, most farm groups believe they've taken an inordinately large hit, and a few want to get rid of the Secretary of Agriculture! But they'll be okay if the rest of the package is real, and if it brings about a reduction in interest rates," he wrote. "We emerged from the farm bill debate with positive vibes on both sides of the political aisle, so we'd like to do a nice signing ceremony, perhaps here at USDA."[93]

Getting the bill passed required a heavy personal touch by Yeutter. He worked one-on-one with Washington legislators—including Republicans from farm states who had long been wedded to domestic subsidies—and he made persuasive economically based arguments about the value of boosting exports that won most legislators over, Sununu recalls. "Clayton really was the point man."[94]

The 1990 bill did not go as far as Yeutter and others in the Bush administration would have liked, says former USDA under secretary Crowder.[95] Such bills, after all, ultimately are the work of Congress, and the administration has limited input. But the measure did give farmers more autonomy to choose the mix of crops they would grow and set the stage for a later measure, the Freedom to Farm bill of 1996, which went much farther toward ending the government's supply management efforts. As grain surpluses soared in the following two years, however, the pendulum on policy swung back, and Congress wound up enacting measures through 1998 that repudiated much of what farmers took to deriding as the "Freedom to Fail" bill.[96] One major culprit was the Asian financial crisis of 1997, which drove the collapse of the commodity markets, rendering inadequate the direct payments to farmers that were sketched out under the 1996 legislation and ratcheting up farm foreclosures.[97]

Soon after getting the Farm Bill of 1990 approved and signed, Yeutter resigned as secretary of agriculture, effective March 1, 1991, to assume the chairman's post at the Republican National Committee. In his January 25, 1991, memo of resignation, Yeutter admitted that the bill was "not a perfect piece of legislation." However, he said, "it is certainly a respectable work product that balances well innumerable sensitive and divergent interests," with "aggressive export assistance programs, increased research efforts, and added production flexibility for farmers. The new act also encourages tree plantings through your America the Beautiful initiative, and fosters our domestic food assistance programs that help so many needy Americans."[98]

For his part, Bush responded that he was pleased with the measure, telling Yeutter it was something "of which we can both be proud." Bush wrote, "It is a market-oriented bill that keeps our farmers competitive, keeps our rural areas environmentally sound, and lets farmers make more of their own production decisions." The president also complimented Yeutter on other achievements, including the development of ethanol, encouragement of rural economic development, increased opportunities for women and minorities at the USDA, boosts to the Women, Infants and Children food program and similar programs, "and bringing balance and good common sense to a number of delicate food safety and environmental issues."[99]

Yeutter's time as ag secretary infuriated critics who couldn't abide the market-oriented changes he pressed for, shifts in entrenched policies that they had long tried to preserve. Some derided both the 1990 Farm Bill's tilt away from government support and Yeutter's efforts to open foreign markets. At an NFO convention in late 1990, the organization's president, DeVon Woodland, branded Yeutter "an internationalist at heart" and argued that his efforts to promote world trade had failed. He assailed Yeutter as "a bureaucrat with no loyalty to U.S. farmers" who was out to "make millions pursuing his goal of a new world economic order devoid of family farmers." Woodland argued that the farm bill would "not give family farmers even minimum wage." Although "it protects the environment, it protects food stamps and nutritional programs, [and] it protects ag research," he said, the bill "has nothing for the farmer."[100]

Woodland's broadsides drew a sharp rebuke from Yeutter, who said he expected better of the farm-group leader, whom he apparently knew. Yeutter called his comments "simply untruthful" and "nonsense." If he had no loyalty to U.S. farmers, for instance, Yeutter said he would have left government early on "rather than making the family, personal and financial sacrifices that have been involved in spending the past two years in my present position. There are not many Americans who have devoted the time and energy to U.S. agriculture that I have over the past forty years. If all of those sixteen-hour days constitute 'no loyalty,' I've certainly miscalculated." And he said opening foreign markets would give U.S. farmers the chance to boost their income.[101]

In fact, Yeutter made great financial and personal sacrifices in several jobs in government, which paid far less than his work at the Chicago Mercantile Exchange or in practicing law. As *Successful Farming* magazine noted in its November 1989 profile of Yeutter, the $99,500 that the secretary of agriculture position's paid annually was a fraction of what he could have earned in the private sector. And the work—at least, Yeutter's approach to it— was brutal, with eighteen-hour days, seven days a week. "For five weeks this spring he had only two free evenings at home," the magazine reported about his work life in that busy year.[102] He had turned down lucrative opportunities at law firms—including one from a Chicago-based firm that would have paid him more than $750,000—along with offers from several Wall Street brokerage houses and universities.[103] His potential workplaces had included Wall Street's Drexel Burnham Lambert, the Hill & Knowlton public relations firm, Land O'Lakes, and the Omaha-based law firm of Kutak, Rock & Campbell.

Even as he felt keenly drawn to public service, as a child of the Depression Yeutter was mindful of money. He rallied to the defense of his youngest son, Van, when a parking slipup threatened to prove costly in Chicago at the time of Van's wedding in early 1991. Yeutter protested a $110 towing fee that the city of Chicago levied when his son's car was towed from a no-parking area on a snowy day. He argued that the charge was not fair, citing the weather and perhaps nervousness that Van felt because of his impending wedding. "We had no choice but to pay the towing charge the following day, but it was not a happy experience under the circumstances," Yeutter wrote, pleading for reconsideration.[104]

Always frugal, Yeutter also wound up getting audited by the IRS for his 1986 tax return, though that may have been because he had overpaid the government some $60,000 that year (and $38,000 the following year), when he was earning big paychecks from the Chicago Mercantile Exchange.[105] Recalls his longtime

Nebraska friend Allen Beermann, "He watched his dollars."[106] The Yeutters didn't live ostentatiously. Van remembers that his parents didn't buy fancy cars and bought comfortable but not showy houses. Yeutter didn't send Van or his sister to the exclusive private schools that some upper-end Chicago executives picked for their children, and the older boys went to public high school in Nebraska. Elitism "wasn't his approach," says Van. "My dad was salt of the earth for sure."[107]

And he remained an economics teacher, giving NFO chief Woodland a lesson in his response to his caustic comments. "Well managed family farm operations are doing mighty well today, as you already know, and I have ample confidence that they'll continue to do well in the future," he wrote. "In a capitalistic society we will always have attrition, among farmers and all other businesses. That is the way it should be, for those of us who believe in that system as compared to socialism or other comparable systems. That's what made this country great, and that's why you and I and most other Americans have a much better quality of life than people in most other countries of the world."

Ending his retort to Woodland on a personal note, Yeutter mentioned that he would leave the Department of Agriculture shortly, as he planned to take up the chairmanship of the Republican National Committee. "I am deeply disappointed that your final message to me is the one articulated above," Yeutter said. "Life for all of us has enough challenges as it is. We ought to be able to treat our fellow man with more decency than your statement evidences."[108]

Despite the attacks of such naysayers, Yeutter stuck to his guns in preferring marketplace solutions to government programs. As he left the department, he wrote to a friendly columnist from Florida, Barbara A. Leinberger, to summarize his views. He said that people in many agricultural organizations saw things differently than they claimed publicly. "Many will concede privately that traditional farm programs are rapidly going the way of horse-drawn machinery. You are correct in asserting that American agriculture must learn to depend on its own efficiencies and competitiveness, and worry less about government safety nets. Safety nets will remain for a time, but they'll clearly shrink in magnitude and importance as time passes. The political support for them no longer exists, and what support remains will diminish over time."[109] Indeed, during the farm bill debate a couple of months earlier, Yeutter told former secretary of agriculture Butz in a memo that the administration was "getting farm bill flak from the groups who are most addicted to government programs, but nothing really troublesome."[110]

But Yeutter also made clear in his letter to Leinberger that the changes didn't mean that government had no role in helping farmers. Government was central to such tasks as negotiating with other governments in the Uruguay Round, along with selected bilateral bargaining. "Once the doors are open through negotiations it then becomes essentially a private sector challenge to produce what consumers around the world want to buy, and sell skillfully to them," Yeutter asserted.[111]

Indeed, Yeutter's global push at the Department of Agriculture to boost trade was applauded in many circles. For instance, the *Journal of Commerce* editorialized in January 1991 that the U.S. government had lost a "powerful spokesman for free trade" with his departure. "It took someone with his high international profile and blustery manner to stand tough before the European Community on agricultural subsidies," the newspaper said. "U.S. expectations in agriculture have been deflated since the Uruguay Round of GATT talks foundered. But any movement by our GATT partners toward more market-oriented agriculture can be credited largely to Mr. Yeutter's bold blow for free trade at the outset."[112] Yeutter responded with a letter thanking the editor for the comments and adding that most Americans did not understand how much was at stake in the Uruguay Round in all fields, including agriculture. He advised the editor to have his reporters watch the upcoming negotiations closely, for they could prove to be a major turning point—as indeed they would, but not for a few years yet.[113]

Even more than wrestling with old policies and the farmers who clung to them, Yeutter was preoccupied throughout his time as ag secretary—and, indeed, all through his time earlier as U.S. trade representative and afterward in several roles—with the Uruguay Round of tariff reduction talks. They took many twists as the European Community fought changes Yeutter pressed for. In November 1990 Yeutter wrote to his old friend, former secretary of agriculture Butz, "The Uruguay Round has now become an incredible brawl, with the European Community being as intransigent as ever. France and Germany are the principal villains in the piece. The next month will tell the tale of that exercise."[114]

Soon after, the Uruguay Round talks fell apart in Brussels, a short but sharp plunge in their roller-coaster ride. At that point, Yeutter was still serving as secretary of agriculture, and his main role was supporting his successor, U.S. trade representative Carla Hills. "As I came through Brussels a week later it was evident that the Community was terribly embarrassed by what had occurred," Yeutter advised President Bush in December 1990. "With the exception of Japan and Korea (both of whom hid behind the EC's skirts) everyone in the world was appalled by the Community's stonewalling on agriculture for four solid days. [EC president] Jacques Delors complained that we were treating the EC like a leper by lining up the world against them, but they brought that problem on themselves."[115]

No one on either side was seeing eye to eye in Brussels, says Crowder. The parties disagreed on all the major points and met only because a preset timetable called for a meeting. "We were not ready for that meeting—no one was," Crowder recalls. "We did not agree on tariffication, we did not agree on export subsidies, and [on] domestic support levels. We did not agree on any of it."[116]

Nonetheless, Yeutter believed that attitudes among many members of the European Commission, the executive group of the twelve-nation EC, had changed, saying that many leaders wanted a deal on agriculture and on the talks overall. But he noted the French, who had to contend with sometimes violent protests by their farmers, and the Germans persisted in obstructionism. "It is obvious that [German] Chancellor [Helmut J. M.] Kohl is sensitive to concerns—particularly in France—that Germany may begin to dominate all of Europe," he wrote to Bush. "To assuage those concerns he had embarked upon a handholding exercise, particularly with [French president François M.] Mitterrand, and specifically on agriculture. That is jeopardizing the entire Round, of course, but so far that seems to be a price Kohl is willing to pay. Unless we or others can change his mind it will be impossible to bring the Round to a successful conclusion."[117]

Much of the round's fate would turn on such complex economic issues and the powerful constituencies that each side had to deal with. But putting those aside, much of Yeutter's success turned on his personal chemistry with other ministers. For instance, he got on well with Ray MacSharry, the European commissioner for agriculture and rural development from 1989 to 1993, according to Crowder. MacSharry, who at one point posed for a magazine photo arm-wrestling with Yeutter, proved to be "a key player" in scaling back some of the community's protectionist approach to agriculture, Crowder says.[118]

In the round's elaborate diplomatic chess match, Yeutter wrote, the game plan he and Hills were following was to cut a deal on agriculture and the other issues with the European Commission leaders, "bring the rest of the world along too, and then force the EC hierarchy to respond." He added, "I find it hard to believe that France and Germany would have the political arrogance to reject such a package."[119] The American demands in agriculture were stiff, however: a 90 percent cut in export subsidies, a 75 percent cut in import barriers, and a 75 percent cut in "distortive internal support programs" over ten years. The EC and Japan balked, seeking smaller cuts, with Japan wanting to stick with a total import ban on rice.[120] For its part, the EC proposed a 30 percent cut in farm subsidies, which translated into a 15 percent cut from current levels because it was based on levels in 1986, when the Uruguay Round started.[121]

EC officials had better ways to support their farmers than the trade-distorting export subsidies, Yeutter argued. He pointed to environmental set-asides, programs that would pay farmers to take vulnerable land out of production and put it into conservation— something the United States had long done. They could also provide direct payments to farmers, unlinked to production, he maintained. Or they could create rural development programs. All such efforts would interfere less with markets than subsidies on exports did. "All that is needed in the EC or anywhere else, is the creativity to respond to this policy challenge in a manner that is sensitive not only to one's own farmers, but to farmers everywhere," Yeutter wrote to the editor of the *International Herald Tribune* after the paper published an article on the collapse of the Uruguay Round.[122]

Nonetheless, Yeutter hoped to nail down a deal by the end of January 1991. As it happened, the frictions remained too great and the talks dragged on until November 1992, when the European Union and the United States resolved most differences in the Blair House Accord. That accord—in which the all-important agricultural issues were resolved—"was the deal that cut the Gordian knot in the talks," recalls Council on Foreign Relations senior fellow Edward Alden. U.S. Trade Representative Michael "Mickey" Kantor cemented the deal with his global colleagues in Geneva in December 1993.[123]

The trade officials finally signed the pact in Morocco in 1994, a formality that established the World Trade Organization to replace the former system on January 1, 1995. In the end, the many years and winding turns of negotiations yielded a major breakthrough that liberalized exports from the United States to most of the world and scaled back the drive toward export subsidies among many of the country's trading partners. "We have now stopped that export subsidy train that has been hurtling toward us, and we have turned it around and it is now moving slowly (but, hopefully, inexorably) in the right direction," Yeutter wrote to a USDA official in January 1995. "That in itself is just an immense accomplishment."[124]

Yeutter's successes in prying open foreign markets took time and patience, things many hard-pressed farmers didn't have when he was secretary of agriculture. But for each critic who wanted him out of that position, others were troubled by his plans to quit the job in early 1991. "You have begun a secular change in agriculture that must be continued," a New Jersey farmer wrote him, pleading for him to stay at Ag. "We need free markets on a global basis. Your conviction and courage to stand up and fight for this important American need (particularly at this latest GATT round) is crucial in the process."[125]

Responding, Yeutter wrote that the administration's "relentless pressure for reform" in agricultural policy worldwide was then just beginning to bear fruit. He reassured the farmer that he would stay in the fight even as he moved to lead the Republican National Committee, saying, "That organization has been essentially rudderless since Lee Atwater's illness, and that is not a good way to prepare for the 1992 election cycle. So it is essential that I move, but I will try to provide some counsel from the sidelines as the agricultural reform process continues to unfold."[126]

Yeutter almost always took the time to reply to those who sent him letters, whether they slammed or praised him. In mid-1989 a nine-and-half-year-old girl from Eureka, California, Serena Forbes, wrote to him about her problems as the youngest in her class after skipping a grade. She was a year younger than her fellow fifth graders and complained in her handwritten note, "They always put me down," and said the others wouldn't let her play handball. She also was, by her account, one of the smartest in the class.[127] After reading her note to the senior staff at the Department of Agriculture, Yeutter sympathized with Serena about how difficult other children could be: "I suspect that some of them may be just a little jealous of your excellent mind too. Kids often pick on schoolmates who are smarter than they are, but deep down they are envious, and they wish there were as smart as you are. . . . I had some of the same problems you have when I was a little kid, and my advice, for whatever it is worth, is to just keep doing the right thing, study hard, be friendly, and practice the Golden Rule and you'll be just fine."[128]

11

No Professional Machiavellian

The period from the middle of 1990 through the opening of 1993 proved to be harrowing for the country and particularly for the GOP. War and recession preceded economic malaise that ultimately ended the one-term presidency of George H. W. Bush. For Yeutter, the years brought rapid back-to-back career changes—leadership of the Republican National Committee, a post as domestic counselor to President Bush in the White House, and a role as deputy campaign manager for Bush's reelection effort—as well as a major global success and a big disappointment for him. In the end, he wound up outside of government again, for the last time.

Much of the early period was colored by the most momentous event of President Bush's tenure, the war with Iraq. After Iraqi president Saddam Hussein invaded neighboring Kuwait in August 1990, Bush rallied Western nations to send a coalition of military forces—mostly American troops—to the Middle East. The Persian Gulf War's defining events included Operation Desert Shield, a military buildup in August 1990 in Saudi Arabia, followed on January 17, 1991, by the fast-moving Operation Desert Storm to crush Iraq's defenses and war-making facilities, and then on February 24 by the launch of Operation Desert Sabre, a move on Iraq that smashed its crippled forces in just three days.[1]

Yeutter backed the war effort. He sent the president a commentary from Nebraska's *Lincoln Journal* in which a former classmate of his, Gerald E. Matzke, compared Bush to President Abraham Lincoln. Matzke wrote that Bush "must know that the agony of following his own and the conscience of the world may bring him temporary denigration and public dissent. We know, however, that history and mankind will bless him in later and more peaceful days, even as we now revere and respect President Lincoln's refusal to retreat from his resolute dedication to his principles during our Civil War."[2] At first many Americans opposed the war, with a Gallup poll in late 1990 reporting that 55 percent said they wanted to avoid war when given a choice among withdrawal, waiting for sanctions to work, or starting a war if Iraq did not leave Kuwait; a slight majority, 53 percent, favored war when given only the options of going to war or not doing so.[3] Legislators were similarly split, as a dramatic vote on Capitol Hill on January 13, 1991, showed. The U.S. Senate narrowly authorized Bush to go to war by a 5-vote margin—a vote of 52 to 47, with 45 Democrats opposing the effort. In the House, the vote was more favorable but still split, with 250 for the war and 183 against.[4]

Public sentiment shifted dramatically as the war proceeded, however. Eighty-four percent of Americans quizzed by Gallup supported Bush's decision to move forward with the ground war on February 24, 1991, and even a year after the lightning-quick victory, polls indicated that 63 percent believed the war was worth fighting. For his part, President Bush basked in that victory, receiving the highest job approval rating—89 percent—that any president had gotten since Gallup began asking the question in the 1930s. His approval rating after the cease-fire in the fighting even eclipsed that given President Truman (87 percent) in June 1945, after Germany's surrender in World War II.[5]

But there were critics, and they included Nebraska Democratic senators Robert Kerrey and James Exon, among many other Democrats. Yeutter lambasted his fellow Nebraskans. When a Norfolk, Nebraska, woman sent Yeutter a letter defending their criticisms of the war as part of "an honest discussion or debate," Yeutter bristled, saying he was holding them and other Democrats who opposed the war resolution accountable for their vote. "They did pick the wrong side, Mrs. Bradford, for in the absence of a timely response by the President the war would have lasted longer and we would have lost more American lives," he wrote to the woman, Jo Ann Bradford.

> In your letter you comment that my remark was an attack on the judgment of Senator Kerrey and Senator Exon, and that is assuredly the case. Neither Senator demonstrated good judgment in analyzing the Persian Gulf situation, and Senator Kerrey in particular made some unfortunate statements about the President during the debate on this issue. Our two Senators, and a good many other Democrats in Congress (and to be fair) along with a few Republicans, had an opportunity to demonstrate support for the President, unity of the American people, and a commitment to confront aggression in the world, but they chose not to do so.[6]

Indeed, Kerrey—a frequent target of Yeutter's—had criticized Bush during the second half of 1990 in the leadup to the ground assault. "I believe that if we launch a military offensive, we will sustain thousands of casualties without military necessity, moral justification or public endorsement," the senator, who had personally been badly scarred by his experiences in Vietnam years earlier, said in written testimony to the Senate Armed Services Committee in November 1990. He, along with other Democrats, did rally to Bush's side after the vote. After the victory, Kerrey went so far as to hail the troops in a series of speeches and praise Bush for rousing the American people into a moral crusade. But for Yeutter, then mindful of the possibility that Kerrey could run against Bush for president, that was too little, too late. He scoffed at Kerrey's "negative and depressed viewpoints."[7]

The euphoria over the quick victory in Iraq, however, would not sustain Bush. The economy performed poorly in 1990, as the Federal Reserve kept interest rates high to curb inflation and oil prices soared during the buildup to the Iraq actions. The United

States slipped into recession in July 1990, and when the economy emerged from recession in March 1991, the rebound was lackluster, with unemployment worsening for fifteen months after the recovery officially began, through June 1992.[8] The economic doldrums, a jobless recovery, guaranteed an uphill fight for Bush in his reelection effort in 1992. With the war behind him, Bush's approval rate eventually slipped to 39 percent by February 1992 (before bottoming at 29 percent in August 1992).[9]

As a Republican who hewed to market-based conservative principles but was willing to compromise, Bush was in a tough spot. Conservatives in the party were angry at him for reneging on his 1988 Republican National Convention pledge of "Read my lips: no new taxes." Some rallied around right-wing columnist and broadcaster Patrick J. Buchanan, who mounted a rare primary challenge to the sitting president beginning in December 1991. Bush also lacked the charisma of his predecessor, Reagan, and was slow to get out and press the flesh in campaigning. Bush dispatched Buchanan, taking all the primary contests nationwide, but his margins were less than expected, and the fight weakened the president on the party's right flank. The 1990 budget agreement in which Bush breached the no-new-taxes pledge "devastated the Bush presidency," Yeutter said in the spring of 1993 at a forum at the University of Virginia.[10]

Bush also championed legislation that would have sat well with Yeutter's belief in government activism of specific sorts but likely offended some on the right wing.[11] The measures included the Americans with Disabilities Act, which prohibited discrimination against the disabled in employment and in the purchase of goods and services, and the Clean Air Act revisions of 1990, which used markets to curb emissions—the "cap and trade" approach—and reduced acid rain.[12] The capper was the controversial budget agreement, with more taxes, that paved the way for federal surpluses under President Clinton. "This was a presidency and an administration—and Clayton fit perfectly into it—that was there to get things done," says John Sununu, Bush's chief of staff.[13]

To make matters worse for the GOP under Bush, the Republican National Committee was in disarray the year before the race. Harvey LeRoy "Lee" Atwater, the hard-charging political operator who had piloted Bush's victory as his campaign manager in the 1988 election, had chaired the RNC ever since Bush took office. But in the spring of 1990 Atwater was diagnosed with a fatal brain cancer, and for the rest of that year the committee slipped into tumult and financial distress. Republicans cast about for a successor to Atwater, first turning to William J. Bennett, Bush's drug czar who oversaw the Office of National Drug Control Policy. But Bennett backed out in December 1991, citing financial concerns that the post's $125,000-a-year salary could not alleviate.[14]

So Bush reached out to Yeutter, whose work on the farm bill was over. Yeutter was eager to move back into the private sector at the time, but—as he had done before—he answered his president's call. "It wasn't something he wanted, but it was something he recognized the president needed," recalls Sununu, who was deeply involved in the RNC chief selection. "He knew that there were big issues that had to be addressed and he addressed them by making sure you were going in the right direction and paid attention to the details."[15]

When Yeutter accepted the post, speculation abounded about his motives. As a journalist for *Farm Futures* magazine reported, some said he wanted to be ready to take a more lucrative job in the industry he had presided over, others said the move would set him up to run for governor or senator from Nebraska or even to replace J. Danforth "Dan" Quayle as a vice presidential candidate with Bush in the 1992 election, and still others said he was "motivated by a Midwesterner's reverence for the American system of government and for the office of the president."[16] Howard G. Buffett, son of famed Nebraska investor Warren E. Buffett and a friend of Yeutter's, sent Yeutter a copy of the magazine article, pointing in a note to the final option on that list and saying, "You have my vote." In thanking Buffett in a memo, Yeutter said the writer, Jonathan Harsch, did "a good job. I was fascinated by all the speculations re my RNC motivations. You picked the right one!" Yeutter doubled down on his motivation in a letter to relatives in Germany, saying, "I made the switch simply because the President asked me to do so."[17]

Yeutter knew from the outset that the job would be daunting. He told an Omaha friend that the RNC had "deteriorated a lot because of Lee Atwater's illness," saying, "I have a major rebuilding project to do as soon as I get over there on March 1."[18] Just before moving into the job, he wrote to another friend, the U.S. ambassador to Greece, that the RNC had been "essentially rudderless since Lee Atwater's illness." He added, "It has begun to fall apart in a lot of ways. Fundraising has dropped dramatically, primarily related to the budget summit fiasco and about a third of the staff has to be laid off. So I have a lot of rebuilding to do."[19]

After President Bush named him to the RNC chairmanship, on January 7, 1991, Yeutter graciously responded, "I hope I can do the job half as well as you did while there." But he also alerted the president that he would stick to his moderate stances and approaches. "I'll not be as stridently partisan as some Republicans would prefer, but I do not believe that one must be strident in order to be politically persuasive," he wrote in a memo. "No one will replace Lee Atwater as a strategist, but between John Sununu and me, and our respective staffs and political contacts, we should be all right in that respect."[20] Perhaps fittingly, given his moderate stances, the RNC at the time was headquartered in the Dwight D. Eisenhower Republican Center in Washington DC.

Indeed, Atwater's stiletto-edged tactics offended many— including the regret-filled Atwater himself as he neared his death. As campaign manager in 1988 for Bush, Atwater tied Democratic opponent Michael S. Dukakis to a murderer and rapist, Willie Horton, in ads because Dukakis, as governor of Massachusetts, had vetoed a bill banning furloughs for murderers. He later apologized to Dukakis: "In 1988, fighting Dukakis, I said that I 'would strip the bark off the little bastard' and 'make Willie Horton his running mate.' I am sorry for both statements because it makes me sound racist, which I am not." He admitted to having been one of the most "ardent practitioners" of negative politics, saying he was "dogged" by his reputation as a fierce and ugly campaigner.[21] In Atwater's wake, Yeutter saw his role, in part, as helping "raise the level of political debate in this country while electing a lot of Republicans in the process."[22]

As with any task he took on, Yeutter would set his shoulder to the plow. "The RNC job will be a tough one, because things have deteriorated there over the past several months because of Lee Atwater's illness. The White House now recognizes that they made a mistake in [that] their earlier nomination was not universally popular, so my task is to repair all the wounds and try to get on top of things before the 1992 campaigns roll around," he wrote to Richard "Dick" Herman, an editor at Nebraska's *Lincoln Journal* who had published an editorial praising Yeutter's RNC appointment. "We'll work hard at it though, it should be a rewarding experience, and when the coach want[s] you to change positions, you change."[23]

Yeutter's appointment was hailed in some conservative circles. *National Review*, for instance, said the choice was "winning kudos all around," continuing,

> Yeutter is not a professional Machiavellian, like Atwater, nor yet a bare-knuckle philosopher, like William Bennett. But he has been in politics and government since the Nixon years. He is a conservative without being a prickly pear, and he has few enemies—an important point, given the ill feeling that has festered ever since President Bush broke the tax pledge. Finally, as someone who has worked in the Agriculture Department (under Nixon and Bush) and the U.S. trade representative's office (under Ford and Reagan), he has cut his teeth on farmers and protectionists. Republicans and Democrats should be a relief.[24]

As he had for many years, Yeutter leaned to the left of some Republican colleagues on key social issues. Feeding the needy and taking care of the helpless through welfare were high on his personal list throughout his career. He also sought a moderate course on such explosive issues as abortion. On taking the RNC post, he wrote to a friend, referring to a FarmHouse fraternity brother, psychiatrist Robert V. Radin, who evidently was concerned about the party's extremists: "Tell Bobby that I'll try to keep the Republican party from endorsing any of the extreme abortion positions going either direction. That will be a delicate balancing act, as you can tell. I've yet to be persuaded that it ought to be a political issue at all!"[25] It was no wonder, perhaps, that a Democratic Chicago political consultant, Grace Kaminkowitz, wrote about Yeutter at the time:

> Although he's conservative, Mr. Yeutter is no ideologue. He's loyal to President Bush and Chief of Staff John Sununu, but he may have a problem accommodating his neo-conservative wing. Mr. Yeutter's conservatism is in fiscal matters. He has no trackable record on so-called "social" issues that rank high on the right-wing agenda. In the Nixon administration, however, he headed the food stamp and WIC (Women, Infants, Children nutrition) programs. Earlier, he directed an agricultural assistance mission in Colombia for two years, so he shows the compassion and empathy to serve the disadvantaged. That never has been a priority of the right.[26]

From his first days in Washington, Yeutter was so easy to work with that some Democrats thought his party affiliation was almost irrelevant. "Basically, he's a pragmatist, and he's not strictly ideological," Joseph A. Kinney, a Chicago-based agricultural consultant and former legislative assistant to Democratic senator Hubert H. Humphrey, said of Yeutter in 1985. Kinney, who had worked with Yeutter in the mid-1970s, added, "If he had grown up in Detroit or Philadelphia, [he] would probably have grown up a Democrat and would have been a secretary of labor in a Democratic Administration by now. He's a Republican mainly from his background in Nebraska rather than from any ideological conviction."[27] Indeed, Yeutter had little use for ideologues, as he made clear in an address to the Republican National Committee in January 1991: "I'm a pragmatist. And I try to be practical because we have a lot of ideologues in the world who never accomplish anything," he said. "It's great to be pure, but if that means that one doesn't achieve anything, then there isn't a whole lot of reward for ideological purity or purity in any other case. So one does have to be practical and pragmatic."[28]

Such pragmatism marked him throughout his working life. "He was focused on the issue and not the politics of it," says Allen J. Beermann, a former secretary of state for Nebraska who had worked with Yeutter back in the days of the Tiemann governorship and remained friends with him throughout his life. "Clayton was always focused on the mission, not your politics. Political luminaries come and go."[29]

Yeutter saw the GOP as the better vehicle for the causes and ideas he valued, though even as RNC chairman until the end of January 1992 he swam against the party's rightward current at times. For instance, Yeutter personally opposed abortion but also felt it was not something government should be involved with.[30] Nonetheless, the 1992 GOP platform reaffirmed support for a human life amendment to the Constitution and endorsed legislation to make clear that the Fourteenth Amendment's provisions would apply to children. "We believe the unborn child has a fundamental individual right to life that cannot be infringed," the platform said, and it opposed the use of public revenues for abortion, as well as funding for organizations that advocated that.

While serving as deputy chairman for the Bush-Quayle campaign for a few months before the November 1992 election, Yeutter wrote to a Texas woman concerned about abortion to share Bush's view that he opposed abortion except in cases of rape or incest, or where the mother's life was in danger. Yeutter acknowledged that the party platform left such exceptions unclear but said the party would not take a position inconsistent with its leader's stance.[31] Bush himself had long been pro-choice, abandoning that stance only when he became Reagan's running mate in 1980.[32] The platform also derided welfare as "the enemy of opportunity and stable family life," calling it "anti-work and anti-marriage."[33]

Yeutter's tenure at the RNC was short, and some critics panned it, inaccurately, as uneventful. "But even admirers say he isn't a conceptual thinker," a reporter for the *National Journal* wrote disdainfully when Yeutter moved to the White House. "As Republican National Committee chairman for the past year, a job for which he seemed ill-suited, he left little trace."[34] The latter jab, particularly, proved to be off base, as Yeutter's work in redistricting and various tempests would show. In tapping Yeutter, Bush had bypassed a longtime campaign aide and Atwater adviser, Richard N. Bond, among other candidates. Even though Bond was seen as politically more savvy—more familiar with the details of building an organization, fundraising, and getting out the vote—Bush wanted someone with stature and gravitas for the job, the *Washington Post* reported. He got that in Yeutter, and when Yeutter left, Bond took the helm at the RNC.[35]

Certainly, Yeutter brought his usual high level of energy to the RNC post. He traveled to nearly forty states, speaking at more than one hundred events, Yeutter reported in reviewing his work at a January 1992 RNC meeting. He stabilized the staff after cutbacks that preceded his arrival at the committee. He put fundraising on target and "enhanced" relations with African Americans, Hispanics, Asian Americans, and Americans with disabilities, though he said party leaders had "no unrealistically high expectations" about successes with such constituencies. And he predicted success in reelecting Bush at the end of that year—something which was not to be.[36]

He dealt with plenty of challenges at the committee. One was the embarrassment—and for a short time, the threat—posed by David E. Duke, the former Ku Klux Klan leader and a Republican member of Louisiana's House of Representatives. Duke ran for the governor's post in Louisiana in 1991. Early on, the election looked like a toss-up, with Democratic incumbent Edwin W. Edwards drawing just 33.7 percent of the vote to Duke's 31.7 percent in the October 1991 first round, setting up a runoff in mid-November. Yeutter warned President Bush in a memo that Duke had "effectively conned both the media and the people of Louisiana. . . . He's a populist, protest candidate and anyone of that ilk has considerable appeal when things aren't going well. And they haven't been going well economically in Louisiana for several years."[37]

A couple of weeks before the final voting in Louisiana, Yeutter cautioned Bush, "Anyone who predicts a winner in the Edwards/Duke race is flying blind. Immense amounts of money are now flowing into that race, on both sides, with a lot of Jewish money going to Edwards and a lot of blacks having registered in recent days. But it should be obvious by now that Duke is a very skillful demagogue, particularly in mounting an economic protest appeal. . . . A heavy black vote for Edwards will probably wipe out nearly all, if not all, Republican candidates for state offices."[38] President Bush weighed in against Duke in the final weeks of the campaign, calling Duke "an insincere charlatan" and rejecting his claims that he had undergone a Christian conversion and turned away from bigotry.[39]

Yeutter was unequivocal about Duke the week before the November 1991 election in Louisiana. If voters chose the former KKK chief as governor, he said, the GOP would "ignore him" and "condemn him as a reprehensible representative of the American public." Yeutter predicted no good could come of such a choice: "We hope that the people of Louisiana will have the good judgment not to permit their state to self-destruct next Saturday. In my judgment, a Duke election would mean severe economic losses for that state over time because of the impact on investment and business activity. But beyond that, to have someone of that ilk governing a major state in this country or any office, for that matter, is simply indefensible."[40] In the end, Duke lost the runoff, garnering 38.8 percent of the vote, while Edwards trounced him with 61.2 percent.

But Duke generated attention. Writer Michael Kinsley, in an essay in *Time* magazine shortly after the gubernatorial election, called him "the face of American decline" and warned about how Duke was tapping into anger among "white people who feel they are being cheated of their American birthright by blacks, immigrants, liberals, New Yorker and similar bogeys." Kinsley—in what might have been an eerie bit of prescience for the 2016 election of Donald J. Trump as president—wrote that Duke was "the political expression" of economic decline, the stalling of the steady rise in the average person's prosperity that had previously been the course for many Americans.[41] Yeutter congratulated Kinsley on "a very perceptive piece." He added, "We need to make sure we don't talk ourselves into having an inferiority complex as a nation, but we also need to begin to realize that we can't have our cake and eat it too in economic policy. You delivered those and other messages in superb fashion."[42]

Duke continued to be a pest for the party. He had run in the 1988 presidential primaries as a Democrat, drawing few votes, and then had run unsuccessfully for the U.S. Senate as a Republican in 1990. After losing the race for the governorship in Louisiana in 1991, he ran again for the presidency as a Republican. In December 1991 he told Yeutter that he was disinclined to run as anything but a Republican, but he threatened to mount a third-party candidacy if party leaders denied him the right to appear on the ballot. "For party bosses to set themselves up as the Commissars of 'political correctness' is arrogant, heavy-handed and unconscionable," Duke thundered. "If it ever comes to the widespread attention of the public, it will backfire on you."[43] He did run and wound up garnering less than 1 percent of the vote. He ran for several offices afterward, failing each time, making headlines again in 2016 when he backed Trump for president.

While Yeutter had no use for the fringe likes of Duke, he remained a gentleman with many political opponents. For instance, he traded cordial letters with an economics giant, Harvard professor John Kenneth Galbraith, a liberal stalwart. When Galbraith learned from a 1991 news account that Yeutter had earned his undergraduate degree in animal husbandry and his doctorate in agricultural economics, he popped Yeutter a friendly note about how they had earned similar undergraduate degrees. "So may I say, have I; I am the first senior Harvard professor for some years, perhaps ever, to be so sanctioned in, as it was called at the Ontario Agricultural College, An. Hub.," wrote Galbraith. "Obviously with these common qualifications one or the other of us has strayed from the strictly indicated course of academic discipline and political belief. And, alas, on this there would, I suppose, be no agreement. I'm sure we do agree on our so wisely chosen preparation."[44]

Delighted at their similar backgrounds, Yeutter wrote back and told Galbraith he felt he was "in great company." He said it was probably their undergraduate degrees that made them "both so determined (perhaps bullheaded would be the term applied by many!)." Yeutter added that one of the most valuable courses he ever took was livestock judging, "because it taught me to be decisive, concise, and hopefully persuasive (My wife says I have since forgotten the concise part!)." He struck a diplomatic tone with the eighty-two-year-old Canadian-born economist, who had served in the administrations of four Democratic presidents, starting with FDR: "We may have drawn apart a bit academically and politically, but that's what makes our society exciting and challenging. I suspect our fundamental objectives in life are essentially identical. Irrespective of our views I must add that I've been an everlasting admirer of your prose. You are unquestionably the finest writer the economics profession has ever produced."[45]

As an economist, Yeutter had to battle economic ignorance even at high levels within his own party at times. When the economy was in the doldrums in November 1991, a year before the Bush-Clinton election, Yeutter saw the malaise as the major threat to the president's reelection. In a memo circulated among other GOP leaders, he advised Bush to address that, drawing attention to the fact that the Reagan-Bush years included the longest peacetime recovery ever (to that point). And as any good economist might, he noted that the economy was cyclical, with recessions to be expected "from time to time." Secretary of Housing and Urban Development Jack F. Kemp, a friend whom Yeutter at times saw in church, annotated the memo by hand and sent it back to Yeutter, calling that observation "Bull 'feathers,'" and claiming it was "not true at all and anti-American!"[46] In fact, there had been ten recessions since World War II at that point.[47] (Kemp, who was often at odds with the White House even as he served in the cabinet, also asked Yeutter why he wasn't defending him "against the crap out of W.H.")

Yeutter managed to maintain good relations among warring factions in the White House and outside. As a general rule, he seemed to value personal relations over political ones. For instance, he congratulated Democrat Jay Rockefeller of West Virginia on his reelection to the Senate in 1990 in a letter that Rockefeller described as "typical of you, Clayton—generous and warm." Further, Rockefeller in his handwritten response added, "And do you know what—I don't think your heart was really anything but 'for' me. We have just become too good friends." Striking a bipartisan note, Rockefeller said, "Anyway, if there has to be Republicans (as I once told my Uncle David), they should all be like you, Clayton. I'm rooting for Nebraska! Jay."[48]

Even when the stakes were the highest, Yeutter proved to be as gracious in defeat as he was in victory. When Bill Clinton beat incumbent Bush in the fall of 1992, Yeutter, then Bush's deputy campaign manager, offered his "heartiest" congratulations in letters to Clinton and his running mate, Al Gore. "We worked mighty hard over these past several weeks, but you and your organization ran a splendid campaign," he wrote. "After all those primaries and a long, hard general election campaign, you and your family certainly deserve to savor the win and get a little rest before assuming the most challenging job in the world. As a part of the loyal opposition, I wish you great success over the next four years. Just remember that problems here and abroad are formidable, but never insurmountable."[49]

Respectful of many of his political opponents, Yeutter also could look past partisan differences to befriend people on both sides of the aisle, to the point of spending leisure time together. As RNC chairman, for instance, he got along well with Ronald H. Brown, who chaired the Democratic National Committee at the time. The two appeared on TV interview programs together, debating issues. When Yeutter stepped down from the RNC to take a position at the White House, he wrote to Brown in February 1992, joking that he would "try hard to cause [Brown] more trouble at the White House than [he] might have at the RNC!" But Yeutter also waxed serious:

I have really enjoyed sharing these political party responsibilities with you this past year, and I was looking forward to doing so the rest of the way. Having a sound, credible party structure is important to the operation of our democratic society, and I truly believe we were both making positive contributions in that direction. . . . Jeanne and I both cherish our friendship with you and Alma, and I am glad we had at least a little time together in Hawaii a couple of weeks ago. I fear we'll not have that opportunity again until November, but we can then look forward to renewing that friendship irrespective of the political outcome.[50]

He got along well, too, with E. Benjamin Nelson, a Democrat who served as governor of Nebraska all through the 1990s and as a two-term U.S. senator from the state until 2013. Nelson had known Yeutter since Yeutter's graduation from law school in Nebraska. "I had great respect for his intellect and his capacity to get things done," Nelson says. He credits Yeutter with paving the way for the growth of trade, particularly in agriculture, between Nebraskans and the world. Nelson led seven trade missions to Asia as governor, moves that helped boost global exports from the state by more than 300 percent. Yeutter "certainly had a hand in making that a possibility," Nelson asserts. "He had a big hand in opening the trade lanes for agriculture."[51]

Throughout his time in partisan politics, Yeutter remained the gregarious, back-slapping midwesterner he had always been. But that approach—and the 1950s-male attitude he sometimes exhibited toward women—could hit flat notes. In one case, in early 1992, he infuriated a California businesswoman who had contributed $100,000 to President Bush's reelection effort by walking up to her at a reception for big donors and saying, "And who do you belong to, little lady?" The businesswoman, Kathryn G. Thompson, responded with a sharply worded column in the *Los Angeles Times.* "Well, Mr. Yeutter, I've managed to get myself out of the kitchen long enough to climb to the top of the Orange County home-building business, and if you read the paper, you'll note that I'm quoted from time to time on economic and business matters."

She pointed out that she had not been appointed to her job, unlike Yeutter. "I learned early that any success I would achieve had to be earned. So I and many other successful women have developed something our leaders in this nation don't have and desperately need, an ethic of success through struggle."[52]

Yeutter could handle fair criticism, and he was both apologetic and nuanced in his response. He said he didn't recall making the comment and added, "But if you quoted me accurately, that was an insensitive comment, and your criticism was appropriate. At the same time, I wonder whether such a fierce counter attack was really necessary." He bristled at the implication, moreover, that he had not earned his success. "Kathryn, I learned that lesson long before you did, when I was growing up as a farm boy in the middle of Nebraska in the Dust Bowl of the 1930s. I may have had some appointments through the years, but I've had far more achievements in the non-appointive category, all of which have come from a lot of blood, sweat, and tears."

Far from being someone who did nothing to "afford women an opportunity to advance on their own," he argued that he had done as much to advance opportunities for women as almost any leader in the country. For example, he counted five women in subcabinet posts when he was secretary of agriculture, and he had worked to get one named executive director of the World Food Program in Rome, one of the highest international spots ever achieved by an American woman. He also had a lot to do with Barbara H. Franklin being named secretary of commerce. "In summary," Yeutter concluded, "the next time you do an article of this nature I hope you'll do a little more checking to find out whether you really want to twist the dagger quite that much."[53] Terry Savage, a former TV reporter and commentator who knew Yeutter when he ran the Chicago Mercantile Exchange, pushed back on Thompson's criticism in an interview with me, praising Yeutter's personal warmth and saying that he was "always charming and respectful."[54]

At times during Yeutter's leadership of the RNC, issues he cared most about and the troublesome stances of longtime opponents coalesced. In February 1992 *Wall Street Journal* columnist Paul A. Gigot wrote a piece attacking "the illusory politics of protectionism," which he suggested presidential hopeful Robert Kerrey practiced. The Nebraskan aired a campaign commercial of himself striding onto a hockey rink, saying, "What's happening in the world economy is like a hockey game where others guard their goal and keep our products out, while we leave our net open. . . . I'll tell Japan if we can't sell in their market, they can't sell in ours. And if they don't get the message, they'll find out this president is ready to play a little defense too." But as Gigot argued, such protectionism and economic nationalism were failing as a campaign theme, and blaming foreigners for domestic economic woes was a nonstarter—something a leading rival Democratic presidential contender, Senator Paul E. Tsongas of Massachusetts, acknowledged in his ads. Kerrey pulled his commercial a week and a half later, after it drove down his poll numbers, and he admitted it was a mistake.[55]

Yeutter dropped Gigot a note, complimenting him for "another exceptional job on an issue dear to my heart." Even though some Democrats attacked protectionism, Yeutter wrote, "As your article implies, the Democrats are just chomping at the bit to make protectionism work for them in 1992, but so far they are not having any more luck than they did in 1988. Let's hope that continues. Thanks for doing such a fine job of putting that issue in its proper perspective."[56]

He could also point to enduring contributions as RNC chairman, some of which look questionable in light of later events. He oversaw the once-every-decade redistricting effort, which contributed to Republican state and congressional victories in many states for years afterward. Columnist and CNN host Rowland Evans Jr. in May 1991, referring to the effort to redraw political boundaries, said, "You might even call it the Yeutter plan." Evans pointed to efforts in Alabama to put Black voters into specific voting areas so they would have their own Congress members, thus creating Black and white districts but also locking in Republican seats. At the time, although 25 percent of the Alabama population was African American, no Congress member from the state was Black. Yeutter, in an appearance with Evans and cohost Robert D. S. Novak, argued his plan would work to benefit minorities. "But I don't see it as being, in essence a quota bill," Yeutter said. "I see it as leveling the playing field that has clearly been tilted against Republicans and minorities for the last ten years. And it seems to me correcting that tilt is in everybody's interest."[57]

Later, in a January 1993 letter to David S. Broder, a columnist for the *Washington Post*, Yeutter called redistricting "one of the big political stories of the past two years that is still not well recognized." He wrote, "We quietly went about winning about 90% of those battles, just the opposite of what occurred a decade earlier. As a consequence, the Republican party (assuming good candidates) should win state legislative and House races in the '90s just as the Democrats did in the '80s."[58] Indeed, at the end of 1994 Yeutter told a friend in Nebraska, "One thing we did do right during my RNC tenure in 1991 was redistrict." While the results were masked by Bush's defeat in 1992, he said, "We got those benefits big time in 1994, and that had a lot to do not only with our gaining control of the House of Representatives, but also control of a whole host of state legislatures. Hopefully, that will permit us to really build this party into a tower of strength over the remainder of the decade."[59]

Yeutter and his RNC team didn't invent redistricting, of course, but they did seem to master it in ways that endured beyond his time. Derisively called gerrymandering, the technique has been used at times by both parties to ensure success at the polls. By drawing district lines carefully (if often oddly), state legislators seek to protect their partisan advantages. In recent years it has become a cause célèbre among good-government advocates, as groups such as the Conference Board condemned redistricting for its "unprecedented levels of severity." In a 2018 policy brief, the board's Committee for Economic Development said:

> Both parties have thus been able to gain additional seats by crafting maps to their advantage. Republicans achieved the greater

benefit from the 2010 districting because they had control of more states where legislatures are responsible for districting, including 10 of the 15 states that gained or lost seats through reapportionment based on population shifts, and controlled more of the larger states with a greater number of congressional districts. According to an analysis of the 2016 US House races by the Associated Press, the Republicans gained as many as 22 additional US House seats as compared to the average vote share in congressional districts due to the partisan advantage achieved through the districting process.[60]

After Yeutter stabilized the RNC and officials reached out to the more nuts-and-bolts oriented Bond to run it, Bush moved to bring Yeutter closer by installing him at the end of January 1992 in the White House as a counselor for domestic policy, a new cabinet-level spot.[61] That meant he oversaw a broad range of issues on which he advised the president, including the political ramifications such policies would have in the election year. The post brought a host of new challenges, at times putting him in conflict with ambitious and sharp-elbowed White House insiders—some of whom lacked the genteel style that was second nature to Bush and Yeutter. Indeed, Yeutter once referred to "jungle warfare" in the presidential mansion.

Like Bush, Yeutter believed in good manners, unlike at least one other high-ranking person in the administration, William P. Barr, who was then serving his first stint as attorney general (he returned to the job under President Donald J. Trump). In June 1992 Yeutter got crosswise with the forty-two-year-old Barr, who was twenty years his junior, in a contentious phone call. Barr hung up on Yeutter, prompting Yeutter to scold the brusque New Yorker: "Bill, I've held three Cabinet posts and three sub-Cabinet posts in the government of this country, and I've never slammed the phone down on a colleague in all those years. In my judgment that is inexcusable personal conduct. It reflects an immaturity and impatience that should not emanate from a Cabinet officer, and a tarnishing of relationships with the White House that cannot serve the President well."[62] Yeutter copied White House chief of staff Samuel K. Skinner on the memo. Barr later "profusely" apologized, as Yeutter told Skinner in a follow-up note.[63]

A few days before the phone flap, Barr had made crime-related budget proposals that Richard G. "Dick" Darman, director of the Office of Management and Budget, thought were too costly that year. And it appeared that Barr and Darman had a prickly relationship, which Yeutter, in his well-mannered way, sought to assuage. "For whatever reason Dick is not enthusiastic about giving Barr's programs an additional boost," Yeutter wrote to Skinner in late May 1992. "In addition, he raised the question of why he wasn't invited to the meeting, an issue about which he is super sensitive, as you know. I'd suggest, Sam, that you host another session involving the two of us, Darman and Barr to see if we can make some progress on this."[64]

But Yeutter sometimes fell victim to the infighting. A few weeks before the Barr contretemps, a piece appeared in the *New Republic* accusing the Bush White House of "inertia, dithering, cynicism, and fear of failure among Bush's senior aides and Cabinet," which the author said made it difficult for Bush to package "an appealing, newsworthy domestic program." The piece said a group of advisers pressed for welfare reform, for example. When Wisconsin governor Tommy G. Thompson sought a waiver to create a state program in line with that reform drive, aimed at getting welfare recipients to work and marry, one such adviser helped speed it through, the magazine reported. "Still, there were kvetchers. Clayton Yeutter, the new domestic policy czar, suggested that the White House wait for a bigger event than the Wisconsin waiver to play up welfare reform. He was overruled. Again, Skinner gets the credit. He overruled Yeutter, figuring that if welfare reform is a good idea, why wait?"[65]

Yeutter complained to Edith E. Holiday, who as secretary of the cabinet served as primary liaison between the White House and the cabinet and federal agencies. In a memo to her, Yeutter called the magazine story "another example of the kind of petty backbiting that Pres. Bush was talking about this afternoon." Yeutter added, "This story had to have come from someone fairly close to the welfare reform announcement, and it just astounds me that some of our people would engage in this jungle warfare. It does a terrible disservice to the President."[66]

As was his wont when media outlets published work he either disputed or liked, Yeutter also wrote to the journalist, Frederic W. Barnes, about the piece. Some of the information, he said, was "completely off base." For instance, he said he was never overruled, though there were several courses of action about releasing the news discussed. "We're a lot better organized, Fred, than this article would indicate," Yeutter told the journalist. "No White House operates to perfection, particularly when experiencing the vagaries of an election year, but this one's performing a lot more smoothly today than most I've observed over the last 22 years, notwithstanding some petty internal sniping." Starting his note with a complimentary touch, Yeutter called Barnes "one of the most admired and responsible journalists around," but he then shot down all the article's core points.[67]

And Yeutter sometimes found himself in the crosshairs even of fellow Republicans on the Hill. Iowa senator Charles E. "Chuck" Grassley in March 1992 was angry that ethanol was left out of a statement of the national alternative fuels policy. The senator told a reporter for Nebraska's *Lincoln Journal* that Bush had ordered Yeutter to include ethanol. When a story about it—unflattering to Yeutter—appeared in the newspaper, Yeutter fired off a memo to William G. Rosenberg, assistant administrator of the Environmental Protection Agency, saying, "Bill, this guy may be a Republican Senator but he is a total pain in the derriere on this issue. You need not draft a response for my signature, but if you'll give me the ammunition to use I'll get a response off to him. If he keeps up, we're going to declare him persona non grata here in the White House!"[68]

Then Yeutter was indignant in his response to Grassley. "I don't appreciate being crucified in my home town newspaper, particularly when the comments are erroneous," Yeutter wrote. Bush hadn't ordered Yeutter to do anything on ethanol, he said, and the actions he took to "get the issue back on track" were completed when the president and Senator Dole called him about it. "Chuck, you shouldn't be spreading negative stories on anyone without verifying their accuracy," Yeutter said. "And you probably shouldn't be spreading them period. Finally, I sure don't believe you score points on this earth by throwing daggers at friends."[69]

As domestic counselor, Yeutter mostly focused on policies at home, but his responsibilities sometimes bled into the international arena—such as on global environmental issues of the sort that had dogged him in his ag secretary job. He kept an eye on the lead-up to the global climate change discussions at the Rio de Janeiro Earth Summit, for instance, when U.S. officials met in New York with representatives of other countries to develop a text that would be presented for adoption by more than one hundred countries at the June 1992 summit. "Congratulations on a splendid performance as the climate change negotiations over the past couple of weeks!" he wrote to Robert Reinstein, the deputy assistant secretary of state for environment, health, and natural resources, who represented the United States. "I wonder if an American negotiator has ever had the odds so heavily stacked against him! This was the United States versus the rest of the world, and the U.S. won. What a marvelous achievement, and what a testimony to your preparation, patience, and basic negotiating skills."[70]

Indeed, while substantial numbers of scientists were seeing climate change as a worrying phenomenon, some Republicans were less convinced.[71] Fearing that economic growth would be stultified, the Bush administration wanted to avoid making commitments to specific targets and timetables for restrictions on carbon dioxide emissions in any agreement that would emerge from the Rio meeting. So the agreement Reinstein hammered out in the preliminary talks sidestepped such targets. As Yeutter explained in a letter to Wyoming Republican senator Malcolm Wallop, U.S. representatives carefully chose the word *aim* in reference to language in the text about cutting greenhouse gases to 1990 levels by 2000. "As a nation, we will do our share, perhaps more than our share, but that is because we already have the process already well underway, and not because of any compulsion emanating from this proposed document," Yeutter wrote. "The word 'aim' was carefully chosen, and it does not constitute a commitment, binding or otherwise. Nor does this sentence prescribe or imply any kind or timetable."[72]

Intentionally vague as it was, the language infuriated environmentalists. Senator Gore, for instance, at a September 1992 hearing about the Rio meeting before the Senate Foreign Relations Committee, vented his anger at the administration. Gore at the time was running for vice president with presidential candidate Clinton. "As we all are now all too well aware, the Bush administration was throughout these negotiations the single largest obstacle to progress," Gore argued. "In the end, our intransigence meant that the final agreement is completely devoid of any legally binding commitments to action."

Gore, who chaired the U.S. Senate delegation to the summit and had been at odds with Yeutter, saw the environmental challenges raised at the summit in far more dire terms than did Yeutter and Bush. "The real meaning of the Earth Summit itself was also lost on President Bush. It was a true turning point in history," Gore said. "Leaders of nearly every nation on earth gathered together for the first time in a profound awareness of the true nature and magnitude of the global environmental crisis we face. Perhaps even more significantly, they realized that the alleviation of human suffering around the globe is inextricably intertwined with our efforts to relieve the building pressures on the environment. They understood that to combat the poverty, suffering and pain that afflicts so many in the world today we have to pursue economic growth that is not harmful to the environment."[73]

Years later, in 2007, Gore's environmental efforts drew praise in global circles. He shared the Nobel Peace Prize with the Intergovernmental Panel on Climate Change "for their efforts to build up and disseminate greater knowledge about man-made climate change, and to lay the foundations for the measures that are needed to counteract such change."[74]

But during the arguments of the early 1990s, Yeutter had little use for Gore's passions for environmental protection and the need to combat climate change. When a friend in Florida wrote about appearances by both men on television news program, Yeutter responded, "As you could tell, Senator Gore spends about half of his life demagoguing environmental issues, so he is a real pain on programs such as that. It is difficult to resist the temptation to really blast him!"[75] Yeutter shared his annoyance with Gore directly about a Sunday TV appearance in which the senator suggested that polluters had "a back door to the White House." Yeutter wrote to Gore, "Al, that is just untrue. In all the Earth Summit discussions I have chaired over the past several weeks, never has an argument of that nature arisen, and never have any of the 'polluters' been in to see me. It is statements like yours, Al, that cause American citizens to be cynical about their government, and that hurts everyone, including you and all other Members of Congress. All of us need to work harder at being positive about public service and public servants, rather than negative."[76]

Yeutter was concerned especially about how the issue was playing in the business community and sought to generate positive press about it. He wrote to a public liaison official in the White House in May 1992 that the climate change agreement that emerged from the New York negotiations "came out exceptionally well from our standpoint." Yeutter added, "Our business community was petrified during most of these negotiations because they thought we'd sell our souls to the Europeans and the third world. We did not do so, and they should now be mighty pleased." He said that Bush wanted to make sure the White House got the message out to the business community "so they'd start applauding such efforts, instead of criticizing us."[77]

Coming when economic conditions in the United States were poor, the timing of the Rio summit was problematic. The last thing policymakers wanted to do was depress economic growth further, particularly when they were laboring to reelect Bush. "America is in a hole. It would be as deep a hole as the Great Depression of 1929 were it not for the federal guarantees that stabilize the banking system and the $400 billion deficit," Mortimer B. Zuckerman, editor-in-chief of *U.S. News & World Report*, wrote in a commentary in July 1992:

> George Bush still doesn't get it. The White House inner circle, by all accounts, argues whether he should project optimism about the so-called recovery or concerned realism about its weakness. . . . The increase in wealth per citizen over the past two decades has been the lowest and slowest of the major industrial nations, with our lifestyle sustained only because most households now contain two wage earners. And things are getting worse. Unemployment approaching 10 million is the highest in eight years. Reaganomics has failed, as demonstrated by a new study by the Federal Reserve Bank of New York.[78]

Continuing his practice of writing to journalists when their work impressed or troubled him, Yeutter told Zuckerman he "enjoyed and appreciated much of what" the editor wrote. Diagnosing the ills in the economy was more complex than the writer could convey in a short space, and his attack on Reaganomics was "inordinately harsh," Yeutter said, but the challenges Zuckerman named for the future were real, particularly the need to control entitlement spending on health care and Social Security and to invest in education and training. Yeutter maintained that Bush was addressing such major issues and argued that what he needed was "a little more leverage on Capitol Hill," which he hoped to win in the election in November 1992.[79] Zuckerman responded a week later: "This is the first time in almost four years that I have had the opportunity to have an intelligent conversation with someone from the administration on its domestic policy. I thank you for it."[80]

Believing in his messages in each of his roles, Yeutter tended to be open and accessible with the media, those who worked with him recalled. His bluntness sometimes got him in trouble, as happened with the Canadians and his quip about culture at the 1987 Brookings Institution conference on trade, and it often left his press aides shaking their heads.[81] "He used to move the market all the time too," remembers Kelly Semrau, who worked in media relations for Yeutter at the Office of the U.S. Trade Representative (USTR) and followed him to the Department of Agriculture. "He would say things and I would be in the back of the room going, 'Oh no, there goes the corn market, there goes the wheat market.' Clayton was so honest, he would answer every question. . . . He was human. . . . He said to me, 'My mother always said it was rude not to answer.'"

Yeutter knew that the media could help him advance his agendas by putting a spotlight on problems and the solutions he put forward. Candor, he figured, paid off. "He's a study in how to work with reporters," Semrau says. "The reason he was so successful is because that man knew how to work with the press. . . . That man worked the press. . . . Now, did the press frustrate him sometimes with misquotes or whatever? Of course . . . but he knew that was part of what he had to do to shape policy, move policy, make changes, and he was willing to do it."[82]

As domestic policy counselor, Yeutter advised Bush and others about reelection strategy—and the subjects sometimes were surprising, even idiosyncratic, and occasionally involved Jeanne, his wife. When a White House official, Todd Buchholz, had dinner with Gerald L. McRaney, the star of the TV sitcom *Major Dad*, he wrote to another official, Ron Kaufman, and copied Yeutter on the note. McRaney backed Bush and volunteered to campaign for him. Dropping a note to Kaufman, Yeutter chimed in, "Ron, my wife thinks this guy is the greatest thing ever to hit the TV screen. We really ought to get him out on the campaign trail." Kaufman wrote back, saying McRaney would be at the Republican Convention in August 1992, where the actor would introduce Second Lady Marilyn T. Quayle. McRaney also spoke at several other events. The campaign enlisted other stars as well, including Cheryl Ladd of *Charlie's Angels*, Bruce Willis, and Arnold Schwarzenegger.[83]

Jeanne, whom Yeutter seemed to have won over to the GOP, had other impressions that Yeutter shared with campaign officials at times. In July 1992 he wrote to Bush's national campaign chairman,

Robert M. Teeter, about Jeanne's sense of the Clinton family. "They just don't seem like a family; it is as if they are three totally independent individuals who are rooming together," she felt, according to Yeutter. "There is quite a contrast between the way they act toward each other and the way the Gore family does. . . . There's something that just doesn't ring right about this group, and that could make a big difference in the response of the American public to them as a potential first family." Yeutter said Jeanne had "very good political instincts."[84]

Yeutter thought little of Clinton and worse of the other presidential contender, H. Ross Perot, in the three-way race shaping up for the White House in 1992. "Clinton is another mediocre Governor, just as Carter was, and he'll end up bending as far left as any other Democrat candidate—even though he may not talk that way," Yeutter told former Nebraska governor Charles Thone in June 1992. "And Perot is just a loose cannon. People who know him well feel that he'd be an absolute disaster as a President."[85]

Nonetheless, feelings about Bush's reelection chances were running low among some staffers in the White House in mid-1992, and Yeutter shared that sense with Chief of Staff Skinner. In a June 1992 memo to Skinner, Yeutter mentioned that an aide had told him, "Low level staffers here in the White House are feeling depressed these days. They see and hear all the negative political news, and it is hard for young people to keep that in perspective. If our folks are depressed, I suspect the same condition prevails in most of the departments." He suggested that scheduling events that brought out the president and vice president and a military band would "pick these folks up and give them some motivation for the final stretch of the campaign."[86]

Even Yeutter seemed discouraged about the election prospects. In early July Yeutter sounded gloomy in a letter to U.S. attorney general Richard L. Thornburgh, who had lost a special-election race for the U.S. Senate the prior November in an upset by an anti-Bush Democrat, Harris L. Wofford Jr.[87] "You can imagine how busy we are trying to live through this presidential election year! I told Jeanne I wish we could fast forward through November 3, just to get it over with, but maybe we need all the time we can get to persuade people to vote rationally," Yeutter told Thornburgh, who was serving at the United Nations as under-secretary-general. "The first inkling of the kind of funk they are in came in your campaign, but we see it everywhere now, and at all levels of government. The anti-incumbent fervor is the most ferocious I have ever seen, and it is not just a U.S. phenomenon. A lot of other countries are going through the same experience we are."[88]

It was clear to many in the White House that the future looked bleak for the GOP. "There was a sense of doom months in advance," recalls Gary Blumenthal, Yeutter's former chief of staff at the U.S. Department of Agriculture (USDA) who also served in a couple of roles in the Bush White House. In the end, he added, "Obviously, all of us in the White House were hugely disappointed, but not surprised."[89]

As the outlook for Bush's reelection grew increasingly dreary, the president switched Yeutter out of the White House and into a role as deputy campaign chairman for the Bush-Quayle reelection committee from August 31, 1992, through the November 3 election.[90] Tapping into Yeutter's talents on the stump, the campaign reached out to him as a "super surrogate" who could give speeches on behalf of Bush and Vice President Dan Quayle. According to an analysis by David E. Lynch, a reporter for the *Lincoln Journal*'s Washington bureau, Yeutter shouldered a lot of the blame for the failure of the team led by Chief of Staff Skinner to pull the Bush presidency out of its post–Persian Gulf War slump. Farmers, for instance, blamed Yeutter for initially rejecting a plan to provide export supports for a major pork sale to the Soviet Union and for EPA clean air rules that made ethanol infeasible in high smog areas. Bush ultimately reversed his stand on the pork sale supports but sided with a curious coalition of oil and environmentalist interests opposed to ethanol.[91]

But Skinner, who had succeeded the aggressive John Sununu in December 1991 after a travel expenses scandal took Sununu down, endured most of the heat for Bush's decline. Even as early as June 1992, the *Washington Post* reported that Skinner's honeymoon in the job had ended quickly: "The president's polls continued to drop, and his staff continued what seemed like a long line of amateurish political mistakes. Republicans—including Skinner's colleagues inside the White House—began anonymously knifing the new chief of staff, describing him as an odd man, aloof and overwhelmed, unable to avoid the simplest political sand traps."[92]

The cards seemed stacked against Skinner, Yeutter, and Bush, as Yeutter's experience in trying to build good relations with minorities suggested. Because shoring up the modest support the party had among African American voters was one of his initiatives, he befriended activist Jean Howard-Hill, but in the end he lost her backing of the GOP. Just days before the November 1992 vote, Howard-Hill wrote to Yeutter to say that she and her organization, the National Impact Coalition of Politically Active Women, would back Clinton and Gore in a press conference. "During that conference I also will be announcing that I will no longer be a part of the Republican Party," she said. "I have seen a great deal of suffering among the poor and working class, as well as racial and gender indifference. This has greatly disturbed me as I sometimes felt totally helpless to effectuate any substantial change as a female or black participant within the party."

Howard-Hill, who had dismantled her National Coalition of Black Republican Women and converted it into the nonpartisan National Impact Coalition, was unsparing in her assessment of some Republicans: "Although I have been welcomed by so many of you within the party, I cannot totally ignore those times when I have been called a n—— or made to feel that my presence and motives were suspect, despite the pureness of my motives to simply attract blacks to the Republican party. . . . I believe our friendship will survive my political decision and will hope that you will feel the same."[93] Yeutter wrote back to reassure her of their continuing friendship and warn her away from "the Democrat Party, with its heavy emphasis on programs that generate dependence on government," adding that he doubted it would appeal to her over time.[94] Howard-Hill, a lawyer and professor of political science at the University of Tennessee–Chattanooga, later rejoined the GOP, chairing its National Republican African American Caucus, and she ran unsuccessfully for Congress several times.

In his final months working for Bush, Yeutter still had agriculture on his plate. Troublesome global surpluses in wheat persisted, so worries about low wheat prices spilled over into the election arena in September 1992, when the distress prompted President Bush to unveil a $1 billion subsidy program for wheat farmers. The government paid $40 per ton to make their wheat competitive with subsidized European Community grain, and Bush echoed Yeutter's comments that there would be "no unilateral disarmament" by the United States, even as it attacked subsidies by the Europeans in the Uruguay talks. In addition, Bush announced plans to provide $755 million in disaster aid to such farmers hurt by drought and frost in the Midwest, cotton growers in Texas who were flooded out, and sugarcane growers in Louisiana hurt by a hurricane. Administration officials denied that the aid was designed to shore up lagging support for Bush among farmers, but Democrats saw reelection pandering at work. "This is really an example of the Bush administration's cynicism at its worst," an aide to Democratic senator Thomas A. Daschle of South Dakota told the *Washington Post*.[95] Of course, Democrats over the years had pandered to their constituents for electoral advantage as well.

As it turned out, the financial support for wheat wasn't robust enough. While the plan called for subsidies on a billion bushels of wheat to sell it to twenty countries, projections by the Department of Agriculture suggested buyers would take up only some fifty million bushels more in exports. Farmers were troubled by the huge expected shortfall and complained. Yeutter, who was by then serving as deputy campaign chairman for President Bush's reelection effort, drew flak when he criticized the farmers, writing a memo to the National Association of Wheat Growers that said, "One wonders how ungrateful some folks can be! President Bush has just given their market a big shot in the arm but they seem not to be very appreciative." Democrats accused Yeutter of being condescending and argued that the campaign was pandering because

Bush was trailing Clinton in farm states such as South Dakota and Kansas, states that normally were sure bets for the GOP.[96]

Despite Yeutter's best efforts, Bush lost to Clinton in a November landslide. Clinton took 370 Electoral College votes and 43.01 percent of the popular vote, and Bush snared just 168 Electoral College votes and 37.45 percent of the popular vote, with Perot garnering 18.91 percent of the popular vote and no Electoral College votes. The election broke a twelve-year hold on the White House by the GOP. Bush, as always, was gracious in conceding, so much so that Clinton applauded both his opponent's "lifetime of public service" and the "grace with which he conceded this election."[97] While the Republicans picked up a handful of seats in the House, thanks largely to the redistricting effort Yeutter oversaw, Democrats swept into control of both chambers of Congress as well as the White House.

Postmortems on Bush's campaign were brutal. Stephen Knott, a professor of national security affairs at the U.S. Naval War College, wrote that "Bush ran a lifeless campaign that seemed to lack focus and energy; many observers felt he was ineffective at communicating to the public about his achievements." He cited observers who blamed the absence of Atwater for the lackluster performance since, for good or ill, Atwater had invigorated the 1988 campaign. Bush, Knott said, "seemed to be repeatedly caught off guard by the energetic Clinton-Gore campaign."[98]

For his part, Yeutter in 1991 had wanted Bush to begin his campaign earlier than he did. And much like Knott, he noted that Bush didn't feel compelled to make a strong case for his reelection beyond letting his record speak for itself. "What he was saying to the American public was 'I have just done a heck of a good job as President of this country; I deserve a second term and I shouldn't have to go through all this hassle to get there,'" Yeutter said, according to author David Mervin.[99] That view was echoed by a co-chairman of Bush's campaign, Representative John Vincent "Vin" Weber of Minnesota. "He was a good man, he was a good President," Weber said. "But he thought that if he simply did the right thing, people would understand. Whereas I think Reagan understood the need to communicate your vision."[100] Some Republicans, moreover, thought Clinton's tainted history with women would cost him enough votes to keep Bush in power, a view in which they were mistaken, even as Clinton's proclivities would later threaten his presidency.[101]

Yeutter's analysis of his president's problems in governing was similarly on point. He asserted that Bush had never been sufficiently aggressive with Congress. "He never realized that those folks were doing him in," Yeutter said, according to Mervin. "He had so many good friends over there and, on a one-to-one basis, they all loved George Bush and he loved them and it was marvelous. But he was never able to separate the personal relationships with the Congress from the political relationships. He couldn't comprehend that those who were great friends were doing him in politically every day of the week."[102]

Privately, Yeutter could be scathing in his political assessments, as he was of Quayle in the 1988 campaign, in which the forty-one-year-old U.S. senator from Indiana first became Bush's running mate. "It seems to me that your much larger challenge with Quayle is whether or not he can demonstrate to the American public that he is of Presidential caliber," Yeutter wrote to a friend involved in the campaign. "So far he has not shown the poise, maturity, and judgment that is necessary to achieve that objective. But he has time, if he handles himself well."[103] Later, as vice president, Quayle was given to gaffes—misspelling *potato* on a school visit, stumbling when discussing the Holocaust, and botching the United Negro College Fund's slogan—which prompted critics including commentators William F. Buckley Jr. and George F. Will to suggest Bush should drop him from the ticket and draft someone such as Department of Housing and Urban Development secretary Kemp.

In the runup to the 1992 election, however, Yeutter as RNC chairman publicly backed Quayle, even when polls showed that Americans by a two-to-one margin didn't think he was qualified to be president. Yeutter argued in a May 1991 appearance on CNN's *Evans & Novak* that 99 percent of the vice president's problem was that the media was unfair to him, pouncing on his every slip. Much of what Quayle did to help the administration, Yeutter said, took place behind the scenes, with Congress and in Republican Party fundraising. But perhaps suggesting Quayle was less than a major plus in the public eye, Yeutter did not agree when cohost Evans bruited the idea that Bush should elevate Quayle's profile with more visible tasks. "There's no doubt in my mind that he is performing in an outstanding fashion," Yeutter said. "It's just that most of the people of America do not see that." Adding that Quayle had "earned his spurs," Yeutter maintained that Bush should stick with his vice president, as Bush did. When the ship sank, however, Quayle wound up ousted from public office for good.[104]

Quayle considered a run for the White House in 1996 but opted against it, something Yeutter praised. "Please tell Dan he made the correct move by choosing not to run for the Presidency in the coming year," Yeutter wrote in an April 1995 memo to Marilyn Quayle. "As tempting as that prospect may be, and as important a position it is, the timing for Dan would not have been right. At his relatively young age, he will be far better off continuing to build a track record, either in the private sector or in public service in Indiana, for a number of years prior to contemplating a possible return to Washington, D.C."[105] Quayle briefly made a run at the presidency in 1999 but withdrew in favor of George W. Bush.[106]

Of all his roles in Washington, Yeutter most enjoyed his USTR post, where he made the biggest impact and which was a job he could have stayed in for years, says Cristena Bach Yeutter.[107] He likely enjoyed his post-USDA government-related tasks the least of all, several former colleagues told me. Unlike professional political operatives, he didn't live and breathe politics for its own sake, but rather he saw government as a means to accomplishing ends, such as trade liberalization. According to some of his friends, the cut and thrust of politics and jockeying for power left him cold. Politics "is a down in the mud sport," says Blumenthal, who had also worked for a time at the Republican National Committee. "And I just don't think it was his nature."[108]

12

A Second Chance

ife after government brought fresh accomplishments for
Yeutter. During his last quarter century, he saw much of
his professional legacy come to fruition, as most of the
world came around to his views on trade and economics and pros-
pered accordingly. But the time also brought crushing personal
tragedy, as well as surprising joy.

Ever energetic, Yeutter had no intention of coasting into a cozy
retirement after his nearly eight-year stint in government and partisan politics. Indeed, the coming years would prove to be a time
when he would be fairly paid for his broad and deep expertise, for
which he had been comparatively underpaid in government and
party work. After sorting through his many professional options
in the wake of Bush's loss at the polls in the fall of 1992, Yeutter
settled first on serving on corporate boards on which his international trade expertise would be useful. Moving quickly, by the
spring of 1993 he joined the boards of seven companies for which
he had served as a corporate director before his return to government, including Caterpillar, ConAgra, FMC, and Oppenheimer
Funds; he then added Texas Instruments, Lindsay Manufacturing, and the British diversified tobacco company BAT Industries.

Each board met at least six times a year, requiring at least forty-
two days of travel, including abroad, and providing him with

plenty of homework. In addition, he signed up with a speakers' bureau, the Leigh Bureau of New Jersey, to give paid speeches mostly on trade and agricultural policy around the world, particularly in Japan and Europe. He also consulted for Vigoro Corporation, an export-minded agricultural chemical company in Chicago. "We've settled easily back into the private sector, and there are not many gaps in my schedule," he wrote to a contact in the Chicago office of the Heidrick & Struggles executive search firm.

Busy as that schedule kept him, Yeutter wanted to do even more. He wrote to his headhunting contact about adding one or two more corporate boards, perhaps including a major bank or a financial company such as American Express. He was interested, too, in serving as a director of the forest products company Weyerhaeuser because he had overseen the U.S. Forest Service at the U.S. Department of Agriculture, as well as Louisiana Pacific, another building products company. He also was intrigued about a potential university presidency, though he said it would have to be something "absolutely irresistible" because he would have to revamp his corporate involvements. He mentioned Michigan State and noted that he was being pressed by the University of Nebraska, "though they've not yet opened a search process." And he was considering joining a law firm on an "of counsel" basis— either Sidley & Austin of Chicago or Hogan & Hartson in Washington DC.[1]

In the end, he turned down the university possibilities and joined the Washington-based law firm on June 1, 1993, while sticking with the corporate boards he had joined and then occasionally moving on or off boards. In time, he added Weyerhaeuser, Farmers Insurance (at the time owned by BAT), Covanta Holding Corporation, American Commercial Lines, Burlington Capital Group, Neogen, and Mycogen, among others. And he chaired the New York Board of Oppenheimer Funds. He eventually swapped out BAT Industries for Zurich Financial Services when the tobacco company merged its financial businesses with Zurich Insurance.[2]

Yeutter also offered his opinions on issues of the day to friends and publications and stayed at least somewhat politically active. For instance, he couldn't abide President Clinton, who had unseated President Bush. When Martin S. Feldstein, who chaired the Council of Economic Advisers under President Reagan, wrote an op-ed in the *Wall Street Journal* titled "Clinton's Path to Wider Deficits" in February 1993, Yeutter popped Feldstein a note, saying, "I just hope we can get through the next four years without too much structural damage, but with sufficient evidence to demonstrate to the American public that they're being fed snake oil!"[3] (As it happened, the federal government narrowed its deficits each fiscal year from 1994 through 1997, then ran surpluses from 1998 through 2001, during Clinton's second term.)[4]

Similarly, when *Fortune* ran a special feature on "Clintonomics" in March 1993, predicting various tax hikes, Yeutter sent a note to author Ann Reilly Dowd. He gave her a classic Nebraska "compliment sandwich," featuring attaboys on the top and bottom, with criticisms as the meat in the middle. In his opening paragraph, he called the piece "the most thorough exposition of the present economic policy picture (and the most readable!) I've seen anywhere." And at the end he called Dowd "a fine journalist, and a terrific person!" In between, he offered detailed comments about how she should have posed a few more hard questions and suggested that she "gave the Clinton program more of a free ride than it deserves." Echoing his comment to Feldstein, he added, "There's a lot of snake oil being peddled; hopefully the American public will eventually recognize it."[5]

But the summer of 1993 also brought a stunning personal blow to Yeutter and his four adult children, some of whom had children of their own. Jeanne, Yeutter's wife of four decades, died in her sleep of a presumed heart attack on August 24, 1993, only four days after she turned sixty-two. "She was truly an extraordinary person, and I will miss her tremendously for the rest of my life," Yeutter told a friend late the following year. "As you might expect, her activities were thoroughly entwined with mine, and she was a true partner in every sense of the word. When someone commented a few months ago that Jeanne was 'one in a billion,' a lady standing nearby intervened to comment that such a ratio did her a disservice. I truly believe the latter person was correct, for she possessed warmth and selflessness beyond that of any person I have ever seen."[6]

Jeanne's death left him alone and unmoored. After all, she had encouraged him in his earliest days to leave the farm and pursue the graduate studies that led to his achievements. "She elevated my dad," recalls Van A. Yeutter, their youngest son. "She helped him become the giant of a man he was. And he wouldn't have become the giant he was if she wasn't who she was." As he dealt with people of all sorts along the way in his career ascent, Van adds, she was often a shrewd judge of character who could help him assess them—at times seeing faults that Yeutter, who tended to see the best in people, may have missed. One could not overestimate the pain and loss her death caused for his dad, Van says.[7]

Jeanne's death also stirred Yeutter's long-standing religious sentiments anew. His letters to friends were filled with references to "her unexpected departure from this earth" and phrases such as "When God placed her on this earth He made a special contribution to all of us, and especially to me."[8] He referred to losing his wife in a letter consoling Warren H. Maruyama on the death of his colleague's father. "There is just no way for the world ever to be quite the same again," Yeutter wrote. "The occasion is a happy one in the sense that your father has now finished his tasks on this earth, and I'm sure he did them well. So his eternal reward is now before him, whereas the rest of us still have work on this planet to do. . . . Faith carries us through these times and into the future, and faith supports the proposition that life on this earth is only a small part of the eternal life cycle—meaning that you'll assuredly see your father again."[9]

He struck similar notes in a letter to another friend who had lost his wife, nicknamed Boots: "By our faith we know that she'll continue to be able to communicate her love to all of you, and vice versa, though none of us will ever understand quite how. Only God knows that answer, though He'll share it with us one day. God understands how hard this is, and He'll comfort you as the days unfold. . . . We also know that life passes quickly, so we'll see Jeanne and Boots again, perhaps sooner than we now contemplate. By faith we know that too will be a joyful day indeed."[10] And to yet another friend who had lost his wife, Sheila, Yeutter wrote, "I'll wager that Jeanne was in the initial greeting party when Sheila arrived at the gates to heaven last week. I can just imagine the big smiles that were flashed and the joy they experienced when that occurred. Both of us now have two guardian angels taking care of us, and what a pair they are."[11]

Yeutter never abandoned his memories of his late wife. But still a vibrant and charismatic personality, he did find someone else to join his life with. Yeutter had met Cristena Bach in 1986 when they worked out at the same times in the White House gym while serving under President Reagan. Cristena then was handling intergovernmental relations in the White House and had worked for Donald P. Hodel when he served as secretary of energy and then as secretary of the interior. They stayed in touch intermittently and got further reacquainted after Jeanne died, though courting was a challenge for him. "The relationship is not by any means a 'done deal,' at this point, and moving in that direction sure was hard. There just isn't anybody like Jeanne on the face of this earth!" he wrote to a longtime friend in January 1995. "But I do want you and Cynthia to meet Cristy. You'll like her—especially her politics!"[12]

Yeutter and Cristena married a bit over two years after Jeanne's death, on October 21, 1995, while she was working as executive director of the Chicago-based Council of Great Lakes Governors. It surprised them both. "The idea of getting married was totally shocking to both of us, because when we met it obviously wasn't even on the screen," Cristena told a writer for the *Washington Lawyer*.[13] Until May 1996 theirs was a commuter marriage, as Cristena tied up loose ends in her job in Illinois. The couple split their time between Chicago and Washington, with Yeutter occasionally working out of her Chicago office, until they could return full-time to their home in McLean, Virginia.[14] For the sixty-four-year-old

Yeutter, remarrying was difficult, though he was devoted to and delighted by his new bride, then thirty-six, as he would be with the three girls they later adopted.

"A lot of additional joy has come from my wedding," he told a friend in Illinois two months after they married. "We deliberately kept the wedding low profile in nature," Yeutter wrote, adding, "Because of my enormous love and respect for Jeanne, and all the joy our 40 years together brought both of us, I just felt that this was the proper modus operandi. . . . All this was a tremendously emotional decision for me, of course, for it will forever be impossible to replace Jeanne. . . . But Cristy fills a huge void, and I am certainly far more content with life than before she came onto the scene."[15]

To another friend, he wrote of his second marriage, "That was a huge emotional hurdle for me, as you might expect, for it is one that I never anticipated in my lifetime. No one can ever replace Jeanne, but Cristy fills that huge void in a wonderful way."[16] And to yet another friend, he described Cristena as "a wonderful lady," adding, "so I have been blessed a second time in my life." But he didn't gloss over the challenges involved, especially since Cristena was twenty-eight years younger than he and younger than his two older sons. "Remarrying was an emotional process for me, though, and it was also difficult for the children. But we had a beautiful wedding, all the children participated, and Cristy and I are now looking forward to productive and rewarding years ahead."[17]

Blunt perhaps to a fault, as always, Yeutter was most revealing about his complicated feelings in a Christmas greeting letter he sent to friends at the end of 1995—a letter to which he appended Cristena's name as well:

The past two Christmases have been rather solemn occasions for me, though I comprehend fully that God has heaped blessings on me for a lifetime. Absent Jeanne's warmth, kindness and funloving spirit, the holidays just aren't the same. And the world will never be the same without that sensational lady. But

Cristy has made life vital and vibrant again, and with our marriage on October 21 I have now been twice blessed. She is a bright, attractive 37-year-old, and that is a challenge in itself! . . . As you can tell, Cristy has restored happiness to my life—and the pampering I think I deserve! At the same time those magnificent memories of life with Jeanne continue forever.[18]

Indeed, Yeutter and his family, including Cristena, made sure to honor his first wife's memory. In early May 1996 they dedicated the Jeanne Yeutter Memorial Garden, which he endowed, at the University of Nebraska–Lincoln (UNL). The garden consisted of a planted berm and an oval rock garden ring.[19] Yeutter also endowed a seminary fellowship in Jeanne's honor at Fourth Presbyterian Church in Bethesda, Maryland, the church he was affiliated with later in his life.[20]

Jeanne was honored at the U.S. Arboretum in Washington as well. A grove there reflects her love of trees, which she began planting on Arbor Day as a child in Nebraska and continued to do to celebrate births, marriages, and anniversaries. She had worked in Washington to set aside a thirty-acre tract at the arboretum to contain trees from all fifty states and the District of Columbia. She called the effort the Trees-Mend-Us project, which was dedicated as the National Grove of State Trees in 1993.[21] A wooden entrance arbor at the grove commemorates her work.

Yeutter's colleagues were often touched by Jeanne's kindnesses. Alan F. Holmer, for instance, recalls that Yeutter once let his family use Yeutter's getaway condo in Clearwater, Florida, in the late 1980s. "Later on, I learned that before we left, Jeanne made a special trip from D.C. to make sure the condo was set for our visit, including children's books, puzzles, coloring books, crayons, etc. What generosity and hospitality!"

At Jeanne's "celebration of life" memorial ceremony on September 11, 1993, Holmer read excerpts of letters from people who knew her. One, from a Nebraska woman who was a freshman at UNL when Jeanne, a senior, was her counselor, said, "I was frightened by my new experience at college; she was calm and secure.

She always had all the time I needed—to listen to me, to encourage me, to challenge me." Another, from her friend Honey Skinner, said, "I cannot recall an event in Washington in which Jeanne did not deny the town's 'code' by being warm and loving to everyone, happy and cheerful no matter how grim the day and—of course—elegant and beautiful."[22]

While Yeutter and his family honored Jeanne with the garden at UNL, officials in Nebraska wanted to similarly create permanent memorials for Yeutter. In late 1996 they designated the two-lane State Highway 21 linking Cozad and Eustis the Clayton Yeutter Highway, naming in his honor the road he had driven hundreds of times to and from his family farm. "I always thought that kind of recognition comes along only after one had departed from this earth," Yeutter wrote to Governor E. Benjamin Nelson, the Democrat who had signed off on the designation as part of a nonpartisan effort among proud Nebraskans. "So it will be a special privilege now to drive past those signs when we head to Dawson County to visit our farm."[23]

Eighteen and a half years later, in the fall of 2014, the university installed a larger-than-life statue of Yeutter in a green space north of Filley Hall on the school's East Campus, home of the agriculture program.[24] It accompanies those of three other former U.S. secretaries of agriculture from Nebraska: J. Sterling Morton, Clifford M. Hardin, and Michael O. Johanns.[25]

Throughout the twenty-one years Yeutter and Cristena were married, life proved to be different with a wife who hailed from a different generation and had different expectations. The couple adopted three children, Victoria, Elena, and Olivia—from Russia, Kazakhstan, and Guatemala, respectively. "Clayton told me that it was clear I was born to be a mother and I would hate his guts if we didn't have children," Cristena recalls. "That was a very generous and selfless decision, and I think he was right."[26]

As their lives together unfolded, Yeutter had to do things he hadn't done much of before, such as emptying dishwashers and taking care of other domestic chores, along with tending to babies' needs. While Jeanne had taken a more traditional approach, running life on the home front and letting Yeutter focus on his almost nonstop work, Cristena says she was determined that Yeutter would be a twenty-first-century father and husband—something he agreed to.[27] As Cristena put it to *Omaha World-Herald* columnist Michael Kelly in 1997, when the couple adopted their first child, "Clayton likes to say he's a man of the '50s thrust into the '90s, and I'm making him do that with a vengeance. He changes diapers, feeds a bottle, rocks the baby and burps her."[28]

When Victoria was seventeen months old and had been with them for a year, he wrote to a couple of friends that she was an absolute joy. "I probably have changed her diaper more frequently than all of the other four children combined, perhaps even for their entire lifetimes!" Yeutter told Ned and Essie Raun. "I am not quite sure why fathers did little of that in the 'good old days,' but life just isn't like that anymore! . . . As Ned will recall, we were always so busy we just didn't have a chance to do that in the early years of our careers. Though I am still busy, I now have so much more flexibility in controlling my own schedule and establishing my own priorities."[29]

By all accounts, Yeutter warmed to the modern father's role, cherishing the years he had with his girls, even as he acknowledged the challenges of parenting as a self-described senior citizen. According to Cristena, his second family was something of a second chance; indeed, he told his wife he felt bad that he hadn't realized how hard Jeanne had to work to care for their four youngsters.[30] As his infant daughters grew to become toddlers, he joined them for tea parties, wearing a pink feather boa around his neck and clip-on earrings dangling from his ears, Cristena told the *Omaha World-Herald*. He also puttered about his yard, coming in looking as though he'd rolled in dirt.[31]

Indeed, Yeutter had confessed to his colleague, Gary Blumenthal, that he felt his decades of long workdays, frequent separate living arrangements, and constant travel had exacted a cost on his family life the first time around. "He said to me one day that he had one regret in life: that he hadn't spent more time with his first [set of] children," Blumenthal recalls. "He focused so much on work and professional success that he probably had not done as good a job as he should have as a father."[32] For his part, Yeutter told a journalist in early 2000, "I have absolutely adored the experience of being a far more active father than was possible for me when my first four children were growing up."[33]

13

The World Will Thank You

As time moved on for Yeutter, he saw some of his life's work bear still more fruit. But he also saw much of his legacy jeopardized by fellow Republicans, first in the mid-1990s and in 2000 by a presidential hopeful he had resisted, Patrick J. Buchanan, a man who appealed to GOP extremists whom Yeutter had long rejected. And then in his final years, Yeutter saw some of his accomplishments put at risk in domestic political upheaval, as the party's extremists rallied behind a man the ever-moderate, global-market-oriented, well-mannered, and religious Yeutter could not support, Donald J. Trump.

While Yeutter tried to focus more on life at home, the tug of his professional life was intense. He made time along the way to tie up major loose ends left from his days as U.S. trade representative (USTR) and as secretary of agriculture. For instance, he had worked with Bush's USTR, Carla Hills, when officials in Mexico, beginning in 1991, sought to set up a free trade agreement similar to that with Canada. As the talks proceeded, the three countries decided to set up the North American Free Trade Agreement, based largely on the U.S.-Canada Free Trade Agreement that Yeutter had brokered in the late 1980s.

The leaders came to agreement on the North American Free Trade Agreement (NAFTA) by the fall of 1992. But it took until late

1993—during President Clinton's term—to get the deal approved; it went into effect on January 1, 1994. Yeutter lent a hand, mainly on agricultural issues, to persuade Americans to support NAFTA. "He was meeting regularly with farm groups," recalls Hills, who notes that American farmers feared being undercut by foreign imports and Yeutter tried to school them on the benefits it would bring them in exports. "That was his mission."[1]

Yeutter also paid close attention to the wrap-up of the ongoing Uruguay Round of global trade talks that he had kicked off years before, in the fall of 1986 in Punta del Este. With Yeutter's help, the United States and the European Union had settled most of their differences on agriculture in the Blair House Accord in November 1992—coincidentally, the same month that American voters turned Bush out of the White House. Negotiators named by Clinton and led by USTR Michael Kantor picked up the ball, and by July 1993 the Quad group—the United States, the European Union, Japan, and Canada—announced progress on tariffs and market access issues. By December 1993 almost all the outstanding issues were resolved, and the deal was signed by ministers of most of the 123 participating countries in Morocco in April 1994.[2] NAFTA had provided some of the impetus for global leaders outside of North America to finally come to terms on the Uruguay Round changes, as they saw the potential such an agreement could bring, according to Hills.

Clinton's staff invited Yeutter to a signing ceremony for the Uruguay Round agreement. He begged off, citing a commitment in New York, but he congratulated the president on sealing the deal, while drawing attention to the prior work that made it possible. "As you have said on numerous occasions, this agreement is an immense achievement, by far the most comprehensive multilateral trade agreement in history. It also attests to the merits of bipartisanship on international trade issues, for Ambassador Kantor was able to build upon a first-rate foundation established during the Reagan and Bush administrations, and then finish off the Agreement in fine fashion," Yeutter wrote to Clinton in late 1994. "You played a major role in bringing this exercise to a successful conclusion, in the face of lots of reprehensible demagoguery, some on the left and some on the right. The world will someday thank you, and so will this country, but I want to thank you now."[3]

He told Kantor in a separate note that although the pact was not perfect, it was nonetheless "a huge improvement over the status quo, and should be recognized as such. Without doubt it is the finest negotiating achievement ever in the sphere of international commerce."[4]

In a private letter to a friend, however, Yeutter found fault with the Clinton administration negotiators. While he called the pact "a very good agreement" overall, he added, "The agreement could have been even better, and should have been better, in agriculture and a number of other areas. We clearly were out-negotiated by the Europeans in those final days, and particularly by the French, who played the situation beautifully."[5]

The United States did not get all that it wanted, he suggested, but it nonetheless made great progress in reshaping the world trading order. The quantity of exports to be subsidized by any given country was cut 21 percent over six years, which Yeutter called "probably the single most important achievement of the Uruguay Round for American farmers." The trim would be heaviest in the later years of the agreement, something the French demanded. Further, the United States insisted that all the world's import quotas, licensing schemes, and other nontariff barriers be converted into tariffs. Such "tariffication" meant that the barriers could be negotiated downward over time, perhaps to zero. The United States had gotten the same sort of conversion for Japanese beef and citrus imports years before, and Yeutter said that had worked well. The negotiators also agreed that barriers to trading agricultural products on grounds of health and food safety would have to have a scientific basis, which Yeutter said was important because when "nations cannot impede food imports in any other way, they often find an alleged health reason for doing so." He said the agreement also set up a better dispute settlement mechanism, the World Trade Organization (WTO).

"As I review the Uruguay Round, I conclude that we did well on export subsidies, reasonably well on market access (though the jury is still out), and not terribly well on internal supports," wrote Yeutter, a tough grader. "I give a passing mark to the combination, though certainly not an A. But since we've been somewhere between a D and an F in past negotiations, that's progress!"[6]

If anything, Yeutter underestimated the round's success and his effect in driving it. In merchandise alone, exports worldwide grew from $2.14 trillion in 1986, when the meeting at Punta del Este kicked off the trade liberalization discussions, to $19.45 trillion in 2018, according to the WTO. Tariffs worldwide had been driven down to an average of 9 percent, perhaps one-third of their post–World War II levels.[7] Along with that breathtaking growth in trade, developing countries such as China rose from widespread poverty to join the ranks of the industrialized nations. Starvation rates also plunged as trade in food grew.[8]

The sharp growth in trade—and particularly the emergence of China and other parts of Asia as the world's factory for so many goods—created much upheaval. Jobs disappeared in some countries, notably in industrial areas of the United States, as places with lower-cost production supplanted more expensive regions (and the jobs moved accordingly). Yeutter, as a classical economist, wasn't blind to the downside of comparative advantage, and he often warned that net benefits enjoyed by most people would disrupt the livelihoods of some. But such efforts as retraining, he contended, could mitigate that. He would have been mindful, too, of Austrian political economist Joseph A. Schumpeter's theory of creative destruction, the relentless process of improvement that, often with turmoil, drives much economic growth both in industry and in agriculture. As an optimist, Yeutter focused on the improvements and the overall gains.

Despite any disappointment Yeutter might have felt in not breaking down agricultural trade barriers altogether, just getting agriculture into the trade talks to begin with was a breakthrough, and then rolling back many of the restrictions on agricultural trade was a seminal achievement. Almost certainly, colleagues say, that would not have occurred had Yeutter not been serving as USTR with his friend Dick Lyng, who was secretary of agriculture at the time of the preliminary talks in Punta del Este and later on. The late Carole Brookins, the trade consultant Yeutter often worked with, called his appointment to the USTR post "a destiny job," saying it turned out for the best that Yeutter had been passed over the first time for the top ag position. Brookins, who served as executive director of the World Bank, added, "If Clayton had been at Ag and some guy from Microsoft at USTR, we never would have gotten the Uruguay Round in agriculture done." Yeutter's expertise in agriculture, familiarity with markets from his time at the Chicago Mercantile Exchange, and knowledge of global trade issues from his time in Washington, she said, all combined to make him the essential man of the moment.[9]

The Uruguay Round proved to be the last successful global effort at trade talks. After that, the Doha Round, launched in the fall of 2001, was a massive failure.[10] Many other leaders around the globe played key roles in the Uruguay Round's success—indeed, global collaboration was essential—but Yeutter was one of its chief architects. "The global trade regime, which is still operating, was put in place by virtue of the will of one person—his name is Clayton Yeutter," says Roger Bolton, his former assistant trade representative at the USTR office. "It's safe to say that hundreds of millions of people around the world have had economic opportunity that they would not otherwise have had, and the world is better off—poverty is lower, middle class is growing. . . . One of the fundamental causes of [the] developing world [moving] from abject poverty into the middle class was the Uruguay Round."[11]

Michael Johanns, the former governor of Nebraska who served as secretary of agriculture under President George W. Bush and later as a U.S. senator, was similarly effusive about Yeutter's impact. "Clayton really was the first person who starting kicking the door down when it came to agricultural trade," Johanns said in a 2015 video for the Clayton K. Yeutter Institute of International Trade and Finance at the University of Nebraska–Lincoln. "So much of the work I did was really following in his footsteps." Johanns added that the establishment of the World Trade Organization reflected Yeutter's vision for how institutions should operate. "It would be a system based upon rules; it would not be a system based upon the whims of whoever was in office at the time," Johanns said. "We owe our modern-day trading efforts to that belief, that we could do agricultural trade based upon principles and rules."[12]

Yeutter attended a celebratory luncheon in December 1994 at the Treasury Department at the invitation of Secretary Lloyd Bentsen, who had labored to persuade the U.S. Senate to support the agreement that emerged from the Uruguay Round. It was another occasion for Yeutter to strike a moderate tone and to applaud someone whose work he admired, even though Bentsen was a Democrat. "The final vote on the Round was splendid, and a lot of the credit for that goes to you. We knew the vote would be strong in the House, but the Senate was a question mark in light of all the right wing/left wing demagoguery that was in the air. You, Bob Dole, and a few others merit special accolades for overcoming all that negativism. You served the country well!" Yeutter wrote. "You've served it mighty well in lots of other ways too, not only as the star of the Clinton Cabinet, but over many years of superlative service in the Senate as well. You and your family can be terribly proud of the record you've accumulated in public service, and you still have much more to give, whatever you undertake in the future."[13]

Coincidentally, Yeutter got a laugh at that time from another invitation he received. The president of the National Democratic Club in Washington sent him a personalized form letter, inviting him to join the club as a special VIP member. The official, former representative Dawson Mathis of Georgia, bragged that the club, which counted more than two hundred Democratic members of Congress on its roster, would be the social center for party leadership activities in 1995 and beyond.[14] Writing back, Yeutter jokingly said he felt honored, adding, "I know that November 8 was a tough day for you folks, but you are reaching when a former Republican National Chairman and former Republican Cabinet officer is on your mailing list!" He told Mathis, whom he called a longtime friend, that he would not forward the invitation to the *Washington Post* to generate a snarky news item, as he said would usually happen with such snafus. "I'd not do that to anyone," the ever-gentlemanly Yeutter wrote, wishing Mathis a happy new year.[15]

But much as he got along with some Democrats, Yeutter didn't abandon his partisanship. He made time to lend a hand on the 1996 campaign of Bob Dole and Jack Kemp to try to unseat President Clinton and Vice President Gore. By backing Dole, Yeutter once again reaffirmed his moderate stance, as Dole, the former Senate majority leader and clear establishment figure, fended off GOP primary challengers including Pennsylvania senator Arlen Specter on the left and NAFTA opponent Buchanan, an economic nationalist, on the right. H. Ross Perot, also a NAFTA opponent, took another stab at the presidency that year, heading the Reform Party ticket.

Yeutter shared some of his thoughts with a reporter at the *Journal of Commerce* who had written a scathing opinion piece titled "Buchanan: Playing on Fear," which attacked the candidate's "message of nationalism, xenophobia, and intolerance" and likened his approach to that of Hitler and Mussolini. Yeutter called the journalist's work "superbly done, and right on target." He added, "Buchanan is so destructive, not only to the Republican Party but to the country as a whole, and it is imperative that the media begin to hold him accountable for what he says. As you well know, the Buchanan/Perot combination had a lot to do with President Bush's political demise in 1992. It would be ironic indeed if either or both of them would do the same to Senator Dole in 1996. Those two seem to be President Clinton's best political friends."[16]

Deep as his distaste was for Buchanan, he was scorching about the Clinton White House. In mid-1995 he referred to Clinton in a letter to a globally minded friend, John C. Whitehead: "I think about you every time the Clinton Administration foreign policy team bungles another international issue! They certainly have not had many successes, and some of the blunders are likely to cost us dearly in the decades ahead."[17] Whitehead, deputy secretary of state under President Reagan, also had co-chaired the investment firm Goldman Sachs.

In early 1995 Yeutter had also used his access to the media to press for global trade to be liberalized still further, building on the Uruguay Round's successes. He and Maruyama, at that point his colleague at the Hogan & Hartson law firm, wrote a commentary published by the *Wall Street Journal* that called for a free trade agreement between the United States and the European Union that would eliminate all barriers to trade and investment between them.[18] After a friend complimented him on the piece, he wrote back to say that such a pact would likely take a long time to develop but that he and Maruyama felt "it was time to get that pot stirring."[19]

Keeping his hand in global matters and politics, Yeutter served on GOP candidate Dole's task force on international trade and investment and took on a job as an honorary chairman in a Nebraska Dole fundraiser, but his busy schedule limited the roles he could play in the campaign.[20] He saw Dole as having "the best leadership qualities of anyone in either political camp." While he acknowledged that Dole had "downsides," as he called them, he said Dole's new campaign was much better managed than his prior efforts to win the White House.[21] Cristena Bach Yeutter also lent a hand, helping prep vice presidential candidate Kemp to debate Gore and set up a transition of administrations.[22]

For the Yeutters, the campaign did have its high points. One of them came when the Dole campaign asked the couple to join a campaign bus caravan trip in the Central Valley of California. Since the Yeutters would be nearby celebrating their first anniversary, they agreed. When Yeutter learned that part of the trip would include appearances with Bo Derek, the voluptuous star of the 1979 movie *10*, Yeutter "didn't sleep all night," recalls Cristena. The next day, as a "clearly braless" Derek got on the bus, Yeutter said, "Oh, Ms. Derek," and the star responded, "Please call me Bo." Cristena then chimed in: "And I said to her, 'Please call him Mr. Yeutter.'"[23]

Even by mid-1996, though, Yeutter seemed to doubt Dole's chances. Dole's road was "an uphill climb," he told a couple of Swiss friends. "Senator Dole has far more leadership potential than does President Clinton, so we hope the American public will recognize that before November, but there is not yet much evidence that they have or will," Yeutter wrote. "So at the moment we can be no more than cautiously optimistic. The conduct of the Clintons is so deplorable that we are discouraged by the prospect of having him govern our country for four more years."[24]

Nonetheless, that was the outcome, as Clinton handily bested Dole in the November election, winning a second term. "It is just exceptionally difficult to defeat an incumbent when the economy is perceived to be good (even when the incumbent had nothing to do with that!)," Yeutter wrote to a friend after the election. "In addition, the sleaziness of the present Administration (which goes beyond anything I have ever observed in my lifetime) did not begin to resonate with voters until the last ten days or so. It may resonate a lot more in the future, in which case we will have another global leadership vacuum."[25]

Yeutter also made note in his letter to the Swiss couple of a curious bit of political skulduggery by staffers in the Clinton White House. They got hold of FBI files of Republicans who had served GOP presidents, including that of Cristena Bach Yeutter. "Cristy's FBI file, by the way, was one of those obtained improperly by the White House as they sought to find 'trash' to use against Republicans in the campaign. That has at least provided a conversation piece for our family!" Investigating the scandal known as "Filegate," a House committee lambasted the Democrats for improperly combing through "the most private and personal information" of the GOP staffers.[26] Democratic officials apologized for what one, a former White House counsel, called "a serious mistake," and the Clinton administration's director of personnel security took responsibility for the affair and resigned.[27]

In that same mid-1996 letter, Yeutter admitted he continued to be quite busy, particularly with corporate board meetings. But, he added, "Cristy is attempting to slow the schedule a bit. I have actually made modest progress in that respect, but need to do a bit more."[28]

As it turned out, for a while Yeutter did not seem to ratchet down his time working, both for the Hogan & Hartson law firm and elsewhere. He estimated that he spent about 40 percent of his time in 1995 on firm-related activities. But his work continued to be extensive, and a letter summarizing his efforts that year for one of the firm's leaders filled five and a half pages. The clients or prospective clients he dealt with (often as a rainmaker drumming up business for the firm) included Fuji Bank, Burger King, Monsanto, FMC, National Milk Producers Federation, North American Export Grain Association, Farm Credit Banks of Texas, Farmland Issues, American Forest & Paper Association, National Cattlemen's Beef Association, Glaxo, and ConAgra. In addition, he gave speeches or took part in conferences and events at forty-three organizations, ranging from the conventions of the Pickle Packers Association in Kansas City and the National Pork Producers in Florida to an investment conference cosponsored by the European Union and the U.S. Embassy in Brussels and a meeting of the Swiss-American Chamber of Commerce in Geneva.[29]

The next couple of years were busier still. He quit the IMC Global board in 1997 but picked up the presidency of the International Food and Agribusiness Management Association, planning to preside over its annual conference, coincidentally in Punta del Este, Uruguay, in June 1998, marking his first trip to the resort town since he launched the Uruguay Round of global trade talks there in 1986. He reported to Hogan & Hartson that he did at least as much public speaking in 1997 as he had in 1996 and a lot more writing. "If one were to combine the articles with the prepared texts for speeches, they'd amount to about half a book," he said. "That's the most professional writing I've done in a long time." In the same letter, however, he noted that because he and Cristena had adopted a daughter, he planned to cut back his time at the firm to one-third and was regarding 1998 as a "phaseout year," possibly extending that to June 1, 1999, marking six years at the law firm.[30] Nonetheless, he maintained his association with the firm, which developed in 2010 into the global firm of Hogan Lovells, serving as a senior adviser for international trade until the end of 2015.

His busy schedule did change a bit in the late 1990s, though. To focus even more on their home lives—and to pursue a warmer climate—the Yeutters left McLean, Virginia, the Washington suburb where they lived on the cheerfully named Merrie Ridge Road, for a home in Scottsdale, Arizona, in the fall of 1998. He still worked, however, keeping up his board memberships even as he scaled down his work for Hogan & Hartson. "The geographic shift is somewhat limiting in that regard, but less so than I had anticipated," he wrote to a friend. "It is amazing what one can do through e-mail, faxes, and the telephone. And these are mighty pleasant surroundings in which to work!"[31] After missing the vibrancy of Washington DC, he and Cristena returned a couple of years later, settling in the suburb of Potomac, Maryland.

Throughout this period Yeutter also kept his eye on global affairs. In mid-1997 he joined USTR Kantor and three other former USTRs in writing a letter to Clinton supporting his decision to renew "most favored nation" status with China, noting that the country was seeking to join the World Trade Organization and to bring its trading system "into line with the international standards and WTO rules."[32] Under most favored nation status, China was treated the same as most other countries the United States dealt with in terms of tariffs and trade barriers.

And when Senator John W. Warner, a Republican from Virginia, asked President Clinton in late 1998 to set up a national bipartisan commission to review U.S.-Cuba policy, with a view toward ending the embargo of the country, Yeutter signed a letter endorsing the idea.[33] He wrote to the head of the U.S.-Cuba Foundation, arguing that engagement with Cuba would be more successful than the American embargo, which dated back to 1962. "I do believe that it is time for increased dialogue between our two countries, and I am persuaded that our longstanding embargo of Cuba has been a mistake. Had we followed a more enlightened policy toward that government over the past couple of decades, I believe Mr. Castro would no longer be leading Cuba today."[34] Clinton opted not to pursue the bipartisan commission, however.[35]

He also contributed a chapter in late 1998 to *Economic Casualties*, a book published by the Libertarian-oriented Cato Institute. In the chapter, titled "Unilateral Sanctions: A Politically Attractive Loser," Yeutter argued that sanctions America imposed on other countries to attack conduct such as drug trafficking, religious persecution, human rights violations, or nuclear proliferation often did little good and should be the "exception rather than the rule in dealing with deplorable conduct in other nations." It would be better to use diplomacy and rally the world behind the effort to drive changes in troublesome countries, he suggested. True to his economics training, he called for careful study: "And let us make sure the implementation of sanctions is a considered decision, made after careful calculation of the probable costs and benefits. In a nutshell, let us stop taking wild swings with unilateral economic sanctions. We have been hitting ourselves in the chin far too often."[36]

Yeutter also remained interested in domestic politics, if not as active as he had been. In early 1999, for instance, he backed Texas governor George W. Bush, President George H. W. Bush's eldest son, in the race for the presidency against Vice President Gore. "My schedule is still so hectic that I will not be able to help him a lot, but I will provide some behind the scenes support in both trade and agricultural policy," Yeutter wrote to a friend in June 1999. "Barring any major surprise, he will be the nominee, and I believe he will be an excellent candidate. He will never be the communicator that Ronald Reagan was, but he has good political instincts and a lot of that Reagan likeability."[37]

Nonetheless, Yeutter was mindful of the younger Bush's shortcomings compared with his father, a World War II veteran who had served in several top global government positions. But he was gratified that young Bush was getting some schooling from Robert B. Zoellick, who had served as the elder Bush's deputy chief of staff and then as president and chief executive officer of the Center for Strategic and International Studies. "I am pleased that you have been involved in tooling him up on some of the international issues, for he certainly needs to enhance his knowledge base in that area," Yeutter wrote in a note that proved prescient. "But he will get there, and he'll be an outstanding candidate. I also look for him to be the nominee, and right now I would see him as the winner in November 2000. As well you know, we do badly need a change, particularly in view of what has transpired (or not transpired) in things international these past few years. The next President will have no choice but to shift his administration's emphasis from domestic challenges to international ones."[38]

As someone who valued personal morality, Yeutter found that his revulsion at the Clinton administration deepened as word of Clinton's sexual misadventures between 1995 and 1997 came to light. "I am very disappointed in the performance of the executive branch these days, and certainly hope we can change all that the 2000 election," he told a friend in Virginia in early February 1999, as Clinton was being tried—and eventually acquitted—in the U.S. Senate over lying about his relationship with intern Monica S. Lewinsky. "As you know, this is just a very sleazy White House, and I hope the American public will eventually recognize that. I don't expect to see a change in the presidency in the coming months, but I do hope the nation will soon have a better moral compass than it has displayed recently."[39] He was similarly blistering in a note to another friend: "I continue to be astonished—and dismayed—that the American public does not seem to recognize the amoral, and often immoral, nature of this presidency. The performance of the economy has certainly given President Clinton infinitely more cover than he deserves."[40]

As it turned out, George W. Bush narrowly defeated Gore in 2000. The election was ultimately decided by the Supreme Court because of balloting questions in Florida.[41] Bush served two terms, leaving the White House in January 2009, after the GOP lost the White House to Illinois senator Barack H. Obama II, who also served two terms before yielding the presidency in 2017 to Donald J. Trump.

Some of Yeutter's longtime friends in Omaha briefly thought things could have turned out quite differently as far back as 1996, the time of the Dole-Clinton race. Notwithstanding his lack of elective office experience and his small-state roots, they thought he could do a better job in the Oval Office than any of the contenders in the mix. Given Yeutter's sterling résumé, global political experience, and stretches of service in and around several presidential administrations, businessman Michael B. Yanney approached him and Cristena about his making a presidential run. According to Yanney, the chairman emeritus of Burlington Capital, Yeutter was "one of the brightest and most capable people that I've seen in the political arena, locally or nationally or internationally. His ability to look at a problem from 50,000 feet and grasp it brilliantly and then hone in at 500 feet was awesome."[42]

After Cristena bluntly suggested divorce would be the likely outcome if Yeutter made a presidential bid, he declined. Before they agreed to marry, she had asked if he wanted to run for office or return to government. "If he wanted to do that, then we shouldn't get married, because given our age difference, time was our most precious commodity," she says. "I didn't think it made sense to get married if I was never going to see him."[43]

Years earlier, Yanney had broached the idea of Yeutter running for the Nebraska governor's post or the U.S. Senate, though Yeutter demurred. Others had similarly approached him, only to be turned down. Yanney, who had known Yeutter ever since he was a freshly minted lawyer working for Nebraska governor Tiemann, said Yeutter had long felt he was more effective laboring in support of elected officials. He excelled at advising such leaders as Presidents Reagan and Bush and making them look good with the results he delivered.

Part of the problem may have been the need elected officeholders chronically have to focus on reelection. "My personal view is that the constant campaign mode would have been annoying to him, that he would just want to go get stuff done," says Darci L. Vetter, a friend of Yeutter's and veteran of USTR, the USDA, and Capitol Hill who dealt with him mostly after he left government. "I see him as so much more of an implementer than a campaigner. . . . I don't know if he would have enjoyed the campaign for the campaign's sake. I think he would have been looking past the campaign and wanting to get to work on the policy."[44]

Yeutter's daughter Kim holds similar views of her father: "He was not a politician. He was a policy guy. My dad cared about ideas, people and policies."[45] Cristena adds, "He was an executive, and legislative jobs (House and Senate) are not executive."[46]

Yeutter's braininess might have hurt him in a political run, notes Gary Blumenthal, his longtime colleague at the USDA and the White House. "He was a little too intellectual for a politician. . . . There aren't very many intellectual politicians," Blumenthal observes. "Other than [T. Woodrow] Wilson, how many other Ph.D. presidents have we had? You don't have a Congress filled with PhDs; you have a Congress filled with lawyers. Yeutter was a lawyer, but I don't think he was ever as much a practicing lawyer as he was a practicing academic, and I say that as a term of discipline and knowledge."[47]

In fact, Yeutter shone most brightly when working on complex topics that were often dealt with out of the public eye, as Yanney remembers from an episode in the mid-1970s, a period when the Soviet Union was importing American grain. Earl Butz, the secretary of agriculture at the time, asked Yanney to help him school Soviet ambassador Anatoly F. Dobrynin about American agriculture. With the help of a friend who ran the Omaha-based Union Pacific Railroad, Yanney arranged for the ambassador and his wife and granddaughter to take a special executive train to North Platte, Nebraska, and then flew them out to a ranch in the western part of the state before returning to a dinner at Omaha's Joslyn Art Museum. Yeutter, who was then working for Butz, joined them on the long trip and all along the way "had the ambassador mesmerized with his knowledge of agriculture and his knowledge of politics," Yanney recalls.[48]

The Dobrynin trip led to the creation of the international division of Yanney's Burlington Capital firm, on whose board Yeutter later served. The firm undertook several major agricultural efforts in the Soviet Union, involving companies including Deere & Company, the Pioneer Seed Company, and Valmont Industries, as well as the University of Nebraska and Iowa State University—all making inroads into the Soviet Union, despite the Cold War.[49]

Along with his cerebral approach, Yeutter's moderate stances might also have cost him in a general election, where shades of gray rarely draw votes. He argued, for instance, that Republicans should be supportive of those who need help, as he had as far back as his early days in the Nebraska government. Former vice president Quayle and Tennessee senator Andrew Lamar Alexander Jr. got under his skin in 1999 when they attacked the term "compassionate conservatism," which then-candidate George W. Bush embraced. They contended it was insulting, saying it was created by liberal Republicans as code "for surrendering our values and principles." Senator Richard J. Santorum of Pennsylvania, in turn, criticized them, writing, "The Republican Party has a proud tradition of being both compassionate and conservative, and we should embrace and promote both."[50] Yeutter seconded Santorum, telling him in a letter, "You were right on target, for if we Republicans do not begin to demonstrate compassion to accompany our conservatism, we will continue to dissipate our support among the American people."[51] (To be sure, Santorum's interpretation of compassion differed from that of many Democrats, including the ideas of "restoration of dignity through welfare reform" and "defense of the unborn.")

Yeutter kept up a lively correspondence, sharing his thoughts on trade, electoral politics, and sometimes journalism. A friend shared a harsh review in 1999 from the *New York Times* of journalist Bob Woodward's book *Shadow: Five Presidents and the Legacy of Watergate*, which concluded it was "an overlong inside-the-Beltway collage" that tended toward gossip, and Yeutter wrote back with a shot at the reporter, even as he confirmed some of Woodward's observations:

> I have not read Woodward's book, and probably will not do so. In my view, he is not a very talented journalist. I suspect that the final sentence of the review, concluding that the book was more gossip than anything else, was fairly accurate. He is on target with the Bush comments, though one could add a number of other shortcomings that ultimately led to President Bush's 1992 defeat. Basically Bush wanted to be President but hated the prerequisite—a presidential campaign. Ironically, President Clinton is almost the exact opposite. Whereas Bush was effective at governance but inept at campaigning, Clinton is brilliant as a campaigner and seemingly disinterested in governance.[52]

Over the following decade and a half, Yeutter continued working as a top trade adviser for the Hogan Lovells law firm, whose global reach made him much in demand. He traveled the world giving talks and appearing on panels about subjects that intrigued him, particularly in trade. In April 2002, for instance, he moderated a session in Geneva for the WTO that brought together some of the people he had worked with years before on trade issues. Then in early 2003 he spoke in Brussels at a German Marshall Fund session about genetically modified food, transatlantic relations, and the hunger crisis in Southern Africa, before returning to Washington to discuss global trade law at the Georgetown University Law Center.

Closer to home, he spoke at sessions such as "Fiesta Americana: The Americas; Unity for Prosperity Forum," sponsored by the U.S.-Mexico Chamber of Commerce, the Greater America Business Coalition, and the Johns Hopkins University Paul H. Nitze School of Advanced International Studies, a session that coincidentally took place in the Ronald Reagan Building in Washington in March 2002. For the Inter-American Development Bank, he took part in roundtable discussions about Central American countries negotiating a free trade agreement with the United States and then about U.S. trade policy generally for the Organization of American States, both in June 2002. He keynoted an Inter-American Development Bank session on agricultural liberalization in October 2002, the same month that he traveled to Southern Illinois University to discuss agriculture- and food-related issues. The following month he was in Indianapolis to lecture at a national convention of the American Society of Agronomy, the Soil Science Society of America, and the Crop Science Society of America, and then, two days later, he appeared at New York City's Waldorf Astoria Hotel to discuss corporate governance for the Directorship Search Group.

His crowded schedule would have been impressive for a younger man and didn't daunt him in his early seventies, a time when friends said he seemed as fit as someone in his fifties. Cristena Bach Yeutter tells of a retirement ceremony for directors at FMC Corporation in which Yeutter, at age seventy, strode up to the podium "like he's fifty," chest forward and grin in place, while another seventy-year-old director struggled with a walker and oxygen to get to his award.[53] In the spring of 2003 he stopped by the Watergate Hotel in Washington to discuss the Doha Round of global trade talks for the National Association for Business Economics. That May he spoke to the Texas Agricultural Lifetime Leadership organization at an early morning breakfast meeting. The next month he addressed a meeting of the Consumers for World Trade. And in November Yeutter met with reporters at a trade press luncheon sponsored by the Committee for Economic Development. In such events, Yeutter spoke extemporaneously, drawing on hand-scrawled outlines.[54]

He was proud of his strength and stamina. To mark his seventy-fifth birthday in the winter of 2005, he asked his four adult children to join him skiing in Colorado, a favorite hobby of the family for many years when he owned a condo at the Keystone Resort. While he avoided the challenging black diamond runs that he had charged down years before, he zipped down the midlevel blue runs, recalls his daughter Kim. "He skied as he lived—he skied hard and fast and happy," she says, noting that Yeutter was a self-taught skier who on an earlier family trip took a tumble that dislocated his shoulder.[55]

Soon after, however, Yeutter faced the most formidable challenge of his life. In about 2007 he was diagnosed with colon cancer. Yeutter had rarely, if ever, been ill; indeed, Cristena credits his exceptional good health to the immunities he developed from his early life on a farm where he was exposed to all sorts of bacteria and toxins. "He grew up on a farm; he ate dirt," she says. He fought the cancer with surgery and chemotherapy, was set back for a short time, but eventually succeeded so well that the doctors declared him cancer-free.[56]

His victory freed him to focus again on his work and, perhaps more important, even more on his home life. He paid closer attention than ever to his three youngest daughters, doubling down on attending their school and sporting events. He volunteered to help on school trips, assisted in homework, and gave driving lessons, as daughters Elena, who was twenty-one in mid-2020, and Olivia, fifteen that year, warmly recall. He took Elena, the middle child, to nightly tae kwon do practices and tournaments from ages six to eleven, often helping out by holding wooden boards she would break, efforts that led to her earning a black belt at age eleven. Yeutter, a notoriously bad driver, asked Elena at age fourteen if she wanted to drive on one trip near home and let her do so; from then on, she routinely drove home from school when he came to pick her up. (As a child, Yeutter had driven farm machinery at an even younger age.)[57] Elena's driving was a father-daughter secret, kept from her mother.[58]

For her part, Olivia had fond memories of breakfasts the two of them shared at McDonald's. He also routinely got together with his youngest daughters and a couple of his adult children and their families in the Washington area to watch Cornhuskers football games in one another's homes—with many of them sporting bright red Huskers gear. Indeed, Olivia says she was considering attending the University of Nebraska and later going to law school, perhaps following in her father's footsteps.[59] Her father's love of the state may have rubbed off on her, since it was deep, according to his children. "My dad loved Nebraska," recalls his son Van. "He loved everything about it: the food, the people, the football, the land, the university, just everything about Nebraska my dad loved, even though he lived most of his life in DC after that."[60] In 2006 Yeutter and Cristena adopted a rescue dog and named him Husker.[61]

At home in Maryland, his three youngest girls regularly saw him working in his office, sometimes as they sat nearby, coloring or playing. "He was very persistent about work," remembers Olivia. "Once he started something, he always made sure to finish it."[62]

And Yeutter did continue working. As ever, he paid attention to world trade and politics. He teamed up with Maruyama in November 2010 to write an op-ed for the *Wall Street Journal*, "Japan as a Trade Crossroads," which urged Japan to pursue "a more dynamic future" by joining the Trans-Pacific Partnership (TPP), then under discussion. The TPP, planned as a regional free trade pact that would include North America, a couple of South American countries, and much of Asia, except for China, would give Japan even more access to foreign markets, the men wrote. Echoing Yeutter's passionate belief in free markets, they argued, "But TPP is also an opportunity to expand foreign investment, boost domestic competition, eliminate costly internal barriers, promote innovation, and bring along new companies and industries in high technology, the life sciences, finance, and environmental goods and services that can support dynamic growth and jobs."[63] (As things turned out, Japan did join in what became the world's largest free trade deal, initially including twelve countries, but the United States, under President Trump in 2017, withdrew from the pact.)[64]

Yeutter also kept up his correspondence with writers and journalists whose work impressed him. In late 2010 journalist and German Marshall Fund Trans-Atlantic Fellow Bruce Stokes wrote a piece in the *National Journal* about the WTO. "The WTO is, by far, the busiest and the most powerful international dispute settlement institution in history, having handled more than 400 disagreements and having ruled on everything from trade in apples to computer chips," Stokes said. "When the WTO was created nearly two decades ago, many worried about the potential loss of national sovereignty and had grave doubts as to whether the United States would comply with international dispute settlement. These concerns have turned out to be overblown."[65] Yeutter popped him an email complimenting him for "the best summary I've seen anywhere re what has been happening with that key WTO function." He reminded Stokes that improving the GATT dispute settlement mechanism was one of the key objectives he had in the Punta del Este meeting in 1986, noting it turned out to be "the major achievement" a few years later.[66]

As he aged, Yeutter's religious convictions seemed to strengthen even more. In mid-2010, when he was seventy-nine, he dropped a note to a friend who had gone through tough financial times years before, just to stay in touch. "God obviously found a way to provide the guidance and direction that you needed during those trying times, though it might have been impossible to discern just what was happening," Yeutter wrote, reflecting his congenital optimism. "As you well know, God's ways are mysterious, but He seems to find a way to make things come out as they should."[67]

Yeutter himself, along with more than 40 officials from the United States and more than 150 from New Zealand, may have felt blessed for surviving a disaster in February 2011 when a powerful earthquake struck the city of Christchurch as a two-day United States–New Zealand Partnership Forum was wrapping up there.[68] For several years Yeutter had been a leader in the forum—co-chairing its meetings several times since its first in 2006—as American and New Zealand officials sought to repair a breach in relations between the countries that had opened when the Kiwis refused in 1985 to allow nuclear-powered or nuclear-armed ships to dock in the country. As a lawyer, Yeutter had represented some New Zealand agricultural interests in Washington.

The 2011 session, co-chaired on the U.S. side by Senator Birch Evans "Evan" Bayh III and former USTR Susan C. Schwab and on the New Zealand side by former prime minister James B. Bolger and former deputy prime minister Sir Michael J. Cullen, dealt with matters of security and trade, particularly the TPP, which most forum attendees supported. While much of the forum took place in a rugby stadium, participants spread throughout Christchurch on the final day, February 22, for nine small-group lunches. Yeutter's group met at the ANZCO Foods headquarters, a low-rise building outside the city center—which proved crucial when the quake, measuring 6.3 on the Richter scale, toppled towers such as the spire on the ChristChurch Cathedral, where forum attendees had met for evensong just two days earlier.

The lunch host, ANZCO founder and leader Sir Graeme T. Harrison, credited Yeutter with opening the Japanese market to New Zealand agricultural exports and was eager to welcome him to the gathering. He wanted to thank Yeutter for expanding Japan's horizons to such goods, recalls Edward J. Farrell, a Washington lawyer for New Zealand agricultural interests who was in the group.

According to Farrell, Yeutter was among a dozen people who were sitting down to lunch just as the quake struck. As the drop ceiling fell on them, the diners dove under the table and waited for the building to stop shaking to leave. Several powerful aftershocks made the event even more harrowing, and because of debris on the streets, it was impossible to get a ride to the rugby stadium, where the group was to assemble. So Yeutter, Farrell, and two other forum participants set out on a two-and-a-half-hour walk through the shaken city. "One thing I learned about earthquakes is this phenomenon called liquefaction . . . very heavy, muddy liquid that rises to the surface. It almost looks like wet concrete," Farrell notes. "Between the damage in the street and the liquefaction, it was a challenging walk, to say the least."

They joined other participants at the stadium and were bused out to the airport. Though it was closed, the authorities provided a couple of Lockheed C-130 Hercules military transports to airlift the dignitaries off to Wellington and Auckland on the country's north island, finding hastily arranged lodging with locals. Without changes of clothes, documents, or their luggage—which was back in the destroyed conference hotel—they had to make do, shopping for amenities to make their way back to the United States on flights out of Auckland. "It was really remarkable, the reaction of the Kiwis in Christchurch . . . the level of cooperation and concern of everybody we ran into in the street . . . it was really remarkable how kind and considerate the Kiwis were and how efficient their government was and their military was in getting us out," Farrell says, adding that the U.S. embassy worked hard to get documents for those whose passports were missing.[69]

In the end, no one connected with the conference was seriously hurt. The cuts and bruises some suffered were nothing compared with what the New Zealanders had lost. At least 185 people were reported killed, along with thousands injured and more than one thousand center-city buildings and ten thousand homes destroyed. Damage was estimated at $25 billion.[70] In the wake of the disaster, members of the forum raised and committed more than $1 million in relief aid for Christchurch.[71]

Perhaps driven by such events, Yeutter made more time for friends and colleagues as he moved into his eighties. Just as he had been mentored by others, so did he return the favor, especially to those associated with the University of Nebraska. One mentee, for instance, was Darci L. Vetter, who served in top jobs for Yeutter's old Office of the U.S. Trade Representative from 2001 to 2007, as an international trade adviser to the Senate Finance Committee until 2010, as a deputy under secretary of agriculture at the USDA until 2014, and then as chief agricultural negotiator for the USTR office from late 2013 until Obama's term ended in 2017. Vetter then was named a diplomat in residence at University of Nebraska–Lincoln (UNL), a title that allowed her to lay the groundwork over nine months for the Clayton Yeutter Institute of International Trade and Finance.

Another mentee was Ronnie D. Green, who had served as the national program leader for animal production research at the USDA and as executive secretary of the White House's interagency working group on animal genomics before becoming a global executive at Pfizer Animal Health, then moving to UNL for top positions in its Institute of Agriculture and Natural Resources. With Yeutter's staunch backing, Green was appointed chancellor of UNL in May 2016. Both Vetter and Green often sought Yeutter's counsel; among other things, Green and he shared the experience of being first-generation college students for whom academics made all the difference.[72]

As Yeutter moved through his final years, he was distressed at seeing threats arise against much of the progress he had made in breaking open the world for more trade. He was troubled by the criticisms of open markets, as trade agreements such as NAFTA and the TPP were assailed by critics on both the right and left, despite the gains such deals could provide. He was unsettled by the general direction the GOP was headed in. "I'm quite certain that he would not feel the same way about the Republican Party today that he did when he was doing his public service," says his youngest son, Van. "It's not the same party. . . . A core of who my dad is is honesty, integrity, tell the truth, and do the right thing— all those things—which is not happening today."[73]

Indeed, shortly before the November 2016 election, Yeutter teamed up with colleagues Maruyama and Matthew J. Slaughter, a member of the President's Council of Economic Advisers, to write an op-ed that slammed both Trump and Clinton for their hostile stances on major U.S. trade pacts. "The Biggest Loser from Trump's Trade Wars and Hillary's Waffling on TPP Would Be the American Worker" was their headline on the draft. "In the emotion of a political campaign it is not unusual to hear that the answer to fixing the U.S. economy is a trade war, but that's a conflict that nobody wins," the trio wrote in the unpublished commentary. "Trade requires leadership and we have seen little of that in either Presidential campaign. As always, it will be ordinary American workers—the ones who pay taxes, fight our wars, and look to their government to create economic conditions that support economic growth and good jobs—who will pay the price of leadership folly. They deserve better."[74]

Washington lawyer Farrell, who had accompanied Yeutter in New Zealand, calls it the "ultimate irony" that Yeutter's career-long efforts to open Japan to exports from such Pacific area countries as New Zealand have done more for such countries than for the United States because of American abandonment of the TPP. "New Zealand is enjoying the fruits of that negotiation while the U.S. is not fully," Farrell says, noting that a bilateral "minideal" the Trump administration made with Japan was helping provide some U.S. agricultural access to the country's markets. The TPP, he adds, was the ultimate product of Yeutter's work with Japan and other countries, of the U.S.–New Zealand forum, and of many individual efforts, and that was benefiting the countries that had joined the deal, but not the United States.

Farrell praises Yeutter's work, calling him "the best" trade representative the United States has had, while noting that several have been very good at the job. "Clayton had a combination of extraordinary energy and a personal manner that was very engaging, and he had a very clear concept of where he wanted to go in terms of ag trade," he says. Sadly, Farrell adds, much of that work was thrown into jeopardy in the years leading up to 2020. The global trade environment had become "as tenuous as it's been post–World War II, given the U.S. lack of leadership and some of the negative impact U.S. actions have had on the international trade frame-work." Looking ahead, though, Farrell suggests the damage is not irreparable, hoping that the Joseph R. "Joe" Biden Jr. administra-tion will move trade relations forward again.[75]

Perhaps because of his stance as a moderate who believed in civility in government and in free trade—and perhaps because of his sense of morality—Yeutter bridled at Trump as the GOP's standard-bearer in 2016. Yeutter used to tweak his friend and fel-low Nebraskan Vetter about her loyalty to the Democratic Party, but when they spoke shortly before Yeutter died, she says, "he was just beside himself" at where the Republican Party had moved. He valued basic decency, courtesy, and grace, but "he didn't see it in the current leadership. That frustrated him greatly." In addi-tion, she says, Trump's attacks on such important trade arrange-ments as NAFTA and the TPP troubled him.[76] Says Blumenthal, "Donald Trump was not his type of person."[77]

But Yeutter could not bring himself to vote for Hillary R. Clinton, the Democratic candidate in 2016 and First Lady to a president he disliked. Instead, he wrote in his vote for Mitchell E. Daniels Jr., the former governor of Indiana, Cristena says.[78] Daniels had worked in Washington for Presidents George W. Bush and Reagan, and Cristena had worked for him in the Reagan White House; Daniels had been mentioned as a presidential contender in 2012 and then again in 2016. Daniels begged off a White House run, instead tak-ing a job as president of Purdue University in 2013. After Trump won, one of his first acts was to issue an executive order pulling the United States out of the TPP, which Trump called "a rape of our country."[79] The new president then scrapped NAFTA, only to replace it with the United States–Mexico–Canada Agreement.[80] He also did much to alienate allies, including the leaders of many countries with whom Yeutter had labored to build bridges.

Although he had seemed to beat colon cancer in 2008, Yeutter took ill with another, more serious bout of the disease in about 2013. He told many of his friends about it in an email, letting them know he might live perhaps six months to a year longer.[81] But as he fought the disease, the years moved on, and during that time he continued to advise his colleagues and clients at his law firm about international trade matters, a task he kept up through 2015. He also made still more time for family: though he was weakened by his illness, he and his four children from his first marriage traveled to Illinois in September 2016 to watch the Nebraska team beat the Northwestern University Wildcats in Evanston, next door to Chicago, and to visit sites in the area that had been part of what his son Van calls "a magical time" for the family three decades before. That final visit, which included getting together with old friends, was "awesome," Van says.[82]

Yeutter succumbed to the cancer at home in Potomac, Maryland, on March 4, 2017, at age eighty-six. Several years earlier, he had sent a note to his son Gregg that included a newspaper clipping of a review of a book about former UN ambassador Jeane Kirkpatrick. Yeutter had suggested that a sentence in the review was how he would like to be remembered: Kirkpatrick, an Oklahoma native who died in 2006, "was not as much a political leader as she was a model citizen, a woman from the heartland who helped shape the time in which she lived."[83]

But a different leader may come to mind when pondering Yeutter's legacy. Because of his military service, both Yeutter and his first wife, Jeanne, were buried in Arlington National Cemetery in a section bordered partly by a road named for Dwight D. Eisenhower. Though Yeutter never served that president, they had a lot in common. As moderate Republicans and level-headed pragmatists raised in the Midwest, they shunned extremism. They could work hand in hand with cooperative Democrats to do great things, harnessing government and the private sector to make a profound difference in American and global lives. They also saw a well-defined activist role by government as something to be embraced, not diminished. That was true whether it was a matter of building an interstate highway system or overhauling the global trading order. Moderate as they proudly were, they both changed the world—radically and for the better.

ACKNOWLEDGMENTS

My thanks go first to Cristena Bach Yeutter for fostering this project, in conjunction with the Clayton K. Yeutter Institute of International Trade and Finance. I am obliged to University of Nebraska–Lincoln chancellor Ronnie D. Green and his chief of staff, Michael J. Zeleny, as well as Yeutter Institute director Jill Kosch O'Donnell, for asking me to undertake the effort. I am indebted to my former interim dean, Amy Struthers, for allowing me the time for this research, and I am grateful to the Huse family for endowing the professorship that supports my work. I much appreciate the careful review provided by Edward Alden of the Council on Foreign Relations. My hat is off, too, to Donna A. Shear, director of the University of Nebraska Press, and editor Tom Swanson, who midwifed the book, as well as to my exacting copyeditor Joyce Bond. We all are indebted to Katie M. Jones, who organized thousands of documents in the Yeutter papers for the UNL Libraries.

Clayton Yeutter's colleagues and friends generously shared their time and reminiscences, adding depth and color to this account. Judith H. Bello, Alan F. Holmer, and Warren H. Maruyama, in particular, were immensely helpful in providing useful edits and additions to several chapters and in fleshing out complex trade matters. The kindness Yeutter's colleagues demonstrated as they gave of their time to share memories and reflections was a measure of the deep impressions that the Nebraska farm boy turned globetrotter made on them.

APPENDIX A

Clayton Yeutter's Final Résumé

Résumé has been slightly edited for style and clarity.

Clayton Yeutter

Personal Data

Date of Birth: December 10, 1930

Birthplace: Eustis, Nebraska

Spouse: Cristena Bach Yeutter

Children: Brad, Gregg, Kim, Van, Victoria, Elena, Olivia

Home Address:

Potomac, Maryland

Office Address:

Hogan Lovells LLP

555 Thirteenth Street NW

Washington DC 20004-1109

Academic Data

EDUCATION

High School: Eustis High School, Eustis, Nebraska, 1948

University: University of Nebraska, Lincoln NE, BS, 1952

University of Wisconsin, Madison, one semester of graduate work in agricultural economics, 1960

University of Nebraska, Lincoln, JD in law, 1963

University of Nebraska, PhD in agricultural economics, 1966

SCHOLASTIC RECORD

BS with High Distinction: Highest scholastic honor given by the University of Nebraska. Ranked first in College of Agriculture graduating class. Named by the Block & Bridle Club as outstanding animal husbandry graduate in the United States.

JD Cum Laude: Ranked first in graduating class. Named outstanding law graduate in Midwest by Phi Delta Phi legal fraternity. Editor, *Nebraska Law Review*.

PhD: Named outstanding graduate student in agricultural economics. Above an A average for entire graduate program.

PROFESSIONAL AND FRATERNAL SOCIETIES

Agriculture: Alpha Zeta (scholastic), chancellor of local chapter as undergraduate

Gamma Sigma Delta (scholastic)

FarmHouse (social), president of local chapter as an undergraduate

Law: Order of the Coif (scholastic)

Phi Delta Phi (social and professional)

Employment History

February 1993–Present: Senior Adviser, International Trade, Hogan Lovells, LLP, Washington DC, one of the nation's oldest and largest law firms. Previously of counsel. Involved in expanding the firm's already extensive trade practice, which now encompasses

15 foreign offices. Also involved in the firm's food and agriculture practice, since the firm represents numerous U.S. companies and agribusiness trade associations.

1992: Counselor to the President for Domestic Policy. A cabinet-level post established in the White House, responsible for the development and coordination of all administration initiatives in the domestic policy arena. During 1992 the White House undertook more than 60 domestic policy initiatives, some of which helped lay the groundwork for the healthy economic recovery in the last half of that year and on into the 1990s.

1991: Chairman, Republican National Committee. Responsible for all fundraising and party communications on a national basis and for coordination with and support of all 50 state party organizations. This was the most successful off-year election cycle in party history. The RNC's vigorous redistricting efforts laid the groundwork for many of the Republican successes in congressional and state legislative races throughout the ensuing decade.

February 1989–February 1991: Secretary of Agriculture. Responsible for administration of the fourth largest department of the United States in budget terms (nearly $50 billion) and sixth largest in employment (more than 100,000). The USDA's jurisdiction extends to a myriad of programs: price and income supports, export expansion, Food for Peace, inspection and grading functions, food stamps, school lunches, agricultural credit, rural development, forestry, and soil conservation. It has one of the most diverse agendas in all of government, one in which there are many crosscurrents involving competing constituencies. Agriculture is still by far the nation's largest industry.

July 1985–January 1989: U.S. Trade Representative, Executive Office of the President, a cabinet post reporting directly to the president of the United States on all trade matters. The primary responsibility of this position is to develop an overall trade policy for the nation, and then generate and coordinate a U.S. position on all individual trade issues of importance to our country. The U.S. Trade Representative is also responsible for the strategy and tactics that are followed in the conduct of both bilateral and multi-lateral trade negotiations.

July 1978–June 1985: President and Chief Executive Officer, Chicago Mercantile Exchange, the world's second-largest futures market. The CME conducts futures trading in (1) all the major international currencies; (2) interest rate contracts for Treasury bills, bank certificates of deposit, and Eurodollars; (3) stock indices, such as the s&p 500; and (4) agricultural contracts, such as fat cattle, feeder cattle, and hogs. The exchange also offers options trading in several of these products. It has been the fastest-growing futures exchange in the world in recent years and probably has a larger dollar turnover (many billions each day) than any other private sector entity in the world.

April 1977–June 1978: Senior partner of the law firm Nelson, Harding, Yeutter & Leonard in Lincoln, Nebraska. The firm had additional offices in several other cities. Responsible for the firm's agriculture-related practice and for coordinating all elements of the practice where Washington DC or international interests were involved.

June 1975–February 1977: Deputy Special Trade Representative, Executive Office of the President. This was an ambassadorial post with responsibility for conducting trade negotiations on behalf of the president and the U.S. government. It involved contacts and negotiations with representatives of many foreign governments, as well as coordination of U.S. policy positions with other federal departments, Congress, and numerous private sector advisory committees.

March 1974–June 1975: Assistant Secretary (now Undersecretary) of Agriculture for International Affairs and Commodity Programs. Responsible for all activities of the U.S. Department of Agriculture in the following agencies: Agricultural Stabilization and Conservation Services, Foreign Agriculture Service, Federal Crop Insurance Corporation, and Commodity Credit Corporation.

January 1973–March 1974: Assistant Secretary of Agriculture for

Marketing and Consumer Services. Responsible for essentially all regulatory and domestic market service functions in the U.S. Department of Agriculture. Agencies included Animal and Plant Health Inspection Service, Agricultural Marketing Service, Commodity Exchange Authority, Food and Nutrition Service, and Packers and Stockyards Administration.

January 1972–December 1972: Regional Director, Committee for the Reelection of the President. Responsible for all facets of the president's campaign in seven midwestern states. Also served as Director of Agriculture with responsibility for the agricultural portion of the campaign in all 50 states.

October 1970–December 1971: Administrator, Consumer and Marketing Service, U.S. Department of Agriculture. Responsible for such programs as meat and poultry inspection, the grading of agricultural products, development of product standards, market news, the administration of market orders, and procurement of food for commodity distribution and school lunch programs.

September 1968–October 1970: Director, University of Nebraska Mission in Colombia. The largest agricultural technical assistance program in the world at that time. Involved the participation of six midwestern land grant universities, with funding by AID, the Kellogg Foundation, and the Ford Foundation. Assistance was provided at the graduate and undergraduate levels in teaching, research, and extension in all major agricultural fields. Recipient agencies were the Colombian Agricultural Institute (which somewhat approximates the USDA) and the National University.

January 1966–September 1968: Executive Assistant to the Governor of Nebraska. Responsible for coordination between the governor and numerous agencies of state government, including the Department of Agriculture and all state educational institutions. Handled all legislative liaison work, including drafting of legislation to broaden the state tax base and to provide for state aid to education. Other major legislation enacted included the creation of a state department of economic development, establishment of a minimum wage, merger of the University of Nebraska and the

University of Omaha, and establishment of a state telecommunications commission.

January 1960–January 1966: Faculty member, Department of Agricultural Economics, University of Nebraska. This position involved a combination of teaching, research, and extension responsibilities in agricultural economics and agricultural law. The major professional area was resource economics (i.e., land and water). Taught part-time while completing the requirements for a PhD and JD, then served full-time in 1965 and 1966.

1957–75: Operator of a 2,500-acre farming/ranching/cattle feeding enterprise in central Nebraska.

1952–57: United States Air Force. Enlisted as a Basic Airman upon graduation from the University of Nebraska. Later received a direct commission in medical administration. Ranked first in graduating class in Basic Course in Medical Administration, Gunter AFB, Alabama. Was a recipient of numerous military awards. Continued in the active reserve until 1977.

Directorships

MEMBER, BOARD OF DIRECTORS, OF THE
FOLLOWING CORPORATIONS:

Burlington Capital Group, Omaha, Nebraska

Neogen Corporation, Lansing, Michigan

Rural Media Group, Omaha, Nebraska

MEMBER, BOARD OF DIRECTORS, OF THE FOLLOWING
ENTITIES OR NONPROFIT ORGANIZATIONS:

Advisory Board, Center for Trade Policy Studies, Cato Institute, Washington DC

Honorary Director, Swiss Commodity and Futures Association, Geneva, Switzerland

Board of Advisors, U.S.–New Zealand Council, Washington DC

FORMER MEMBER, BOARD OF DIRECTORS, OF THE
FOLLOWING CORPORATIONS:

American Commercial Lines (Chairman), Jeffersonville, Indiana

BAT Industries, London, England

Caterpillar, Peoria, Illinois

Chicago-Tokyo Bank, Chicago, Illinois

ConAgra, Omaha, Nebraska

Covanta Energy, Morristown, New Jersey

Cropsolution, Morrisville, North Carolina (former Chairman)

Farmers Insurance Company, Los Angeles, California

FMC Corporation, Chicago, Illinois

IMC Global, Northbrook, Illinois

Kislak, Miami Lakes, Florida

Lindsay Manufacturing Company, Lindsay, Nebraska

Mycogen Corporation, San Diego, California

OppenheimerFunds, New York, New York (former Chairman)

Texas Instruments, Dallas, Texas

Tri-Valley Growers, San Francisco, California

Vigoro Corporation, Chicago, Illinois

Weyerhaeuser Company, Federal Way, Washington

Zurich Financial Services, Zurich, Switzerland

FORMER MEMBER, BOARD OF DIRECTORS,
OF THE FOLLOWING ENTITIES:

Advisory Board, Board IQ, New York, New York

Agricultural Roundtable, Oak Brook, Illinois (former Chairman)

Advisory Board, Canadian American Business Council, Washington DC

Chicago Association of Commerce and Industry, Chicago, Illinois (former Chairman)

Chicago Council on Foreign Relations, Chicago, Illinois

Cordell Hull Institute, Washington DC (former Chairman)

Farm Foundation, Oak Brook, Illinois

Garrett-Evangelical Theological Seminary, Evanston, Illinois

Board of Visitors, Georgetown University School of Business Administration, Washington DC

Independent Directors Council, Washington DC

International Food and Agribusiness Management Association (former President)

Japan-America Society, Chicago, Illinois

Meridian International Center, Washington DC

President's Export Council, Washington DC

Swiss Commodity Industry Association, Zurich, Switzerland

U.S. Meat Export Federation, Denver, Colorado

Winrock, Morrilton, Arkansas

Other Significant Awards

HONORARY DOCTORATE DEGREES

Clemson University

DePaul University

Georgetown University

Nebraska Wesleyan University

Santa Clara University

University of Arizona

University of Maryland Eastern Shore

University of Nebraska

Chairman, Agricultural Development Task Force to Peru, appointed by President Reagan in response to U.S. commitments made at Third World Summit in 1981

First American businessman invited to Japan (in 1982) under Japanese government program to improve trade relationships with the United States

Israeli Prime Minister's Medal for longtime friendship to Israel and support for its economic development

American Farm Bureau Federation Distinguished Service Award

FarmHouse "Master Builder of Men" Award, the highest honor granted an alumnus of that fraternity

Fowler-McCracken Commission Leadership Award for Government

Distinguished Public Service Medal, Center for the Study of the Presidency

National 4-H Alumni Award

Service to American/World Agriculture Award, National Association of County Agricultural Agents

Mike Mansfield Award, the highest public service award granted by the U.S. Meat Export Federation

American Agricultural Editors' Association Distinguished Service Award

Distinguished Nebraskalander Award

Ak-Sar-Ben Court of Honor Award for Public Service, the first such award ever granted

Consumers for World Trade Hall of Fame, Washington DC

International Food Executive of the Year

American Society of Agricultural Consultants Distinguished Service Award

Chicago Farmers Distinguished Service to Agriculture Award

Fraternity of Alpha Zeta Centennial Honor Roll

Purdue University, Lafayette, Indiana, Old Masters award

University of Nebraska's comparable Masters Award

US-NZ Torchbearer Award from the United States–New Zealand Council, the first award presented by the council in recognition of contributions made in promoting global leadership on issues of importance to both nations

Fellow Award 2003 from the International Food and Agribusiness Management Association (IFAMA), the first award presented by IFAMA in recognition of outstanding and sustained contributions to the success of IFAMA and demonstrated leadership in the food and agribusiness industry

Champion for Rural America Award presented by Partners for Rural America

Nominee, Mutual Fund Trustee of the Year, 2003 (three nationwide)

Special Service Award given for support of international agriculture and rural development initiatives from the Association for International Agriculture and Rural Development, 2005

St. Duke Alexander Nevskiy Award given for development of cooperation in agriculture and trade from the Russian Academy of Security, Defence, and Law Enforcement, 2005

Trustee of the Year, Mutual Fund Industry, 2005

Selected for inclusion in the 2007 (and later) editions of *The Best Lawyers in America* for international trade and finance law

Leader in Agriculture Award presented by Agriculture Future of America, 2006

By order of the Queen, named Honorary Officer of the New Zealand Order of Merit

APPENDIX B

Yeutter's Major Accomplishments, as He Saw Them

The U.S.-Canada Free Trade Agreement

As U.S. trade representative (USTR), Ambassador Yeutter was responsible for this historic negotiation. Prior to this endeavor, only one free trade agreement had ever been negotiated by the United States, the much smaller U.S.-Israel Free Trade Agreement (FTA), concluded earlier in the Reagan administration. The U.S.-Canada FTA is still one of the largest bilateral free trade agreements ever concluded by anyone, and perhaps the most successful. (Trade volumes between the U.S. and Canada have quadrupled since it went into effect.) This was an exceedingly difficult negotiation, since it made headlines in Canada nearly every day for eighteen months or so. Mexico was later added to the agreement to constitute what then became the North American Free Trade Agreement. Most of that negotiation was conducted by Ambassador Carla Hills, who succeeded Ambassador Yeutter as USTR when George H. W. Bush became president and Dr. Yeutter became secretary of agriculture.

Launch of the Uruguay Round of GATT Negotiations

The Uruguay Round is the most extensive and most successful multilateral (many nation) trade negotiation ever conducted. But getting it launched was a formidable task. Ambassador Yeutter's predecessor had sought to do so in the early 1980s but failed. So American prestige was on the line in a big way when he sought to get the approximately one hundred member nations of the General Agreement on Tariffs and Trade (GATT) to agree to this exercise. Ambassador Yeutter and his delegation, which included several other cabinet members and a number of high-level U.S. business and agricultural officials as guests, accomplished that objective in Punta del Este, Uruguay, in September 1986. The United States had five major objectives for the negotiating agenda and secured approval to negotiate all five. Ambassador Yeutter slept about eight hours in five days, but that dedication paid off. For all practical purposes, agriculture made the agenda for the first time, as did intellectual property protection and services, two other areas of immense importance to U.S. global trade. At the end of the round, the World Trade Organization was created to replace the GATT, which had become outmoded.

The U.S.-Japan Semiconductor Agreement

Semiconductors are at the heart of high-technology products. Just consider the number of semiconductors in an airplane, an automobile, or a tank. When Dr. Yeutter became USTR, the U.S. industry was dying. In the view of many key U.S. government officials, the explanation was predatory practices on the part of Japanese semiconductor firms. Ambassador Yeutter decided to make an all-out attempt to counter such practices, for both economic and national security reasons. That led to a contentious negotiation between the two countries and ultimately to retaliation by the United States against certain practices of the Japanese industry. The final outcome was a bilateral agreement that has been an enormous success for the United States, having played a major role in the huge technology explosion the United States experienced in the 1990s. Today the United States has a semiconductor industry that is the envy of the world.

The U.S.-Japan Beef and Citrus Agreements

In the post–World War II period, Japan was immensely protectionist in agriculture. U.S. penetration of the Japanese market was minimal in almost every agricultural product. Japan had sky-high tariffs on agricultural products and also had put in place an institutional structure that made it possible to hold imports at levels that were among the most restrictive in the entire world. Ambassador Yeutter and his colleagues attacked all facets of that protectionism, especially in beef and citrus, and emerged from that endeavor with agreements in those two products. That not only has led to increased beef and citrus exports to Japan but also has made it possible to obtain improved access for other agricultural products. Our friends in Australia and New Zealand loved this effort, for it opened up important new market opportunities for them as well. They rode in on our coattails, but that's okay!

Reforms of the Common Agricultural Policy

The United States has fought more battles over the Common Agricultural Policy (CAP) of what is now the European Union than over any other agricultural policy structure in the world, including the Japanese policies just discussed. We expended a huge amount of effort in these struggles, going all the way back to the Tokyo Round during the Nixon and Carter administrations. Dr. Yeutter was involved in those early battles and then continued his involvement from the sidelines when he headed the Chicago Mercantile Exchange in the early 1980s. These issues continued to be on his personal agenda when he became USTR, and they received attention in the Uruguay Round and in a host of bilateral negotiations. The EU long argued that the CAP was sacrosanct and couldn't be touched, but that argument finally began to collapse in the late 1980s and on into the 1990s. The United States deserves no more than partial credit for the reforms that have occurred over the past thirty years, but our relentless pressure certainly had an impact. It was EU agriculture commissioner Ray Macsharry of Ireland who deserves much of the credit, and we are grateful for what has occurred. Would those reforms have emerged without intense U.S. pressure, more from Ambassador Yeutter than from anyone else? Perhaps, but the world is much better off for what has occurred.

The 1990 Farm Bill

One cannot expect other nations to follow sensible, open agricultural and trade policies if one is unwilling to do the same at home. With all the demands for reform that we placed on other nations throughout the world in the late 1980s, it was imperative that we pass a farm bill in 1990 that would uphold our share of this open trade bargain. We did that with bipartisan cooperation of the Congress. That farm bill was more market-oriented than any such bill the United States had put in place for half a century. It served us well as we expanded U.S. ag exports in subsequent years, and it took away any opportunity for our trading partners to accuse us of hypocrisy on the trade front.

A NOTE ABOUT THE YEUTTER INSTITUTE

Seeking to launch a world-class institute to enable students to navigate a global economy, Clayton and Cristena Bach Yeutter created the Clayton Yeutter Institute of International Trade and Finance at the University of Nebraska–Lincoln (UNL) in early 2015, winning formal approval from the university's Board of Regents in December 2017. The Yeutters chipped in $2.5 million, which the Nebraska State Legislature matched, and they attracted another $3 million, which was earmarked for establishing endowed faculty chairs, fellowships for students, and global trade conferences that drew major names in the field to Lincoln.

"More than ten years before the Institute was established, Clayton and I began discussing how we could expand the knowledge of how international trade impacts the world," Cristena says. "We wanted to create something tangible, that would prepare UNL students for leadership roles around the globe."

Their goal was twofold: to expose students to the challenging, important, and little-understood world of global trade and to help populate the field with talented, well-trained, and economically knowledgeable people. Yeutter learned the field by working in the world of global trade from its earliest days and blazing new paths; the institute could bring students up to speed in the field far more quickly, equipping them to make profound marks on it.

"Ultimately, Clayton and I hoped that the Yeutter Institute would produce trade negotiators, and government and corporate policy makers, who understand how integral free and fair trade is to growing the global economy," Cristena says.[1]

To explain the institute's mission, director Jill Kosch O'Donnell cites a letter former president George H. W. Bush sent to UNL chancellor Green in which the president called Yeutter a "game-changer" in global trade. "When I think about the Yeutter Institute, I think about building an institute that's a game-changer for students," she adds. Like that of the university overall, the institute's mission includes education, research, and public engagement, says O'Donnell, who took the helm as its first director in July 2018. When it comes to students, she adds, the institute is "about opening their eyes to how trade works and to what possibilities exist for them . . . what career paths are possible, exposing them to that and to people who've been very successful in that field."[2]

A student fellowship program, launched in the fall of 2020, brought thirteen undergraduates from an array of disciplines into the institute's programming. Students wrote briefing papers and memos on a variety of trade policy topics and explored trade-related career paths through networking opportunities, with some landing internships in the field for the summer of 2021. Earlier that year, the organization created the Steve Nelson Yeutter Institute International Trade Internship Award, providing $6,000 yearly for a student to intern during summers at the Washington International Trade Association (WITA). The award is a partnership among the institute, the Nebraska Farm Bureau, and WITA, which had bestowed a lifetime achievement award on Yeutter. Nelson retired at the end of 2020 as president of the state farm bureau, which he had led since 2011. Following their work with WITA, each intern will organize a public discussion on an agriculture trade policy topic important to Nebraska. The institute also launched the Yeutter Student Scholar Award Fund to support students doing unpaid or modestly paid internships in trade-related organizations.

The institute also created opportunities for students, irrespective of their academic majors, to learn about the field. These included courses laying the groundwork for a minor degree and a graduate specialization in international trade and finance, and eventually a possible major degree. O'Donnell was scheduled to teach one such course in the fall of 2021, focusing on international trade policy and politics.

Pursuing its mission of fostering research, the institute funded professorships, hiring John C. Beghin as the Michael Yanney Chair in the UNL Department of Agricultural Economics in 2019 and Edward J. Balistreri as the Duane Acklie Chair in the Department of Economics at the university's College of Business in 2020. Matthew Schaefer, the Veronica A. Haggart and Charles R. Work Professor of International Trade Law in the College of Law, also became an integral part of the institute. Early interdisciplinary research collaborations among these three core faculty members included the cost of the U.S.-China trade war and the impact of the Market Facilitation Payment program on the U.S. and Nebraska economies (Beghin and Balistreri) and gene-edited agricultural regulation (Beghin and Schaefer). As of this writing, the institute also planned to fill an endowed faculty position in the College of Law. In the meantime, it brought in two visiting law professors to teach one-credit courses on specialized international trade law topics. Overall, the approach reflected the many interests Yeutter had in his life: law, agriculture, economics, business, education, and above all, trade.

"I am very enthused by the unique opportunity created by Clayton Yeutter's vision with the named institute and the Michael Yanney Chair," Beghin said when he joined UNL. "I foresee much potential to develop programs for students interested in globalization and international trade, to undertake applied economic research on Nebraska's agriculture and allied industries, and to engage with stakeholders in the state and the Midwest." As the university noted in a press release when he joined, Beghin's expertise in international agriculture and food markets economics suited him for the UNL position. He studied nontariff measures, trade and the environment, and global food security and was a fellow of the Agricultural and Applied Economics Association, the main professional association of agricultural economists.[3] In early 2021 Beghin created a new course in international agricultural trade. He also was slated to work with four students on a pair of projects for the Minnesota-based Cargill Corporation over the summer of 2021 in an applied economics research internship program.

Balistreri, a former research economist at the U.S. International Trade Commission and consultant, worked with legal teams in analyzing trade pacts and disputes, at times focusing on agricultural products important in Nebraska. "For me the institute represents a unique conduit for advancing the field of international trade and finance from both a legal and economic perspective," Balistreri said when he took the chair. "As the Duane Acklie Chair I foresee contributing practical policy analysis that is informative to students and stakeholders. I hope to capitalize on this opportunity to contribute to the team's far-reaching education and outreach activities from here in America's heartland."[4]

The institute also developed a far-reaching podcast series called *Trade Matters*, in which experts discussed trade issues. Renee Bowen, an economics professor at the Center for Commerce and Diplomacy at UC San Diego, spoke about the World Trade Organization (WTO) and U.S. domestic politics in one episode. In another, Wendy Cutler of the Asia Society Policy Institute, who had negotiated the Trans-Pacific Partnership trade deal for the United States, discussed how the United States should engage the Asia-Pacific region. Clete R. Willems, a former White House trade adviser, argued for reforming the WTO in yet another episode. And in still another, Kenneth Smith Ramos, Mexico's point man on the renegotiation of the North American Free Trade Agreement, detailed the bargaining that led to the United States–Mexico–Canada Agreement. Other episodes featured U.S. Navy admiral (ret.) James G. Stavridis, U.S. chief agricultural negotiator ambassador Gregg Doud, Salman Ahmed of the Carnegie Endowment for International Peace, Senior Trade Commissioner Carl Pilon of the Consulate General of Canada in Minneapolis, and Michael G. Plummer of the Johns Hopkins School of Advanced International Studies, among many others.

Relationships that Yeutter developed around the world helped put the institute on solid footing, as academics, trade officials, and businesspeople came forward to join its advisory council. Darci Vetter, a former U.S. chief agricultural negotiator, served on the council and played a key role in assembling the inaugural thirteen-member group, which included a retired CEO from Weyerhaeuser Company, an international trade association director, a top executive of Cargill, an academic from the Georgetown University Law Center, a top executive from CME Group, a major trade lawyer, the creator of a popular trade policy website, and others. Still others, including top trade academics and diplomats, came forward to take part in conferences the institute held (initially in person at UNL, but sessions in 2020 and early 2021 were virtual because of the COVID-19 epidemic).

Speakers at institute presentations in the fall of 2020 included a panoply of experts. Ambassador Marc Grossman, formerly the third-ranking U.S. State Department official as under secretary of state for political affairs, discussed reshaping the U.S. Foreign Service. Former trade negotiators and former White House trade advisers discussed new approaches to trade negotiations and delved into the impact of Chinese industrial subsidies on trade. Top academics from law schools at the University of Miami, UCLA, and Nebraska examined the questionable future of the WTO. Business leaders from Cargill, CME Group, and Rabobank detailed the management of risk in agricultural trade. Experts from the University of Cambridge and the University of Michigan spelled out the special trade relationship between the United States and the United Kingdom.

Also in 2020 the institute hosted a bipartisan, off-the-record discussion on congressional trade priorities featuring Katherine C. Tai, chief trade counsel for the House Ways and Means Committee, and Mayur Patel, chief trade counsel for the Senate Finance Committee. President-elect Joe Biden later nominated Tai to be U.S. trade representative, and she was sworn in to the post in March 2021.

In a 2019 session a top businessperson from Deere & Company reviewed global growth and agricultural trade. In another session that year, Edward Alden of the Council on Foreign Relations gave a keynote address, placing the uncertainty surrounding U.S. trade policy at the time into historical context. And in 2018, at the inaugural conference of the institute's CME Symposium, Canada's deputy ambassador, Kirsten Hillman, joined Vetter on a panel that explored changing trade alliances. These are just a few examples of the many sessions.

The institute's ability to pull in such marquee names in global trade reflected Yeutter's broad range of friends and colleagues. "I cannot overemphasize how many people I have met (or run into virtually during the COVID pandemic) all over the country and the world who remember Clayton with tremendous respect both for how he treated them and what he achieved in his career," O'Donnell says. "Even people who met him only once remember exactly when and where that was and the impression he made on them. The tremendous amount of goodwill he sowed around the country and the world paved the way for the Yeutter Institute."[5]

And much as Yeutter had to adapt to unexpected challenges as he worked to open the world's trading system, institute officials had to prove flexible amid the COVID-19 pandemic. In the summer of 2020, for instance, five UNL interns were ready to go to work at a global food and agriculture company through an arrangement with the institute. When that became impractical, the institute set up partnerships with Nebraska state offices and other agencies to give the students hands-on experience under Beghin's mentorship. Some of the students analyzed the impact of the pandemic on Nebraska's nonprofit sector, while others created a searchable database of manufacturing exporters for the Nebraska Department of Economic Development. As they mastered data management skills, the university reported, the students made a practical difference by developing a database that allowed businesses to explore sourcing or selling products globally—an effort of which the ever-practical Yeutter likely would have been proud.[6]

"You must prepare yourselves to live in a world that will never look like the one that has been occupied by your parents and grandparents," Yeutter told students in a prescient 1989 lecture at Kansas State University. He added:

> The world is changing more rapidly today than ever before, and you are going to have to adjust to that. It is not a time, students, for people to go out on jobs with an attitude that is one of timidity. It is not a time to be averse to risk. It is not a time to be resistant to change. If you fit in those categories you will experience a very frustrating life indeed. If, on the other hand, you are prepared to be a courageous risk-taker, and you have a bit of the pioneer spirit that we saw in this country one hundred years ago, and if you are prepared to be broad and creative and global in your thinking, you should have a very productive and rewarding career indeed.[7]

PEOPLE INTERVIEWED

Allen J. Beermann

Judith H. Bello

Gary Blumenthal

Roger Bolton

John S. Bottimore

Kim Y. Bottimore

William E. Brock III

Carole L. Brookins

Derek H. Burney

Leonard W. Condon

Richard T. Crowder

Ray R. Easterday

Edward J. Farrell

Ronnie D. Green

Carla A. Hills

Alan F. Holmer

J. Robert Kerrey

John J. Lothian

People Interviewed

Barbara Marschang-Hendry

Warren H. Maruyama

Leo Melamed

E. Benjamin Nelson

Susan K. Nelson

Jill Kosch O'Donnell

E. Wesley F. Peterson

William A. Reinsch

Charles E. "Chip" Roh Jr.

John F. "Jack" Sandner

Terry Savage

Kelly Semrau

Mildred Stagemeyer

John H. Sununu

A. Ellen Terpstra

Carol Lee Tucker-Foreman

Darci L. Vetter

John M. Weekes

Michael B. Yanney

Cristena Bach Yeutter

Elena Yeutter

Gregg S. Yeutter

Olivia Yeutter

Van A. Yeutter

NOTES

1. Rugged Times

1. State of Nebraska Certificate of Birth, Clayton K. Yeutter, U.S. Secretary of Agriculture Papers (MS 0360), Archives and Special Collections, University of Nebraska–Lincoln Libraries (hereafter cited as Yeutter Papers).

2. Timothy Hutchens, "He Spends His Weeks in White House and His Weekends on the Range," *Washington Star,* 1975; Jay Richter, "Yeutter (Rhymes with Fighter) Takes on Global Trade Chaos," *Farmland News,* August 15, 1986, Yeutter Papers. Richter quotes Yeutter as saying, "I walked to school with holes in my shoes and sheets of cardboard filling the holes. Those were rough days."

3. The Great Depression comprised two recessions, with the first stretching from August 1929 to March 1933. A feeble recovery followed until May 1937, when another recession lasted until June 1938, followed by slow recovery. See "US Business Cycle Expansions and Contractions," National Bureau of Economic Research, last updated June 8, 2020, https://www.nber.org/research/data/us-business-cycle-expansions-and-contractions.

4. During the 1930s drought and wind dried out the land across the Great Plains, at times spawning massive dust storms in Nebraska and elsewhere. The *Hastings Tribune* in March 1935 reported on one such storm in the area, less than a hundred miles east of Eustis, which was marked by a sixty-mile-per-hour gale that "struck with tornadic fury." Piles of dust were soon covered by snow. See "Timeline Tuesday: Dust and Snow in 1935 Hastings," *History Nebraska Blog,* https://history.nebraska.gov/blog/timeline-tuesday-dust-and-snow-1935-hastings; "Dust Bowl Migration," *Rural Migration News* 14, no. 4 (October 2008), https://migration.ucdavis.edu/rmn/more.php?id=1355.

5. Dennis J. Opatrny, "Motivation Carried Clayton Yeutter from Farm to Position of Influence," *Lincoln Journal,* February 25, 1967, Yeutter Papers.

6. Hutchens, "He Spends His Weeks."

7. "A Great Man's Journey: Trip Home Reminds Yeutter of His Great Nebraska Roots," Donor Stories, UNL, University of Nebraska Foundation, February 10, 2016, https://nufoundation.org/a-great-mans-journey-trip-home-reminds-yeutter-of-his-great-nebraska-roots/.

8. Clayton Yeutter, email to Orion Samuelson, April 12, 2013, shared with the author by Gregg S. Yeutter.

9. Cristena Bach Yeutter, email to the author, July 10, 2020.

10. "A Man in Perpetual High Gear," *Today's 4-H*, December 31, 1987, Yeutter Papers.

11. "Great Man's Journey."

12. Tim Anderson, editor's note, *Sunday Omaha World-Herald Magazine of the Midlands*, August 4, 1985, Yeutter Papers.

13. Clayton Yeutter, note to Marlene Timmermann, April 6, 1967. See also letter to County Extension Agent Harold Stevens, March 8, 1967, acknowledging a 4-H Alumni Recognition nomination. Both in the Yeutter Papers.

14. "Great Man's Journey."

15. Clayton Yeutter, email to Orion Samuelson, April 12, 2013, shared with the author by Gregg S. Yeutter.

16. Clayton Yeutter, "Washington's Historic Sights Impress Nebraska Visitors," *Omaha World-Herald*, undated, Yeutter Papers.

17. *Cloverleaf* Staff Medal Winners, June 1946, Yeutter Papers.

18. Barbara Marschang-Hendry, conversation with the author, February 13, 2020.

19. Mildred Stagemeyer, conversation with the author, February 14, 2020.

20. Madison Yeutter, "The 1940's: Interview with Clayton Yeutter," April 2006, Yeutter Papers.

21. Marschang-Hendry, conversation, February 13, 2020.

22. Ray R. Easterday, conversation with the author, January 31, 2020.

23. See Frank, *What's the Matter with Kansas?*, 15–32.

24. Hutchens, "He Spends His Weeks."

25. Clayton Yeutter, letter to Cliff W. Burkhead, April 23, 1992, Yeutter Papers.

26. Clayton Yeutter, email to Orion Samuelson, April 12, 2013, shared with the author by Gregg S. Yeutter.

27. J. Robert Kerrey, conversation with the author, October 28, 2019.

28. Lincoln Bureau, "Income Tax Bill Author Is Tiemann's Top Aid [*sic*]," *Omaha World-Herald*, November 23, 1966, Yeutter Papers.

29. "Meet C&MS Administrator Clayton Yeutter," *Meat Management*, May 1971, Yeutter Papers.

30. "Man in Perpetual High Gear."

31. Cristena Bach Yeutter, conversation with the author, November 14, 2019, and email December 3, 2020.

32. Clayton Yeutter, interview with George S. Round at the University of Nebraska–Lincoln, January 6, 1975, Yeutter Papers.

33. "Man in Perpetual High Gear."

34. Anderson, editor's note.

35. Clayton Yeutter, memorandum for the president, May 4, 1989, Yeutter Papers.

36. Announcement of a Centennial Breakfast at the United Methodist Church of Seward, Nebraska, Yeutter Papers.

37. Clayton Yeutter, letter to Rev. Richard H. Englund, May 31, 1967, Yeutter Papers.

38. Van A. Yeutter, conversation with the author, June 22, 2020.

39. Clayton Yeutter, "Doers Profile," *Washington Times*, July 28, 1992, Yeutter Papers; Kelly Semrau, conversation with the author, November 5, 2019.

40. Jay Richter, "Energy Runs in the Family," *Farmland News*, August 15, 1986, sidebar to "Yeutter (Rhymes with Fighter) Takes on Global Trade Chaos," Yeutter Papers.

41. Ambassador Clayton Yeutter, of Nebraska, prepared statement, "Nomination of Clayton Yeutter, of Nebraska, to be Secretary of Agriculture," *Hearing before the Committee on Agriculture, Nutrition, and Forestry, United States Senate*, February 2, 1989, University of Minnesota Depository Pubn. U.S.-G.P.O.-D-301-A, St. Paul Campus Libraries, 50, https://www.google.com/books/edition/Nomination_of_Clayton_Yeutter/FVAkQXmEokcC.

42. "Biographical Sketches of Nominees: Clayton Yeutter," *Nominations of Richard C. Holmquist, Clayton Yeutter, and William N. Walker, Hearings Before the Committee on Finance, United States Senate*, May 14–15, 1975, 18, https://www.google.com/books/edition/Nominations_of_Richard_C_Holmquist_Clayt/uFESAAAAIAAJ.

43. Cristena Bach Yeutter, email to the author, December 3, 2020.

44. "Resume of Dr. Clayton K. Yeutter," *Hearing before the Committee on Finance, United States Senate, Ninety-Ninth Congress, First Session, on Nomination of Dr. Clayton K. Yeutter to Be the U.S. Trade Representative*, June 25, 1985, 26, https://www.finance.senate.gov/imo/media/doc/HRG99-216.pdf.

45. Clayton Yeutter, vita, Yeutter Papers.

46. Clayton Yeutter, letter to Mr. and Mrs. Jack Brothers, August 30, 1999, Yeutter Papers.

47. Clayton Yeutter, letter to Jack R. Bol, January 18, 1991, Yeutter Papers.

48. Yeutter, letter to Bol, January 18, 1991.

49. Letter to Stevens, March 8, 1967.

50. Clayton Yeutter, letter to The Honorable Frank B. Morrison Sr., June 16, 1999, Yeutter Papers, UNL Libraries.

51. J. James Exon, a U.S. Senator from Nebraska, witness statement, *Hearing before the Committee on Finance, United States Senate*, June 25, 1985, 4, https://www.finance.senate.gov/imo/media/doc/HRG99-216.pdf.

52. Linda Schotsch, "Resume of a Trade Rep," *Top Producer*, June 1985, Yeutter Papers.

53. Clayton Yeutter, interview with George S. Round, January 6, 1975, Yeutter Papers.

54. "Biographical Sketches of Nominees: Clayton Yeutter," 18.

55. Hon. J. Robert Kerrey, a U.S. Senator from Nebraska, prepared statement, "Nomination of Clayton Yeutter, of Nebraska, to Be Secretary of Agriculture," *Hearing before the Committee on Agriculture, Nutrition, and Forestry, United States Senate*,

February 2, 1989, University of Minnesota Depository Pubn. U.S.-G.P.O.-D-301-A, St. Paul Campus Libraries, 8, https://www.google.com/books/edition/Nomination _of_Clayton_Yeutter/FVAkQXmEokcC.

56. Clayton Keith Yeutter, "The Administration of Water Law in the Central United States: A Legal-Economic Critique of Laws and Administrative Procedures in Colorado, Kansas, Nebraska, and Iowa" (PhD diss., University of Nebraska–Lincoln, 1966), ProQuest Dissertations Publishing, 4, https://www.proquest.com /docview/302222803.

57. Clayton Yeutter, remarks, Annual Conference of the Nebraska Association of Soil and Water Conservation Districts, Kearney, Nebraska, September 1966, Yeutter Papers.

58. "Waters of the West," editorial, *Wall Street Journal*, April 20, 1992; Clayton Yeutter, memorandum for Bob Bartley, April 20, 1992, Yeutter Papers.

59. "Tiemann, Governor Norbert (Nobby)," obituary, *Lincoln Journal Star*, July 13, 2012, https://journalstar.com/lifestyles/announcements/obituaries/tiemann-governor -norbert-nobby/article_c0bd39a2-1537-5082-a173-5606ac3eb114.html.

60. "Governor's Top Counsel," editorial, *Tri-City Tribune* (Cozad NE), November 29, 1966, 2.

2. The Clayton Grin

1. "Governor's Top Counsel," editorial, *Tri-City Tribune* (Cozad NE), November 29, 1966, 2.

2. "Nebraska 1966 Ballot Measures," BallotPedia, https://ballotpedia.org/Nebraska _1966_ballot_measures.

3. Dick Herman, "The Tiemann Administration's First Year—II: '67 Unicam OKd Most of Governor's Proposals," *Lincoln Evening Journal and Nebraska State Journal*, December 19, 1967, 3, Yeutter Papers.

4. Don Walton, "50 Years Ago, Nebraskans 'Aroused to the Point of Fury' over Taxes," *Lincoln Journal Star*, April 10, 2017, https://journalstar.com/news/state-and -regional/govt-and-politics/years-ago-nebraskans-aroused-to-the-point-of-fury-over /article_15e33f6b-3709-5338-8139-42ce726cfb1f.html; Matt Schudel, "Sen. J. James Exon Dies at 83," *Washington Post*, June 12, 2005, https://www.washingtonpost.com /archive/local/2005/06/12/sen-j-james-exon-dies-at-83/2608f86c-ec56-456d-b683 -bd7e330634b4/.

5. Michele Brown, "Ex-Gov.: Alternative to Taxes Was Economic Death," *Kearney Hub*, December 20, 2006, https://www.kearneyhub.com/news/local/ex-gov-alternative -to-taxes-was-economic-death/article_f7d35cad-cd97-520d-8a82-bff89b583ffc.html.

6. See William F. Buckley, "Goldwater, the John Birch Society, and Me," *Commentary*, March 2008, https://www.commentarymagazine.com/articles/goldwater -the-john-birch-society-and-me/.

7. "Wasting No Time," editorial, *Lincoln Star*, November 24, 1966, Yeutter Papers.

8. Rowland Evans and Robert Novak, "Nebraska's Gov. Tiemann: A Symbol of G.O.P. Schism," *Des Moines Register*, June 29, 1967, Yeutter Papers.

9. "New Way to Spell Nebraska," *Time*, April 28, 1967, 23, Yeutter Papers.

10. Clayton Yeutter, letter to Herb Zwink, March 9, 1967, Yeutter Papers.

11. Clayton Yeutter, letter to Prof. Neil E. Harl, May 26, 1967, Yeutter Papers.

12. Madeline Brown, "Vietnam War Protests at the Disapproval of the Nebraska Legislature," *Nebraska U: A Collaborative History*, Fall 2019, http://unlhistory.unl.edu/exhibits/show/vietnam-war/vietnam-war.

13. See Maurine Biegert, correspondence from "Nebraska Democrats Care," letter to Nebraska senator William R. Skarda, November 7, 1967, in Yeutter Papers. The letter asked that he oppose a boost in the state sales tax from 2 to 3 percent as advocated by Governor Tiemann and included a copy of a resolution to that effect adopted by the Democratic State Executive Committee on November 2.

14. Clayton Yeutter, letter to Dr. Bert Evans, April 11, 1967, Yeutter Papers.

15. Allen J. Beermann, conversation with the author, February 10, 2020.

16. Undated and unidentified newspaper clip, Yeutter Papers.

17. Clayton Yeutter, letter to Dr. and Mrs. Gerald J. Bergman, April 23, 1968, Yeutter Papers.

18. Dr. William K. Clark, "Political Blackmail," letter to the editor, Public Pulse, *Omaha World-Herald*, March 28, 1968; Lincoln Bureau, "Yeutter Says Kearney Talk No Blackmail," *Omaha World-Herald*, April 2, 1968, both in Yeutter Papers.

19. Clayton Yeutter, letter to Prof. A. W. Epp, University of Nebraska, March 26, 1968, reacting to an article by Darrell Petska, "'Opportunities Limited for Ag Econ Majors': Economists Get Better Jobs—Yeutter," *Daily Nebraskan*, March 18, 1968, 3, both in Yeutter Papers.

20. Ellen Sim (Mrs. Robert) Dewey, correspondence with Clayton Yeutter, April 13, 1968, Yeutter Papers.

21. Clayton Yeutter, letter to Mrs. Robert Dewey, April 17, 1968, Yeutter Papers.

22. Clayton Yeutter, letter to Beverly Schroeder, April 19, 1968, Yeutter Papers.

23. Clayton Yeutter, letter to Mrs. Rita Shaw, January 3, 1968, Yeutter Papers.

24. Clayton Yeutter, letter to Gary Johnson, January 4, 1968, Yeutter Papers.

25. Clayton Yeutter, letters to Dick Herman and to Don Walton, January 3, 1968, Yeutter Papers.

26. Clayton Yeutter, letter to Bill Dobler, *Lincoln Star*, July 10, 1968, Yeutter Papers.

27. Clayton Yeutter, letter to Jack Hart, *Lincoln Journal*, August 29, 1968, Yeutter Papers.

28. Ron Hull, letter to Clayton Yeutter, Nebraska Educational Television Commission, July 8, 1968, Yeutter Papers.

29. Clayton Yeutter, letter to Ron Hull, July 11, 1968, Yeutter Papers.

30. "Meet C&MS Boss: Dr. Yeutter (as in 'Fighter')!," *Broiler Industry*, July 1971, 19, Yeutter Papers.

31. Clayton Yeutter, excerpts from an August 25, 1968, talk at Christ United Methodist Church in Lincoln, supplement, *Together*, November 1968, A1–3, Yeutter Papers.

32. Bob Warden, "Chicago Economist Says Program for Poverty Ill Conceived, Fails," *Chicago Daily News*, March 1, 1968, Yeutter Papers.

33. Clayton Yeutter, letter to Mrs. Carl Rickertsen, April 17, 1968, Yeutter Papers.

34. Dennis J. Opatrny, "Motivation Carried Clayton Yeutter from Farm to Position of Influence," *Lincoln Journal*, February 25, 1967, Yeutter Papers.

35. Clayton Yeutter, letter to Dennis J. "Pat" Opatrny, January 2, 1968, Yeutter Papers.

36. Yeutter, letter to Opatrny, January 2, 1968.

37. Carl Nolte, "Dennis Opatrny, Veteran SF Reporter of Crime and Courts, Dies," SFGATE, June 25, 2016, https://www.sfgate.com/bayarea/article/Dennis-Opatrny -veteran-SF-reporter-of-crime-and-8325088.php.

38. "1968 Republican Party Presidential Primaries," Wikipedia, last modified January 11, 2021, https://en.wikipedia.org/wiki/1968_Republican_Party_presidential _primaries; Gene Kopelson, "The 1968 Nebraska Republican Primary," *Nebraska History* 95 (2014): 162–72, https://history.nebraska.gov/sites/history.nebraska.gov /files/doc/publications/NH2014Republican.pdf.

39. "Meet C&MS Administrator Clayton Yeutter," *Meat Management*, May 1971, 28, Yeutter Papers.

40. Cristena Bach Yeutter, conversation with the author, November 14, 2019.

3. More Self-Help

1. Clayton Yeutter, interview with George S. Round, January 6, 1975, Yeutter Papers.

2. Country Profile—Colombia, *New Agriculturalist*, January 2010, http://www .new-ag.info/en/country/profile.php?a=1056.

3. World Bank, Colombia, 2021, https://data.worldbank.org/country/colombia.

4. Clayton Yeutter, interview with George S. Round, January 6, 1975, Yeutter Papers.

5. Clayton Yeutter, letter to Rex Messersmith, July 10, 1968, Yeutter Papers.

6. Clayton Yeutter, letter to Michael V. Smith, July 24, 1968, Yeutter Papers.

7. Clayton Yeutter, letter to Dr. Dale Flowerday, University of Nebraska Mission in Colombia, August 29, 1968.

8. "Yeutter Tells Education Impact on Colombians," *Lincoln Evening Journal and Nebraska State Journal*, undated clip, Yeutter Papers.

9. World Factbook, Central Intelligence Agency, February 25, 2021, https://www .cia.gov/the-world-factbook/countries/colombia/.

10. See Oscar Medina, "Mexican Drug Cartels Now Make Their Own Cocaine, Colombia Says," Bloomberg, May 15, 2019, https://www.bloomberg.com/news/articles /2019-05-15/mexican-drug-cartels-now-make-their-own-cocaine-colombia-says.

11. Conor Friedersdorf, "Why the War on Cocaine Still Isn't Working: U.S. Policy Continues to Harm Colombia While Failing to Prevent Immense Quantities of Cocaine from Reaching American Soil," *Atlantic*, June 21, 2020, https://www .theatlantic.com/ideas/archive/2020/06/why-the-war-on-cocaine-still-isnt-working /613297/. See also Muse, *Kilo*.

12. Ruth Thone, "Jeanne Is Lonely for Her Friends in Colombia," *Omaha World-Herald*, September 20, 1970, Yeutter Papers.

13. Gregg S. Yeutter, conversation with the author, June 25, 2020.

14. Clayton Yeutter, "Here's the Story behind the Story on This One," note for personal biographical file, April 20, 2015, Yeutter Papers.

15. "The Plumbers," *New York Times*, July 22, 1973, https://www.nytimes.com/1973/07/22/archives/the-plumbers.html.

16. "Resume of Dr. Clayton K. Yeutter," *Hearing before the Committee on Finance, United States Senate, Ninety-Ninth Congress, First Session, on Nomination of Dr. Clayton K. Yeutter to Be the U.S. Trade Representative*, June 25, 1985, 27, https://www.finance.senate.gov/imo/media/doc/HRG99-216.pdf.

17. Yeutter, "Here's the Story."

18. Clayton Yeutter, "The 70s," note to Mary Boote Roth, July 31, 2016, Yeutter Papers.

19. "C&MS Prepares for Future Shock," *Meat Management*, May 1971, 27, Yeutter Papers.

20. "Inspection's Super-Boss Airs His Philosophy," *Broiler Industry*, July 1971, 16–17, Yeutter Papers.

21. "Inspection's Super-Boss," 20, 27, 21, 22.

22. See Turner, *Chemical Feast*; Philip M. Boffey, "Nader's Raiders on the FDA: Science and Scientists 'Misused,'" *Science* 168, no. 3929 (April 17, 1970): 349–52.

23. Roger Hirsch, "Yeutter: Society Must Accentuate Positive," *Lincoln Journal*, May 1, 1971, 8–9, Yeutter Papers.

24. "Inspection's Super-Boss," 27.

25. "Meet C&MS Administrator Clayton Yeutter," *Meat Management*, May 1971, 29, Yeutter Papers.

26. Dennis J. Opatrny, "Motivation Carried Clayton Yeutter from Farm to Position of Influence," *Lincoln Journal*, February 25, 1967, Yeutter Papers.

27. "Deadlines Put Pressure on Yeutter in New Job," *Lincoln Evening Journal and Nebraska State Journal*, Jan. 27, 1971, 23, Yeutter Papers.

28. Van A. Yeutter, conversation with the author, June 22, 2020.

29. Yeutter, "The 70s"; Associated Press, "Yeutter Is Expected to Resign Post as the Head of Consumer Services," *Lincoln Journal*, November 15, 1971, Yeutter Papers.

4. Character Flaws

1. Arthur M. Eckstein, "How the Weather Underground Failed at Revolution and Still Changed the World," *Time*, November 2, 2016, https://time.com/4549409/the-weather-underground-bad-moon-rising/.

2. Clayton Yeutter, letter to Ray Lyne, April 21, 1972, Yeutter Papers.

3. "Resume of Dr. Clayton K. Yeutter," *Hearing before the Committee on Finance, United States Senate, Ninety-Ninth Congress, First Session, on Nomination of Dr. Clayton K. Yeutter to Be the U.S. Trade Representative*, June 25, 1985, 27, https://www.finance.senate.gov/imo/media/doc/HRG99 216.pdf.

4. Clayton Yeutter, personal files, June 29, 2015, Yeutter Papers.

5. See Bernard Brenner, "Funeral Forecast Termed Premature," *Lubbock Avalanche-Journal*, December 19, 1971; Dominic Costello, "Yeutter: Nixon Seeking Farmers' Votes in Virtually Every State," *Lincoln Journal*, undated, both in Yeutter Papers.

6. Bernard Brenner, "Farm 4–14," April 17, 1971, Yeutter Papers.

7. Brenner, "Farm 4–14."

8. "Republicans Pledge More If President Nixon Is Re-Elected" and "Democrats Outline Plans for Farmers If Sen. McGovern Wins," undated and unsourced comparison of party platforms, Yeutter Papers. For a full discussion of parity, see Peterson, *Billion Dollars a Day*, 130–31.

9. DeVan L. Shumway, "Agriculture Organized in 50 States to Support President Nixon," News from the Committee for the Re-election of the President, October 24, 1972, Yeutter Papers.

10. Edward Cowan, "Mandatory Wage-Price Controls Ended Except in Food, Health, Building Fields; Nixon Call for Voluntary Compliance," *New York Times*, January 12, 1973, https://www.nytimes.com/1973/01/12/archives/mandatory-wageprice-controls-ended-except-in-food-health-building.html.

11. See "Nixon and the End of the Bretton Woods System, 1971–73," Office of the Historian, U.S. Department of State, https://history.state.gov/milestones/1969-1976/nixon-shock.

12. Gene Healy, "Remembering Nixon's Wage and Price Controls," DC *Examiner*, republished by the Cato Institute, August 16, 2011, https://www.cato.org/publications/commentary/remembering-nixons-wage-price-controls.

13. Yergin and Stanislaw, *Commanding Heights*, lxxxi.

14. See "US Business Cycle Expansions and Contractions," National Bureau of Economic Research, last updated June 8, 2020, https://www.nber.org/research/data/us-business-cycle-expansions-and-contractions.

15. See "Nixon and the End of the Bretton Woods System, 1971–73," Office of the Historian, U.S. Department of State, https://history.state.gov/milestones/1969-1976/nixon-shock.

16. Katherine Hatch, "Big Campaign by McGovern for Farmer Vote Expected," *Sunday Oklahoman*, undated clip, Yeutter Papers.

17. Dominick Costello, "Yeutter: Nixon Seeking Farmers' Votes in Virtually Every State," *Lincoln Journal Star*, undated clip, Yeutter Papers.

18. Don Kendall, "Farmers-GOP 450," Associated Press, undated clip, Yeutter Papers.

19. Charles Carter, no headline, *Denver Post*, undated clip, Yeutter Papers.

20. Carter, no headline.

21. "The 1972 Nixon Agricultural Campaign," undated document, Yeutter Papers.

22. Associated Press, "Farm Strategy Gets Back Seat to War Policy," *Atlanta Journal and Constitution*, May 21, 1972, Yeutter Papers.

23. Clayton Yeutter, Committee for the Re-election of the President, correspondence to Mr. and Mrs. William M. Brown of Atmore, Alabama, November 15, 1972, Yeutter Papers.

24. "Resume of Dr. Clayton K. Yeutter."

25. Economic Research Service/USDA, "Legislative and Regulatory History of the WIC Program," *The WIC Program: Background, Trends, and Economic Issues, 2009 Edition*, https://www.ers.usda.gov/webdocs/publications/46165/17227_err73c

_3_pdf?v=0; "First w1c Program Slated for San Diego," *West Side Index* (Newman ca), September 6, 1973, Yeutter Papers.

26. Clayton Yeutter, unaddressed letter in a biography file, June 29, 2015, Yeutter Papers.

27. Yeutter, unaddressed letter, June 29, 2015.

28. Nixon Foundation, "8.10.1973—rn Signs Agriculture and Consumer Protection Act," Richard Nixon Foundation, August 10, 2010, https://www.nixonfoundation .org/2010/08/8-10-1973-rn-signs-agriculture-and-consumer-protection-act/.

29. Clayton Yeutter, "The New American Agriculture," address at Food Update 74 in Scottsdale, Arizona, April 24, 1974, Yeutter Papers.

30. See Alice Popovici, "Watergate: Who Did What and Where Are They Now?," *History Stories*, October 16, 2018, https://www.history.com/news/watergate-where -are-they-now.

31. See "The Watergate Scandal: A Timeline," *History Stories*, October 9, 2018, https://www.history.com/topics/watergate-scandal-timeline-nixon.

32. Bart Barnes, "Nixon Vice President Spiro T. Agnew Dies," *Washington Post*, September 19, 1996, https://www.washingtonpost.com/archive/local/1996/09/19 /nixon-vice-president-spiro-t-agnew-dies/6616ed01-311a-4b13-8051-dd0ce3782552/.

33. "Richard Nixon's Top Domestic and Foreign Policy Achievements," Richard Nixon Foundation, https://www.nixonfoundation.org/richard-nixons-top-domestic -and-foreign-policy-achievements/.

34. Milton Friedman, "Commanding Heights," interview with pbs, wgbs, October 1, 2000, https://www.pbs.org/wgbh/commandingheights/shared/minitext/int _miltonfriedman.html#8.

35. "President Nixon Arrives in Moscow for Historic Summit," *This Day in History: May 22*, last updated May 20, 2020, https://www.history.com/this-day-in-history /president-nixon-in-moscow.

36. Michael C. Jensen, "Soviet Grain Deal Is Called a Coup," *New York Times*, September 29, 1972, https://www.nytimes.com/1972/09/29/archives/soviet-grain-deal-is -called-a-coup-capitalistic-skill-surprised.html.

37. Clayton Yeutter, "National Food Policy—A Broad Perspective," Proceedings, address at the National American Wholesale Grocers Assn., Midyear Executive Conference, October 1, 1977, Yeutter Papers.

38. "Richard Nixon's Top Domestic and Foreign Policy Achievements," Richard Nixon Foundation, https://www.nixonfoundation.org/richard-nixons-top-domestic -and-foreign-policy-achievements/.

39. "Tiemann-Yeutter Sad over Nixon Resignation," *Lincoln Journal*, August 9, 1974, Yeutter Papers.

40. Richard Nixon, correspondence to Clayton Yeutter, January 28, 1991, Yeutter Papers.

41. Clayton Yeutter, correspondence to Richard Nixon, March 27, 1991, Yeutter Papers.

42. Jenna Riemenschneider, "Interviewee: Clayton Yeutter," December 12, 2005, transcript of a taped interview, Yeutter Papers.

5. Free Farmers

1. "Unemployment Rate," Federal Reserve Bank of St. Louis, https://fred.stlouisfed .org/series/UNRATE; "Historical Inflation Rates: 1914–2020," U.S. Inflation Calculator, https://www.usinflationcalculator.com/inflation/historical-inflation-rates/.

2. Richard Norton Smith, interview with Alan Greenspan, Gerald R. Ford Presidential Foundation, December 17, 2008, https://geraldrfordfoundation.org/centennial /oralhistory/alan-greenspan/.

3. "Resume of Dr. Clayton K. Yeutter," *Hearing before the Committee on Finance, United States Senate, Ninety-Ninth Congress, First Session, on Nomination of Dr. Clayton K. Yeutter to Be the U.S. Trade Representative*, June 25, 1985, 27, https://www .finance.senate.gov/imo/media/doc/HRG99-216.pdf.

4. Clayton Yeutter, "Prices: Power to the People," *Vital Speeches of the Day*, speech to the American Association of Agricultural College Editors, West Lafayette, Indiana, July 16, 1974, Yeutter Papers.

5. Clayton Yeutter, letter to the editor, *St. Petersburg Times*, March 18, 1974, Yeutter Papers.

6. See Cora Peterson, "Evaluating the Success of the School Commodity Food Program," *Choices* 24, no. 3 (2009), http://www.choicesmagazine.org/UserFiles/file /article_84.pdf.

7. Clayton Yeutter, "Freer Trade: Key to the Future for Grain," speech to the Federation of Grain Cooperatives, April 25, 1974, Yeutter Papers. Yeutter's work centered on opening markets around the world, but he was not an absolutist and tolerated some protectionism, as the title of his talk suggested. This led associates such as Judith H. Bello to regard him as a believer in "freer" markets, a term she preferred as more precise.

8. Clayton Yeutter, "Old Reruns Are Not the Future," speech at the Merchants Exchange of St. Louis, May 3, 1974, Yeutter Papers.

9. Clayton Yeutter, "Producing in a World Economy," speech at the annual meeting of the Animal Health Institute at Marco Island, May 10, 1974, Yeutter Papers.

10. Clayton Yeutter, "U.S. Agriculture in an International Setting," speech at the Kern County Farm Bureau annual banquet, Bakersfield, California, May 28, 1974, Yeutter Papers.

11. Clayton Yeutter, "We Have Learned Our Lesson," speech at the American Soybean Association, Houston, Texas, August 12, 1974.

12. Clayton Yeutter, "U.S. Should Not Consider Export Controls," speech at the Champaign County Farm Day, Champaign, Illinois, August 17, 1974.

13. James Risser and George Anthan, "Why They Love Earl Butz," *New York Times*, June 13, 1976, https://www.nytimes.com/1976/06/13/archives/why-they-love -earl-butz-prosperous-farmers-see-him-as-the-greatest.html.

14. Jim Jones, "Taxpayer Revolt Predicted If 100% Parity Is Granted," *Minneapolis Star*, February 15, 1978, Yeutter Papers.

15. Risser and Anthan, "Why They Love Earl Butz."

16. See Dan Morgan, "The Shadowy World of Grain Trade," *Washington Post*, June 10, 1979, https://www.washingtonpost.com/archive/business/1979/06/10/the -shadowy-world-of-grain-trade/354b11cd-6dc2-4ac0-b047-51dd7e9ffe83/.

17. Clayton Yeutter to Lewis Leibowitz, "1972 Farm Campaign," email, December 3, 2015, Yeutter Papers. See also Don Walton, "Yeutter Keeps Busy on Job despite Cabinet Speculation," *Lincoln Star*, undated; Andy Montgomery, "Yeutter Ties May Push Him Out with Butz," August 25, 1974, *Lincoln Sunday Journal and Star*, Yeutter Papers.

18. Associated Press, "Yeutter Nomination Just in Time," *Lincoln Star*, April 17, 1975, Yeutter Papers.

19. "Clayton Yeutter: A Versatile Man," *North Platte Telegraph*, February 1, 1981, Yeutter Papers.

20. Clayton Yeutter, "Here's the Story behind the Story on This One," note for personal biographical file, April 20, 2015, Yeutter Papers.

21. Kim Y. Bottimore, conversation with the author, June 24, 2020.

22. "Resume of Dr. Clayton K. Yeutter."

23. Office of the Special Representative for Trade Negotiations, "Yeutter Sees Rising U.S. and World Demand for Beef; Urges Domestic Cattlemen to Expand Exports," press release, February 11, 1976, Yeutter Papers.

24. Office of the Special Representative for Trade Negotiations, "Yeutter Urges Focus on Specifics to Achieve World Trade Objectives," press release, May 20, 1976, Yeutter Papers.

25. Steven Greenhouse, "Man in the News: A Tough Trade Negotiator," *New York Times*, April 4, 1985, https://www.nytimes.com/1985/04/04/business/man-in-the-news -a-tough-trade-negotiator.html?scp=28&sq=clayton+yeutter&st=nyt.

26. Clayton Yeutter, "What EC Subsidies Have Cost U.S. Farmers," *Farm Journal*, February 18, 1983, Yeutter Papers.

27. Clayton K. Yeutter, "Issues Facing U.S. Farmers and Their Cooperatives," address at the 49th AIC National Institute on Cooperative Education, Texas A&M University, August 18, 1977, https://digitalcommons.unl.edu/cgi/viewcontent.cgi ?article=1002&context=yuetter.

28. John R. Crook, "Jackson-Vanik Amendment Repealed; Magnitsky Provisions Draw Russian Ire and Termination of Adoption and Anticrime Agreements," *American Journal of International Law* 107, no. 2 (April 2013): 449–52.

29. Warren H. Maruyama, conversation with the author, November 14, 2019.

30. Richard Lawrence, "World Trade: Has the US Really Prepared Itself for Tough Trade Negotiations like Those in Geneva?," *Journal of Commerce*, July 29, 1976, Yeutter Papers.

31. Douglas P. Bennett, director of the Presidential Personnel Office at the White House, responding to John William Megown's recommendation for Yeutter to serve as secretary of agriculture, October 20, 1976, Yeutter Papers.

32. See Rick Steigmeyer, "Fire Yeutter, Say Wheatgrowers," *Wenatchee (WA) World*, October 5, 1990, Yeutter Papers.

33. Earl Butz, correspondence to Clayton Yeutter, Fall 1990, Yeutter Papers.

34. Clayton Yeutter, memorandum for Richard Douglas, June 16, 1992, Yeutter Papers.

35. "Historical Inflation Rates: 1914–2020," U.S. Inflation Calculator, https://www.usinflationcalculator.com/inflation/historical-inflation-rates/.

36. Labor Force Statistics from the Current Population Survey, U.S. Bureau of Labor Statistics, 1975–76.

37. "Resume of Dr. Clayton K. Yeutter."

38. J. Phil Campbell, under secretary, U.S. Department of Agriculture, letter to John P. Noonan, secretary of the presidential advisory search committee, Kansas State University, February 5, 1975, Yeutter Papers.

39. Ralph J. Knobel, Knobel Farms, letter to Paul Schorr III, chairman of the University of Nebraska Presidential Search Committee, September 1, 1976, Yeutter Papers.

40. Gerald F. Corrigan, Spencer Stuart, letter to Clayton Yeutter, November 17, 1987; Clayton Yeutter, letter to R. William Funk, Heidrick & Struggles, October 11, 1988, both in Yeutter Papers.

41. Clayton Yeutter, letter to Frederick B. Wells, Asian Fine Arts, December 30, 1988, Yeutter Papers.

42. William J. Bowen, Heidrick & Struggles, letter to Clayton Yeutter, September 14, 1990; Clayton Yeutter, letter to Don Blank, Chairman of the Board of Regents, University of Nebraska, August 7, 1990; Esther N. Capin, University of Arizona, letter to Clayton Yeutter, December 21, 1990, all in Yeutter Papers.

43. Conrad Leslie, letter to William Slover, Miami University, August 18, 1992, Yeutter Papers.

44. William J. Bowen, Heidrick & Struggles, letter to Clayton Yeutter, April 13, 1993; Clayton Yeutter, letter to William J. Bowen, Heidrick & Struggles, March 6, 1993, both in Yeutter Papers.

45. Harvey Perlman, letter to Clayton Yeutter, June 14, 1993, Yeutter Papers.

46. Clayton Yeutter, letter to Dr. Robert Finley, College of Agriculture, Food & Natural Resources, University of Missouri, July 8, 1996, Yeutter Papers.

47. Clayton Yeutter, letter to William J. Bowen, Heidrick & Struggles, April 25, 1993, Yeutter Papers.

48. Clayton Yeutter, letter to Norman G. P. Krausz, March 27, 1991, Yeutter Papers.

49. Clayton Yeutter, letter to President Ford, January 18, 1977, Yeutter Papers.

50. Peter T. Kilborn, "Washington Talk: Those in Power and Out Share Pearls and Barbs," *New York Times*, June 26, 1989, https://www.nytimes.com/1989/06/26/us/washington-talk-those-in-power-and-out-share-pearls-and-barbs.html.

6. Juicy Corn-Fed Nebraska Sirloin

1. Clayton Yeutter, letter to Brazil ambassador Luis Augusto Pereira Souto Maior, May 16, 1977, Yeutter Papers.

2. Clayton Yeutter, letter to Kendall L. Manock, August 2, 1977, Yeutter Papers.

3. Yeutter, letter to Souto Maior, May 16, 1977.

4. Clayton Yeutter, letter to Dave Knau, March 21, 1978, Yeutter Papers.

5. Clayton Yeutter, letter to T. V. Hansen, Bonner Packing Co., May 1, 1978, Yeutter Papers.

6. Clayton Yeutter, memorandum for Clyde Nef, "Discussion with Ambassador Alan Wolff of the Office of the Special Representative for Trade Negotiations," May 9, 1978, Yeutter Papers.

7. Clayton Yeutter, memorandum for Alan Wolff, "Mexican Trade Trip," May 5, 1978, Yeutter Papers.

8. Clayton Yeutter, memorandum for Jud Carter, "An Export Subsidy Code," May 10, 1978, Yeutter Papers.

9. Clayton Yeutter, memorandum for Bill Geimer, Jim Lake, and Alison Heath, June 13, 1978, Yeutter Papers. See also Stanley J. Glod, letter to Yeutter, April 11, 1978, Yeutter Papers.

10. Yeutter, memorandum for Clyde Nef, May 9, 1978.

11. Clayton Yeutter, memorandum for Jud Carter, "Discussion with Richard Rivers, General Counsel, Office of the Special Trade Representative," March 27, 1978, Yeutter Papers.

12. Clayton Yeutter, letter to Janos Nyerges, April 26, 1978, Yeutter Papers.

13. Clayton Yeutter, letter to Hector Hernandez Cervantes, October 4, 1977, Yeutter Papers.

14. Alvaro da Costa Franco, letter to Clayton Yeutter, June 12, 1978, Yeutter Papers.

15. Clayton Yeutter, letter to Ambassador Arthur Dunkel, June 1, 1978, Yeutter Papers.

16. William A. Reinsch, conversation with the author, November 1, 2019.

17. Clayton Yeutter, memorandum to file, June 7, 1978, Yeutter Papers.

18. Clayton Yeutter, memorandum for Jim Lake and Alison Heath, "My Recent Conversation with Jim Starkey," June 6, 1978, Yeutter Papers.

19. Clyde V. Prestowitz Jr., Alan Tonelson, and Robert W. Jerome, "The Last Gasp of GATTism," *Harvard Business Review* 69, no. 2 (March–April 1991): 130–38, https://hbr.org/1991/03/the-last-gasp-of-gattism.

20. James R. Hagerty, "Alonzo McDonald, Former McKinsey Chief, Found Theological Mission," *Wall Street Journal*, December 18, 2019, https://www.wsj.com/articles/alonzo-mcdonald-former-mckinsey-chief-found-theological-mission-11576692584.

21. Clayton Yeutter, memorandum for Clyde Nef, "Assessment of the Multilateral Trade Negotiations," June 5, 1978, Yeutter Papers.

22. Edward Alden, review of draft of this book, shared with the author by email, November 16, 2020.

23. Clayton Yeutter, memorandum to file, "File—Dubuque Packing Company," January 27, 1978, Yeutter Papers.

24. Clayton Yeutter, letter to Dr. Robert Angelotti, February 15, 1978, Yeutter Papers.

25. Clayton Yeutter, memorandum to file, "Meeting on January 19, 1978 with Dr. Fred Fullerton," Yeutter Papers.

26. Clayton Yeutter, memorandum to file, "USDA Meeting re Dubuque Pack," January 30, 1978, Yeutter Papers.

27. Clayton Yeutter, "Meeting with Dr. Robert Angelotti," memorandum to file, Feb. 14, 1978, Yeutter Papers.

28. U.S. Department of Agriculture (USDA), "USDA Proposes Changes in Meat Grading and Labeling; Public Hearings Scheduled," press release, January 20, 1978, Yeutter Papers.

29. USDA, "Note to Correspondents," press release, July 15, 1977, Yeutter Papers.

30. Clayton Yeutter, memorandum for Chuck Stolz, Dubuque Packing Co., August 9, 1977, Yeutter Papers.

31. Carol Lee Tucker-Foreman, email to the author, March 11, 2020.

32. Clayton Yeutter, memorandum for Erving H. Priceman, MBPXL, "My Conversation with Assistant Secretary of Agriculture Carol Foreman," April 10, 1978, Yeutter Papers.

33. Clayton Yeutter, letter to Carol Tucker-Foreman, May 4, 1978, Yeutter Papers.

34. Clayton Yeutter, letter to Irving [sic] H. Priceman, May 4, 1978, Yeutter Papers.

35. Tucker-Foreman, email, March 11, 2020.

36. Clayton Yeutter to Dennis E. Stringer, March 7, 1978, Yeutter Papers.

37. Clayton Yeutter, letter to Betty Olson, October 17, 1977, Yeutter Papers.

38. As of early 2021 CME Group was the third-largest such exchange, after two Asian exchanges surpassed it. The group bills itself as the leading and most diverse derivatives exchange, as it has futures products in every investible asset class. Anita Liskey of CME Group, email to the author, February 22, 2021.

7. Our Fellow Man

1. Tim Fernolz, "The Great Chicago Onion Ring: Why Selling Onion Futures Is against Federal Law," *Good*, April 6, 2012, https://www.good.is/articles/the-great-chicago-onion-ring-why-selling-onion-futures-is-against-federal-law.

2. Leo Melamed, conversation with the author, March 24, 2020. Melamed, who was eighty-eight when we spoke, details his dealings at the CME and his pursuit of Yeutter in his 1996 memoir, *Escape to the Futures*, written with Bob Tamarkin.

3. See Ron Grossman, "There's No Place like a Home in Golfview Hills," *Chicago Tribune*, September 1, 1984, Yeutter Papers.

4. Clayton K. and Lillian J. Yeutter, "Farm & Ranch Loan Application," August 9, 1985, Yeutter Papers.

5. See Clayton Yeutter, letter to Mr. and Mrs. Al Gilbert, December 24, 1974, Yeutter Papers.

6. Allen J. Beermann, conversation with the author, February 10, 2020.

7. See Andy Montgomery, "U.S. Agriculture's Continued World Market Sways Yeutter," *Lincoln Journal*, April 16, 1975, 21, Yeutter Papers.

8. Don Pieper, "Yeutter Keeping Political Options Open in New Job," *Lincoln Journal*, November 21, 1977, Yeutter Papers. See also "Dr. Yeutter Is Named President of Chicago Mercantile Exchange," *Lincoln Journal*, November 17, 1977, Yeutter Papers.

9. Clayton Yeutter, letter to Ab Hermann, assistant to the chairman of the Republican National Committee, April 14, 1977, Yeutter Papers.

10. Clayton Yeutter, letter to Roger Semerad, Republican National Committee, February 17, 1978, Yeutter Papers.

11. Earl Butz, handwritten note on a letter to Yeutter from Roger D. Semerad of the Republican National Committee, April 14, 1978, Yeutter Papers.

12. Clayton Yeutter, letter to Bill Brock, Republican National Committee, May 31, 1979, Yeutter Papers.

13. See Jack W. Germond and Jules Witcover, "From Farm to GOP Zoo Newswatch . . . on Politics Today," *Baltimore Evening Sun*, January 9, 1991, https://www .baltimoresun.com/news/bs-xpm-1991-01-09-1991009143-story.html.

14. See Mark DePue, "Interview with John R. Block," Abraham Lincoln Presidential Library, July 9, 2009, https://www2.illinois.gov/alplm/library/collections /OralHistory/agriculture/modern/Documents/BlockJohn/Block_John_4FNL.pdf.

15. Dan Morgan, "Illinois Agriculture Chief Is Pushed to Head USDA," *Washington Post*, November 19, 1980, Yeutter Papers.

16. Darwin Olofson, "Dole Does About-Face on Ex-Nebraskan," *Omaha World-Herald*, April 8, 1985, Yeutter Papers.

17. Clayton Yeutter, letter to Douglas Bereuter, January 14, 1981, Yeutter Papers.

18. Clayton Yeutter, letter to Kyu Sung Bae, January 9, 1981, Yeutter Papers.

19. Clayton Yeutter, letter to Mamoru Sawabe, December 30, 1980, Yeutter Papers.

20. Clayton Yeutter, letter to Lawrence K. Taber, Canners League of California, January 12, 1981, Yeutter Papers.

21. Clayton Yeutter, letter to Donald G. Ogilvie of the American Bankers Association, June 3, 1985, Yeutter Papers.

22. See Gerald M. Boyd, "Reagan Picks New Trade Chief," *New York Times*, April 3, 1985, https://www.nytimes.com/1985/04/03/business/reagan-picks-new-trade-chief .html.

23. Hon. Robert Dole, a U.S. Senator from Kansas, prepared statement, "Nomination of Clayton Yeutter, of Nebraska, to Be Secretary of Agriculture," *Hearing before the Committee on Agriculture, Nutrition, and Forestry, U.S. Senate*, February 2, 1989, 18, https://www.google.com/books/edition/Nomination_of_Clayton _Yeutter/FVAkQXmEokcC.

24. Nelson Warfield, "Dole Campaign Announces Formation of Two Additional Economic Policy Task Forces," Dole/Kemp campaign press release, October 29, 1996; Clayton Yeutter, letter to Dr. and Mrs. Michael Boskin, June 1, 1995, both in Yeutter Papers.

25. Clayton Yeutter, letters to Katherine Graham, July 9, 1987, and September 25, 1996, Yeutter Papers.

26. Clayton Yeutter, letter to the Honorable Manuel Ulloa Elias, prime minister of Peru, June 4, 1982, Yeutter Papers.

27. Clayton Yeutter, letter to David Bathrick, USAID, January 11, 1983, Yeutter Papers.

28. Jonathan Kandell, "Augusto Pinochet, Dictator Who Ruled by Terror in Chile, Dies at 91," *New York Times*, December 11, 2006, https://www.nytimes.com/2006/12 /11/world/americas/11pinochet.html.

29. Charles H. Percy, letter to James A. Baker III, chief of staff at the White House, April 30, 1982, Yeutter Papers.

30. William Robbins, "Spotlight: New Man at the Reins of the Merc," *New York Times*, July 30, 1978, https://www.nytimes.com/1978/07/30/archives/spotlight-new -man-at-the-reins-of-the-merc-competition-heats-up.html.

31. Clayton Yeutter, letter to Dr. Chen Ding, January 9, 1981, Yeutter Papers.

32. Clayton Yeutter, letter to Mr. and Mrs. Charles Wang, January 9, 1981, Yeutter Papers.

33. Clayton Yeutter, letter to Mr. and Mrs. Charles Wang, January 22, 1991, Yeutter Papers.

34. Clayton Yeutter, "Negotiations on the Five-Year Grain Agreement with the Soviet Union," memorandum for David Macdonald, June 16, 1981, Yeutter Papers.

35. Clayton Yeutter, letter to Shintaro Abe, June 28, 1982, Yeutter Papers.

36. Clayton Yeutter, letter to Federico Uranga, July 28, 1982, Yeutter Papers.

37. Clayton Yeutter, letter to John J. McCloy, American Council on Germany, August 16, 1983, Yeutter Papers.

38. Clayton Yeutter, letter to Jeane J. Kirkpatrick, October 5, 1981, Yeutter Papers.

39. Jeane J. Kirkpatrick, letter to Clayton Yeutter, October 15, 1981, Yeutter Papers.

40. Gregg S. Yeutter, email to his siblings, June 15, 2012, shared with the author.

41. Clayton Yeutter, letter to Carol Tucker-Foreman, January 19, 1982, Yeutter Papers.

42. Tony Coelho, letter to Clayton Yeutter, February 3, 1982, Yeutter Papers.

43. Clayton Yeutter, letter to Tony Coelho, January 19, 1982, Yeutter Papers.

44. Tamarkin, *Merc*, 280.

45. Tamarkin, *Merc*, 281.

46. Keith Schneider, "Dan Rostenkowski, Lawmaker, Is Dead at 82," *New York Times*, August 11, 2010, https://www.nytimes.com/2010/08/12/us/politics/12rostenkowski.html.

47. Timothy R. Smith, "Jim Wright, House Speaker Who Resigned amid an Ethics Investigation, Dies at 92," *Washington Post*, May 6, 2015, https://www.washingtonpost .com/politics/jim-wright-texas-democrat-who-was-speaker-of-the-house-dies-at-92 /2015/05/06/2b5d116c-f406-11e4-bcc4-e8141e5eb0c9_story.html.

48. Michael Oreskes, "Coelho to Resign His Seat in House in Face of Inquiry," *New York Times*, May 27, 1989, https://www.nytimes.com/1989/05/27/us/coelho-to -resign-his-seat-in-house-in-face-of-inquiry.html.

49. Clayton Yeutter, letter to Tony Coelho, June 5, 1989, Yeutter Papers.

50. Clayton Yeutter, letter to Ralph J. Knobel, April 11, 1983, Yeutter Papers.

51. Steven J. Dryden, "Clayton Yeutter Speaks Softly and Carries a Big Agenda," *Business Week*, February 2, 1987, Yeutter Papers, 31.

52. Philip M. Boffey, "Edward Zorinsky, 58, Dies; U.S. Senator from Nebraska," *New York Times*, March 8, 1987, https://www.nytimes.com/1987/03/08/obituaries/edward -zorinsky-58-dies-us-senator-from-nebraska.html; Washington Bureau, "Zorinsky Praises Yeutter Nomination," *Omaha World-Herald*, April 3, 1985, Yeutter Papers.

53. Clayton Yeutter, letter to John J. Roche, December 17, 1990, Yeutter Papers.

54. John J. Lothian, conversation with the author, March 23, 2020.

55. See Bart Chilton, "Financial Transaction Tax: A Failure in the Making," FOX Business, June 16, 2016, https://www.foxbusiness.com/markets/financial-transaction -tax-a-failure-in-the-making.

56. Susan Abbott, "Clayton Yeutter: From Traders to Trade," *Futures*, June 1985, Yeutter Papers.

57. See Robbins, "Spotlight."

58. See Robbins, "Spotlight."

59. Clayton Yeutter, statement, CFTC *Reauthorization: Hearings before the Subcommittee on Conservation, Credit and Rural Development of the Committee on Agriculture, House of Representatives*, February 23, 24, and 25, 1982, 168, https://www.google .com/books/edition/CFTC_Reauthorization/c4cmxwEACAAJ?hl=en.

60. Tamarkin, *Merc*, 291.

61. See Robbins, "Spotlight."

62. Susan B. Stoffle, "New Merc Head Seeks Public Trust," *Kansas City Star*, December 13, 1977, Yeutter Papers.

63. See Kim Iskyan, Stansberry Churchouse Research, *Business Insider*, May 17, 2016, https://www.businessinsider.com/hunt-brothers-trying-to-corner-silver -market-2016-5.

64. Tamarkin, *Merc*, 241.

65. John F. "Jack" Sandner, conversation with the author, March 18, 2020.

66. Alexandra Horos, CME Group, email to the author, March 23, 2020.

67. Rodengen, *Past, Present & Futures*, 74, 87–90.

68. Tamarkin, *Merc*, 288–90.

69. Tamarkin, *Merc*, 280.

70. Leo Melamed, conversation with the author, March 24, 2020.

71. Clayton Yeutter, letter to Abraham Sharir, December 1, 1986, Yeutter Papers.

72. Melamed, *Escape to the Futures*, 322–25.

73. Leo Melamed, conversation with the author, March 24, 2020.

74. Lucia Mouat, "Mayor-Council Standoff May Have a Lasting Effect on Chicago," *Christian Science Monitor*, June 12, 1984, https://www.csmonitor.com/1984 /0612/061236.html.

75. "Mayor Harold Washington Biography," Chicago Public Library, https://www .chipublib.org/mayor-harold-washington-biography/.

76. Terry Savage, conversation with the author, March 19, 2020. Savage, also a financial planner, is the author of *The Savage Truth on Money*.

77. Laurie Cohen and Richard Orr, "12 Farmers Arrested at Board of Trade," *Chicago Tribune*, January 22, 1985; David Greising, "35 Arrested at Merc," *Chicago Sun-Times*, January 23, 1985, both in Yeutter Papers.

78. Savage, conversation, March 19, 2020.

79. Laurie Cohen and Richard Orr, "12 Farmers Arrested at Board of Trade," *Chicago Tribune*, January 22, 1985.

80. Richard Orr and Laurie Cohen, "Police Seize 35 in 2nd Day of Farm Protest," *Chicago Tribune*, January 23, 1985, Yeutter Papers.

81. David Greising, "35 Arrested at Merc," *Chicago Sun-Times*, January 23, 1985.

82. Rod Smith, "Farm Policies Must Be Redirected: Helms, Yeutter," *Feedstuffs*, January 21, 1985, Yeutter Papers.

83. See Eric N. Berg, "Ex-Chicago Merc Chief Is Barred," *New York Times*, May 26, 1990, https://www.nytimes.com/1990/05/26/business/ex-chicago-merc-chief-is -barred.html.

84. J. James Exon and J. Robert Kerrey, letter to Clayton Yeutter, November 9, 1989, Yeutter Papers.

85. Jerry Knight, "Yeutter's Testimony for Friend Smacks of Political Interfer-ence," *Washington Post*, December 12, 1989, https://www.washingtonpost.com/archive /business/1989/12/12/yeutters-testimony-for-friend-smacks-of-political-interference /4c30e6c2-0445-47fd-967f-c746a12ea7f4/.

86. Jerry Knight, "Friends in High Places: Yeutter's Testimony in Investigation Raises Questions," *Wichita Eagle*, December 17, 1989, Yeutter Papers.

87. Clayton Yeutter, letter to Mr. and Mrs. Ronald Davis, January 9, 1990, Yeut-ter Papers.

88. Clayton Yeutter, letters to J. James Exon and J. Robert Kerry [*sic*], Novem-ber 28, 1989, Yeutter Papers.

89. Clayton Yeutter, letter to Robert Kerry [*sic*], November 16, 1988, Yeutter Papers.

90. Clayton Yeutter, letter to Thomas H. Dittmer, February 5, 1990, Yeutter Papers.

91. Monieson v. Commodity Futures Trading Com'n, opinion, No. 92-3014, decided June 7, 1993, Casetext, https://casetext.com/case/monieson-v-commodity-futures -trading-comn.

92. William J. Brodsky, letter to Clayton Yeutter, December 20, 1989, Yeutter Papers.

93. Clayton Yeutter, character affidavit for the U.S. Justice Department, April 24, 1990, Yeutter Papers.

94. Tamarkin, *Merc*, 222–23.

95. Clayton Yeutter, letter to Leo Melamed, July 2, 1990, Yeutter Papers.

96. Clayton Yeutter, letter to Don Wycliff, *Chicago Tribune*, January 16, 1996, Yeutter Papers.

8. Macho Man of Trade

1. Clayton Yeutter, letter to Marilee Menard of the Cosmetic, Toiletry, and Fra-grance Association, May 28, 1985, Yeutter Papers.

2. Clayton Yeutter, letter to Earl M. Scudder Jr. of Nelson & Harding, June 3, 1985, Yeutter Papers.

3. Clayton Yeutter, letter to James M. Stone, Plymouth Rock Assurance Corp., June 3, 1985, Yeutter Papers.

4. Clayton Yeutter, letter to Milton Friedman, July 31, 1985, Yeutter Papers.

5. Clayton Yeutter, letter to Yoshifusa Watanabe, Tokyo Commodity Exchange for Industry, May 29, 1985, Yeutter Papers.

6. Gerald M. Boyd, "Reagan Picks New Trade Chief," *New York Times*, April 3, 1985, Yeutter Papers. See chapter 5 for a discussion of the cheese war.

7. "A Great Man's Journey: Trip Home Reminds Yeutter of His Great Nebraska Roots," video interview, *Donor Stories*, University of Nebraska Foundation, February 10, 2016.

8. Clyde H. Farnsworth, "Office of the Trade Representative: Nimble Soldiers of the Commercial Wars," *New York Times*, November 16, 1987, Yeutter Papers.

9. Steven J. Dryden, "Clayton Yeutter Speaks Softly and Carries a Big Agenda," *Business Week*, February 2, 1987, Yeutter Papers.

10. Susan K. Nelson, conversation with the author, June 12, 2020.

11. Roger Bolton, conversation with the author, November 13, 2019.

12. Alan F. Holmer, email to the author, July 17, 2020.

13. "U.S. Trade in Goods and Services—Balance of Payments (BOP) Basis," 1960–2019, U.S. Census Bureau, Economic Indicator Division, March 6, 2020, https://www.census.gov/foreign-trade/statistics/historical/gands.pdf.

14. Clyde H. Farnsworth, "Tide of Protectionism in Congress," *New York Times*, July 4, 1985, https://www.nytimes.com/1985/07/04/business/tide-of-protectionism-in-congress.html.

15. David Broder, "Fiddling as Protectionism Rages," *Chicago Tribune*, June 17, 1985, Yeutter Papers.

16. Bernard Weinraub, "Reagan Rejects Shoe Import Curb," *New York Times*, August 29, 1985, https://www.nytimes.com/1985/08/29/business/reagan-rejects-shoe-import-curb.html.

17. Clayton Yeutter, letter to Samuel R. Mitchell, Chicago Association of Commerce and Industry, August 26, 1986, Yeutter Papers.

18. United Press International, "Yeutter Picked as Trade Rep" and "Senate Committee Votes for Trade Retaliation," *Mid-Illinois Newspapers*, April 3, 1985, Yeutter Papers.

19. Farnsworth, "Tide of Protectionism."

20. Boyd France, Ronald Grover and John N. Frank, "Trial by Fire for Reagan's New Negotiator," *Business Week*, April 15, 1985, Yeutter Papers.

21. Art Pine, "Nominee for Trade Post to Seek Shift in U.S. Policy, Cites Dollar for Problems," *Wall Street Journal*, June 26, 1985, Yeutter Papers.

22. Holmer, email, July 17, 2020.

23. Judith H. Bello, conversation with the author, November 14, 2019.

24. Philip Geyelin, "Pasta War," *Washington Post*, July 24, 1985, https://www.washingtonpost.com/archive/politics/1985/07/24/pasta-war/588ed130-4008-4037-b31e-9893e8d97ba5/; Peter T. Kilborn, "U.S., Europe Reach Truce in Pasta Rift," *New York Times*, July 9, 1985, https://www.nytimes.com/1985/07/09/business/us-europe-reach-truce-in-pasta-rift.html; Oswald Johnson, "Republican Mixes Pragmatism and Persuasiveness: Yeutter—Apostle of Free Trade," *Los Angeles Times*, August 16, 1985, Yeutter Papers.

25. See Art Pine, "U.S., E.C. Set Tentative Pact on Pasta Flap," *Wall Street Journal*, July 15, 1985, Yeutter Papers.

26. Leonard W. Condon, email to the author, June 9, 2020.

27. United Press International, "U.S. and Europe Settle Pasta and Citrus Dispute," August 11, 1986, *New York Times*, https://www.nytimes.com/1986/08/11/business/us-and-europe-settle-pasta-and-citrus-dispute.html.

28. Elaine S. Povich, "U.S., Europe Avert Pasta Trade War," *Chicago Tribune*, August 6, 1987, https://www.chicagotribune.com/news/ct-xpm-1987-08-06-8702270357-story.html.

29. David S. Broder, "Ford Chief Backs Retaliatory Tariff," *Washington Post*, August 20, 1985, Yeutter Papers.

30. Clayton Yeutter, letter to Donald E. Petersen, August 20, 1985, Yeutter Papers.

31. Jane Seaberry, "Reagan Puts Off Ruling on Shoe-Import Curbs," *Washington Post*, August 10, 1985, https://www.washingtonpost.com/archive/business/1985/08/10/reagan-puts-off-ruling-on-shoe-import-curbs/bef9c1a3-0216-4689-b443-af91410bee7b/.

32. Bernard Weinraub, "Reagan Rejects Shoe Import Curb," *New York Times*, August 29, 1985, https://www.nytimes.com/1985/08/29/business/reagan-rejects-shoe-import-curb.html.

33. Charles E. "Chip" Roh Jr., conversation with the author, December 9, 2020.

34. Norman D. Sandler, "Reagan Rejects Shoe Quotas," United Press International, August 28, 1985, https://www.upi.com/Archives/1985/08/28/Reagan-rejects-shoe-quotas/9779494049600/.

35. Clayton Yeutter, memorandum for Robert H. Tuttle, August 28, 1985, Yeutter Papers.

36. Judith H. Bello, email to the author, July 5, 2020.

37. William E. Brock III, conversation with the author, December 2, 2019.

38. "Trade in Goods with Israel," U.S. Census Bureau, https://www.census.gov/foreign-trade/balance/c5081.html.

39. Thomas L. Friedman, "U.S. Trade Accords: Success in Israel . . . ," *New York Times*, October 12, 1987, Yeutter Papers.

40. "Trade in Goods with Israel."

41. See Herzog Fox & Neeman, "'Substantial Transformation' under the Israel-US Free Trade Agreement," March 30, 2020, https://www.lexology.com/library/detail.aspx?g=b68a5837-f0d3-4c73-bbbd-a1e588e9278b.

42. Brock, conversation, December 2, 2019.

43. Clayton Yeutter, letter to Mr. and Mrs. Arven Eggert in Burnaby, Canada, June 26, 1985, Yeutter Papers.

44. Clayton Yeutter, letter to Lloyd C. Atkinson, June 4, 1985, Yeutter Papers.

45. "United States–Canada Free Trade Agreement (FTA) Resources," Georgetown Law Library, https://guides.ll.georgetown.edu/c.php?g=363556&p=3662927.

46. See Dryden, *Trade Warriors*; Brian Mulroney and L. Ian MacDonald, "Leveraging Canada-US Relations 'to Get Big Things Done' (Interview)," *Policy Options*, March 1, 2011, https://policyoptions.irpp.org/magazines/canada-us-conversations-and-relations/leveraging-canada-us-relations-to-get-big-things-done-interview/.

47. Dryden, *Trade Warriors*, 340–41. See also Douglas Martin, "Despite U.S. Actions, Canada Seeks Freer Trade," *New York Times*, October 23, 1986, Yeutter Papers.

48. Helen Ericson, "US-Canadian Corn Row Threatens Trade Talks," *Journal of Commerce*, undated, Yeutter Papers.

49. Warren H. Maruyama, email to the author, June 24, 2020.

50. Dryden, *Trade Warriors*, 342.

51. Derek H. Burney, conversation with the author, February 25, 2020. See also Dryden, *Trade Warriors*, 342.

52. Charles E. "Chip" Roh Jr., conversation with the author, July 10, 2020.

53. John Ferguson, "Honeymoon Definitely Over for Loud-Mouthed Yeutter," *Ottawa Citizen*, February 5, 1987, https://news.google.com/newspapers?id= GK8yAAAAIBAJ&sjid=ku8FAAAAIBAJ&pg=5518,2424921&dq=yeutter&hl=en.

54. John M. Weekes, conversation with the author, November 19, 2019.

55. Burney, conversation, February 25, 2020.

56. Holmer, email, July 17, 2020.

57. Maruyama, email, June 24, 2020.

58. Roh, conversation, July 10, 2020.

59. Nader et al., *Case against "Free Trade,"* 94.

60. Bureau of National Affairs, "Trade Policy: Canadian Negotiator Walks Out on Free Trade Talks, Leaving Future of Accord in Jeopardy," undated, Yeutter Papers.

61. Burney, conversation, February 25, 2020.

62. James A. Baker III, Oral History transcript, Presidential Oral Histories, Ronald Reagan Presidency, University of Virginia Miller Center, June 15, 2004, https:// millercenter.org/the-presidency/presidential-oral-histories/james-baker-iii-oral -history.

63. Maruyama, email, June 24, 2020.

64. Roh, conversation, July 10, 2020.

65. Burney, conversation, February 25, 2020; Baker, Oral History.

66. Maruyama, email, June 24, 2020.

67. See Charles Lewis, *America's Frontline Trade Officials: Office of the United States Trade Representative* (Washington DC: Center for Public Integrity, 1990), 129, 124, https://cloudfront-files-1.publicintegrity.org/legacy_projects/pdf_reports /AMERICASFRONTLINETRADEOFFICIALS.pdf.

68. Holmer, email, July 17, 2020.

69. Clayton Yeutter, *United States–Canadian Free-Trade Agreement, Hearing before the Committee on Agriculture, House of Representatives*, February 25, 1988, https:// www.google.com/books/edition/_/ALbh_Ftls-IC?hl=en&gbpv=0, 4–6.

70. Holmer, email, July 17, 2020.

71. Ronald Reagan, letter to Clayton Yeutter, October 17, 1988, Yeutter Papers.

72. James A. Baker III, letter recounted in Clayton Yeutter tribute video, University of Nebraska, Clayton Yeutter Institute for International Trade and Finance, https://www.youtube.com/watch?v=hPY8a1p3l7c.

73. Clayton Yeutter, letter to Donald E. Petersen, October 20, 1987, Yeutter Papers.

74. Warren H. Maruyama, conversation with the author, November 14, 2019.

75. Burney, conversation, February 25, 2020.

76. Clayton Yeutter, transcript of speech at the Brookings Institution conference on building a Canadian-American free trade agreement, February 3, 1987, Univer-

sity of Nebraska–Lincoln Digital Commons, https://digitalcommons.unl.edu/cgi/viewcontent.cgi?article=1013&context=yuetter.

77. Oswald Johnston, "Republican Mixes Pragmatism and Persuasiveness: Yeutter—Apostle of Free Trade," *Los Angeles Times*, August 16, 1985, Yeutter Papers.

78. Clyde H. Farnsworth, "U.S.-Canada Trade Pact's Details Listed," *New York Times*, December 12, 1987, Yeutter Papers. See also "Key Elements of U.S.-Canada Free-Trade Accord," *Congressional Quarterly*, October 10, 1987, 2467, Yeutter Papers.

79. Larry Rohter, "U.S. and Mexico in Trade Pact," *New York Times*, November 6, 1987, Yeutter Papers.

80. "Trade in Goods with Canada," U.S. Census Bureau, https://www.census.gov/foreign-trade/balance/c1220.html.

81. Burney, conversation, February 25, 2020.

82. Clayton Yeutter, letter to Brian Mulroney, March 13, 1993, Yeutter Papers.

83. Ronald Reagan, "Transcript of Speech to Business and Government Leaders," *New York Times*, September 24, 1985, https://www.nytimes.com/1985/09/24/business/transcript-of-speech-to-business-and-government-leaders.html.

84. Reagan, "Transcript of Speech."

85. Clyde H. Farnsworth, "Yeutter: The Nation's Macho Man of Trade," *Santa Rosa (ca) Press Democrat*, February 22, 1987, Yeutter Papers.

86. Clyde H. Farnsworth, "Washington Talk: Working Profile: Clayton K. Yeutter; a Trade War Veteran with Tales to Tell," *New York Times*, February 14, 1987, https://www.nytimes.com/1987/02/14/us/washington-talk-working-profile-clayton-k-yeutter-trade-war-veteran-with-tales.html.

87. Cristena Bach Yeutter, email to the author, December 3, 2020.

88. Maruyama, email, June 24, 2020.

89. "Who Wants What This Time Round," *Economist*, September 13, 1986, 66, Yeutter Papers. See also Yu, *Punta*, 1.

90. Leonard W. Condon, conversation with the author, November 14, 2019.

91. Yu, *Punta*, 5.

92. Stephen Koepp, Gisela Bolte, and Frederick Ungeheuer, "A Launch for the Uruguay Round," *Time*, September 29, 1986, Yeutter Papers.

93. Frances Williams, "Uruguayan Trade-Off: Gatt Ministers Agree to Talk—on US Terms," *Far Eastern Economic Review*, October 2, 1986, 100, Yeutter Papers.

94. Yu, *Punta*, 4–6.

95. Condon, conversation, November 14, 2019.

96. Roh, conversation, December 9, 2020.

97. Yu, *Punta*, 8–11.

98. Koepp, Bolte, and Ungeheuer, "Launch for the Uruguay Round."

99. Williams, "Uruguayan Trade-Off," 100.

100. Oxley, *Challenge of Free Trade*, 144.

101. Roh, conversation, July 10, 2020.

102. Walter S. Mossberg and Ellen Hume, "U.S. Proposes Nations Cease Farm Subsidies," *Wall Street Journal*, July 7, 1987, Yeutter Papers.

103. Condon, email, June 9, 2020.

104. Condon, conversation, November 14, 2019, and email on June 5, 2020.

105. "The Uruguay Round," World Trade Organization, last modified December 17, 2018, https://www.wto.org/english/thewto_e/whatis_e/tif_e/fact5_e.htm.

106. "Uruguay Round."

107. "President Yeutter," *Wall Street Journal*, undated, Yeutter Papers.

108. Holmer, email, July 17, 2020.

109. Hobart Rowen, "What's Wrong with the Gephardt Amendment," *Washington Post*, May 28, 1987, https://www.washingtonpost.com/archive/opinions/1987/05/28/whats-wrong-with-the-gephardt-amendment/a9f3b861-d53e-47c8-9c9f-cd48c4866ac1/.

110. Maruyama, email, June 24, 2020.

111. See Clark Parkard, "Congress Should Take Back Its Authority over Tariffs," *Foreign Policy*, May 4, 2019, https://foreignpolicy.com/2019/05/04/congress-should-take-back-its-authority-over-tariffs-trump/.

112. Warren H. Maruyama, letter to Yeutter, undated, for a book of letters compiled by friends Bert Pena and Burt Eller, Yeutter Papers.

113. Ronald A. Cass, "Velvet Fist in an Iron Glove: The Omnibus Trade and Competitiveness Act of 1988," *Regulation* (Winter 1991), 50–56, https://web.archive.org/web/20121012020405/http://www.cato.org/pubs/regulation/regv14n1/v14n1-5.pdf.

9. Saving a Major Industry

1. Michael Maiello, "The Japanese Just Bought Jim Beam. Remember When They Owned the Empire State Building?," *Esquire*, January 13, 2014, https://www.esquire.com/food-drink/drinks/news/a26838/japanese-bought-jim-beam/.

2. Roger Bolton, email to the author, July 7, 2020.

3. "Trade in Goods with Japan," U.S. Census Bureau, https://www.census.gov/foreign-trade/balance/c5880.html.

4. Jane Seaberry, "Trade Nominee Testifies on Hill," *Washington Post*, June 26, 1985, Yeutter Papers.

5. Clayton Yeutter, memorandum for Secretary Malcolm Baldrige, August 27, 1985, Yeutter Papers.

6. Clayton Yeutter, memorandum for Secretary James A. Baker III, August 27, 1985, Yeutter Papers.

7. Dryden, *Trade Warriors*, 317–20.

8. George Russell, "Trade Face-Off: A Dangerous U.S.-Japan Confrontation," *Time* 129, no. 15 (April 13, 1987), 28–32, 35–36, Yeutter Papers.

9. Louise Kehoe, "Japanese 'Flouting Chip Trade Accord," *Financial Times*, October 27, 1986, Yeutter Papers.

10. Stuart Auerbach, "Remark Fires U.S. Campaign to Retaliate against Japan," *Washington Post*, March 26, 1987, Yeutter Papers.

11. Stuart Auerbach, "Japan Taking Harder Line in Trade Talks," *Washington Post*, February 15, 1987, Yeutter Papers.

12. Stephen Koepp, Gisela Bolte, and Neil Gross, "Fighting the Trade Tilt: The U.S. Fires Protective Tariffs at Japanese Electronics Products," *Time*, April 6, 1987, Yeutter Papers.

13. David Pauly, David Newell, and Thomas M. DeFrank, "No More Mr. Nice Guy: The U.S. Proposes Stiff Tariffs on Japanese Imports," *Newsweek*, April 6, 1987, Yeutter Papers.

14. Associated Press, "U.S. Official Quits over Trade Issue," *Asahi Evening News*, April 21, 1987, Yeutter Papers.

15. Steve Johnson, "Gerald Marks, Maverick Official," *Chicago Tribune*, September 6, 1987, https://www.chicagotribune.com/news/ct-xpm-1987-09-06-8703070523 -story.html.

16. "Yeutter Lays Down Law on U.S. Penalty Tariffs" and "Yeutter Urges Japan to Import Rice," *Asahi Evening News*, April 21, 1987, Yeutter Papers.

17. Ronald E. Yates, "U.S.-Japan Agriculture Talks Yield Frustration," *Chicago Tribune*, undated clip, Yeutter Papers.

18. Stuart Auerbach, "Japanese Aide Cites Health, Religious Reasons for Slackening U.S. Beef Imports," *Washington Post*, December 18, 1987, Yeutter Papers.

19. Jane Seaberry, "Bat Men Strike Out in Japan," *Washington Post*, April 15, 1982, https://www.washingtonpost.com/archive/business/1982/04/15/bat-men-strike-out -in-japan/a59fcca7-e97a-4d01-9e9e-105847dca136/.

20. Don Oberdorfer, "Reagan, Nakasone Conclude Talks without Plan to Lift Trade Sanctions," *Washington Post*, May 2, 1987, Yeutter Papers, https://www.washingtonpost .com/archive/politics/1987/05/02/reagan-nakasone-conclude-talks-without-plan-to -lift-trade-sanctions/3cf0932f-e7a9-490a-a5e2-a7a659b9bd23/.

21. Oberdorfer, "Reagan, Nakasone Conclude Talks."

22. John Yemma, "Tough US Attitude on Trade," *Christian Science Monitor*, June 15, 1987, Yeutter Papers.

23. Alan Wm. Wolff, letter to Clayton Yeutter, October 12, 1990, Yeutter Papers.

24. Office of the United States Trade Representative, "Foreign Share of the Japanese Semiconductor Market Reaches Record 29.6%," press release, March 19, 1966, Yeutter Papers.

25. Sam Jameson, "Japan OKs Ending Quotas on U.S. Beef and Oranges," *Los Angeles Times*, June 20, 1988, https://www.latimes.com/archives/la-xpm-1988-06 -20-mn-3512-story.html.

26. Warren H. Maruyama, email to the author, June 25, 2020.

27. Leonard W. Condon and A. Ellen Terpstra, conversation with the author, November 14, 2019.

28. Warren H. Maruyama, conversation with the author, November 14, 2019.

29. Jim Gransbery, "Japan Bit Bullet, Negotiator Says," *Billings (MT) Gazette*, July 10, 1988, Yeutter Papers.

30. See Clayton Yeutter, letters to Max S. Baucus and Ben Nighthorse Campbell, November 7, 1990, Yeutter Papers.

31. A. Ellen Terpstra, conversation with the author, November 14, 2019.

32. Cristena Bach Yeutter, email to the author, July 3, 2020.

33. Darci L. Vetter, conversation with the author, October 21, 2019.

34. Ron Yoder, "Clayton Yeutter Receives Honor from Japan," University of Nebraska–Lincoln Institute of Agriculture and Natural Resources News, January 8, 2018, https://ianrnews.unl.edu/clayton-yeutter-receives-honor-japan.

35. Shinzo Abe, letter to Yeutter family members, April 2017, personal papers of Cristena Bach Yeutter.

36. Kim Y. Bottimore, conversation with the author, June 24, 2020.

37. John S. Bottimore, conversation with the author, June 24, 2020.

38. John S. Bottimore, conversation, June 24, 2020. Yeutter shared the story with the Bottimores on a tour of the USTR offices.

39. Charles E. "Chip" Roh Jr., conversation with the author, July 10, 2020, and an email on July 23, 2020.

40. Gransbery, "Japan Bit Bullet."

41. Clayton Yeutter, letter to Koji Deguchi, Nissho Iwai American Corporation, August 16, 1995, Yeutter Papers.

42. Susumu Yamaji, *Japan Times*, 1986, Yeutter Papers.

43. Yoichi Funabashi, "An Unexpected Ally for the U.S.: A Japanese Took the U.S. Side in the Trade Dispute over Liberalization of Rice Imports," *Asahi Shimbun*, November 8, 1986, in a digest of news accounts in the Yeutter Papers.

44. "Tokyo's Rice Policy," *Wall Street Journal*, May 14, 1990, Yeutter Papers.

45. See John Burgess, "Rice Trade Dispute Is Boiling Up: Japan Resisting U.S. Effort to Open Its Market to Imports," *Washington Post*, October 21, 1986, Yeutter Papers.

46. Keith Schneider, "U.S. Plays Down Rice Dispute: No Move Seen against Japan," *New York Times*, October 24, 1986, https://www.nytimes.com/1986/10/24/business/us-plans-no-action-on-japan-rice-dispute.html.

47. See Clayton Yeutter, memos to Jack Rosenthal of the *New York Times*, John Anderson of the *Washington Post*, and Arnaud de Borchgrave of the *Washington Times*, November 7, 1988, Yeutter Papers.

48. Earl L. Butz, letter to Clayton Yeutter, October 29, 1988, Yeutter Papers.

49. "Trade Job Appeals to Iacocca," *Detroit Free Press*, undated clip, Yeutter Papers.

50. Clayton Yeutter, letter to Douglas F. Duchek, November 21, 1988, Yeutter Papers.

51. Ronald Reagan, letter to Noboru Takeshita, October 28, 1988, Yeutter Papers.

52. Roh, conversation, July 10, 2020.

53. Clayton Yeutter, "Press Conference with US Trade Representative Clayton Yeutter, Regarding Japanese Rice Situation," *Federal News Service*, October 28, 1988, Yeutter Papers.

54. Clayton Yeutter, memorandum for the president, November 1, 1989, Yeutter Papers.

55. Jude Wanniski, letter to President George H. W. Bush, October 13, 1989, Yeutter Papers.

56. President George H. W. Bush, letter to Jude Wanniski, October 30, 1989, Yeutter Papers.

57. Clayton Yeutter, memorandum for the president, April 26, 1990, Yeutter Papers.

58. Clayton Yeutter, memorandum for the president, August 31, 1990, Yeutter Papers.

59. Clayton Yeutter, letter to Hajime Tamura, a member of Japan's House of Representatives, January 7, 1991, Yeutter Papers. See also Charles Lewis, *America's Frontline Trade Officials: Office of the United States Trade Representative* (Washington DC: Center for Public Integrity, 1990), 93, https://cloudfront-files-1.publicintegrity.org /legacy_projects/pdf_reports/AMERICASFRONTLINETRADEOFFICIALS.pdf.

60. Lewis, *America's Frontline Trade Officials*, 94–95.

61. Lewis, *America's Frontline Trade Officials*, 94–95.

62. Clayton Yeutter, "Remarks of Clayton Yeutter, Secretary of Agriculture, at the Farm Women's Leadership Forum, Holiday Inn, Capitol Hill," June 8, 1989, transcript, Yeutter Papers.

63. David E. Sanger, "Japan Shuts U.S. Rice Exhibition," *New York Times*, March 18, 1991, https://www.nytimes.com/1991/03/18/business/japan-shuts-us-rice-exhibition .html.

64. President Bush, memorandum for Ed Madigan, Jim Baker, Bob Mosbacher, Carla Hills, and Brent Scowcroft, March 18, 1991, Yeutter Papers.

65. David Graves, president of the Rice Millers' Association, letter to Clayton Yeutter, February 1, 1991, Yeutter Papers.

66. Nathan Childs, *Rice Situation and Outlook Yearbook*, Economic Research Service, U.S. Department of Agriculture, November 2003, https://www.google.com /books/edition/Situation_and_Outlook_Yearbook/yi_3kCJofX0C, 11.

67. Maruyama, conversation, November 14, 2019.

68. Bloomberg, "Rice Excluded from Trade Accord U.S. and Japan Aim to Ink Soon," *Japan Times*, September 18, 2019, https://www.japantimes.co.jp/news/2019/09 /18/business/rice-excluded-trade-accord-u-s-japan-aim-ink-soon/#.Xpc8wZp7nOQ.

69. Carole L. Brookins, conversation with the author, November 10, 2019. Brookins died in the COVID-19 pandemic in March 2020. See https://www.nytimes.com /2020/04/22/obituaries/carole-brookins-dead-coronavirus.html.

70. Nelson Graves, "Koop Urges Curbs on RJR Nabisco's 'Smokeless Cigarette,'" Reuters, 1988, Yeutter Papers.

71. Clayton Yeutter, letter to Dr. C. Everett Koop, November 21, 1988, Yeutter Papers.

72. Judith H. Bello, email to the author, July 6, 2020.

73. Clayton Yeutter, letter to Hamish Maxwell, January 19, 1989, Yeutter Papers.

74. Lewis, *America's Frontline Trade Officials*, 93.

75. Lewis, *America's Frontline Trade Officials*, 92–93.

76. Clayton Yeutter, "To the Directors of B.A.T. Industries P.L.C.," letter of resignation, September 1998, Yeutter Papers.

77. Kelly Semrau, conversation with the author, November 5, 2019.

78. Carla A. Hills, conversation with the author, November 15, 2019.

79. Clayton Yeutter, "Accomplishments and Setbacks," interview at a forum at the Miller Center of Public Affairs, University of Virginia, April 30, 1993, transcript in personal papers of Cristena Bach Yeutter, 46.

80. Clayton Yeutter, email to Steve Krikava, March 1, 2012, personal papers of Cristena Bach Yeutter.

81. Ronald J. Hansen, "Sandra Day O'Connor's Path to the Supreme Court Included Help from Surprising Places," *Republic*, March 15, 2019, updated March 18, 2019, https://www.azcentral.com/story/news/local/phoenix/2019/03/15/sandra-day-oconnor -path-supreme-court-included-help-surprising-places/3156960002/; Cristena Bach Yeutter, email, July 3, 2020.

82. Kim Y. Bottimore, conversation, June 24, 2020.

83. George Bush, "Remarks at the Swearing-In Ceremony for Clayton Yeutter as Secretary of Agriculture," American Presidency Project, February 16, 1989, https:// www.presidency.ucsb.edu/documents/remarks-the-swearing-ceremony-for-clayton -yeutter-secretary-agriculture.

84. Christopher Graybill, "Horatio Alger Crops Up in the Cabinet," *Wall Street Journal*, January 4, 1989, Yeutter Papers.

85. Clayton Yeutter, memorandum for Christopher Graybill, January 18, 1989, Yeutter Papers.

10. We Barely Survived

1. Sue Kirchhoff, "Ag Secretary Yeutter Finds Praise Is Scarce," *Fresno Bee*, September 21, 1990, Yeutter Papers.

2. Kirchhoff, "Ag Secretary Yeutter."

3. Gary Blumenthal, conversation with the author, November 13, 2019.

4. Carole L. Brookins, conversation with the author, November 10, 2019.

5. Charles E. "Chip" Roh Jr., conversation with the author, July 10, 2020.

6. Blumenthal, conversation, November 13, 2019.

7. Kirchhoff, "Ag Secretary Yeutter."

8. Richard T. Crowder, conversation with the author, November 13, 2019.

9. John H. Sununu, conversation with the author, December 4, 2019.

10. Gene Johnston, "Dear Clayton Yeutter," open letter, *Successful Farming*, April 1989, Yeutter Papers.

11. Clayton Yeutter, letter to Gene Johnston, July 12, 1989, Yeutter Papers.

12. Jack Anderson, "No Friend to Family Farmers," in *Formulation of the 1990 Farm Bill: Hearings before the Subcommittee on Domestic Marketing, Consumer Relations, and Nutrition of the Committee on Agriculture, House of Representatives*, August 8, 1989, 101, https://www.google.com/books/edition/Formulation_of_the_1990_Farm _Bill/Fx1DAQAAMAAJ.

13. Roger J. Baccigaluppi, letter to Clayton Yeutter, August 21, 1989, Yeutter Papers.

14. John H. Sununu, letter to Clayton Yeutter, November 29, 1990, Yeutter Papers.

15. Clayton Yeutter, "To John Sununu," December 18, 1990, Yeutter Papers.

16. Preston Smith, "Ag's Leading Man," *Successful Farming*, November 1989, 18–19, Yeutter Papers.

17. "Secretary Yeutter's Fitness Challenge," USDA internal brochure, Yeutter Papers, May 25, 1990.

18. Clayton Yeutter, memorandum for the president, May 4, 1989, Yeutter Papers.

19. Clayton Yeutter, email to Orion Samuelson, April 12, 2013, shared with the author by Gregg S. Yeutter.

20. Clayton Yeutter, letter to Mrs. Blandena Bovee, June 5, 1989, Yeutter Papers.

21. Clayton Yeutter, memorandum for President George W. Bush, March 13, 1989, Yeutter Papers.

22. "Alar Concerns," USDA staff memorandum for Clayton Yeutter, March 14, 1989, Yeutter Papers.

23. Charles J. Abbott, "Apple Scare Unfair: Official," *Lebanon Democrat*, March 20, 1989, Yeutter Papers.

24. "Joint Statement," FDA/EPA/USDA, March 16, 1989, Yeutter Papers.

25. "Talking Points on Food Safety," undated, Yeutter Papers.

26. "Address of the Hon. Clayton Yeutter, Secretary of Agriculture, Before the National Newspaper Association," USDA, March 17, 1989, transcript in Yeutter Papers, 22–23.

27. Elliott Negin, "The Alar 'Scare' Was for Real'; and So Is That 'Veggie Hate-Crime' Movement," *Columbia Journalism Review* 35, no. 3 (September–October 1996): 13–15, https://www.pbs.org/tradesecrets/docs/alarscarenegin.html.

28. Clayton Yeutter, memorandum for William K. Reilly, July 20, 1989, Yeutter Papers. See also Philip Shabecoff, "E.P.A. Proposing Quicker Action against Suspect Farm Chemicals," *New York Times*, July 19, 1989, Yeutter Papers.

29. Clayton Yeutter, letter to Dr. T. B. Kinney Jr., November 13, 1990, Yeutter Papers.

30. Farm Credit Council, "Yeutter Sees Heavy Environment Debate; Rural Development," *Insider*, undated, Yeutter Papers.

31. Clayton Yeutter, Q&A, USDA transcript, September 15, 1989, Yeutter Papers.

32. David Gram, "Yeutter's Remarks Divide Vermont's Farm Community," *Barre Montpelier Times Argus*, September 13, 1989, Yeutter Papers.

33. Clayton Yeutter, letter to William R. Sayre, October 2, 1989, Yeutter Papers.

34. Bruce Ingersoll, "Suit Attacks Firms' Efforts for Cattle Drug," *Wall Street Journal*, November 30, 1990, Yeutter Papers.

35. "Food Fights, Fouls & Victories," *Consumer Reports*, March 31, 2016, https://www.consumerreports.org/food-safety/food-fights-fouls-and-victories/.

36. USDA *Report to Congress on the Dairy Promotion Program*, July 1, 1992, 28, https://www.google.com/books/edition/USDA_Report_to_Congress_on_the_Dairy_Pro/JhNiVCegfTwC.

37. "Those Terrifying Cows," editorial, *Wall Street Journal*, January 7, 1991.

38. See "Recombinant Bovine Growth Hormone," American Cancer Society, https://www.cancer.org/cancer/cancer-causes/recombinant-bovine-growth-hormone.html.

39. Clayton Yeutter, memorandum for the president, April 6, 1990, Yeutter Papers.

40. Clayton Yeutter, memorandum for the president, September 21, 1990, Yeutter Papers.

41. See Associated Press, "Concern about Spotted Owl Leads to Ban on Timber Sale," *New York Times*, May 25, 1991, https://www.nytimes.com/1991/05/25/us/concern-about-spotted-owl-leads-to-ban-on-timber-sale.html.

42. David Schaefer, "Bush Takes Offensive on Spotted-Owl Debate," *Seattle Times*, May 14, 1992, Yeutter Papers.

43. "Spotted Owl Became Symbol in 1990s Controversy," *Seattle Times*, April 27, 2007, https://www.seattletimes.com/seattle-news/spotted-owl-became-symbol-in-1990s-controversy/.

44. Clayton Yeutter, letter to Dr. Robert W. Hahn, July 31, 1993, Yeutter Papers.

45. See "UN Climate Talks," Council on Foreign Relations, https://www.cfr.org/timeline/un-climate-talks.

46. Scott Waldman and Benjamin Hulac, "This Is When the GOP Turned Away from Climate Policy," *E&E News*, December 5, 2018, https://www.eenews.net/stories/1060108785/; Steven A. Holmes, "The 1992 Campaign: The Environmental Debate; Gore Says Bush Is Hypocritical on Ecology Issues," *New York Times*, August 4, 1992, https://www.nytimes.com/1992/08/04/us/1992-campaign-environmental-debate-gore-says-bush-hypocritical-ecology-issues.html.

47. Clayton Yeutter, "U.S. Mission to Poland Feels Challenge of History," November 27, 1989, Yeutter Papers.

48. Daniel Runde, "President Trump Is Visiting Poland, a Staunch US Ally and US Foreign Assistance 'Graduate,'" *Forbes*, July 5, 2017, https://www.forbes.com/sites/danielrunde/2017/07/05/president-trump-visit-poland-us-ally-foreign-assistance-graduate/#30b0b9db2c08.

49. "Poland GDP," Trading Economics, accessed April 18, 2021, https://tradingeconomics.com/poland/gdp.

50. Clayton Yeutter, memorandum for the president, February 9, 1990, Yeutter Papers.

51. Ann Bailey, "Mailing Christmas Cards? Don't Forget Clayton," *Agweek*, December 17, 1990, Yeutter Papers.

52. Clayton Yeutter, letter to Ann Bailey, January 2, 1991, Yeutter Papers.

53. Anonymous wheat farmer, letter to Clayton Yeutter, undated, Yeutter Papers.

54. Rick Steigmeyer, "Fire Yeutter, Say Wheatgrowers," *Wenatchee (WA) World*, October 5, 1990, Yeutter Papers.

55. Roy Hemman, "Yeutter Cares Little for Farmers," *Hutchinson (KS) News*, undated clip, Yeutter Papers.

56. Clayton Yeutter, letter to Ray Hemman, October 29, 1990, Yeutter Papers.

57. Leonard W. Condon, conversation with the author, November 14, 2019.

58. Brookins, conversation, November 10, 2019.

59. Neal Blewett and John Kerin, letter to Clayton Yeutter, January 18, 1991, Yeutter Papers.

60. Clayton Yeutter, letter to John Allwright, National Farmers Federation of Australia, January 10, 1991, Yeutter Papers.

61. Daniel L. Dudden, letter to Clayton Yeuter, February 6, 1991, Yeutter Papers.

62. Blumenthal, conversation, November 13, 2019.

63. Clayton Yeutter, letter to Marvin Barnett, October 29, 1990, Yeutter Papers.

64. Keith E. Portenier, letter to Clayton Yeutter, September 24, 1990, Yeutter Papers.

65. Clayton Yeutter, letter to Keith E. Portenier, October 8, 1990, Yeutter Papers.

66. Clayton Yeutter, memorandum for Dick Crowder, August 31, 1990, Yeutter Papers.

67. Terpstra, conversation, November 14, 2019.

68. Clayton Yeutter, letter to Viveca Arnst, January 30, 1991, Yeutter Papers.

69. Leland Swanson, letter to Clayton Yeutter, November 13, 1990, Yeutter Papers.

70. Clayton Yeutter, letter to Leland Swanson, November 26, 1990, Yeutter Papers.

71. Clayton Yeutter, letter to Leland Swanson, March 26, 1990, Yeutter Papers.

72. Clayton Yeutter, letter to Delvin Jech, March 21, 1990, Yeutter Papers.

73. Clayton Yeutter, letter to Henry Bellmon, March 21, 1990, Yeutter Papers.

74. Clayton Yeutter, letter to Wayne Nielsen, February 28, 1993, Yeutter Papers.

75. Clayton Yeutter, "Remarks Prepared for Delivery by Clayton Yeutter, Secretary of Agriculture to the Chicago Farmers," September 14, 1990, in *Acreage Limitation Program for the 1991 Crop of Wheat: Hearing before the Subcommittee on Wheat, Soybeans, and Feed Grains of Committee on Agriculture, House of Representatives,* September 17, 1990, 18, https://www.google.com/books/edition/Acreage_Limitation_Program_for_the_1991/GjdrvjzTCT4C.

76. National Milk Producers Federation, "NMPF 'Disappointed' in Yeutter's Attack on Farm Programs," press release, September 14, 1990, Yeutter Papers.

77. George Mueller, letter to Clayton Yeutter, September 24, 1990, Yeutter Papers.

78. Clayton Yeutter, letter to George B. Mueller, October 1, 1990, Yeutter Papers.

79. John R. Block, letter to Clayton Yeutter, September 18, 1990, Yeutter Papers.

80. Clayton Yeutter, letter to John R. Block, September 27, 1990, Yeutter Papers.

81. J. Robert Kerrey, letter to Clayton Yeutter, undated, Yeutter Papers.

82. Clayton Yeutter, memorandum for the president, August 30, 1991, Yeutter Papers.

83. Clayton Yeutter, memorandum for the president, September 27, 1991, Yeutter Papers.

84. Clayton Yeutter, memorandum for the president, October 3, 1991, Yeutter Papers.

85. J. Robert Kerrey, letter to Clayton Yeutter, September 3, 1998, Yeutter Papers.

86. Clayton Yeutter, letter to J. Robert Kerrey, September 8, 1998, Yeutter Papers.

87. J. Robert Kerrey, conversation with the author, October 28, 2019.

88. Albert R. Hunt, "Bob Kerrey, Long-Distance Medalist," *Wall Street Journal,* January 30, 1997, https://www.wsj.com/articles/SB854578067241533000.

89. Clayton Yeutter, letter to J. Robert Kerrey, February 3, 1997, Yeutter Papers.

90. Associated Press, "Harkin Says Yeutter 'Kissed Off' Iowa," undated newspaper clip, Yeutter Papers.

91. Clayton Yeutter, memorandum for Sen. Thomas R. Harkin, April 21, 1989, Yeutter Papers.

92. Clayton Yeutter, letter to the Honorable Michael G. Sotirhos, August 7, 1990, Yeutter Papers.

93. Clayton Yeutter, memorandum for the president, October 18, 1990, Yeutter Papers.

94. Sununu, conversation, December 4, 2019.

95. Crowder, conversation, November 13, 2019.

96. See Harwood D. Schaffer and Daryll E. Ray, "Remember When 'Freedom to Farm' Became 'Freedom to Fail'?—Commentary," *AgFax*, August 2, 2018, https://agfax.com/2018/08/02/remember-when-freedom-to-farm-became-freedom-to-fail-commentary/.

97. Blumenthal, conversation, November 13, 2019.

98. Clayton Yeutter, letter to President Bush, January 25, 1991, Yeutter Papers.

99. George Bush, letter to Clayton Yeutter, January 25, 1991, Yeutter Papers.

100. "Woodland Predicts Yeutter's Resignation," NFO *Reporter*, December 1990, Yeutter Papers.

101. Clayton Yeutter, memorandum for Devon Woodland, January 10, 1991, Yeutter Papers.

102. Smith, "Ag's Leading Man," 18–19.

103. See Allan B. Muchin, letter to Clayton Yeutter, November 18, 1988, Yeutter Papers.

104. Clayton Yeutter, letter to City of Chicago, January 22, 1991, Yeutter Papers.

105. Clayton Yeutter, memorandum for Ira Marcus, November 25, 1988, Yeutter Papers.

106. Allen J. Beermann, conversation with the author, February 10, 2020.

107. Van A. Yeutter, conversation with the author, June 22, 2020.

108. Clayton Yeutter, memorandum for Woodland, January 10, 1991.

109. Clayton Yeutter, letter to Barbara A. Leinberger, February 4, 1991, Yeutter Papers.

110. Clayton Yeutter, letter to Earl Butz, November 5, 1990, Yeutter Papers.

111. Clayton Yeutter, letter to Leinberger, February 4, 1991.

112. "Tough Talker," editorial, *Journal of Commerce*, January 29, 1991, Yeutter Papers.

113. Clayton Yeutter, letter to Robert Harris, February 5, 1991, Yeutter Papers.

114. Yeutter, letter to Earl Butz.

115. Clayton Yeutter, memorandum for Bush, December 1990.

116. Crowder, conversation, November 13, 2019.

117. Clayton Yeutter, memorandum for Bush.

118. Richard T. Crowder, email to the author, June 15, 2020; photo by Paul Fetters in "Down to the Count: Time Is Running Out on Farm Trade Talks," *Top Producer* (November 1990): 20, Yeutter Papers.

119. Clayton Yeutter, memorandum for the president, December 20, 1990. Yeutter Papers.

120. Clayton Yeutter, memorandum for the president, October 18, 1990, Yeutter Papers.

121. See Barry James, "Europe Takes Farm Peace over Trade," *International Herald Tribune*, undated, Yeutter Papers.

122. Clayton Yeutter, letter to Robert J. Donahue, January 4, 1991, Yeutter Papers.

123. Edward Alden, review of draft of this book, shared with the author by email, November 16, 2020.

124. Clayton Yeutter, letter to Charles J. "Joe" O'Mara, January 6, 1995, Yeutter Papers.

125. Michael C. Nolan, letter to Clayton Yeutter, January 7, 1991, Yeutter Papers UNL Libraries.

126. Clayton Yeutter, letter to Michael C. Nolan, January 22, 1991, Yeutter Papers.

127. Serena Forbes, letter to Clayton Yeutter, May 6, 1989, Yeutter Papers.

128. Clayton Yeutter, letter to Serena Forbes, June 5, 1989, Yeutter Papers.

11. No Professional Machiavellian

1. "Persian Gulf War," *History*, last updated January 17, 2020, https://www.history .com/topics/middle-east/persian-gulf-war.

2. Gerald E. Matzke, "Bush's Anguish Resembles Lincoln's," *Lincoln Journal*, February 16, 1991, Yeutter Papers.

3. David W. Moore, "Americans Believe U.S. Participation in Gulf War a Decade Ago Worthwhile," *Gallup News*, February 26, 2001, https://news.gallup.com/poll /1963/americans-believe-us-participation-gulf-war-decade-ago-worthwhile.aspx.

4. Adam Clymer, "Confrontation in the Gulf; Congress Acts to Authorize War in Gulf; Margins Are 5 Votes in Senate, 67 in House," *New York Times*, January 13, 1991, https://www.nytimes.com/1991/01/13/world/confrontation-gulf-congress-acts -authorize-war-gulf-margins-are-5-votes-senate.html.

5. Moore, "Americans Believe."

6. Jo Ann Bradford, letter to Clayton Yeutter, February 24, 1991; Clayton Yeutter, letter to Mrs. James Bradford, March 19, 1991, both in Yeutter Papers.

7. Robin Toner, "The Unfinished Politician," *New York Times Magazine*, April 14, 1991, https://www.nytimes.com/1991/04/14/magazine/the-unfinished-politician.html.

8. Jennifer M. Gardner, "The 1990–91 Recession: How Bad Was the Labor Market?," *Monthly Labor Review* 117, no. 6 (June 1994): 3–11, https://www.bls.gov/opub /mlr/1994/06/art1full.pdf.

9. Doug Sosnick, "Groucho Marx's Republican Party," *Politico*, March 17, 2014, https://www.politico.com/magazine/story/2014/03/sosnik-memo-republican-party -future-104749.

10. Clayton Yeutter, "Accomplishments and Setbacks," interview at a forum at the Miller Center of Public Affairs, University of Virginia, April 30, 1993, transcript in personal papers of Cristena Bach Yeutter, 47.

11. See Daron Acemoglu and Joshua Angrist, "Consequences of Employment Protection? The Case of the Americans with Disabilities Act," National Bureau of Economic Research, https://www.nber.org/digest/dec98/w6670.html.

12. See "Introduction to the ADA," U.S. Department of Justice, https://www.ada .gov/ada_intro.htm; "The Clean Air Act: Highlights of the 1990 Amendments," Environmental Protection Agency, https://www.epa.gov/clean-air-act-overview/clean-air -act-highlights-1990-amendments.

13. John H. Sununu, conversation with the author, December 4, 2019.

14. Maureen Dowd, "Bennett Rejects Top G.O.P. Post, Adding to White House Disarray," *New York Times*, December 14, 1990, https://www.nytimes.com/1990/12/14/us/bennett-rejects-top-gop-post-adding-to-white-house-disarray.html.

15. Sununu, conversation, December 4, 2019.

16. Jonathan Harsch, "Moving On: Yeutter's Legacy Includes a New Farm Bill and Movement on the International Trade Scene. As the Republican National Committee Chairman, Will He Abandon Ag?," *Farm Futures*, February 1991, Yeutter Papers.

17. Clayton Yeutter, letter to Mr. and Mrs. Otto Bassler, March 8, 1991, Yeutter Papers.

18. Clayton Yeutter, letter to Dr. Gail Yanney, Yeutter Papers.

19. Clayton Yeutter, letter to Michael Sotirhos, January 22, 1991, Yeutter Papers.

20. Clayton Yeutter, memorandum for the president, January 10, 1991, Yeutter Papers.

21. Associated Press, "Gravely Ill, Atwater Offers Apology," *New York Times*, January 13, 1991, https://www.nytimes.com/1991/01/13/us/gravely-ill-atwater-offers-apology.html.

22. Clayton Yeutter, letter to Pierre S. du Pont IV, March 11, 1991, Yeutter Papers.

23. Clayton Yeutter, letter to Dick Herman, January 22, 1991, Yeutter Papers.

24. "The Week," *National Review*, January 28, 1991, personal papers of Cristena Bach Yeutter.

25. Clayton Yeutter, letter to Norman G. P. Krausz, March 27, 1991, Yeutter Papers.

26. Grace Kaminkowitz, "Underestimate Yeutter? Chicago Knows Better," *Crain's Chicago Business*, undated clip, Yeutter Papers.

27. Oswald Johnson, "Republican Mixes Pragmatism and Persuasiveness: Yeutter—Apostle of Free Trade," *Los Angeles Times*, August 16, 1985, Yeutter Papers.

28. Clayton Yeutter, "Transcript of Remarks of Clayton Yeutter, Chairman, Republican National Committee," January 25, 1991, Yeutter Papers.

29. Allen J. Beermann, conversation with the author, February 10, 2020.

30. Cristena Bach Yeutter, email to the author, December 3, 2020.

31. Clayton Yeutter, letter to Ruth E. Davis, September 25, 1992, Yeutter Papers.

32. Mervin, *George Bush*, 221.

33. AllPolitics, "The 1992 Republican Platform," CNN and *Time*, https://www.cnn.com/ALLPOLITICS/1996/conventions/san.diego/facts/past.platforms/gop92/index.shtml.

34. Burt Solomon, "Send In the Clones," *National Journal*, March 21, 1992, Yeutter Papers.

35. Ann Devroy and David S. Broder, "Bush Moves to Shift RNC Leadership; Yeutter Gets New Post; Longtime Aide Bond Due to Replace Him," *Washington Post*, February 1, 1992, Yeutter Papers.

36. Clayton Yeutter, "January 1991 RNC Meeting," Yeutter Papers.

37. Clayton Yeutter, memorandum for the president, October 24, 1991, Yeutter Papers.

38. Clayton Yeutter, memorandum for the president, November 1, 1991, Yeutter Papers.

39. Roberto Suro, "The 1991 Election: Louisiana; Bush Denounces Duke as Racist and Charlatan," *New York Times*, November 7, 1991, https://www.nytimes.com /1991/11/07/us/the-1991-election-louisiana-bush-denounces-duke-as-racist-and -charlatan.html.

40. Clayton Yeutter and Ron Brown, appearance on *Newsmaker Sunday*, CNN, November 10, 1991, transcript in Yeutter Papers.

41. Michael Kinsley, "David Duke and American Decline," *Time*, November 25, 1991, Yeutter Papers.

42. Clayton Yeutter, letter to Michael Kinsley, November 20, 1991, Yeutter Papers.

43. David Duke, letter to Clayton Yeutter, December 10, 1991, Yeutter Papers.

44. John Kenneth Galbraith, letter to Yeutter, January 8, 1991, Yeutter Papers.

45. Clayton Yeutter, letter to John Kenneth Gailbraith [*sic*], January 22, 1991, Yeutter Papers.

46. Jack Kemp, annotated memorandum for the president from Clayton Yeutter, November 18, 1991, Yeutter Papers.

47. See "US Business Cycle Expansions and Contractions," National Bureau of Economic Research, last updated June 8, 2020, https://www.nber.org/research/data /us-business-cycle-expansions-and-contractions.

48. John D. Rockefeller IV, note to Clayton Yeutter, December 26, 1990, Yeutter Papers.

49. Clayton Yeutter, letter to President-Elect William J. Clinton, November 4, 1992, Yeutter Papers.

50. Clayton Yeutter, letter to Ron Brown, February 20, 1992, Yeutter Papers.

51. E. Benjamin Nelson, conversation with the author, June 16, 2020.

52. Kathryn G. Thompson, "Erase the 'Little Lady' Frame of Mind," Column Right, *Los Angeles Times*, February 2, 1992, Yeutter Papers.

53. Clayton Yeutter, letter to Kathryn G. Thompson, February 14, 1992, Yeutter Papers.

54. Terry Savage, conversation with the author, March 19, 2020.

55. Paul A. Gigot, "In New Hampshire Protectionists Slip on the Ice," Potomac Watch, *Wall Street Journal*, February 7, 1992, Yeutter Papers.

56. Clayton Yeutter, memorandum for Paul A. Gigot, February 10, 1992, Yeutter Papers.

57. Clayton Yeutter, interview on *Evans & Novak*, CNN, May 25–27, 1991, transcript in Yeutter Papers.

58. Clayton Yeutter, letter to David Broder, January 17, 1993, Yeutter Papers.

59. Clayton Yeutter, letter to Dr. Jerry Schenken, December 21, 1994, Yeutter Papers.

60. "Let the Voters Choose: Solving the Problem of Partisan Gerrymandering," Committee for Economic Development of the Conference Board, March 13, 2018, https://www.ced.org/reports/solving-the-problem-of-partisan -gerrymandering.

61. See Ann Devroy and David S. Broder, "Bush Moves Yeutter, Picks New Party Chief," *Washington Post*, February 1, 1992, https://www.mcall.com/news/mc-xpm -1992-02-01-2844024-story.html.

62. Clayton Yeutter, memorandum for Attorney General Barr, June 16, 1992, Yeutter Papers.

63. Clayton Yeutter, memorandum for White House chief of staff Samuel K. Skinner, June 17, 1992, Yeutter Papers.

64. Clayton Yeutter, memorandum for Sam Skinner, May 27, 1992, Yeutter Papers.

65. Fred Barnes, "Logjam," *New Republic*, May 11, 1992, 10–11, Yeutter Papers.

66. Clayton Yeutter, memorandum for Ede Holiday, April 23, 1992, Yeutter Papers.

67. Clayton Yeutter, memorandum for Fred Barnes, April 24, 1992, Yeutter Papers.

68. Clayton Yeutter, memorandum for Bill Rosenberg, April 2, 1992, Yeutter Papers.

69. Clayton Yeutter, memorandum for Senator Charles E. "Chuck" Grassley, April 2, 1992, Yeutter Papers.

70. Clayton Yeutter, letter to Robert Reinstein, May 13, 1992, Yeutter Papers.

71. See J. T. Houghton, B. A. Callander, and S. K. Varney, ed., *Climate Change 1992: The Supplementary Report to the IPCC Scientific Assessment*, Intergovernmental Panel on Climate Change (Cambridge: Cambridge University Press, 1992), https://www .ipcc.ch/site/assets/uploads/2018/05/ipcc_wg_I_1992_suppl_report_full_report.pdf. The report drew on the work of 118 scientists from twenty-two countries and had its work reviewed by 380 scientists from sixty-three countries. It concluded that "emissions resulting from human activities are substantially increasing the atmospheric concentrations of the greenhouse gases: carbon dioxide, methane, chlorofluorocarbons, and nitrous oxide," further noting that the atmosphere had warmed over the last century and that the warming was "anomalously high" in the late 1980s, leading to 1990 and 1991 being the "warmest years in the record" at that time, February 1992.

72. Clayton Yeutter, letter to Malcolm Wallop, May 14, 1992, Yeutter Papers.

73. United Nations Convention on Climate Change, C-Span, September 18, 1992, https://www.c-span.org/video/?32561-1/united-nations-convention-climate-change.

74. Nobel Peace Prize 2007, https://www.nobelprize.org/prizes/peace/2007 /summary/.

75. Clayton Yeutter, letter to E. L. Howe, June 12, 1992, Yeutter Papers.

76. Clayton Yeutter, letter to Albert Gore, June 11, 1992, Yeutter Papers.

77. Clayton Yeutter, memorandum for Sherrie Rollins, May 14, 1992, Yeutter Papers.

78. Mortimer B. Zuckerman, "No Myopia for the Masses!," *U.S. News & World Report*, July 20, 1992, Yeutter Papers.

79. Clayton Yeutter, letter to Mortimer B. Zuckerman, July 21, 1992, Yeutter Papers.

80. Mortimer B. Zuckerman, letter to Clayton Yeutter, July 29, 1992, Yeutter Papers.

81. John Ferguson, "Honeymoon Definitely Over for Loud-Mouthed Yeutter," *Ottawa Citizen*, February 5, 1987, https://news.google.com/newspapers?id= GK8yAAAAIBAJ&sjid=ku8FAAAAIBAJ&pg=5518,2424921&dq=yeutter&hl=en. See chapter 8.

82. Kelly Semrau, conversation with the author, November 5, 2019.

83. Roger Simon, "Got to Admire Bush: He Eats with His Fingers," *Baltimore Sun*, August 21, 1992, https://www.baltimoresun.com/news/bs-xpm-1992-08-21 -1992234058-story.html.

84. Clayton Yeutter, memorandum for Bob Teeter, July 17, 1992, Yeutter Papers.

85. Clayton Yeutter, memorandum for Charlie Thone, June 29, 1992, Yeutter Papers.

86. Clayton Yeutter, memorandum for Sec. Samuel K. Skinner, June 17, 1992, Yeutter Papers.

87. See Michael Decourcy Hinds, "The 1991 Election; Wofford Wins Senate Race, Turning Back Thornburgh: G.O.P. Gains Edge in Trenton," *New York Times*, November 6, 1991, https://www.nytimes.com/1991/11/06/us/1991-election-wofford-wins-senate -race-turning-back-thornburgh-gop-gains-edge.html.

88. Clayton Yeutter, letter to the Honorable and Mrs. Dick Thornburgh, July 9, 1992, Yeutter Papers.

89. Gary Blumenthal, conversation with the author, November 13, 2019.

90. Tony Mitchell, "Yeutter to Join Bush/Quayle '92 Campaign Staff," Bush/Quayle '92 campaign press release, August 31, 1992, Yeutter Papers.

91. David E. Lynch, "Yeutter to Move to Campaign Trail," *Lincoln Journal*, August 1992, Yeutter Papers.

92. Marjorie Williams, "The President's Straight Man," *Washington Post*, June 7, 1992, https://www.washingtonpost.com/archive/lifestyle/magazine/1992/06/07/the -presidents-straight-man/a7cc3adc-a7b8-4b3c-98c4-3bb2bc7738d8/.

93. Dr. Jean Howard-Hill, letter to Clayton Yeutter, October 28, 1992, Yeutter Papers.

94. Clayton Yeutter, letter to Dr. Jean Howard-Hill, November 3, 1992, Yeutter Papers.

95. Ruth Marcus, "Bush Unveils Wheat Export Subsidy," *Washington Post*, September 3, 1992, Yeutter Papers.

96. Philip Brasher, "Bush Campaign Officials Calls Farmers Ungrateful," *Bismarck (ND) Tribune*, October 1, 1992, Yeutter Papers.

97. Robin Toner, "The 1992 Elections: President—The Overview; Clinton Captures Presidency with Huge Electoral Margin; Wins a Democratic Congress," *New York Times*, November 4, 1992, https://www.nytimes.com/1992/11/04/us/1992-elections -president-overview-clinton-captures-presidency-with-huge.html.

98. Stephen Knott, "George H. W. Bush: Campaigns and Elections," University of Virginia, Miller Center, accessed April 5, 2021, https://millercenter.org/president /bush/campaigns-and-elections.

99. Mervin, *George Bush*, 225.

100. Toner, "1992 Elections: President."

101. Cristena Bach Yeutter, email, December 3, 2020.

102. Mervin, *George Bush*, 211.

103. Clayton Yeutter, letter to James H. Lake, September 2, 1988, Yeutter Papers.

104. Yeutter, interview on *Evans & Novak*.

105. Clayton Yeutter, memorandum for Marilyn Tucker Quayle, April 15, 1995, Yeutter Papers.

106. David S. Broder, "Quayle Pulls Out of GOP Race," *Washington Post*, September 27, 1999, https://www.washingtonpost.com/wp-srv/pmextra/sept99/27/quayle092799.htm.

107. Cristena Bach Yeutter, conversation with the author, June 25, 2020.

108. Blumenthal, conversation, November 13, 2019.

12. A Second Chance

1. Clayton Yeutter, letter to William J. Bowen, Heidrick & Struggles, March 6, 1993, Yeutter Papers.

2. Neogen Corporation, "Neogen Names Former Secretary of Agriculture Yeutter to Board," press release, August 1, 2007, https://www.neogen.com/neocenter/press-releases/neogen-names-former-secretary-of-agriculture-yeutter-to-board/. See also Mycogen, "Former U.S. Secretary of Agriculture Clayton Yeutter Elected to Mycogen's Board of Directors," press release, June 11, 1998, Yeutter Papers.

3. Clayton Yeutter, letter to Martin Feldstein, March 6, 1993, Yeutter Papers.

4. Brooks Jackson, "The Budget and Deficit under Clinton," FactCheck.org, February 11, 2008, https://www.factcheck.org/2008/02/the-budget-and-deficit-under-clinton/.

5. Clayton Yeutter, letter to Ann Reilly Dowd, March 13, 1993, Yeutter Papers; Ann Reilly Dowd, "Clintonomics and You—Round I: Higher Taxes for the Rich and Big Corporations. Round II: Higher Taxes for Health Care. Toss in Much Tougher Spending Cuts, and the Payoff Comes down the Road," *Fortune*, March 22, 1993, https://money.cnn.com/magazines/fortune/fortune_archive/1993/03/22/77655/index.htm.

6. Clayton Yeutter, letter to Tina Karalekas, November 4, 1994, Yeutter Papers.

7. Van A. Yeutter, conversation with the author, June 22, 2020.

8. Clayton Yeutter, letter to Gayle Rohrbasser, May 13, 1996; Clayton Yeutter, letter to Bill Deen, December 20, 1995, both in Yeutter Papers.

9. Clayton Yeutter, letter to Warren Maruyama, January 20, 1995, Yeutter Papers.

10. Clayton Yeutter, letter to Bud Morrison, July 10, 1996, Yeutter Papers.

11. Clayton Yeutter, letter to the Honorable James Watkins, September 13, 1996, Yeutter Papers.

12. Clayton Yeutter, letter to Jim Lake, January 12, 1995, Yeutter Papers.

13. John Greenya, "Where Are They Now? Clayton Yeutter and Cristy Bach," *Washington Lawyer*, March–April 2000, personal papers of Cristena Bach Yeutter.

14. Clayton Yeutter, letter to Bob Odle, January 24, 1996, Yeutter Papers.

15. Clayton Yeutter, letter to Bill Deen, December 20, 1995, Yeutter Papers.

16. Clayton Yeutter, letter to Dr. Ron Ritchey, October 16, 1995, Yeutter Papers.

17. Clayton Yeutter, letter to Kay McCarty, December 6, 1995, Yeutter Papers.

18. Clayton and Cristy Yeutter, "Holiday Greetings," Christmas 1995, Yeutter Papers.

19. "History of Maxwell Arboretum," University of Nebraska–Lincoln, Institute of Agriculture and Natural Resources, UNL Gardens, 2017, https://unlgardens.unl.edu/historyofmaxwellarboretum.

20. Clayton Yeutter, letter to Mr. and Mrs. Bill Deen, May 12, 1995, Yeutter Papers.

21. See "Grove of State Trees," U.S. National Arboretum, https://www.usna.usda .gov/discover/gardens-collections/grove-of-state-trees/. See also "Jeanne Vierk Yuetter [*sic*]," Yeutter Papers.

22. Alan F. Holmer, email to the author, July 21, 2020, including letters read at the memorial ceremony.

23. Clayton Yeutter, letter to the Honorable E. Benjamin Nelson, September 24, 1996.

24. The Yeutter statue stands seven feet high. Sculptor Matthew Placzek, email to the author, July 9, 2020.

25. Troy Fedderson, "Sculptures Honor Nebraska's Former U.S. Ag Secretaries," *Nebraska Today*, September 15, 2014, https://news.unl.edu/newsrooms/today/article /sculptures-honor-nebraskas-former-us-ag-secretaries/.

26. Cristena Bach Yeutter, email to the author, December 3, 2020.

27. Cristena Bach Yeutter, conversation with the author, November 14, 2019.

28. Michael Kelly, "Ex-Ag Leader a New Father," *Omaha World-Herald*, August 17, 1997, personal papers of Cristena Bach Yeutter.

29. Clayton Yeutter, letter to Dr. and Mrs. Ned Raun, June 3, 1998, Yeutter Papers.

30. Cristena Bach Yeutter, email, December 3, 2020.

31. Paul Hammel and Mara Klecker, "Clayton Yeutter, Former U.S. Secretary of Agriculture and Native Nebraskan, Dies at 86," *Omaha World-Herald*, March 5, 2017, https://www.omaha.com/news/state_and_regional/clayton-yeutter-former-u -s-secretary-of-agriculture-and-native-nebraskan-dies-at-86/article_1e4d3a82-0134 -11e7-afd4-230f68166c6b.html.

32. Gary Blumenthal, conversation with the author, November 13, 2019.

33. Greenya, "Where Are They Now?"

13. The World Will Thank You

1. Carla A. Hills, conversation with the author, November 15, 2019.

2. "The Uruguay Round," World Trade Organization, last modified December 17, 2018, https://www.wto.org/english/thewto_e/whatis_e/tif_e/fact5_e.htm.

3. Clayton Yeutter, letter to the president of the United States, December 9, 1994, Yeutter Papers.

4. Clayton Yeutter, letter to Michael Kantor, December 9, 1994, Yeutter Papers.

5. Clayton Yeutter, letter to Mr. and Mrs. Preston Smith, February 16, 1994, Yeutter Papers.

6. Clayton Yeutter, postmortem analysis of the Uruguay Round, *Ohio Farmer*, undated, Yeutter Papers.

7. "Evolution of Trade under the WTO: Handy Statistics," World Trade Oganization, last modified September 23, 2020, https://www.wto.org/english/res_e/statis_e /trade_evolution_e/evolution_trade_wto_e.htm.

8. See Joe Hasell and Max Roser, "Famines," Our World in Data, last modified December 7, 2017, https://ourworldindata.org/famines.

9. Carole L. Brookins, conversation with the author, November 10, 2019.

10. See "Uruguay Round"; "The Doha Round," World Trade Organization, last modified April 3, 2017, https://www.wto.org/english/tratop_e/dda_e/dda_e.htm.

11. Roger Bolton, conversation with the author, November 13, 2019.

12. Michael O. Johanns, Clayton Yeutter Institute for International Trade and Finance, Institute of Agriculture and Natural Resources, University of Nebraska, March 19, 2015, YouTube video, https://www.youtube.com/watch?v=WqtqshNWo-A.

13. Clayton Yeutter, letter to the Honorable Lloyd M. Bentsen, December 9, 1994, Yeutter Papers.

14. Dawson Mathis, letter to Clayton K. Yeutter, December 16, 1994, Yeutter Papers.

15. Clayton Yeutter, letter to Dawson Mathis, January 13, 1995, Yeutter Papers.

16. Clayton Yeutter, memorandum for Keith M. Rockwell, March 29, 1996, Yeutter Papers.

17. Clayton Yeutter, letter to John Whitehead, July 5, 1995, Yeutter Papers.

18. Clayton Yeutter and Maruyama, "A NAFTA for Europe," *Wall Street Journal*, May 19, 1995.

19. Clayton Yeutter, letter to John G. Reed Jr., June 19, 1995, Yeutter Papers.

20. Nelson Warfield, "Dole Campaign Announces Formation of Two Additional Economic Policy Task Forces," Dole/Kemp campaign press release, October 29, 1996; Clayton Yeutter, letter to Dr. and Mrs. Michael Boskin, June 1, 1995, both in Yeutter Papers.

21. Clayton Yeutter, letter to Preston Smith, May 8, 1995, Yeutter Papers.

22. Clayton Yeutter, letter to the Honorable Terry Branstad, October 11, 1996, Yeutter Papers.

23. Cristena Bach Yeutter, conversation with the author, June 25, 2020. For more about Derek campaigning for Dole, see Blaine Harden, "Singing a New Tune, He's a Droll Man," *Washington Post*, October 28, 1996, https://www.washingtonpost.com/archive/politics/1996/10/28/singing-a-new-tune-hes-a-droll-man/f2bbf169-59b0-45b4-a26e-1350607824f7/; Michael Olesker, "Politics Has Become a Branch of Entertainment," *Baltimore Sun*, October 31, 1996, https://www.baltimoresun.com/news/bs-xpm-1996-10-31-1996305002-story.html.

24. Clayton Yeutter, letter to Mr. and Mrs. Hanspeter Spaeti, July 19, 1996, Yeutter Papers.

25. Clayton Yeutter, letter to the Honorable Catherine Bertini, December 4, 1996, Yeutter Papers.

26. Yeutter, letter to Mr. and Mrs. Spaeti, July 19, 1996. See *Investigation into the White House and Department of Justice on Security of FBI Background Investigation Files Interim Report*, Committee on Government Reform and Oversight, September 28, 1996, https://fas.org/irp/congress/1996_rpt/fbirep.htm.

27. George Lardner Jr. and Susan Schmidt, "Livingstone Resigns, Denying Ill Intent," *Washington Post*, June 27, 1996, https://www.washingtonpost.com/wp-srv/politics/special/whitewater/stories/wwtr960627.htm.

28. Yeutter, letter to Mr. and Mrs. Spaeti, July 19, 1996.

29. Clayton Yeutter, letter to Bob Odle, January 24, 1996, Yeutter Papers.

30. Clayton Yeutter, letter to Bob Odle, January 6, 1997 [*sic*, actually 1998], Yeutter Papers.

31. Clayton Yeutter, letter to Robert B. Zoellick, April 26, 1999, Yeutter Papers.

32. Michael Kantor, Carla Hills, William Brock, Robert Strauss, Clayton Yeutter, letter to the Honorable William Jefferson Clinton, June 11, 1997, Yeutter Papers.

33. Clayton Yeutter, letter to the Honorable William Jefferson Clinton, October 29, 1998, Yeutter Papers.

34. Clayton Yeutter, letter to Gary L. Jarmin, March 15, 1999, Yeutter Papers.

35. See U.S.-Cuba Foundation, letter to Clayton Yuetter [*sic*], January 25, 1999, Yeutter Papers.

36. Clayton Yeutter, draft chapter in Singleton and Griswold, *Economic Casualties*, Yeutter Papers.

37. Clayton Yeutter, letter to the Honorable William T. Bagley, June 16, 1999, Yeutter Papers.

38. Clayton Yeutter, letter to Robert B. Zoellick, April 26, 1999, Yeutter Papers.

39. Clayton Yeutter, letter to Mr. and Mrs. John Blum, February 2, 1999, Yeutter Papers.

40. Clayton Yeutter, letter to Richard Day, February 2, 1999, Yeutter Papers.

41. See Bush v. Gore, 531 U.S. 98 (2000), Justia/US Supreme Court, https://supreme.justia.com/cases/federal/us/531/98/.

42. Michael B. Yanney, conversation with the author, September 18, 2019.

43. Cristena Bach Yeutter, email to the author, December 3, 2020.

44. Darci L. Vetter, conversation with the author, October 21, 2019.

45. Kim Y. Bottimore, conversation with the author, June 24, 2020.

46. Cristena Bach Yeutter, email, December 3, 2020.

47. Gary Blumenthal, conversation with the author, November 13, 2019.

48. Yanney, conversation, September 18, 2019.

49. See "How International Division Came to Be," Burlington Capital, April 6, 2016, http://burlingtoncapital.com/how-international-division-came-to-be/.

50. Senator Rick Santorum, letter to Senators Dan Quayle and Lamar Alexander, February 4, 1999, Yeutter Papers.

51. Clayton Yeutter, letter to Rick Santorum, February 17, 1999, Yeutter Papers.

52. Clayton Yeutter, letter to William G. Moore Jr., August 10, 1999, Yeutter Papers.

53. Cristena Bach Yeutter, conversation, June 25, 2020.

54. Clayton Yeutter, Yeutter Papers.

55. Kim Y. Bottimore, conversation, June 24, 2020.

56. Cristena Bach Yeutter, conversation, June 25, 2020.

57. Elena Yeutter, conversation with the author, June 25, 2020; Olivia Yeutter, conversation with the author, June 25, 2020.

58. Cristena Bach Yeutter, email, December 3, 2020.

59. Olivia Yeutter, conversation, June 25, 2020.

60. Van A. Yeutter, conversation with the author, June 22, 2020.

61. Cristena Bach Yeutter, email, December 3, 2020.

62. Olivia Yeutter, conversation, June 25, 2020.

63. Clayton Yeutter and Warren Maruyama, "Japan at a Trade Crossroads," *Wall Street Journal*, November 23, 2010, 15.

64. See James McBride and Andrew Chatzky, "What Is the Trans-Pacific Partnership (TPP)?," Council on Foreign Relations, updated January 4, 2019, https://www.cfr.org/backgrounder/what-trans-pacific-partnership-tpp.

65. Bruce Stokes, "WTO Dispute Panels Gain Power," *National Journal*, August 7, 2010, Yeutter Papers.

66. Clayton Yeutter, email to Bruce Stokes, September 8, 2010, Yeutter Papers.

67. Clayton Yeutter, letter to Preston Smith, July 9, 2010, personal papers of Cristena Bach Yeutter.

68. See Associated Press, "NZ Earthquake Death Toll at 75 as Search Continues," *Arkansas Democrat-Gazette*, February 22, 2011, https://www.arkansasonline.com/news/2011/feb/22/nz-earthquake-death-toll-75-search-continues/.

69. Edward J. Farrell, conversation with the author, December 3, 2020.

70. Associated Press, "Comparing 2011 and 2016 New Zealand earthquakes," *AP News*, November 14, 2016, https://apnews.com/article/044edfe0257449af8e224ddab3e7011c.

71. See "2011 Partnership Forum," United States–New Zealand Council, February 20–22, 2011, accessed April 6, 2021, http://usnzcouncil.org/partnership-forum/2011-partnership-forum/.

72. Ronnie D. Green, conversation with the author, September 3, 2019.

73. Van A. Yeutter, conversation, June 22, 2020.

74. Clayton Yeutter, Matthew J. Slaughter, and Warren H. Maruyama, "The Biggest Loser from Trump's Trade Wars and Hillary's Waffling on TPP Would Be the American Worker," unpublished draft op-ed, October 27, 2016, personal papers of Cristena Bach Yeutter.

75. Farrell, conversation, December 3, 2020.

76. Vetter, conversation, October 21, 2019.

77. Blumenthal, conversation, November 13, 2019.

78. Cristena Bach Yeutter, conversation with the author, November 14, 2019.

79. Andrew Glass, "Trump Scuttles Trans-Pacific Trade Pact, Jan. 23, 2017," *Politico*, January 23, 2019, https://www.politico.com/story/2019/01/23/trans-pacific-trade-pact-2017-1116638.

80. Jen Kirby, "USMCA, Trump's New NAFTA Deal, Explained in 600 Words," *Vox*, February 4, 2020, https://www.vox.com/2018/10/3/17930092/usmca-mexico-nafta-trump-trade-deal-explained.

81. Paul Hammel and Mara Klecker, "Clayton Yeutter, Former U.S. Secretary of Agriculture and Native Nebraskan, Dies at 86," *Omaha World-Herald*, March 5, 2017.

82. Van A. Yeutter, conversation, June 22, 2020.

83. Gregg S. Yeutter, email to his siblings, June 15, 2012, shared with the author; Carl Gersham, "Model Citizen, Heartland Born," *Wall Street Journal*, May 26–27, 2012, C7, Yeutter Papers.

About the Yeutter Institute

1. Cristena Bach Yeutter, email to the author, December 8, 2020.

2. Jill Kosch O'Donnell, email to the author, December 14, 2020.

3. University of Nebraska–Lincoln, "Beghin Named Michael Yanney Chair," press release, May 13, 2019, https://news.unl.edu/newsrooms/today/article/beghin-named -michael-yanney-chair/.

4. University of Nebraska–Lincoln, "Balistreri Named Duane Acklie Chair," press release, September 10, 2020, https://ianrnews.unl.edu/balistreri-named-duane-acklie -chair.

5. O'Donnell, email, December 14, 2020.

6. Chandra Spangler, "Yeutter Institute Provides Opportunity after Canceled Internships," *Nebraska Today*, September 21, 2020, https://news.unl.edu/newsrooms /today/article/yeutter-institute-provides-opportunity-after-canceled-internships/.

7. Clayton Yeutter, "Get Sophisticated in Your Education," Landon Lecture Series on Public Issues, Kansas State University, October 3, 1989, https://www.k-state.edu /landon/speakers/clayton-yeutter/transcript.html.

SELECTED BIBLIOGRAPHY

Dryden, Steve. *Trade Warriors*. New York: Oxford University Press, 1995.

Frank, Thomas. *What's the Matter with Kansas? How Conservatives Won the Heart of America*. New York: Henry Holt, 2004.

Melamed, Leo, with Bob Tamarkin. *Escape to the Futures*. New York: John Wiley & Sons, 1996.

Mervin, David. *George Bush and the Guardianship Presidency*. New York: St. Martin's, 1998.

Muse, Toby. *Kilo: Inside the Deadliest Cocaine Cartels—from the Jungles to the Streets*. New York: HarperCollins, 2020.

Nader, Ralph, William Greider, Margaret Atwood, Vandana Shiva, Mark Ritchie, Wendell Berry, Jerry Brown, et al. *The Case against "Free Trade": GATT, NAFTA, and the Globalization of Corporate Power*. San Francisco: Earth Island, 1993.

Oxley, Alan. *The Challenge of Free Trade*. New York: St. Martin's, 1990.

Peterson, E. Wesley F. *A Billion Dollars a Day: The Economics and Politics of Agricultural Subsidies*. West Sussex, UK: Wiley-Blackwell, 2009.

Rodengen, Jeffrey L. *Past, Present & Futures: Chicago Mercantile Exchange*. Fort Lauderdale FL: Write Stuff Enterprises, 2008.

Savage, Terry. *The Savage Truth on Money*. Hoboken NJ: John Wiley & Sons, 2020.

Singleton, Solveig, and Daniel T. Griswold, eds. *Economic Casualties: How U.S. Foreign Policy Undermines Trade, Growth, and Liberty*. Washington DC: Cato Institute, 1999.

Tamarkin, Bob. *The Merc: The Emergence of a Global Financial Powerhouse*. New York: HarperCollins, 1993.

Turner, James S. *The Chemical Feast: Ralph Nader's Study Group Report on Food Protection and the Food and Drug Administration*. New York: Grossman, 1970.

Yergin, Daniel, and Joseph Stanislaw. *The Commanding Heights: The Battle for the World Economy*. New York: Touchstone, 2002.

Yu, Diane, ed. *Punta: An Oral History of the 1986 GATT Ministerial Meeting in Punta del Este, Uruguay*. Washington DC: U.S. Trade Representative Archives, 1987.

INDEX

Eagleton, Thomas, 110

Earth in the Balance (Gore), 184

earthquake (NZ; 2011), 273–74

Easterday, Ray, 5, 6

Eastern European countries, 64–65, 77. *See also* Soviet Union

Economic Casualties (Singleton and Griswold), 263–64

economy: under the Bush administration, 211–12, 221, 232–33; centrally planned systems, 53–54; classical economic theory, 52, 58, 256; under the Clinton administration, 212, 245, 261; comparative advantage principle in, 58, 256; creative destruction theory, 256; under the Ford administration, 51–52, 67; impact of the Uruguay Round on, 256; managed capitalist systems, 54; under the Nixon administration, 40–42, 53–55. *See also* free market economy

education, 10, 18, 24

Edwards, Edwin W., 218–19

EEC (European Economic Community), 190–91

EEP (Export Enhancement Program), 188, 190–91

Ehrlichman, John D., 31–32, 45

Eisenhower, Dwight D., 16, 59, 88, 278

elections: 1964 election, 16; 1968 election, 24–25, 42; 1970 election, 16; 1972 election, 25, 36, 37–43, 285; 1976 election, 52, 67, 92; 1980 election, 25, 89–92, 127, 217; 1984 election, 25; 1988 election, 161, 212, 213, 214–15, 220, 239; 1990 election, 176, 220; 1991 Louisiana gubernatorial election, 218–19; 1992 election, 48, 197, 212, 213, 217, 221, 222, 225, 234–41; 1996 election, 94, 259, 260–61; 2000 election, 264–65; 2016 election, 275–76, 277

electronics industry: CKY investigating unfair trade practices, 137; impact on national security, 148–49; Japanese semiconductor trade dispute, 148–51, 152–54; U.S.-Japan Semiconductor Agreement, 292

Elias, Manuel Ulloa, 94

endangered species, 182–84

England, 97, 105

English, Glenn L., Jr., 156

entertainment industry, 131, 138, 140, 142, 147

environmental issues: Alar-treated apples, 177–79, 180; under the Bush administration, 180, 184–85, 230–32; challenging CKY while ag secretary, 171, 178–84; climate change, 184–85, 230–32, 339n71; in the Farm Bill (1990), 180–81; growth hormone controversy, 181–82; Kyoto Protocol, 185; under the Nixon administration, 46; Paris Agreement, 185; Rio de Janeiro Earth Summit (June 1992), 184–85, 230–32

EPA (Environmental Protection Agency): Alar-treated apples, 177–79, 180; clean air rules of, 46, 236; creation of, 46; relationship with the USDA, 179–80

equity markets, 103

Espy, Alphonso Michael, 156

ethanol, 229–30, 236

European Community (EC): agricultural trading policy reforms, 293; cheese subsidies war, 63, 117, 121; CKY investigating unfair-trade practices of, 137; Common Agricultural Policy (CAP), 63, 138–39, 293; Common Market, 63, 122, 137; export subsidies of, 63–64, 122, 138, 190–91, 205–7, 238; at the Geneva trade talks, 63, 79–81, 91; pasta war, 121–22; at the Punta del Este agenda negotiation talks, 138–40; trade negotiation personality clashes, 76; trade negotiation skills, 75, 80; in the Uruguay Round trade talks, 190, 204, 205–6. *See also* European Union (EU)

European Economic Community (EEC), 190–91

European Union (EU): agricultural policy reforms, 207, 293; Blair House Accord, 207, 254; Brainerd (MN) conference (June 1988), 158; protectionist policies of, 62; in the Quad Group, 158, 254; rBGH milk banned in, 182; signing of Uruguay Round pact, 207, 254; in Uruguay Round trade talks, 254, 255. *See also* European Community (EC)

Eustis (NE): CKY attending school in, 2–3, 4, 282; CKY born in, 1, 281; Clayton Yeutter Highway, 250; family farm in, 2–3, 9, 12;